M000302750

C With Assembly Language

Steven Holzner

BRADY
New York

BRADY

Simon & Schuster, Inc.
15 Columbus Circle
New York, NY 10023

DISTRIBUTED BY PRENTICE HALL TRADE

Manufactured in the United States of America

1 2 3 4 5 6 7 8 9 10

Library of Congress Cataloging-in-Publication Data

Holzner, Steven.
    C with assembly language / Steven Holzner.
        p.   cm.
    ISBN 0-13-010968-1 : $24.95
    1. C (Computer program language)   2. Assembler language (Computer
program language)   I. Title.
    QA76.73.C15H659   1989
    005.26'2—dc20   89-17293
                                                            CIP

Dedication

To my brother Dan, the mad artist. Keep it up.

Acknowledgments

I would like to thank the staff of Brady Books, particularly Marjorie Gursky, my editor, and Tom Dillon, who handled the production of this book.

Limits of Liability and Disclaimer of Warranty

Registered Trademarks

Contents

Introduction

Welcome to programming in C with assembly language. This book will be our guide as we tour through many areas: file handling, graphics, databases, advanced pointers, debugging, and interfacing C to assembly language.

This last topic will be an important one for us—this book is specially designed to include an assembly language primer for C programmers. The reason for including assembly language is that among serious programmers, the most common programming environment today is a mix of C and assembly language. This combination is hard to beat for both speed and ease of programming—the use of high-level languages such as C makes programming easier, and the use of assembly language makes it fast.

This book is dedicated to enabling you to get the most out of C. There are three main areas that we will investigate:

- The C library
- Advanced C techniques
- The C-assembly language interface

The reason for exploring the C library is clear—C is a language built out of functions, and those functions reside in the C libraries. The range and scope of available functions is immense, and without a good knowledge about what functions are available, the C programmer is like a craftsman without tools.

Some of the advanced C techniques discussed in this book include the use of advanced pointer work (including how to write a database program that sorts pointers, not records), how to get a grip on C's use of memory, how to write functions that can take variable numbers of arguments, and the use of a number of professional tricks. The C language itself is an astonishing tool, capable of wonderful speed and precision—and we're going to put it to work.

There is also much to say about assembly language when it comes to speed and precision, of course, but it is difficult to write full-scale programs in assembly language. Instead, assembly language is used with C to form composite programs in which you can accelerate tight loops, speed any graphics, or shorten critical code. Assembly language is much like C in many ways. The exploration of assembly language from the C programmer's point of view is a fruitful approach (especially with respect to the use of pointers).

The Details

The first chapter of this book is dedicated to a review of C. Here we can renew our familiarity with the tools that we'll need. From main() to pointers, this chapter covers a lot of material. The next two chapters explore the C library. That exploration, begins in Chapter 2 with a topic frequently left out of beginning C-level books—file handling. We'll learn about the many file-handling options in the C library, and how to use files to our advantage. The chapter continues on to explore more advanced topics such as the file-position pointer and the use of file records.

Chapter 3 explores what is probably the largest single section of the C library—graphics functions. We'll write a small program to interactively draw graphics figures on the screen, and will finish up with an animation example that uses viewports.

The following two chapters move from an exploration of the C library to advanced programming techniques, and dig deeply into C itself. Chapter 4 discusses the rules for writing database programs and the use of pointers to speed up programs. In this chapter, we'll make the transition from using arrays to using pointers.

Chapter 5 discusses how C uses memory and memory models. We'll learn the special techniques necessary for handling large amounts of data in memory by using Large and Huge pointers. This information will be very important later when we start linking assembly language to C.

Chapter 6 presents debugging techniques in C. A number of good source-level debuggers are available, and we'll get a good feel for the art of debugging.

Chapter 7 turns to assembly language. This chapter and Chapter 8 present the basics of assembly-language programming, and show how to put that knowledge to work. The system resources offered by DOS are also introduced in this chapter.

In Chapter 9, we connect assembly language and C together. The use of inline assembly language, how to link assembly language code into C programs how to link C library functions into assembly language programs are discussed in this chapter. We put that interface to work in many examples.

In the final chapter, Chapter 10, we sharpen our assembly language expertise. This chapter explains the benefits of assembly language with respect to both program speed and program size. We develop some tight code for math manipulations (including a 64-bit by 32-bit divide algorithm) and fast graphics. We also put assembly language routines together into libraries that can be linked to C programs.

Throughout the book, both Quick C and Turbo C are used. Although the emphasis is on Quick C, the book also shows how to do everything in Turbo C. For the most part, the two compilers are very similar (especially where they follow the new ANSI standard), but with respect to both graphics and memory management, they diverge.

Quick C uses the same library functions that Microsoft C uses, so code developed in Quick C is the same as that developed in Microsoft C. The difference between these compilers is that Microsoft C is an optimizing compiler. Program optimization is not needed for the short programs we develop, so we use Quick C. If you use Microsoft C, you can type in the Quick C programs verbatim (with the small exception that Microsoft C does not allow array initializations inside of functions). The versions of the software used in this book are: Quick C 2.0, Turbo C 2.0, CodeView 2.2, Turbo Debugger 1.0, MASM (Microsoft Macro Assembler) 5.1, and TASM (Turbo Assembler) 1.0.

You'll need to use an editor to type in the programs that are developed in this book. Almost any editor will be acceptable (particularly the built-in editors in Quick C and Turbo C). If the editor prints intelligible English, the compilers and assemblers can read it. Word processors that store text in their own proprietary format may not work.

The reason you'll need to use an editor is because this book is filled with examples. Examples are what C books frequently omit—and learning to use C without the examples is like learning to fly by reading a catalogue of plane parts. All too often, books about programming are just like catalogues: long lists of classes of commands, and impenetrable discussions of every available option for each instruction—without any coherent means for tying it all together.

The easiest way to learn C is just by seeing how it works. To a reader earnestly making his or her way through this material, one simple example is worth a thousand descriptions.

Examples can help before you read explanations by whetting your interest. For this reason, sections frequently start with an example that includes a few new lines to help pique your curiosity. And examples help after you read explanations by bringing it all together. Examples often answer many questions—there's the code, and it works—making the use of examples the best way to learn how to program in C and assembly language.

Let's begin with Chapter 1, the review of C.

1
C From Ordinary to Extraordinary

This book is about the C language. In particular, it is about C programming, a subject that can be formal and complicated. In many treatments, this means that you will find yourself reading dry, incomprehensible material, working through such multilayered constructions as: "a pointer to a pointer to a function that returns a pointer to a character" (an exact quotation from a C book). After a hundred or so pages of this material, the mind reels.

On the other hand, formal and complex treatments can be difficult to apply in the real world. It is best to apply what we're talking about immediately, and that is the method of this book. Wherever possible, we will use *examples* to demonstrate the rules that we've been discussing. The use of concrete examples will help you see the rules in action.

We will work deep into the heart of C, learn about memory handling, graphics, file handling, pointer control, advanced pointer control, debugging techniques, how to write databases, and advanced programming methods.

In addition, this book is also about assembly language as seen from the C programmer's point of view. The reason for this is simple: The most common serious programming environment for the IBM PC and PS/2 today is a mix of C and assembly language. Experienced programmers need a good knowledge of both languages, and they need to know how the languages connect. This mix of languages is a particularly easy one, because C is already much like assembly language. This book points out some of the many similiarities between C and assembly language.

C and Assembly Language

C works closely with the machine, and matches assembly language in many ways. For example, counterparts are found in assembly lan-

1

guage for all of these familiar C constructions: one-step increment and decrement operators, bit operators, bit-by-bit shift instructions, macros, and the extensive use of pointers (indirect addressing in assembly language). Both languages share an intimacy with memory usage and allocation.

And, both languages have the reputation of being terse and hard to read. For instance, take a look at this dense expression:

```
char *(**p)();
```

It's the declaration of the object mentioned earlier, a pointer to a pointer to a function that returns a pointer to a character. It's possible to write very dense lines of code in C, and when we work with compact pointer expressions later, it will be unavoidable. Assembly language can be similar. For example, this code is hardly a model of clarity to a beginner:

```
        LEA     SI, BFR
        MOV     DI, OFFSET STR
        POP     CX
REP     SCASB
        JCXZ    ERR
```

In this book, we'll try to make what could be difficult subjects a little easier to understand. If you take your time and work through examples, both languages can come alive without becoming overpowering.

A Review of C

To make sure we know what we're doing, this chapter will review the C language. If you have serious difficulty with the review, this book is probably not for you, and you should work through an introductory C book before continuing here. On the other hand, if you find yourself skimming the details of this review, you may want to go on immediately to Chapter 2 and dig right in.

C programs can be very small. Here is the smallest C program, which provides our starting place:

```
main(){}
```

Usually, there is a good deal more to a C program, but this example shows what is essential. First, there must be a *function* declared as *main*. When a compiled C program runs, control is transferred to this function. This is called the program's *entry point*.

Often, in C, the declaration of a function is followed by a list of variable names enclosed in parentheses. These variables will be used by the function when it runs. Here, main() uses no variables passed to it, so the parentheses are empty.

Following the parentheses in main() is the program body, enclosed in curly brackets. The program body here is remarkably small—it has no length at all. Although this program compiles, it does nothing when it runs. DOS loads the program and calls main(), control is returned immediately to DOS, and the program ends.

> When we disassemble programs later, you will see that the compiler translates even as short a program as this one into many machine-language instructions.

Usually the curly brackets enclose more program lines, as is shown in this program:

```
#include <stdio.h>

main()
{
        printf("Hello, world.");
}
```

This program indicates a few more things about writing C program— especially about the actual format of the program. The curly brackets have been split, and one is directly above the other. The single program line is indented. This format, while not required, helps make C programs easier to use, and is commonly used by C programmers. In addition, lowercase letters are typically used (with a few exceptions that we'll point out later). C is a case-sensitive language—you can't define something as BIGmessage, and then later refer to it as bigMESSAGE. (By contrast, assembly language is not case sensitive). Notice that we have used the #include directive in our program. Here, the file STDIO.H is included, which includes the needed function prototype for the printf() function. How to include *header files* like this is one of the first things that C programmers learn.

This new program prints out the line "Hello, world." on the screen when the progran run (this is the traditional first program of C books). The single program line ends with a semicolon, as do most program lines in C. The printf() function is one of many *library* functions available in C. Rather than having many built-in commands, like FOR-

TRAN or BASIC, C provides a number of libraries with functions. When you refer to one of these functions in your program, the appropriate code is linked in before the program is run. This means that you can tailor C to meet your requirements—if you need to change a library function, you can rewrite it and link your version in instead. We'll see how to do this in assembly language in Chapter 9.

The printf() library function is central in C, and writes to the standard output device (usually the screen). It's one of the basic functions that let a program generate output, and is very important. Variations of this function are used to write to files (fprintf()), to write to strings (sprintf()), or for use with special functions (such as vprintf()).

Output

You can use printf() to format what goes on the screen. For example, the following program prints "Hello,<tab> world. <newline>" where <newline> is a carriage-return and line-feed combination.

```
#include <stdio.h>

main()
{
        printf("Hello,\t world. \n");
}
```

By embedding special sequences—called *escape sequences*—in what you want to print, you can modify what appears on the screen. These escape sequences always start with a backslash, \, and are listed along with their meanings in the following table.

Table 1.1   C Escape Sequences

\a	alert (ring bell)
\n	newline (<cr><lf> pair on screen)
\b	backspace
\r	carriage return
\f	formfeed
\t	tab
\v	vertical tab
\\	backslash (two needed)
\'	single quote mark
\"	double quote mark
\0	null

When you embed one of these escape sequences inside the characters that printf() is to print, the action just described is performed. The characters inside the quotation marks in the call to printf() make up the *format string*. In our example, the string "Hello,\t world. \n" is the format string.

```
#include <stdio.h>

main()
{
        printf("Hello,\t world. \n");
}
```

This string of characters can include more than just escape sequences. printf() can be used to print out the values of variables being used in the program. For example, look at this program:

```
#include <stdio.h>

main()
{
        int i = 12;
        printf("Hello,\t world. \n");
        printf("It is %d o\'clock.",i);
}
```

In this line:

```
printf("It is %d o\'clock.",i);
```

the format string includes %d. This is a *format specification*, and it indicates to printf() that we want a number printed (in this case, an integer). When run, the program prints out this:

```
C>HELLO2
Hello,     world.
It is 12 o'clock. C>
```

The 12 was printed because we included a *parameter* (also called an *argument*) in the call to printf() like this:

```
printf("It is %d o\'clock.",i);
```

The variable i is a decimal integer. To print it, we use a %d in the format string. There are other such format specifications available in

C, matching the other available variable types. The format specifications in C are shown in the following table.

Table 1.2   C Format Specifications

%d	Decimal Integer
%ld	Long Decimal Integer
%i	Integer (same as %d)
%u	Unsigned Integer
%lu	Long Unsigned Integer
%f	Floating Point
%x	Hexadecimal Number
%c	Character
%s	Character String

C allows you to store data in many formats. These format specifications indicate some of those formats. Storing data in different ways, in *variables*, is a big part of any programming language.

> Functions normally require a particular number of arguments. The printf() function is exceptional in that it, along with a few other functions, can take a varying number of arguments. We'll see how to write functions that take varying numbers of arguments later.

Variables

In the beginning of our program, we declared i as an integer variable:

```
#include <stdio.h>

main()
{
→       int i = 12;
        printf("Hello,\t world. \n");
        printf("It is %d o\'clock.",i);
}
```

and we also initialized it to the value 12. The C language demands that you declare all variables and data types used in a program before you use them. An int variable, such as i, takes up 2 bytes of storage. Unless you specify otherwise, declared variables are signed. In other words, i can vary in value from -32,768 to 32,768, not from 0 to 65,535. The variable types available in C are shown in the following table.

Table 1.3   C Variable Types
_____

Declaration	Signed?	Bytes	Range
char	signed	1	-128 to 127
int	signed	2	-32,768 to 32,768
short	signed	2	-32,768 to 32,768
short int	signed	2	-32,768 to 32,768
long	signed	4	-2,147,483,648
long int	signed	4	-2,147,483,648
unsigned char	unsigned	1	0 to 255
unsigned	unsigned	2	0 to 65,535
unsigned int	unsigned	2	0 to 65,535
unsigned short	unsigned	2	0 to 65,535
unsigned long	unsigned	4	0 to 4,294,967,295
enum	unsigned	2	0 to 65,535
float	signed	4	3.4E+-38 [7 digits accuracy]
double	signed	8	1.7E+-308 [15 digits accuracy]

[Note: Some of these are duplicates of each other. For example, int, short, and short int are all names for the same thing.]

ASCII text can be stored character by character in variables declared as *char* (or as entire strings, as reviewed later). Integers can be stored in either *long* (4-byte) or *short* (2-byte) format. The default (which you get by using int) is a signed, 2-byte integer. You can specify whether the number is unsigned by adding the unsigned keyword just before an integer declaration, as in the following code. (Unsigned is valid only with chars, integers, and longs).

```
unsigned    int    bases = 4;
```

If you want very large or very small numbers, you can use the *float* type. Floating point variables come in two lengths: 4 bytes (with the float declaration) and 8 bytes (with the double declaration). They have correspondingly different memory requirements and storage capacities. The default declaration is float, and sets aside 4 bytes for the variable. We will unravel the actual format used for float and double in Chapter 9.

When you declare a variable, you can give it an initial value, as we did with i:

```
# include <stdioh>
main()
}
→   int i = 12;
    printf("Hello,\t world. \n);
    printf("It is %d o'clock",i);
```

Don't make the mistake of assuming that undeclared variables are set to 0—that is not necessarily the case. If we had omitted the initialization of i, its value would have been unpredictable.

C Operators

Other than for the assignment of initial values, you can use an *assignment operator* to give a value to a variable. Here we use the assignment operator =:

```
#include <stdio.h>

main()
{
        int i;
→       i = 12;
        printf("Hello,\t world. \n");
        printf("It is %d o\'clock.",i);

}
```

for the same result as before. C is crammed full of operators; math operators include addition (+), subtraction (-), multiplication (*), division (/), and modulus (%). For example, our program could be written this way to achieve the same result:

```
#include <stdio.h>

main()
{
        int i;
        i = 11;
        i = i - 1;
        i = 2 * i;
        i = i + 4
        i = i / 2;
        printf("Hello,\t world. \n");
        printf("It is %d o\'clock.",i);

}
```

C also has *compound* assignment operators, which is one of its trademarks. The previous program could also be written this way:

```
#include <stdio.h>

main()
{
        int i;
        i = 11;
        i -= 1;
        i *=2;
        i += 4;
        i /= 2;
        printf("Hello,\t world. \n");
        printf("It is %d o\'clock.",i);
}
```

We could even use the comma operator to make things more neat:

```
#include <stdio.h>

main()
{
        int i;
        i = 11, i -= 1, i *=2, i += 4, i /= 2;
        printf("Hello,\t world. \n");
        printf("It is %d o\'clock.",i);
}
```

Operators have two properties: associativity and precedence. Both are important. The following table lists all C operators and their associativity, arranged in groups according to precedence. Members of the top group on the chart have the highest precedence, and precedence decreases as you go down the table. The comma operator has the lowest precedence.

Table 1.4   C Operators and Their Associativity, According to Precedence

Operator	Description	Associativity
( )	function call	left to right
[ ]	array element	
.	structure member	
→	pointer to a structure member	

Table 1.4   *Continued*

!	logical NOT	right to left
~	one's complement	
—	minus (the neg operator)	
++	increment	
——	decrement	
&	address of	
*	contents of	
(vble type)	typecast operator	
sizeof	returns in bytes	
*	multiply	left to right
/	divide	
%	modulus	
+	add	left to right
—	subtract	
<<	left shift	left to right
>>	right shift	
<	less than	left to right
<=	less than or equal to	
>	greater than	
>=	greater than or equal to	
==	equality	left to right
!=	not equal	
&	bit-by-bit AND	left to right
^	bit-by-bit XOR	left to right
¦	bit-by-bit OR	left to right
&&	logical AND	left to right
¦¦	logical OR	left to right
?:	conditional	right to left
=	assignment	right to left
*= /= %= +=	compound assignment	
—= <<= >>=	compound assignment	
&= ^= ¦=	compound assignment	
,	comma operator	left to right

For example, this statement assigns a value of 13 to x, not 15.

x = 3 * 4 + 1

Because * has higher precedence than +, the statement is evaluated this way:

x = (3 * 4) + 1

If two operators are used in the same statement and have the same precedence, the associativity rules is used. For example, consider:

y = 3 * 4 / 2

The * and / operators have the same precedence, so the expressions on the right are evaluated according to their associativity; that is, left to right:

y = (3 * 4) / 2 ·

Usually, associativity and precedence are not big concerns. If you ever have doubts, you can always use parentheses to completely specify things the way you want them. If you forget that z = x % y / 3 will be evaluated like this:

z = (x % y) / 3

you can always put the parentheses in yourself and make sure.

Since this is a review, we will assume that you are familiar with these operators. We'll be using practically every one of them in this book.

Now we've reviewed basic data variables and the C operators. There are no more operators to introduce. (When a number of them are used together, however, especially in compact pointer expressions, their use can become complex.) On the other hand, we've barely begun to examine the ways to store data in C. The next topic is arrays.

Arrays

Variables such as x or i work well if you have a limited amount of data. This is not always the case, however. For example, what if you have

12 dollar amounts, indexed by month? One way that C provides
organization for your data is through the use of arrays. This program
uses an array of integers:

```
#include <stdio.h>
main()
{
        int i = 12;
        int a[20];          ←

        a[i] = 400;
        printf("The %dth element of array a is %d",i+1,a[i]);
}
```

This program shows an elementary use of arrays, and just prints out
an array element. Note that array indexing begins with 0, not 1. That
is, the first term of the array a is a[0], not a[1]. This is a common source
of errors in C. (We'll run into it again in the chapter about debugging
C, Chapter 6.)

Arrays are not limited to one dimension. In this program, the array
a[] has been extended into two dimensions:

```
#include <stdio.h>
main()
{
        int i = 12, j = 3;
→       int a[20][5];

        a[i][j] = 400;
        printf("The term a[%d][%d] is %d",i,j,a[i][j]);
}
```

The array declaration is a[20][5], not a[20,5]. This is particularly confus-
ing if your background is in programming with BASIC or FORTRAN.

The use of arrays and pointers in C sometimes mix. In fact, pointers
can do the same thing as arrays, and just as easily. Many experienced
C programmers prefer to use pointer notation exclusively.

Moreover, using pointers instead of arrays is frequently faster and
makes more efficient use of memory because variable-length entries can
be stored. (In Chapter 4, we'll use pointers more often instead of arrays.)

> Negative subscripts are possible in C, because the language refer-
> ences array locations with pointers. In fact, some of the macros de-
> fined in standard header files (files that end with ".H") purposely use
> negative subscripts; we will see how this works when we use func-
> tions that take varying numbers of parameters.

We can initialize arrays when they are declared. For example, we could have modified our original, one-dimensional array program this way:

```
#include <stdio.h>

main()
{
        int i = 12;
        int a[20] = {23, 32, 11, 32, 213, 324, 55, 56, 247, 899, 10, 211, 400};

        a[i] = 400;
        printf("The %dth element of array a is %d",i+1,a[i]);
}
```

Notice that although the array is declared with 20 elements, we only initialized the first 13. If we leave out the declaration of 20 elements and use this line instead:

```
int a[] = {23, 32, 11, 32, 213, 324, 55, 56, 247, 899, 10, 211, 400};
```

then there are only 13 elements in this array.

In a two-dimensional array, the first index is the *row index*, and the second is the *column index*. We can initialize the rows and columns of a two-dimensional array in this way:

```
#include <stdio.h>

main()
{
        int b[2][4] = {
                        {32, 24, 64, 23,},
                        {66, 14, 98, 55,}
                      };
        printf("%d", b[1][3]);
}
```

C stores the first row in memory first, followed by the second row, and so on. This next program is identical to the previous one:

```
#include <stdio.h>

    main()
    {
            int b[2][4] = { 32, 24, 64, 23, 66, 14, 98, 55,};

            printf("%d", b[1][3]);
    }
```

There is a special type of array that programmers work with frequently—*character strings*. Let's look at them next.

Character Strings

Most modern programming languages (even assembly language) have some provision for handling character strings, and C is no exception. An individual character, such as "a", is stored as one byte of ASCII code. In C, this character has its own data type, char. The char data type is a generic term in C, referring to one byte of memory storage, and beginners in C are often startled to see math operations taking place on an object declared as char.

Groups of characters can be made into a *string*. There is nothing special about a string—it is just an array of type char, where the last char is 0 (ASCII NULL). Strings by themselves have no special merits. What makes them easy to use in C is not the way they are stored, but the fact that there are many functions that expect to receive strings in this format (such as printf()). This program defines a string named hello:

```
#include <stdio.h>

main()
{
char  hello[] = "Hello";                    ←

printf("%s world. \n",hello);
}
```

This next program is the same as the previous program in terms of function:

```
#include <stdio.h>

main()
{
char  hello[] = {'H','e','l','l','o','\0',};

printf("%s world. \n",hello);
}
```

In both programs, we initialize the character array (i.e., the string) named hello, and terminate it with an ASCII NULL byte, \0. Now that we've defined strings, there are many library functions that we can use with them. Some of the library functions are listed in the following table:

Table 1.5   C String Functions

Function	Does
strcat()	concatenates strings
strchr()	finds a char in a string
strcmp()	compares two strings
strcopy()	copies a string to another string
strlen()	returns the string's length (excluding the \0)

Each of the functions expects to operate on character arrays that end with a zero byte. As we'll see in the next chapter, the string functions provide a rich addition to C, making the language easier to use and providing valuable tools.

In addition to variables, arrays, and strings, there is another very popular method of storing data in C data structures.

Structures

In many ways, *structures* are similar to arrays, but the elements of a structure can be of different data types. In order to use a data structure, you must first declare what's going to be inside it:

```
struct customer
{
char    name[20];
int     number;
double  balance;
}
```

After the structure is declared as a data type, you can use it in a program. Instead of using int, double, or char, we use struct customer as the data type to set up a structure named ed:

```
#include <stdio.h>

main()
{
struct customer
    {
char    name[20];
int     number;
double  balance;
    }
```

```
struct customer ed;

strcpy(ed.name,"Edward G. Teller");
ed.number = 2324;
ed.balance = -45424376.89;

printf("Customer %s owes %20.2f\n", ed.name, ed.balance);
}
```

Notice a couple of things here. We reach any element of the data structure ed with the dot operator, ".". This results in expressions such as ed.number = 2324;. However, we could not simply say:

```
ed.name = "Edward G. Teller";   /* Wrong. */
```

because ed.name is the name of an array, not the name of a memory location (in the terminology of C, ed.name is not an *lvalue*). If we say:

```
ed.name[0] = 'E';
```

there is no problem. It is tedious to fill each location in the ed.name array in order to store "Edward G. Teller," however, so we use the string function strcopy() to do it for us.

Another thing to notice is in the format string in the call to printf():

```
printf("Customer %s owes %20.2f\n", ed.name, ed.balance);
```

This prints out ed.balance with a format specification of %20.2f. The f indicates that ed.balance is a floating point number, and the 20.2 specifies to printf() how we want the output to appear on the screen. The 20 indicates that the number should be printed out in a field 20 characters wide. The .2 indicates that we want two places after the decimal point.

You can use these *width* and *precision* numbers in any format that prints out numbers, but they mean different things for integers than they do for floating point numbers.

Arrays of Structures

It is also possible to declare an *array of structures*:

```
#include <stdio.h>

main()
```

```
{
struct customer
{
char    name[20];
int     number;
double  balance;
}

struct customer acme_cust[10];

strcpy(acme_cust[0].name,"Edward G. Teller");
acme_cust[0].number = 2324;
acme_cust[0].balance = -4542327584376.89;

printf("Customer %s owes %.2f\n", acme_cust[0].name, \
acme_cust[0].balance);
}
```

To declare an array of a certain data type, all we need to do is to follow the name of the variable (acme_cust) with the dimension of the array in the array declaration. (Chapter 4 shows that it's possible to omit some indices when declaring an array inside a function.) Here, we are declaring an array of ten structures, each of type customer.

Structures of arrays work as you'd expect—every element of the array is a structure. We can use our new array as easily as we used the data structure ed. Wherever we use ed we just substitute acme_cust[i], where i ranges from 0 to 9.

To fill the customer number of the first element of the array, all that is necessary is a line like this:

```
acme_cust[0].number = 2324;
```

Two more things are worth noticing in this program. The printf() line is long, so we broke it up into two lines using the backslash character "\":

```
printf("Customer %s owes %.2f\n", acme_cust[0].name, \
acme_cust[0].balance);
```

Also, the format specifier has been changed from 20.2 to just .2. This new specifier will print out two places after the decimal point, and be flush left with whatever preceded it (instead of taking a 20 field character field).

Conditional Statements

We've gone through the most popular ways of storing data in C—variables, arrays, and structures. Now we've got to do something with that data.

As programs run, the flow of control through them can take various paths. Only the simplest programs execute sequentially without a break; most programs include branches and conditional statements.

The If Statement

The primary conditional statement for most languages is the if statement. In C, the if statement looks like this:

```
if(kings == 3) {
        printf("hallelujah");
        }
```

The expression in the parentheses is evaluated, and if it turns out to be TRUE (nonzero), the body of the if statement is executed. The curly brackets are optional if only one line follows the if statement. (Note that == is used for conditional checking, and is not the same as the assignment operator = in other languages.)

An if statement can also be followed with an else statement:

```
if(kings == 3) {
        printf("hallelujah");
        }
else        {
        printf("check the calendar");
        {
```

Here, if the variable kings is not 3, the body of the else statement is executed. Let's put this knowledge to work with a brief program called dehex.c, that converts a single typed hexadecimal digit (0 - f) into decimal. To do that, we'll need to read in typed characters.

Input

Here's the program called dehex.c:

```
#include <stdio.h>

main()
{
char x;

scanf("%c",&x);

if(x >= 'a')
        x -= 'a' - 10;
else
        x -= '0';
printf("The hex digit you typed is equal to %d\n", (int) x);
}
```

To read the character from the keyboard, we use the function scanf(). This function also requires a format string. Our format string is very simple—we just inform scanf() that we are going to be reading a character with the format string "%c". This function requires the *address* of the variable(s) that it is to fill. This is because C passes arguments to functions by *value*, not by address. Unless we indicate to scanf() where our character x is in memory by passing its address, scanf() has no way to actually reach the character in order to change its value.

In general, because C passes only copies of arguments to functions, and does not pass their locations in memory, functions have no way to change variables unless they get the variable's address. This is one of the reasons that C relies upon pointers as heavily as it does—with pointers, a calling function can indicate to a called function where it should change the passed arguments in memory.

> Of course, functions can return a single *value*, as we'll see in the coming section on functions. But they cannot change the values of their arguments without help.

To pass the address of our character x to scanf(), we use the address operator, "&." This results in a call such as this:

```
scanf("%c",&x);
```

Using scanf(), we fill the character variable x with a single hexadecimal digit. Now we want to check whether x is in the ASCII range '0' to '9', or whether it's in the range 'a' to 'f'. This is done with an if...else statement:

```
#include <stdio.h>

main()
{
char x;

scanf("%c",&x);

if(x >= 'a')
        x -= 'a' - 10;
else
        x -= '0';
printf("The hex digit you typed is equal to %d\n", (int) x);
}
```

If the character is above the ASCII value for 'a', we assume that the character is in the range 'a' to 'f' (completely omitting error checking), and convert it into a decimal value. This conversion is done by subtracting the ASCII value 'a' and adding 10 to the result, which results in the line x -= 'a' - 10; (because subtracting a negative 10 is the same as adding 10). If the character x is not above 'a' in value, we assume that it is in the range '0' to '9', and subtract ASCII '0' from it.

Subtracting values directly from characters in this way is not unusual for C, but it is not allowed in many other languages, where data types are much more rigorous.

All that remains is to print out the result. If we printed it out as a char, however, it would be converted back to an ASCII character—so we want to print it out as a (possibly two-digit) integer. We do this by converting the type of x from char to int with a *typecast* operator, such as the operator in the end of the printf() statement:

```
printf("The hex digit you typed is equal to %d\n", (int) x);
```

The expression (int) x is an integer. Technically, it is not necessary to include the typecast (int), since the compiler will convert a char (byte) that is pushed on the stack into a word (i.e., a short int) before passing it to a function such as printf(). We include the typecast operator for clarity.

> If you are going to use chars as byte-long numbers in your programs, recall that the default char is treated as if it were signed. You can also define an unsigned char.

You can also nest if. . .else statements, like this:

```
if(      )
        {evaluate me};
```

```
else if(      )
        {evaluate me};
else if(      )
        {evaluate me};
else {evaluate me};
```

Any of the curly brackets can contain as many program statements as you want.

A construction that is similar to the nested if. . .else is the *switch construction*, which we'll review next.

Switch

Switch is a good C construction to use when you have a variety of inputs to sort through. We can implement the file DEHEX.C this way with switch:

```
#include <stdio.h>

main()
{
char x;

scanf("%c",&x);

switch (x)
        {
        case 'a':
                printf("The hex digit is equal to 10");
                break;
        case 'b':
                printf("The hex digit is equal to 11");
                break;
        case 'c':
                printf("The hex digit is equal to 12");
                break;
        case 'd':
                printf("The hex digit is equal to 13");
                break;
        case 'e':
                printf("The hex digit is equal to 14");
                break;
        case 'f':
                printf("The hex digit is equal to 15");
                break;
        default:  {
                x -= '0';
                printf("The hex digit you typed is equal to %d\n", (int) x);
                break;  }
        }
}
```

At the end of every case, there must be either a break or a continue statement. A break statement forces control to exit the switch statement altogether. A continue at the end of a case means that control will fall through to the next case, and execution will continue there. The (optional) default case at the end handles the remaining cases if they do not match any of the previous cases.

Switch is particularly useful when we start to deal with user input, and we'll see more of this construction later.

The Conditional Operator

There is another operator in C that can branch—the *conditional operator*—and it provides another way to convert x from hexadecimal. The conditional operator looks something like this:

```
( cond  ?  exp1  :  exp2  )
```

It returns a value depending upon whether or not cond is TRUE (nonzero). If cond is TRUE, the value of the statement is equal to exp1. If cond is FALSE, the value is equal to exp2.

To convert x from an ASCII character to an integer byte, use this statement:

```
x = ( x >= 'a' ? x-('a'-10) : x-'0' )
```

Translated, the statement says that if x is greater than or equal to 'a', x is set to x-('a'-10). Otherwise, x is set to x-'0'. We can change DEHEX.C to incorporate this new statement:

```
#include <stdio.h>

main()
{
char x;

scanf("%c",&x);

printf("The hex digit you typed is equal to %d", x >= 'a' ? x-('a'-10) : x-'0');
}
```

The use of this type of operator often makes code difficult to read, even if it is more compact. However, it is sometimes just the right operator to use, and then it can't be beat.

We are finished with our review of conditional statements in C—they will be a cornerstone of our study of C. The next topic in the flow of programming control is loops.

*III*BradyLine

Insights into tomorrow's technology from the authors and editors of Brady Books.

You rely on Brady's bestselling computer books for up-to-date information about high technology. Now turn to BradyLine for the details behind the titles.

Find out what new trends in technology spark Brady's authors and editors. Read about what they're working on, and predicting, for the future. Get to know the authors through interviews and profiles, and get to know each other through your questions and comments.

BradyLine keeps you ahead of the trends with the stories behind the latest computer developments. Informative previews of forthcoming books and excerpts from new titles keep you apprised of what's going on in the fields that interest you most.

- Peter Norton on operating systems
- Jim Seymour on business productivity
- Jerry Daniels, Mary Jane Mara, Robert Eckhardt, and Cynthia Harriman on Macintosh development, productivity, and connectivity

Get the Spark. Get BradyLine.

Published quarterly, beginning with the Summer 1988 issue. Free exclusively to our customers. Just fill out and mail this card to begin your subscription.

Name _____

Address _____

City _____ State _____ Zip _____

Name of Book Purchased _____

Date of Purchase _____

Where was this book purchased?   *(circle one)*

Retail Store   Computer Store   Mail Order

**F
R
E
E**

Mail this card for your free subscription to BradyLine

Brady Books
One Gulf+Western Plaza
New York, NY 10023

Loops in C

The ability to handle large, repetitive jobs is a trademark of computers. Both C and assembly language would be of little practical use without the loop commands that let them handle such jobs. There are three primary types of loops in C, and we'll review each of them.

The For Loop

The most frequently used C loop statement is probably the for statement. Here's the way it looks:

```
for(i=0; i<10; i++)
{    printf("array element a[%d] is",i);
          printf("%d\n",a[i]);
}
```

A for statement is divided into these parts:

```
for(initialization exp; conditional exp; end-of-loop exp)
{ body of for statement
};
```

Each expression in the parentheses is optional. When you enter a for loop for the first time, the initialization expression (if there is one) is executed. In the previous example, we set the loop index i to 0 with the expression i = 0;. We can perform a number of actions in the initialization expression. For example, we can do this:

```
for(i=0, j=0, k=0; i<10; i++)
{    printf("array element a[%d] is",i);
          printf("%d\n",a[i]);
}
```

Note that the initialization expression now sets i, j, and k all to 0 (which could have been done with i = j = k = 0;).

The next expression in the parentheses (i<10;) is the for loop's conditional expression. This expression is evaluated each time *before* the loop is executed. If it is TRUE (nonzero), the body of the loop is executed; otherwise, control moves past the for loop in the program.

The final expression in the parentheses (i+ +) is the *end-of-loop expression*. This expression is evaluated at the end of every loop iteration. In our case, it increments the loop index i in preparation for the next loop iteration.

Let's give the for loop a try with an example.

```
#include <stdio.h>

main()
{
int      i;

for( i = 0; i < 100; i += 5)
        printf( "i = %d\n", i);
}
```

This example prints out numbers up to 100 in increments of 5.

In this next example, we omit the end-of-loop expression and the entire body of the for statement. Everything is done inside the parentheses (this is not uncommon for C loops):

```
#include <stdio.h>

main()
{
  for( printf("I'm checking for a <cr>"); getche() != '\r';)
                ;
}
```

This program accepts whatever you type until you press the Enter Key, and then exit. The function getche() gets a single typed character every time through the loop. Notice that the conditional expression here is getche()!= '\r', which handles both reading and checking the character.

We can have even more minimal conditional expressions if we need them. C considers an expression that is zero to be logically false, so we can even use the loop index itself as the conditional expression, terminating when it reaches zero. This program types out "Hello, world." backwards:

```
#include <stdio.h>

main()
{
char     msg[] = {"Hello, world."};
int      n;

for(n = sizeof(msg); n; )
                putch(msg[--n]);
}
```

Again, we could have put the whole thing into the for statement's parentheses:

```
#include <stdio.h>

main()
{
char    msg[] = {"Hello, world."};
int     n;

for(n = sizeof(msg); n; putch(msg[--n]))
                ;
}
```

This program leaves the body of the for loop as only ;, which is the NULL statement.

The While Loop

The next kind of loop is the while loop. The while loop is not difficult to use. Here is an example:

```
#include <stdio.h>

main()
{
i = 0;
while(i < 100)
        { printf("i = %d\n",i++); }
}
```

The body of the while loop is executed while the conditional expression inside the parentheses remains TRUE:

```
initialization exp;
while(conditional exp)
        {       }
```

The condition is evaluated before the loop is executed, so the loop may never be executed at all. This is the same as the for loop, and, in fact, they are interchangeable. The for loop can be made out of a while loop in this way:

```
initialization exp;
while(conditional exp)
        {
```

```
        ...body of loop...
        end-of-loop exp;
        }
```

The while loop, however, can make the code clearer. For example, we can print out the string "Hello world." easily with a while loop:

```
#include <stdio.h>

main()
{
int i = 0;
char hello[] = {"Hello world."};

while(hello[i])
        {putch(hello[i++]);}
}
```

The use of a while loop makes it immediately clear that we want the loop to continue while hello[i] is nonzero—that is, until we reach the NULL character at the end of the string.

The final loop construction is the do while loop. It differs from the for and while loops in that the conditional expression is evaluated at the *end* of the loop, making sure that the loop is executed at least once.

The Do While Loop

There are occasions when you want a loop to execute at least once, or you want to check the conditional expression that keeps the loop going at the end, rather than the beginning, of the loop. For this reason, most computer languages provide loops of both types: *check-first* and *check-last*. The do while loop is C's check-last loop.

The do while is also easy to use. It looks like this and executes as you'd expect.

```
do
{
...body of loop...
} while(conditional expression);
```

Now that we've reviewed the three C loops—for, while, and do while—we can put them to use. Let's work on a program that converts numbers from decimal to hexadecimal.

The DEC2HEX Program

First, start with the essentials:

```
main()
{
unsigned int i = 0, index = 0;
char out_string[10];


}
```

We read a positive integer into i and then convert it to a character string in out_string. We also use an index to keep track of our place in out_string, called index. Get the number to convert with scanf():

```
main()
    {
    unsigned int i = 0, index = 0;
    char out_string[10];

    printf("Type a positive integer please ");
    scanf("%d",&i);

    }
```

Bear in mind that we have to provide scanf() with the address of i, and not just pass the variable itself as a parameter. Now that we have the number, we have to convert it to hexadecimal. To convert a decimal number to hexadecimal, continually divide the number by 16, peeling off successive hexadecimal digits. After each division by 16, take the remainder and convert it into a single ASCII digit.

These ASCII digits are generated in reverse order. In assembly language, to put them in the correct order, they would be stored in the stack, then popped off one by one to be printed (as we'll do in Chapter 8). Here we store them in out_string instead, and then print the string out backwards. Let's use a while loop. First get the character to be stored—the current hexadecimal digit—in a variable called hexdig:

```
#include <stdio.h>

main()
{
unsigned int i = 0, index = 0, hexdig = 0;
char out_string[10];
```

```
printf("Type a positive integer please ");
scanf("%d",&i);

while(i)
        {
→       hexdig = (i%16 > 9 ? i%16-10+'a' : i%16+'0' );
        }
}
```

Next, store hexdig in out_string and divide i by 16 to prepare for the next time through:

```
#include <stdio.h>

main()
{
unsigned int i = 0, index = 0, hexdig = 0;
char out_string[10];

printf("Type a positive integer please ");
scanf("%d",&i);

while(i)
        {
        hexdig = (i%16 > 9 ? i%16-10+'a' : i%16+'0' );
        out_string[index++] = hexdig;
        i /= 16;
        }

}
```

After this loop, out_string contains all of the characters to be printed in backwards order. To print them out properly, decrement index in another while loop:

```
#include <stdio.h>

main()
{
unsigned int i = 0, index = 0, hexdig = 0;
char out_string[10];

printf("Type a positive integer please ");
scanf("%d",&i);

while(i)
        {
        hexdig = (i%16 > 9 ? i%16-10+'a' : i%16+'0' );
        out_string[index++] = hexdig;
        i /= 16;
```

```
              }

→       printf("That number in hexadecimal is ");
→       while(index) putch(out_string[--index]);

      }
```

And there it is, ready to convert numbers into hexadecimal.

The review of loops is finished. Throughout the book, we'll use loops frequently. The same applies to the next C construction that we will examine functions.

Functions

C is a language built out of functions, perhaps more than any other modern programming language. The input and output routines we take for granted in other languages are just functions in C.

The process of using a function is made particularly easy in C. At the end of functions (or subroutines) in other languages, you have to place a return statement to pass control back to the calling routine. C handles that step for you. Return addresses are stored on the stack, and C handles the stack manipulations—no return statement is necessary at the end of a function. On the other hand, you can return a value if you wish, and there is a return statement made just for that purpose.

Let's look at a simple program that contains one simple function:

```
#include <stdio.h>

void finish();

main()
{
printf("Hello ");
finish();
}

void finish()
{
printf("world.");
}
```

In order to use a function, first declare a function prototype, such as in this line from the example program:

```
          #include <stdio.h>

  →       void finish();

          main()
          {
          printf("Hello ");
          finish();
          }

          void finish()
          {
          printf("world.")"
          }
```

This declaration tells the compiler what it can expect from the function finish(). In particular, the keyword void indicates that the function finish() returns no value. For example, if double finish(); is used, then the compiler expects finish() to return a value of length double, and reads the return value out of the appropriate machine registers when finish() returns.

In our case, there is no return value. Here is the function itself:

```
          #include <stdio.h>

          void finish();

          main()
          {
          printf("Hello ");
          finish();
          }

  →       void finish()
  →       {
  →       printf("world.");
  →       }
```

All that this function does is print "world." to complete our "Hello world." string, and then return to main(). No return is necessary at the end of the function, because finish() doesn't return a value.

On the other hand, we can easily write a function that does return a value. Here is an example:

```
#include <stdio.h>

add5();
```

```
main()
{
printf("4 + 5 = %d",add5(4));
}

add5(x)
int   x;
{
return x + 5;
}
```

This function, named add5(), adds 5 to an integer passed to it. Note that a data type, such as int or double, is not included in front of either the prototype or the declaration of add5(). The default data type for functions is int.

At the end of add5(), a value is returned. To return a value, just use a return statement, such as return x + 5.

Multiple Parameters in a Function Call

When a C program calls a function, the values of the arguments are pushed onto the stack in the reverse order that they appear in the function call. This will be very important when we work with assembly language, and it's also important now. For example, consider the following statement:

```
printf("i, i++ = %d %d\n",i,i++);
```

It's important to know that the value of i++ is pushed first. The increment here is a post-increment, which means that if i is 12 when this statement is executed, "i, i++ = 13 12" will appear on the screen. But if we have a statement such as this one, which at first glance seems the same:

```
printf("i++, i = %d %d\n",i++,i);
```

the output is: "i++, i = 12 12", not "13 12". Here's the whole program, called PLUSPLUS.C:

```
#include <stdio.h>
main()
{
int i = 12,j = 12;
printf("i, i++ = %d %d\n",i,i++);
printf("j++, j = %d %d\n",j++,j);
```

```
}

C>plusplus
i, i++ = 13 12
j++, j = 12 12
```

Memory Use in C

It is important to understand what is going on with memory in a C program. Few other high-level languages pay as much attention as C does to memory maintenance and allocation. (Assembly language, of course, is even more memory-conscious than C.)

Memory is divided into several different sections when a C program runs. There is the *Code* area (which corresponds to the *code segment* in assembly language), where the program instructions reside. This area is usually not changed when a program runs. (Some programs do include self-modifying code, but it is unusual. When a program modifies its own code, it is usually done unintentionally.)

The next area is the *Data* area (which corresponds to the *data segment* in assembly language). This area is further divided into two sections, one for initialized data and another for uninitialized data. The latter area is called the *BSS* area (for *Block Started Segment*).

Another memory area is set up at the top of available memory. This region grows towards lower memory as it is filled. This is the *Stack* (which corresponds to the *stack segment* in assembly language).

The final memory area is located in low memory, above the Code and Data areas. This area is called the Heap. It can grow in size just like the Stack, except that it grows towards higher memory, rather than downwards towards lower memory. C itself usually maintains the Stack for us, but the allocation and use of memory on the Heap is our responsibility. A number of library routines are designed to allocate memory space on the Heap, including malloc() and calloc(). We will work more with the Heap in the next chapter.

Here's how the areas might appear in memory:

```
                                    Low Memory
        ┌─────────────────────────┐
        │          Code           │
        │                         │
        ├─────────────────────────┤
        │       Initialized       │
        │          Data           │
        │                         │
        └─────────────────────────┘
```

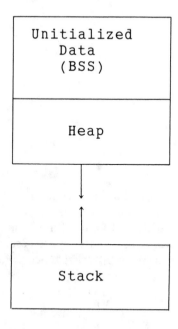

High Memory

Automatic and Static Variables

The use of memory shows itself in the two different types of variables available in C: *automatic* and *static*. All declared variables are automatic by default. There is a keyword auto that you can use before a variable's declaration like this:

```
auto int j = 5;
```

to guarantee that a variable is automatic; Automatic data types are the default, it is not necessary. The reason these variables are called automatic is that memory space for them is automatically allocated when needed.

Memory space on the stack is allocated for automatic variables when the program enters the function or *block* in which they are defined. A block is defined in C as anything within curly braces. For example, look again at the program that uses add5:

```
add5();
main()
{
printf("4 + 5 = %d",add5(4));
}
add5(x)
int   x;
{
return x + 5;
}
```

Here, x is an automatic variable. The executable file for this program contains machine code to allocate storage on the stack for x when add5() is called. If we initialize x, the machine code includes instructions to load the correct value into x after space is set aside for it.

Automatic variables can also appear in blocks. For example, let's add a line to convert decimal to hexadecimal:

```
main()
{
unsigned int i = 0, index = 0, hexdig = 0;
char out_string[10];
printf("Type a positive integer please ");
scanf("%d",&i);
while(i) {
        hexdig = (i%16 > 9 ? i%16-10+'a' : i%16+'0' );
        out_string[index++] = hexdig;
        int b = 12;
        i /= 16; }
printf("That number in hexadecimal is ");
while(index) putch(out_string[--index]);
}
```

The int declaration may look funny inside the while block, but it is legal. It also declares an automatic variable named b. Space for b is set aside on the stack when the block is entered.

> Notice that setting aside and initializing automatic variables when a function is called can add significant amounts of overhead to a program.

On the other hand, this means that because space is newly allocated for automatic variables every time a function or block is entered, their values change every time they are reallocated. Unless they are initalized, we cannot be sure that their values will even be zero. And in some cases, we want a function to retain the values of some of its internal variables between calls.

C also offers *static* variables to address this problem. If you declare a variable static, a new copy of it is not made every time its function or block is entered. Instead, undisturbed space is set aside for the variable in the data area, not on the stack.

Automatic variables are stored on the stack, and static variables are stored in the data area. Static variables can be initialized, like this:

```
static int i = 215;
```

They are then stored in the initialized part of the data area. If they are declared as uninitialized, like this:

```
static int i;
```

then they are stored in the BSS area. In other words, to make a variable static, you must explicitly declare it so, and then its value is stored in the data area. Because the data area is not reallocated whenever a function or block is entered, a static variable's value is just that—static.

Global Variables

Another type of variable that is stored in the data area (either in the initialized data area or in BSS) are *global* variables. Global variables are not declared inside any block or function, and look like this:

```
→    int i = 34;
     main()
     {
     ...program...
     }
```

These variables are called "global" because they may be referenced anywhere in the program. In general, variables may only be referenced inside the block or function where they are declared. Global variables, however, are declared in the *super-block* of the whole program, so they are available anywhere inside it. The reason global variables are stored in the data area, along with static variables, is that control enters the super-block of the whole program only once—there is no reason to have to reallocate or free memory given to a global variable because the program never leaves the block in which it is defined.

It is still possible to have *static global* variables, and they are important. Here, *static* refers not to memory allocation, but to the variable's *scope*. A static global variable looks like this and is *private* to the current file.

```
→    static int i = 34;
     main()
     {
     ...program...
     }
```

The name of any other global variable can be referenced by code in any other file, simply by including the keyword extrn before its declaration. For example, if you write code in one file and you want to reference the int variable, called there, in another file, you only need to include the declaration:

```
extern int there;
```

in the second file. When you link the two files together, the linker looks for the variable there in other files, until it finds the variable.

> For assembly language programmers: The use of extrn is much like the use of EXTRN and PUBLIC in assembly language, except that PUBLIC is not required because variables are PUBLIC by default in C.

Let's add the location of variable storage to our earlier memory chart:

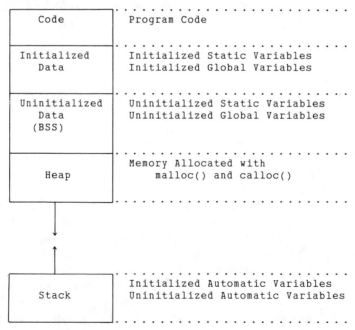

```
┌──────────────┐  . . . . . . . . . . . . . . . . . . . . . .
│     Code     │    Program Code
│              │
├──────────────┤  . . . . . . . . . . . . . . . . . . . . . .
│  Initialized │    Initialized Static Variables
│     Data     │    Initialized Global Variables
│              │
├──────────────┤  . . . . . . . . . . . . . . . . . . . . . .
│ Uninitialized│    Uninitialized Static Variables
│     Data     │    Uninitialized Global Variables
│    (BSS)     │
│              │
├──────────────┤  . . . . . . . . . . . . . . . . . . . . . .
│              │    Memory Allocated with
│     Heap     │        malloc() and calloc()
│              │
│              │  . . . . . . . . . . . . . . . . . . . . . .
│       │      │
│       ↓      │
│              │
│       ↑      │
│       │      │
┌──────────────┐  . . . . . . . . . . . . . . . . . . . . . .
│              │    Initialized Automatic Variables
│    Stack     │    Uninitialized Automatic Variables
│              │
└──────────────┘  . . . . . . . . . . . . . . . . . . . . . .
```

And here's a program that indicates what goes where:

```
int i;                 [Global → BSS]
int j = 5;             [Global → Initialized Data Area]
static int l = 5;      [Static Global → Initialized Data Area]
static int m = 5;      [Static Global → BSS]

main()
{
int n;                 [Automatic → Stack]
int o = 5;             [Automatic → Stack]
static int p;          [Static → BSS]
static int q = 5;      [Static → Initialized Data Area]
}
```

You may wonder why there is an area such as BSS that is separate from the initialized data area. The answer is the speed of execution: C guarantees that uninitialized static and global variables have a value of zero when the program starts. By grouping all such variables together, they can be zeroed all at once.

With all of this memory usage, C must be very good at working with memory. Of course, it is—especially with respect to pointers.

Pointers

For many people, this is a dreaded subject. Yet pointers can make programs faster, easier, and more memory-efficient. Pointers provide C with a method for indirect addressing, and assembly language uses indirect addressing heavily. C places a strong emphasis upon pointers, so we need to get to know them well.

A *pointer* simply holds the address of a memory location.

Two C operators are used with pointers: the indirection operator, "*", and the address of operator, "&." You can declare a pointer in this way:

```
int *pointer_name;
```

That's all there is to it. This declaration sets up a pointer to an integer in memory (the integer that it points to is not yet specified). From now on, when you refer to pointer_name in a program, you are referring to an address. When you use the indirection operator "*", such as in the statement i = *pointer_name, you are referring to the integer that is the contents of that location in memory.

```
pointer_name   → address
*pointer_name  → integer
```

| Pointers are either 16 bits long or 32 bits long; because pointers represent addresses, this should not surprise assembly language programmers. |

Once you have pointer_name declared, you can use it in programs such as this one:

```
main()
{
int *pointer_name;
int i = 5;
```
→
```
pointer_name = &i;        /* assign the address of i to pointer_name */
printf("i = %d, *pointer_name = %d", i, *pointer_name);
}
```

To initialize the pointer, fill it with the address of the variable it points to. Then you can refer to the variable with *pointer_name:

→
```
pointer_name = &i;        /* assign the address of i to pointer_name */
```
→
```
printf("i = %d, *pointer_name = %d", i, *pointer_name);
```

This may seem like a modest gain, yet recall that the way C passes arguments to functions is by value, not by address. If a function is to work directly on data, not on a copy of the data, then the function must know where the data are stored in memory.

Here's a program with a function that sorts two numbers. If the program did not know the number's addresses, it could not do what it does.

```
main()
{
int int1 = 5, int2 = 3;
```

The object here is to set up a function, named sort2(), to sort int1 and int2. We pass the addresses of int1 and int2 (that is, pointers to these two variables) to sort2(), and then print out the sorted integers:

```
main()
{
int int1 = 5, int2 = 3;
```
→
```
sort2(&int1, &int2);
```
→
```
printf("In sorted order, we have: %d, %d",int1, int2);
}
```

Now we need to write the sort2() function. For sort2()'s internal use, let's call the arguments that it receives pointer1 and pointer2. We indicate the type of the arguments in this way:

```
void sort2();

main()
{
int int1 = 5, int2 = 3;

sort2(&int1, &int2);
printf("In sorted order, we have: %d, %d",int1, int2);
}

sort2(pointer1, pointer2)
int *pointer1, *pointer2;
```

This declares pointer1 and pointer2 to be pointers to integers. Now we are free to use those integers in this manner (and to add a temporary variable, temporary):

```
void sort2();

main()
{
int int1 = 5, int2 = 3;

sort2(&int1, &int2);
printf("In sorted order, we have: %d, %d",int1, int2);
}

void sort2(pointer1, pointer2)
int *pointer1, *pointer2;
{
int temporary;
if(*pointer1 > *pointer2) {
        temporary = *pointer2;
        *pointer2 = *pointer1;
        *pointer1 = temporary;   }
}
```

This program lets sort2() affect memory directly through the use of pointers.

Another reason C relies so heavily on pointers is that array use is made much easier and efficient with them, as we'll see later in this book. In fact, the name of an array is really a pointer, and the expression array[i] is really the same as *(array + i).

One more reason we will be using pointers is that command-line arguments are passed to programs in an array of pointers named argv[]. (We will have more to say about argv[] in the following chapter.)

Even though esoteric data structures are possible with pointers (such as circular data buffers, made out of data structures that include pointers to the next structure in the buffer), we will try to keep our feet on the ground. After all, these elements of the C language are meant as tools, and unless we master them, they will be of no use to us.

The goto Statement

The goto statement is the black sheep of programming. For many years, its use was discouraged as bad programming practice because it led to 'spaghetti' code, where the flow of control was not clear. Still, the goto command was too attractive for the designers of C to pass up for a single, simple reason: In certain circumstances, it can increase a program's execution speed.

C is designed to be a fast language, and the goto command can get you out of one particular situation—deeply nested loops—faster than the usual route of making many-level checks. If you are deep inside a many-level loop or an if structure, and are sure you want to leave, use a goto command. This is much faster than waiting for each level to test FALSE and the waiting for control to work its way out of the multiple levels of tests.

You use it like this:

```
goto label;
```

Here labels (or your own name) can be stuck anywhere in a block of code, as in this program:

```
#include <stdio.h>

main()
{
int *pointer_name;
int i = 5;
label:
pointer_name = &i;      /* assign the address of i to pointer_name */
printf("i = %d, *pointer_name = %d", i, *pointer_name);
}
```

That's the end of our lightning-fast review of C. If it's been a little too fast, this book may not be for you. If, however, you are right at home, let's turn to Chapter 2.

2
File Handling

Working with files is rarely covered in beginning texts, yet files are an integral part of any computer system. Unless there was some way of storing data when the power went off, computers would be in trouble. The file-handling capabilities in C are good (and, surprisingly, they are good in assembly language under DOS as well). In fact, the selection of library functions is almost too good: Sometimes it's difficult to wade through all of the available choices.

A File-writing Example

It's easy to make the transition in C from working with keyboard and screen to working with files, because most keyboard-input and screen-output functions have parallel functions for file-handling. In many cases, we can just add f, like this: scanf() becomes fscanf(); getc() (get character) becomes fgetc(); and printf() becomes fprintf(). Let's try a small program that writes the "Hello, world.\n" string to a disk file, named HELLO.TXT:

```
#include <stdio.h>
main()
{
        FILE *file_pointer;
        if( (file_pointer = fopen( "hello.txt", "w") ) != NULL)
        {       fprintf(file_pointer,"Hello, world.\n");
                fclose(file_pointer);
        }
        else printf("Error writing hello.txt\n");
}
```

When you run the program, you'll find a 15-byte file on the disk, and typing it reveals our message. Here's the way it works: First, we include the I/O function header, STDIO.H. Header files, such as this file, give prototypes for library functions and include needed declarations. Next, open the file for writing, with the function fopen():

41

```
#include <stdio.h>

main()
{
        FILE *file_pointer;

→       if( (file_pointer = fopen( "hello.txt", "w") ) != NULL)
        {       fprintf(file_pointer,"Hello, world.\n");
                fclose(file_pointer);
        }
        else printf("Error writing hello.txt\n");
}
```

We specify both the name of the file (HELLO.TXT) and that we intend to write to it, with the character string "w". Six file-opening options with the fopen() function are listed in the following table:

Table 2.1   File-opening Options

File-opening Option	Means
r	Open (existing) file for reading.
w	Open (create if necessary) file for writing.
a	Open (create if necessary) file for appending.
r+	Open (existing) file for reading and writing.
w+	Create and open file for reading and writing.
a+	Open (create if necessary) file for reading and appending.

The fopen() function returns a pointer to a structure of type FILE. Since the details of this structure are handled by the file functions themselves, we won't concern ourselves here with them. If fopen() returns a NULL pointer, the file was not opened. In that case, the program terminates and prints an error message.

We'll call the file pointer file_pointer. Note the typically economical shorthand of C here—we assign the file pointer to file_pointer and check its value in the same step.

> If you want to specify a pathname for the file (for example, c:\hello.txt) note that you need to make the string in fopen() call "c:\\hello.txt", because the single backslash is otherwise interpreted as part of an escape sequence.

If the file is opened successfully, we want to write the data string to it. Since we are most familiar with printf(), let's use its file analog, fprintf(). With this function, you can send formatted output to files in the same way that you can send formatted output to the monitor with printf(). We have to include a format string, as usual. The printf() function only prints to the standard output device (stdout—usually the monitor, unless output was redirected), but a number of files can be open. This means that we have to pass fprintf() the file pointer for the file that we want to use. In this case, the file pointer is file_pointer:

```
#include <stdio.h>

main()
{
        FILE *file_pointer;

        if( (file_pointer = fopen( "hello.txt", "w") ) != NULL)
→       {       fprintf(file_pointer,"Hello, world.\n");
                fclose(file_pointer);
        }
        else printf("Error writing hello.txt\n");
}
```

The fprintf() function does the work. Following it, we close the file (so that DOS may update the file's directory information). To close a file, simply pass the file pointer to the fclose() function.

That's all there is to it. Of course, there are other ways to do it, just as there are other ways to print on the screen. We do not include any formatted output here (just the string 'Hello, world.\n") so we do not really need fprintf(). When you want to send just character strings to the monitor, you can use either printf() or puts(). There is also a file analog for puts(), called fputs(). Here is how the program would have looked with fputs():

```
#include <stdio.h>

main()
{
        FILE *file_pointer;

        if( (file_pointer = fopen( "hello.txt", "w") ) != NULL)
→       {       fputs("Hello, world.\n",file_pointer);
                fclose(file_pointer);
        }
        else printf("Error writing hello.txt\n");
}
```

This program also writes a 15-byte file. There is even an analog for the putc() function, which prints one character at a time—this analog is fputc(). On the other hand, if you had wanted to write numbers or other formatted objects to your file, with fprintf(), since you can specify output with the format string.

A File Reading Example

In a similar way, now that we have the file hello.txt on the disk, we can read it in and print it out. To do that, we have to provide storage space for it in memory. Let's use a string called temp[] for that purpose. The easiest function to use to read a string from the file is fgets(), which is explicitly designed for that purpose from files. Here is our reading program:

```
#include <stdio.h>
main()
{
FILE *file_pointer;
char temp[80];
        if( (file_pointer = fopen( "hello.txt", "r") ) != NULL)
        {
                if( (fgets(temp, sizeof(temp),file_pointer) ) != NULL)
                {
                        printf(temp);
                        fclose(file_pointer);
                }
                else printf("Error reading hello.txt\n");
        }
        else printf("Error opening hello.txt\n");
}
```

First, we define temp[], the buffer for the file's data, and open the file:

```
    #include <stdio.h>
    main()
    {
    FILE *file_pointer;
→   char temp[80];
→           if( (file_pointer = fopen( "hello.txt", "r") ) != NULL)
            {
                    ... get string and print it ...
            }
→           else printf("Error opening hello.txt\n");
    }
```

If we cannot open the file, we print an error message. If we can open the file, our next step is to read in the data. Since our data are simply a character string, we can use fgets(), file get string, which is tailor-made for us. The fgets() function requires three arguments: a pointer to a string buffer, the length of the string buffer in memory, and a file pointer.

The name of an array is really a pointer. This means that the pointer to the buffer in memory is really just the name: temp. C treats a character string (like temp[80]) as an array. We can easily find the size of an array (if we do not already know that it is 80) with the sizeof() function in order to determine the length of the buffer in memory. Finally, the pointer of the file is simply file_pointer. This line gets the string from the file and puts it into temp[]:

```
#include <stdio.h>
main()
{
FILE *file_pointer;
char temp[80];
        if( (file_pointer = fopen( "hello.txt", "r") ) != NULL)
            {
→           if( (fgets(temp, sizeof(temp),file_pointer) ) != NULL)
                {
                    ... print string & close file ...
                }
→           else printf("Error reading hello.txt\n");
            }
        else printf("Error opening hello.txt\n");
}
```

(Note that if fgets() fails, it returns a NULL pointer, and in our program we print out an error message.) All that remains is to print the string now in temp[] and close the file. We can do that easily, and our program is done:

```
#include <stdio.h>
main()
{
FILE *file_pointer;
char temp[80];
        if( (file_pointer = fopen( "hello.txt", "r") ) != NULL)
            {
            if( (fgets(temp, sizeof(temp),file_pointer) ) != NULL)
                {
→                   printf(temp);              /*get character*/
→                   fclose(file_pointer);
                }
            else printf("Error reading hello.txt\n"); /*error*/
            }
        else printf("Error opening hello.txt\n"); /*error*/
}
```

Give it a try—the program will open HELLO.TXT, and print the contents of the file on the screen.

Now we've been able to read in a file that we also created. We may not always know the size of the file we're reading. Let's move from these specific examples to the more general case, where we'll read in from a file until we reach the end of file. After that, we'll go to an even lower level, where the functions we use simply return the number of bytes they've read, and we don't search for the end-of-file marker at all. (This last case is more like assembly language.)

The EOF Marker

When you read in a file, byte by byte, you eventually reach the end of the file. When that happens, the next thing you read is the end-of-file marker. (In C, this is an integer with the value 0FFFFH.) This mark is not actually at the end of a file—it's returned by the C file-reading functions to inform you that there is nothing more to read from the file.

This program demonstrates the use of the EOF mark:

```
#include <stdio.h>

main()
{
int buff1;
FILE *file_pointer;

if( file_pointer = fopen("hello.txt", "r") )
        {
        while( (buff1 = fgetc(file_pointer) ) != EOF)
        printf("%c", buff1);
        printf("\n");
        fclose(file_pointer);
        }
else printf("Couldn't open hello.txt\n");
}
```

This program, like our earlier reading program, reads in the file HELLO.TXT and prints it out on the screen. This program does it byte-by-byte, and does not rely upon the fact that only one character string is in the file. The program stays in the while loop until the read-in character is the end-of-file, or EOF character, as this next program demonstrates:

```
#include <stdio.h>
```

```
main()
{
int buff1;
FILE *file_pointer;

if( file_pointer = fopen("hello.txt", "r") )
        {
→       while( (buff1 = fgetc(file_pointer) ) != EOF)
→       printf("%c", buff1);
→       printf("\n");
→       fclose(file_pointer);
        }
else printf("Couldn't open hello.txt\n");
}
```

Notice that the variable we fill when we read in from the file, buff1, is declared as an integer, and not as a char variable. This is important—if we are testing for the EOF mark, we have to use an integer-sized buffer, even if we only read in one byte at a time. The reason for this is that the EOF mark is one word long, rather than one byte long. In order to test buff1 against EOF, buff1 must be an int.

So far, we've learned that we can write files and we can read them. Also, when we read them in, C will tell us when there are no more data to be read by passing us the EOF mark. However, we still don't have a good feel for what's in a file. Some programs format the files they write under all circumstances: does C? Can we use C to read and write out a file verbatim? Can we store a data structure in a file and retrieve it? Can we section a file up into records? All of these questions remain to be answered.

Binary and ASCII Files

The C language treats files in two different ways: as either ASCII files or binary files. If you specify that a file is to be treated as a binary file, C does not interpret the file's contents when it reads or writes data to or from the file. In this case, the data in the file are just data, nothing more. Soon we are going to write a program that copies one file over into another, and we'll treat the files as binary so that C doesn't do anything fancy.

ASCII files are not radically different—there are only two differences. First, if C finds a ^Z (ASCII 1AH) in the file when it's reading, C treats the ^Z as an end-of-file character and assumes the end of the file has been reached. (Although C does not write these characters at the end of ASCII files, you can explicitly put them in.) The second difference is that on the disk, the newline character \n is stored as an ASCII 0DH 0AH (ASCII <carriage return> and <linefeed>). In memory it is stored only in C's internal format for an end-of-line character, 0AH (ASCII <lf>).

The fact that C stores newline characters internally as ASCII 0AH and on the disk (in ASCII format) as 0DH 0AH has some interesting consequences. When we wrote the original string "Hello, world.\n" out to disk, the file was 15 bytes long. That's because the default file mode is ASCII. If we wrote the string out to match literally what's in memory—in other words, in binary mode—we'd get a file that's only 14 bytes long, since the 0DH character is missing.

To read and write in binary format, it's only necessary to add b to the option string passed to fopen(). For example, here's our first file-writing program converted to write a binary (i.e., uninterpreted) version of the string in memory:

```
#include <stdio.h>

main()
{
        FILE *file_pointer;

→       if( (file_pointer = fopen( "hello.txt", "wb") ) != NULL)
                {       fprintf(file_pointer,"Hello, world.\n");
                        fclose(file_pointer);
                }
        else printf("Error writing hello.txt\n");
}
```

When you run this program, HELLO.TXT ends up being 14 bytes long.

> The reason \n is stored internally as only 0AH is because UNIX—the operating system that fostered C—does it that way. The 0DH is added in disk files so that when you type a file out at DOS level, it prints correctly on the screen.

When do you use ASCII format and when do you use binary format? If you are dealing with only strings, as we have been doing until now, it is best to use only ASCII format (once you pick one format, stick with it throughout the entire program). To see when binary files (that is, literal files without any interpretation of their contents) might be important, let's take an overview of the C file-handling functions. They come in pairs:

Table 2.2   File-handling Functions

Writing	Reading	Used on
fputc( )	fgetc( )	Individual characters
fputs( )	fgets( )	Character strings
fprintf( )	fscanf( )	Formatted ASCII
fwrite( )	fread( )	Binary files
write( )	read( )	Low level binary

In this chapter, we've already worked our way through the top two lines of this list (except for fputc()). The third line, fprintf() and fscanf(), are the functions most commonly used for writing ASCII files. As with their screen counterparts, these functions write ASCII strings to a file. We will use them when we store numbers in our program FILER.C.

Until now, we haven't dealt with non-ASCII output to files. The last two lines in our list, fwrite()/fread() and write()/read(), deal with binary files. We will work with these binary functions after we write FILER.C.

The FILER.C Program

When a file is to be all text, use fprintf() and fscanf(). For example, the FILER.C program asks you for numbers and files them in a file named FILE.TXT:

```c
#include <stdio.h>
main()
{
    FILE *file_pointer;
    int num;
    if( (file_pointer = fopen( "file.txt", "w") ) != NULL)
           {
        printf("Type some integers:\n");
        while(scanf("%d",&num) == 1) fprintf(file_pointer,"%d\n",num);
        fclose(file_pointer);
           }
        else printf("Error writing file.txt\n");
}
```

When we run FILER.C, the screen looks like this:

```
C>filer

Type some integers:
```

As long as we keep typing single integers followed by a <cr>, FILER.C files them in FILE.TXT:

```
C>filer
Type some integers:
1
2
3
4
5
```

However, as soon as we try to pass two numbers to FILER.C, like this:

```
C>filer
Type some integers:
    1
    2
    3
    4
    5
→   6,7
```

we exit the while loop because the value returned by scanf() was no longer 1:

```
#include <stdio.h>

main()
{
  FILE *file_pointer;
  int num;

  if( (file_pointer = fopen( "file.txt", "w") ) != NULL)
  {
        printf("Type some integers:\n");   /*prompt, next, get no.*/
→       while(scanf("%d",&num) == 1) fprintf(file_pointer,"%d\n",num);
        fclose(file_pointer);
  }
        else printf("Error writing file.txt\n"); /*error*/
}
```

> This example would be cleaner if we could have simply type a <cr> and scanf() return a value of 0 (and so exit the while loop), but scanf() returns a value of 1 even if you only type a <cr>.

The program now closes FILE.TXT. The file now exists on disk, written in ASCII mode. Here's the way it looks:

```
C>type file.txt
1
```

```
2
3
4
5
6

C>
```

The file holds what we've typed to it in ASCII. This is exactly right for ASCII format: It stores everything as ASCII characters. (If we use exclusively numerical data, it more efficient to use binary format for the file, especially to store floating point numbers. We'll work with binary format in a moment, but first let's write a program called READER.C that reads our ASCII file.

There are only minor alterations to make to change FILER.C into READER.C. For example, the "w" in the fopen() statement has to become "r" for reading (or else FILE.TXT is zeroed when we open it). Also, instead of using scanf() to read from the keyboard, we use fscanf() to read from the file. And rather than use fprintf() to write to the file, we use printf() to print the ASCII strings we read on the screen. Here is READER.C:

```
#include <stdio.h>
main()
{
    FILE *file_pointer;
    int num;
→   if( (file_pointer = fopen( "file.txt", "r") ) != NULL)
    {
→   while(fscanf(file_pointer,"%d",&num) != EOF) printf("%d\n",num);
        fclose(file_pointer);
    }
    else printf("Error reading file.txt\n");
}
```

Note that as a general rule, you should use the same format string in fscanf() to read the file that you used in fprintf() to write the file. Here that is particularly easy, since the format string is only "%d". Here is the output of READER.C:

```
C>reader
1
2
3
4
5
6
C>
```

Notice that we used the fact here that when fscanf() comes to the end of a file, it returns the EOF integer:

```
#include <stdio.h>

main()
{
   FILE *file_pointer;
   int num;

   if( (file_pointer = fopen( "file.txt", "r") ) != NULL)
      {
→     while(fscanf(file_pointer,"%d",&num) != EOF) printf("%d\n",num);
         fclose(file_pointer);
      }
      else printf("Error writing file.txt\n");
}
```

We're done with ASCII files. When you choose ASCII format, everything is written as ASCII strings, even numbers. This is very wasteful of space, so C offers other options. Let's look again at the earlier table of file-handling functions:

Writing	Reading	Used on
fputc( )	fgetc( )	Individual characters
fputs( )	fgets( )	Character strings
fprintf( )	fscanf( )	Formatted ASCII
fwrite( )	fread( )	Binary files
write( )	read( )	Low level binary

The line after fprintf() and fscanf() is fwrite() and fread(). These are the ANSI standard binary-file writing functions of C (write() and read() are not ANSI standard, but they are very useful in both Microsoft C and Turbo C). Let's put them to the test.

Working With Binary Files

The fwrite() and fread() functions do not interpret what they write or read. When they find the sequence <cr><lf> (0DH 0AH) in the disk file, they do not delete the <cr>. The ^Z (1AH) byte, if read from a file, does not count as the end-of-file mark.

On the other hand, fwrite() and fread() are not as easy to use as the DOS file reading and writing functions in assembly language. There, we simply specify the number of bytes that we want to read or write, and the DOS services read or write that many bytes from or to a file.

The fwrite() and fread() functions request more information. For example, if you want to write an array, farray[], of 15 floating point numbers to a file, the call to fwrite() looks like this:

```
fwrite(farray, sizeof(float), 15, file_pointer);
```

You have to pass fwrite() a pointer to the data, the size of each data item to be written, the number of data items, and an open file's pointer. There are 15 floating point numbers in farray, so our fopen() instruction looks like the instruction just presented.

Let's put this line to work with a small program called NUMBERS.C. Set up an array named farray[] and initialize the first few values:

```
#include <stdio.h>
#define INDEX 15

main()
{
        FILE *file_pointer;
→       float farray[INDEX] = {1.2, 3.78, 1.553, 9.1, -3.14159};

}
```

Next, open a file called NUMBERS.DAT:

```
#include <stdio.h>
#define INDEX 15

main()
{
        FILE *file_pointer;
        float farray[INDEX] = {1.2, 3.78, 1.553, 9.1, -3.14159};

→    if( (file_pointer = fopen( "numbers.dat", "w") ) != NULL)
                        ... write file here ...
→       else printf("Error writing numbers.dat\n");

}
```

And finally, fill the file with farray[] by using fwrite():

```
#include <stdio.h>
#define INDEX 15

main()
{
        FILE *file_pointer;
        float farray[INDEX] = {1.2, 3.78, 1.553, 9.1, -3.14159};
```

```
     if( (file_pointer = fopen( "numbers.dat", "w") ) != NULL)
→             fwrite(farray, sizeof(float), INDEX, file_pointer);
        else printf("Error writing numbers.dat\n");

     fclose(file_pointer);

}
```

When you run NUMBERS.C, it produces NUMBERS.DAT. This file holds the floating point numbers in the same format as if they were in memory—you cannot print them out on the screen. On the other hand, we can use fread() to read them in again.

Here's a small program to do that:

```
#include <stdio.h>
#define INDEX 15

main()
{
        FILE *file_pointer;
        float farray[INDEX];
        int i;

→    if( (file_pointer = fopen( "numbers.dat", "r") ) != NULL)
→            fread(farray, sizeof(float), INDEX, file_pointer);
        else printf("Error reading numbers.dat\n");
     for(i = 0; INDEX - i; i++) printf("number: %f\n",farray[i]);

     fclose(file_pointer);

}
```

Notice that fread() takes the same arguments, in the same order, as does fwrite(). Besides that, we only had to change the "w" in fopen() to "r".

Our file NUMBERS.DAT can hold 15 identical floating point numbers, in floating point (not ASCII) format. But that's not all that such files can do.

File Records

Most languages let you write files in what are called *records*. Data files, for example, are commonly made up of records. Let's say that you have an account book that you want to keep track of on your computer. One record might look like this:

```
Name: "Phileas Fogg"
Owes: $20,000.00
```

Stop Wasting Time!
Order the Program Disk for C With
Assembly Language.

STOP

Don't spend valuable hours keying in the code when you can use this powerful diskette containing all the programs in the book. As you run the programs, followthe explanations in the book. And to learn even more as you conveniently work at your own pace, modify and experiment with the code.

The choice is yours...Why keyboard your fingers to the bone when you can let this powerful diskette handle it for you?

To order your copy, enclose a check or money order for $30.00, plus sales tax, for each disk. Or charge it to your VISA or MasterCard by completing the information below.

This record contains both an ASCII string and a floating point number. In C, we might put together the following data structure for this record:

```
struct entry
{
        char[20] name;
        float owes;
}
```

Now, in order to store such structures, we can build a file of them, one after the next. This is how records are used in data files. Let's give this a try. We can modify our previous program, FILER.C, so that instead of an array of floating point numbers as shown here:

```
#include <stdio.h>
#define INDEX 15

main()
{
        FILE *file_pointer;
  →     float farray[INDEX] = {1.2, 3.78, 1.553, 9.1, -3.14159};
        :
        :
```

we have an array of struct entry:

```
#include <stdio.h>
#define INDEX 15
  struct entry
  {
        char name[20];
        float owes;
  }

main()
{
        FILE *file_pointer;
  →        struct entry farray[INDEX];

    if( (file_pointer = fopen( "numbers.dat", "w") ) != NULL)
  →        fwrite(farray, sizeof(struct entry), INDEX, file_pointer);
        else printf("Error writing numbers.dat\n");

}
```

The only other change we have to make is to change sizeof(float) to sizeof(struct entry) in the fwrite() call. Let's also initialize the first two records in farray:

```
#include <stdio.h>
#define INDEX 15

    struct entry
    {
            char name[20];
            float owes;
    }

main()
{
        FILE *file_pointer;
            struct entry farray[INDEX];

→       strcpy(farray[0].name,"Ebeneezer Scrooge");
→       farray[0].owes = 0.01;
→       strcpy(farray[1].name,"Bob Crachit");
→       farray[1].owes = 312.59;

      if( (file_pointer = fopen( "numbers.dat", "w") ) != NULL)
              fwrite(farray, sizeof(struct entry), INDEX, file_pointer);
          else printf("Error writing numbers.dat\n");
}
```

Again we use strcpy() to fill the character array. Now the file NUMBERS.DAT is on disk. It's about 360 bytes long, and contains 15 records.

Reading Records

We can read NUMBERS.DAT in and print out the first two records. All we need to do is adapt our program to use fread() instead of fwrite(), and then open the file for reading, not for writing. Here is the new program, complete with changes:

```
#include <stdio.h>
#define INDEX 15

    struct entry
    {
            char name[20];
            float owes;
    }

  main()
  {
          FILE *file_pointer;
          struct entry farray[INDEX];

→     if( (file_pointer = fopen( "numbers.dat", "r") ) != NULL)
→             fread(farray, sizeof(struct entry), INDEX, file_pointer);
          else printf("Error writing numbers.dat\n");
```

```
→        printf("%s owes $%.2f\n",farray[0].name,farray[0].owes);
→        printf("%s owes $%.2f\n",farray[1].name,farray[1].owes);

    }
```

When you run this new program, it does just the reverse of FILER.C. It opens NUMBERS.DAT and reads it in, then prints out the first two (formatted) records.

Of course, if you had 3,000 such entries, it would be more difficult to read them all in at once and provide memory space for each one. The C language uses something called a *position pointer* inside a file to solve this problem. With it, we can position ourselves inside the file and read whatever record we want. In that case, since we're only reading one record at a time, we only need to provide memory storage for that record.

The Position Pointer (for use with records)

Let's say we had a file filled with data like this:

The position pointer works like this in a file:

```
                      ┌─────────────────────────────────┐  Record 4
                      │ data data data data data         │
                      │ data data data data data         │
                      └─────────────────────────────────┘
```

It starts at the beginning of the file, but you can place it anywhere with a function called fseek():

```
                      ┌─────────────────────────────────┐  Record 1
                      │ data data data data data         │
                      │ data data data data data         │
                      ├─────────────────────────────────┤  Record 2
                      │ data data data data data         │
                      │ data data data data data         │
position pointer →    ├─────────────────────────────────┤  Record 3
                      │ data data data data data         │
                      │ data data data data data         │
                      ├─────────────────────────────────┤  Record 4
                      │ data data data data data         │
                      │ data data data data data         │
                      └─────────────────────────────────┘
```

You can also return the position pointer to the beginning of the file with a function called rewind().

Let's put this information to work. We could rewrite our program FILER.C to fill only record number 9, like this:

```
#include <stdio.h>
#define INDEX 15

  struct entry
  {
          char name[20];
          float owes;
  }

main()
{
        FILE *file_pointer;
          struct entry farray[INDEX];

→       strcpy(farray[9].name,"Ebeneezer Scrooge");
→       farray[9].owes = 0.01;

    if( (file_pointer = fopen( "numbers.dat", "w") ) != NULL)
            fwrite(farray, sizeof(struct entry), INDEX, file_pointer);
        else printf("Error writing numbers.dat\n");


}
```

Our new version of NUMBERS.DAT contains all uninitialized records—except for record 9. Now we want to read that record from the file. This is a common problem in database programs—how you read, say, record 37,281 in a file of 93,829 records?

Using fseek() to position ourselves in NUMBERS.DAT, the solution is easy. We can modify our reading program so it only has memory space for one record, uses fseek() to set the position pointer in the file, and reads in only one record at a time:

```
#include <stdio.h>
#include <io.h>
#define INDEX 15

  struct entry
  {
            char name[20];
            float owes;
  }

main()
{
        FILE *file_pointer;
        struct entry buffer;
        int rec_num;

     if( (file_pointer = fopen( "numbers.dat", "r") ) != NULL)
            {
            printf("Type the record number to recover:");
            scanf("%d",&rec_num);
      fseek(file_pointer, (long) (rec_num*sizeof(struct entry)), 0);
            fread(&buffer, sizeof(struct entry), 1, file_pointer);
            }
        else printf("Error reading numbers.dat\n");

     printf("%s owes $%.2f\n",buffer.name,buffer.owes);

}
```

This program asks for the name of the record to read, uses fseek() to position us correctly in the file, and then it prints out the record it reads at that position. Let's run it:

```
C>reader

Type the record number to recover:9
Ebeneezer Scrooge owes $0.01
C>
```

That's how we use records in files. Making up a record's structure is up to us—in C, you can use structures as templates for records. Then, you can use fopen() to open files, fread() to read them, fwrite() to write them, fseek() to look around inside them, and fclose() to close them.

Let's take a closer look at the use of fseek():

```
fseek(file_pointer, (long) (rec_num*sizeof(struct entry)), 0);
```

We have already stored the record number to be read in rec_num. To position the file pointer correctly in the file, we have to move rec_num * sizeof(struct entry) bytes into the file. Note that we use a type cast of (long) before passing this product to fseek()—this is because fseek() expects a long value here, allowing you to move through files larger than 64K in size.

The final parameter in our call to fseek() is the *origin* value. This is the initial position in the file; the position pointer is set with respect to this origin. Since we know the number of bytes we want to be away from the beginning of the file (i.e., rec_num * sizeof(struct entry)), we use an origin of zero in this case. In other cases, you can use the present position in the file as the origin and set the position pointer with respect to it.

Although we didn't check it, fseek() returns a value of 0 if the seek was unsuccessful. If we were going to develop our program, we should check the return value as a matter of course. (What if someone requested record 2,432 from our 15-record file?)

Using files in this way—picking out records at random locations in the file—is called *random access*. The other method of file access is *sequential access*. If you are reading a file sequentially, you have to read all of the records in order before coming to the one that you want. With random access, you can just specify a record number and reach in to pick it out. If we didn't have the position pointer, we'd have to use sequential access. The difference is like finding a song on a tape (sequential access) or finding an article in a magazine (random access).

Our error checking hasn't been very good. All we've done is print out rudimentary error messages. Many things can go wrong when you use files, so C provides some error-checking functions that can be helpful. Let's take a brief excursion into error checking; it will be our last topic before we work with low-level file reading and writing

Errno() and Perror()

The two functions errno() and perror() are designed to let you know what's going on if an error occurs. If an error occurs in a file operation,

C places the error number in a variable called errno, declared in errno.h. We can print that number out. The number itself often isn't that much help, so there is another option—we can have C print out the error in English with perror().

For example, we could modify our terse error message in the previous record-reading program to this:

```
#include <stdio.h>
#include <io.h>
#define INDEX 15

extern int errno;
  struct entry
  {
          char name[20];
          float owes;
  }
main()
{
        FILE *file_pointer;
        struct entry buffer;
        int rec_num;
    if( (file_pointer = fopen( "numbers.dat", "r") ) != NULL)
            {
            printf("Type the record number to recover:");
            scanf("%d",&rec_num);
        fseek(file_pointer, (long) (rec_num*sizeof(struct entry)), 0);
                fread(&buffer, sizeof(struct entry), 1, file_pointer);
            }
        else    {
            printf("Error number:%d returned\n",errno);
            perror("Error reading numbers.dat\n");
                }
        printf("%s owes $%.2f\n",buffer.name,buffer.owes);

}
```

Here we are using errno and perror(). Note that because errno is not defined in this program, we had to declare it external (like this: extern int errno;). If we run this program, it will look for NUMBERS.DAT; if the file does not exist, there will be an error. Let's see what happens:

```
D>del numbers.dat

D>reader
Error number:2 returned
Error reading numbers.dat
: No such file or directory

D>
```

A number of error messages were returned. The first one says that errno was set to 2. The second one was the standard error message that we put into the program. The third one, however, is perror()'s explanation of what is going on: ": No such file or directory." This kind of information can be very useful when working with files, and complete error handling is an asset to any program.

Low-level File Handling

Besides the fwrite() and fread() pair, C includes a pair of file functions that operate at an even lower level: write() and read(). Neither write() nor read()—nor the associated low-level functions (lseek(), open(), and close())—are part of the ANSI C standard C library. Yet you can find them in all popular C compilers for the PC and PS/2 (including Microsoft C and Turbo C). The reason is that these low-level functions give you more control over file functions, and they are much faster.

With fread() and fwrite(), data are first transferred to buffers. Only when you close the file (using fclose()), or explicitly flush the buffer (fflush()), are the data written to disk. Both read() and write() are *unbuffered*—that is, when you write five bytes to a file, it goes directly to disk. In addition, these functions work much like the DOS file-handling services in assembly language, so they're worth a look.

Let's take a look at these fast file functions. With them, we can write a program that copies files. The program, COPIER.C, makes a copy of a file for you—you tell it the name of the file to copy and the new filename.

COPIER.C

Before doing anything in COPIER.C, we have to include these header files:

```
#include <stdio.h>
#include <fcntl.h>
#include <sys\types.h>
#include <sys\stat.h>
#include <io.h>

main()
```

The reason there is so much to include is because we are responsible for setting everything up for these low-level functions. We also have to set up a buffer in memory for our data.

In COPIER.C, we should use a large-sized buffer to make reading and writing faster. (Otherwise we would have to read and write many times.) Let's use a buffer size of 32K. But we can't just declare a large data area of 32K without special preparation. If we put it into our program, then buffer[] is an automatic array.

```
→       #define BUFFSIZE 32*1024
        #include <stdio.h>
        #include <fcntl.h>
        #include <sys\types.h>
        #include <sys\stat.h>
        #include <io.h>

        main()
        {
→       char buffer[BUFFSIZE];
```

Space would have to be allocated for it on the stack. However, the default C stack is only about 2K long (4K in Turbo C), and we would get a stack overflow.

Let's use a function that we'll use often later on, malloc().

Malloc()

The malloc() library function allocates memory for use by your program when the program is running. In our case, we need 32K bytes, in a character array named buffer[]. The malloc() function returns a pointer to char (unless you override it like this: (type) malloc()), and an array name is really just a pointer to a char as well. In other words, we can use malloc() in this way:

```
#define BUFFSIZE 32*1024
#include <stdio.h>
#include <fcntl.h>
#include <sys\types.h>
#include <sys\stat.h>
#include <io.h>

main()
{
→ char *malloc();
→ char *buffer;
```

```
→     if((buffer = malloc(BUFFSIZE)) == NULL)
                      {
                      printf("Malloc could not allocate.")
                      exit(1);
                      }
```

If malloc() returns a NULL pointer, it did not allocate memory, so the program terminates. When the program runs correctly, malloc() allocates 32K bytes for our use on the Heap, and supplies us with a pointer to that space (which we name buffer).

Now that we have the space in memory for the data we are going to read in, we have to know what file to read. We have to read that from the keyboard when the program is running. Let's get the information with scanf():

```
#define BUFFSIZE 32*1024
#include <stdio.h>
#include <fcntl.h>
#include <sys\types.h>
#include <sys\stat.h>
#include <io.h>

main()
{
char *malloc();
char *buffer;
char source[50];
char target[50];

if((buffer = malloc(BUFFSIZE)) == NULL)
                  {
                  printf("Malloc could not allocate.");
                  exit(1);
                  }
```
```
→     printf("Source file:");
→     scanf("%s",source);
```

After we use scanf(), the character string named source will hold the name of the file that is to be copied. We also need the name of the destination file or the target file, which is the file that will be created when the copy is made:

```
#define BUFFSIZE 32*1024
#include <stdio.h>
#include <fcntl.h>
#include <sys\types.h>
#include <sys\stat.h>
```

```
#include <io.h>

main()
{
char *malloc();
char *buffer;
char source[50];
char target[50];

if((buffer = malloc(BUFFSIZE)) == NULL)
                {
                printf("Malloc could not allocate.");
                exit(1);
                }
printf("Source file:");
scanf("%s",source);
printf("Target file:");
scanf("%s",target);
```

After we have both names, we can open both files. With the low-level file functions, you use open() to do this. These lines open the files:

```
#define BUFFSIZE 32*1024
#include <stdio.h>
#include <fcntl.h>
#include <sys\types.h>
#include <sys\stat.h>
#include <io.h>

main()
{
char *malloc();
char *buffer;
char source[50];
char target[50];
int s_handle;
int t_handle;

if((buffer = malloc(BUFFSIZE)) == NULL)
                {
                printf("Malloc could not allocate.");
                exit(1);
                }
printf("Source file:");
scanf("%s",source);
printf("Target file:");
scanf("%s",target);

if((s_handle = open(source, O_RDONLY | O_BINARY)) == -1)
                {
                printf("Couldn't open source.");
```

```
→                           exit(1);
→                           }
→       if((t_handle = open(target, O_CREAT | O_WRONLY | O_BINARY,
→                           S_IWRITE )) == -1)
→                           {
→                           printf("Couldn't open target.");
→                           exit(1);
→                            }
```

The open() function takes many flags as parameters. The flags are shown in the following table:

Table 2.3   Open () Function Flags

Flag	The open( ) function flags Means
O_RDONLY	Open for reading only
O_WRONLY	Open for writing only
O_RDWR	Open for reading and writing
O_APPEND	Open to append
O_CREAT	Creates file
O_TRUNC	If file exists, its length is truncated to 0
O_BINARY	Make this a binary file
O_TEXT	Make this a text file

There are many possibilities: We can create files, open them as "read-only" or "write-only," open them for appending, or open them as ASCII or binary files. If we open files for appending, anything we write to them will be placed at the end of the current file on disk. If we open a file with the O_TRUNC flag, the file is truncated to zero length (that is, zeroed) and then opened. These options can be or'ed together, as we have done in our program.

If you use open() to create a new file, you must do two things: You must include the O_CREAT flag in your call, and you must add a third parameter in the call to open(), as we have done here:

```
    if((s_handle = open(source, O_RDONLY | O_BINARY)) == -1)
                {
                printf("Couldn't open source.");
                exit(1);
                }
→       if((t_handle = open(target, O_CREAT | O_WRONLY | O_BINARY,
→                           S_IWRITE )) == -1)
                {
                printf("Couldn't open target.");
                exit(1);
                }
```

We ask for permission to write to the file, so the last parameter is S_IWRITE. The other two possibilities for this parameter are the flags S_IREAD and S_IWRITE¦S_IREAD, which open the newly created file for reading, or for reading and writing, respectively.

The reason that these options exist is that when other programs access the same files that you are using, the situation can get complicated. To forestall confusion, you have to specify the access allowed to a file by other programs when you open the file. With these low-level functions, you have to choose from among all of the choices just offered.

> This is a big concern under the multitasking environment of OS/2, where the file-opening functions use a similar number of flags.

The open() function does not return a pointer to a file structure, but rather (as with assembly language functions) returns a *file handle*. This handle is a short integer, and we can use it with all the low-level file-handling routines, instead of with a file pointer. Let's put the handle to use immediately. Here's the real meat of the program, the two lines that actually do all the copying:

```
#define BUFFSIZE 32*1024
#include <stdio.h>
#include <fcntl.h>
#include <sys\types.h>
#include <sys\stat.h>
#include <io.h>

main()
{
char *malloc();
char *buffer;
char source[50];
char target[50];
int s_handle;
int t_handle;
int num; /*dd*/

if((buffer = malloc(BUFFSIZE)) == NULL)
                {
                printf("Malloc could not allocate.");
                exit(1);
                }
printf("Source file:");
scanf("%s",source);
printf("Target file:");
scanf("%s",target);

if((s_handle = open(source, O_RDONLY ¦ O_BINARY)) == -1)
                {
                printf("Couldn't open source.");
```

```
                    exit(1);
                    }
    if((t_handle = open(target, O_CREAT ¦ O_WRONLY ¦ O_BINARY,
                S_IWRITE )) == -1)
                    {
                    printf("Couldn't open target.");
                    exit(1);
                    }
→   while (num = read(s_handle, buffer, BUFFSIZE))
→               write(t_handle, buffer, num);

    close(s_handle);
    close(t_handle);
    }
```

In the while() statement, we keep reading bytes from the file. The read() function returns the number of bytes actually read, and as long as that number is not 0, we write the bytes out again. When these two lines are completed, we have copied the whole source file into the target file. Except for cleanup, the program is done.

After the files are copied, we close them both. The source file has now been duplicated in the target file. The actual work of the program was accomplished in just two lines. This program, COPIER.C, is able to copy files in large, 32K chunks.

Now that we've finished COPIER.C, we turn from handling data to working with the data. We have been able to get large amounts of data into memory at once—let's make some use of it. C provides an excellent number of string commands (declared in STRING.H), and while we're working with files we should explore them.

As our final large-scale file example, we'll develop a program that reads in files and searches for a specific string. For example, if we had wanted to find the string "needle" in the file HAYSTACK.TXT, we could use our program, named FIND, this way:

```
find haystack.txt needle
```

String Commands

These are some of the string commands in C:

strcpy( )	Compares strings.
strcat( )	Connects strings together.
strchr( )	Scans a string for a character.
strcmp( )	Compares one string to another.
strcmpi( )	Compares one string to another without cases.
strcpy( )	Copies one string to another.

strdup( )	Copies string to memory it allocates itself.
strlen( )	Returns a string's length.
strlwr( )	Converts uppercase chars in a string to lower.
strpbrk( )	Scans a string for one of a number of chars.
strrchr( )	Scans string for last occurance of a char.
strrev( )	Reverses a string.
strstr( )	Scans string for given substring.
strupr( )	Converts lowercase letters in a string to upper.

The program we want to develop searches through a file for a certain string, so strstr() is the function we want. The way to use it is this: strstr(string1, string2). This function scans string1 for string2 and returns a pointer to the match if there is one, and NULL if there is not. We can modify the program we already wrote, COPIER.C, to develop this new program, FIND.C.

To add a sparkle to the program, let's use command-line arguments to pass the name of the file to search and the string to search for. For example, let's say we want to use FIND.C to find "wolf" in a file named LITTLE.RED. We could use it like this:

```
find wolf little.red
```

That means wolf is argv[1] and little.red is argv[2] (find is argv[0]). Putting this knowledge to use, we can begin FIND.C like this:

```
#define BUFFSIZE 32*1024
#include <stdio.h>
#include <fcntl.h>
#include <sys\types.h>
#include <sys\stat.h>
#include <io.h>
#include <string.h>

main(argc, argv)
int argc;
char *argv[];
{
char *malloc();
char *buffer;
char source[50];
char tofind[50];
int s_handle;
int num, i;

strcpy(tofind, argv[1]);
strcpy(source, argv[2]);
```

Using strcpy(), we place the string we are searching for (pointed to by argv[1]) into the character array tofind[], and we place the name of the file to be searched (pointed to by argv[2]) into the array source[]. To use string functions, you have to include the header file STRING.H as we did here, so that the prototype of strcpy() is included.

Next, we set up our data buffer in preparation for reading in the actual data. Here we use malloc() to request additional space on the heap. We read data in 32K sections, so 32K is the size of the buffer we request.

We have to make sure that the data in buffer is treated as a string, because we will use the string functions of C. For that reason, we put a 0 at the end of the read-in data. (We also have to make the buffer one character longer than 32K, in case we have to put the 0 at the very end.) Here's how we start with malloc():

```
#define BUFFSIZE 32*1024
#include <stdio.h>
#include <fcntl.h>
#include <sys\types.h>
#include <sys\stat.h>
#include <io.h>
#include <string.h>

main(argc, argv)
int argc;
char *argv[];
{
char *malloc();
char *buffer;
char source[50];
char tofind[50];
int s_handle;
int num, i;

strcpy(tofind, argv[1]);
strcpy(source, argv[2]);

if((buffer = malloc(BUFFSIZE+1)) == NULL)
{
            printf("Malloc could not allocate.");
            exit(1);
}
```

Next we read in the file as before—but do not open a target file. Instead, the while loop that formerly looped over the 32K chunks of data will change:

```
#define BUFFSIZE 32*1024
#include <stdio.h>
```

```
#include <fcntl.h>
#include <sys\types.h>
#include <sys\stat.h>
#include <io.h>
#include <string.h>

main(argc, argv)
int argc;
char *argv[];
{
char *malloc();
char *buffer;
char source[50];
char tofind[50];
int s_handle;
int num, i;

strcpy(tofind, argv[1]);
strcpy(source, argv[2]);

if((buffer = malloc(BUFFSIZE+1)) == NULL)
                {
                printf("Malloc could not allocate.");
                exit(1);
                }

if((s_handle = open(source, O_RDONLY | O_BINARY)) == -1)
                {
                printf("Couldn't open source.");
                exit(1);
                }
while (num = read(s_handle, buffer, BUFFSIZE))
{
          →
}

close(s_handle);
}
```

This while loop is where the action is. Each time through the loop, we will have more data to search. To prepare that data, we first make sure that it is treated as a string by adding a 0 at the end. (We have read in num bytes, so we want to make sure that the byte after the last byte in memory, buffer[num], is 0):

```
while (num = read(s_handle, buffer, BUFFSIZE))
{
          →                buffer[num] = 0;

}
```

Now the data are all set and we can use strstr() to search for the string tofind[]. There may be more than one match in the current 32K chunk of data, so we need a loop here:

```
while (num = read(s_handle, buffer, BUFFSIZE))
{
    buffer[num] = 0;
    for(match = buffer; match = strstr(match,tofind);++match)
    {

    }
}
```

This loops over matches to the string tofind[] in this chunk of data. The strstr() function returns a pointer to the place where the substring was found in the buffer. We can call this pointer match. Every time we loop in this inner for loop, match is updated.

Once we find a match, we have to print it out. Let's print out 40 bytes surrounding the match. In other words, we want to print 40 characters starting at (match - 20)—but what if (match - 20) takes us before the beginning of the buffer? A better idea is to print 40 characters starting from:

```
((match - 20)<buffer ? buffer : match - 20)
```

> We may also print beyond the end of the buffer. This is only a demonstration program, so let's not worry about that, or about the case where the string straddles chunks of read-in data. In a real program, of course, we'd have to watch it.

Here's where we print, a character at a time, using putch():

```
while (num = read(s_handle, buffer, BUFFSIZE))
{
    buffer[num] = 0;
    for(match = buffer; match = strstr(match,tofind);++match)
    {
        start = ((match - 20)<buffer ? buffer : match - 20);
        for(i = 0;i < 40; i++,start++)
            putch(*start);
            printf("\n");
    }
}
```

Printing a "\n" at the end separates the typed string by a newline. That's all there is to it. When we stop finding matches, strstr() returns 0, and we exit the for loop. If there are no more data to be read, we also exit the outer while loop, and we're done. The C string instructions made the program simple.

Here's the entire program FIND.C:

```
#define BUFFSIZE 32*1024
#include <stdio.h>
#include <fcntl.h>
#include <sys\types.h>
#include <sys\stat.h>
#include <io.h>
#include <string.h> /*add*/


main(argc, argv)
int argc;
char *argv[];
{
char *malloc();
char *buffer;
char source[50];
char tofind[50];
int s_handle;
int num, i;
char *match, *start;

strcpy(tofind, argv[1]);
strcpy(source, argv[2]);

if((buffer = malloc(BUFFSIZE+1)) == NULL)
{
                printf("Malloc could not allocate.");
                exit(1);
}

if((s_handle = open(source, O_RDONLY ¦ O_BINARY)) == -1)
{
                printf("Couldn't open source.");
                exit(1);
}
while (num = read(s_handle, buffer, BUFFSIZE))
{
            buffer[num] = 0; /*next line remove ( add ;)*/
            for(match = buffer; match = strstr(match,tofind);++match)
            {
                start = ((match - 20)<buffer ? buffer : match - 20);
                for(i = 0;i < 40; i++,start++) /*no ; this line*/
                    putch(*start);     /*make putch*/
                    printf("\n");   /*add*/
            }
}

close(s_handle);
}
```

You can use this program with files as we did before (like this: find wolf little.red). Give it a try.

We can work on a new example program to take the next step in data handling: mixing string functions and file records. Let's write a small dictionary program. When you type a word to this program, it will check to see if it has a definition for the word. If so, it prints the definition out. (We'll see this program again when we start to replace arrays with pointers, because pointer storage is more efficient.)

The LOOKUP.C Program

To begin, we have to create a file full of words and their definitions. To do so, we can write a small program that asks for words and the corresponding definitions, then writes them out to the file DEF.TXT. We'll use arrays of strings here, so let's use the semiformatted functions fwrite() and fread().

To keep track of the data, let's start with an array for the words and a corresponding array for the definitions. For each entry in array lword[][], there a corresponding definition with the same first index number in array ldef[][]. Here's how we start in the program to create DEF.TXT, the file of words and definitions:

```
#include <stdio.h>

main()
{
char lword[10][20], ldef[10][80];
int i;
FILE *file_pointer;

        for(i=0; i <= 10; i++)
        {
                printf("\nType word to be defined, q to quit:");
                gets(lword[i]);
                if(lword[i][0] == 'q' && lword[i][1] == '\0') break;
                printf("\nType definition:");
                gets(ldef[i]);
        }
```

This loop loops over the typed-in words and definitions until we type "q" to quit. The program asks for a word and then for its definition. As they are read, these strings are stored in lword[][] and ldef[][]. Note that lword[][] and ldef[][] are two-dimensional arrays. The first index refers to the word number, and the second index refers to the actual letters themselves.

A two-dimensional array is really a one-dimensional array of pointers to one-dimensional arrays (the character strings). This means that we can refer to a character string by omitting one of the indices. In other words, the first word string is lword[0], and the first definition string is ldef[0]. Therefore, we can fill the character strings directly with gets():

```
#include <stdio.h>

main()
{
char lword[10][20], ldef[10][80];
int i;
FILE *file_pointer;

        for(i=0; i <= 10; i++)
        {
                printf("\nType word to be defined, q to quit:");
→               gets(lword[i]);
                if(lword[i][0] == 'q' && lword[i][1] == '\0') break;
                printf("\nType definition:");
→               gets(ldef[i]);
        }
}
```

When we exit the for loop (after ten definitions have been stored), all we have to do is to write out the file DEF.TXT with fwrite():

```
#include <stdio.h>

main()
{
char lword[10][20], ldef[10][80];
int i;
FILE *file_pointer;

        for(i=0; i <= 10; i++)
        {
                printf("\nType word to be defined, q to quit:");
                gets(lword[i]);
                if(lword[i][0] == 'q' && lword[i][1] == '\0') break;
                printf("\nType definition:");
                gets(ldef[i]);
        }

→       if( (file_pointer = fopen( "def.txt", "w") ) != NULL)
→       {
→               fwrite(lword, sizeof(lword), 1, file_pointer);
→               fwrite(ldef, sizeof(ldef), 1, file_pointer);
        }
    else perror("Error writing def.txt\n");
```

```
fclose(file_pointer);

}
```

And that's it. We've stored our dictionary in DEF.TXT.

> Note that we did not have to write out the two arrays, one after the other: We can put them together in structures and then write out ten structures.

Using DEF.TXT

Now we have to concentrate on using this data file in LOOKUP.C. The file DEF.TXT now exists—the next step is to get definitions from it. Let's use the lookup program with command-line arguments like this: lookup word. To do that, we'll have to use *argv[]. Here's the beginning of LOOKUP.C:

```
#include <stdio.h>
#include <string.h>

main(argc,argv)
int argc;
char *argv[];
{
char lword[10][20], ldef[10][80], tofind[20];
int i;
FILE *file_pointer;

strcpy(tofind, argv[1]);
```

The word to be looked up will be put into the character string tofind[]. Next, let's read the file DEF.TXT and fill th lord[][] and ldef[][] arrays:

```
#include <stdio.h>
#include <string.h>

main(argc,argv)
int argc;
char *argv[];
{
char lword[10][20], ldef[10][80], tofind[20];
int i;
FILE *file_pointer;

strcpy(tofind, argv[1]);
```

```
→        if( (file_pointer = fopen( "def.txt", "r") ) != NULL)
→        {
→                fread(lword, sizeof(lword), 1, file_pointer);
→                fread(ldef, sizeof(ldef), 1, file_pointer);
→        }
→   else perror("Error reading def.txt\n");
```

From this point, we just have to find a match for tofind[] in lword[][]. Here's how it goes:

```
#include <stdio.h>
#include <string.h>

main(argc,argv)
int argc;
char *argv[];
{
char lword[10][20], ldef[10][80], tofind[20];
int i;
FILE *file_pointer;

strcpy(tofind, argv[1]);        /* get string */

        if( (file_pointer = fopen( "def.txt", "r") ) != NULL)
        {                          /* fill arrays */
                fread(lword, sizeof(lword), 1, file_pointer);
                fread(ldef, sizeof(ldef), 1, file_pointer);
        }
else perror("Error reading def.txt\n");

fclose(file_pointer);   /* close file */

→        for(i = 0; i <= 10; i++)        /* find a match */
→        {
→        if(strstr(tofind, lword[i]) != NULL && lword[i][0] != '\0')
→                printf("\nDefinition: %s", ldef[i]);
→        }
}
```

We just loop over all words and check for a match with the familiar function strstr(). If there is a match, we print it out.

> Note that we made sure in the strstr() expression that there really was a string to compare to: If there is no second string, strstr() returns not NULL, but a pointer to the first string, tofind[].

We can keep looping over lword[][] until a match is found. If no match is found, LOOKUP.C simply exits. If, however, a match is found, we can use the index number of the match in the array lword[][] to find the corresponding definition in ldef[][], which we print out with printf(). If we were writing a database program (which we will do later), we would use similar methods to search through read-in records for a match to some requested keyword.

To use LOOKUP.C yourself, first type in the data-definition program and run it to establish the data dictionary in DEF.TXT. You'll be asked for ten words and their definitions (or you can change that number to whatever you want). Then type in and run LOOKUP.C; give it a word and, if the word is in the dictionary, LOOKUP.C will dig it out.

That's it for files. We've seen how to write them as either ASCII or binary files, and how to read them as well. We've also examined how to use file records and the position pointer to gain control over data. Sometimes, sequential access is appropriate (for example, if we write text files). At other times, random access using the position pointer is more appropriate (as in databases). There are many options available, represented by a rich assortment of library functions.

The largest single area of library functions in either Microsoft C or Turbo C is graphics—and that is the topic we're going to explore next.

3

Graphics

There are a tremendous number of graphics routines in C for the PC
and PS/2—this is one place where C shines. In this chapter, we will
develop a paint-like program that draws on the screen. As we develop
it, we will explore many of the graphics options available in both the
Microsoft C and Turbo C libraries. Before we're one, we'll draw ellipses and rectangles.

> Graphics is one area of C that is not specified by the ANSI standard.
> Microsoft C and Turbo C diverge here, and we will keep track of both
> of them. On the other hand, everything that we'll do in this chapter
> can be done with either compiler.

Let's begin immediately. Before doing anything else in graphics,
you have to set the screen the way you want it. We'll do that first.

Selecting a Video Mode

There have been many different video standards for the PC, including
CGA, EGA, and VGA. For the purposes of our demonstration program, and because there are so many different types of monitors on
the market, we'll pick a graphics mode that just about any PC with
graphics can support—the CGA low-resolution mode (320 x 200 pixels). We'll investigate other modes later.

Setting the video mode is done differently in the Microsoft C and
Turbo C compilers. In Microsoft C, you use the function _setvide-
omode() and pass it constants predefined in the GRAPH.H header
file. In Turbo C, you use the function setgraphmode(), constants from
the GRAPHICS.H header file, and specify a graphics driver file. We
will investigate the details of setting all video modes under both compilers later. To get our demonstration program going and to set the
video mode to low-resolution CGA mode, we will concentrate first on
Microsoft C. Later, we'll write the whole program in Turbo C.

To use graphics, the include file that has the prototypes and constant definitions that we'll need is GRAPH.H (Turbo C: GRAPHICS.H). We start off by including that file:

```
→   #include <stdio.h>
→   #include <graph.h>

    main()
    {
    }
```

In order to set up graphics mode, we call _setvideomode(). (Turbo C: setgraphmode()). There are a number of different constants already defined in GRAPH.H that we can use with setvideomode(). We will see all of them later, but only use one of them now (_MRES4COLOR) to set up the CGA 4-color mode (Turbo C: mode CGAC3):

```
    #include <stdio.h>
    #include <graph.h>

    main()
    {

→   _setvideomode(_MRES4COLOR);
                    ⋮
                    ⋮
    }
```

Turning a Screen Pixel On

After the video mode is set, we can immediately draw on the screen. Let's start off by turning individual pixels on. We read typed characters and move our position around on the screen. When a 'p' is typed, we turn the pixel at our present position on. When a 'q' is typed, we exit the program.

The cursor keys are a little more tricky. None of the standard character-reading C routines acknowledge the cursor keys as typed keys—but we can work with them by using the getch() function. If you press a cursor key, getch() returns 0. If we see that value, we will use getch() again, and this time, we will get the scan code for the key. We can use the cursor keys easily now. The scan code for the up arrow is 208, the scan code for the down arrow is 200. The scan code for the right arrow

is 205, and the scan code for the left arrow is 203. We'll just check to
see if they've been typed, and we'll be home free.

The way we will keep track of our screen location is in two variables:
xloc and yloc. In the graphics mode we have chosen, the screen is 200
pixels vertically (the y direction) and 320 pixels horizontally (the x
direction). Furthermore, the origin (0,0) is in the upper left-hand corner of the screen. The lower right-hand corner is (320,200):

```
                       xloc  →

  yloc  │ (0,0) Columns increase  →
        │ Rows
    │   │ Increase
    │   │
    │   │    │
    ↓   │    │
        │    ↓
        │
        │                        (320,200)
```

When a 'p' is typed, we'll set the pixel at the current location (xloc,
yloc) with a function named _setpixel(xloc,yloc) (Turbo C:
putpixel(xloc,yloc,1), where 1 is the pixel color). Here's the program
so far:

```c
#include <stdio.h>
#include <graph.h>

main()
{
  int in;
  int xloc = 0, yloc = 0;

  _setvideomode(_MRES4COLOR);

while((in = getch()) != 'q')
{
        if (!in) in = getch() + 128;
        switch (in)
        {
          case 208:
                yloc++;
                break;
          case 203:
                xloc--;
                break;
          case 205:
                xloc++;
                break;
```

```
case 200:
       yloc--;
       break;
case 'p':
       _setpixel(xloc,yloc);
       break;
     default:
              ;
    }
}
}
```

A switch statement works through all of the cases. We can use it already—it will set pixels anywhere on the screen. As you move around with the cursor keys and type 'p', the program turns the pixel on at the cursor's current location.

Adding Lines

Turning on dots on the screen is interesting, but it falls short of exciting. Let's add a few features to our program. First, let's add color. We'll get a more comprehensive discussion of color after we discuss screen modes, but for now, if you include this line:

```
#include <stdio.h>
#include <graph.h>

main()
{
  int in;
  int xloc = 0, yloc = 0;

  _setvideomode(_MRES4COLOR);

→     _setcolor(1);
             :
             :
  }
```

in your program, the pixels you turn on the screen will be cyan, not white (Turbo C: setcolor(1)). Let's take advantage of more C library functions now to draw a cyan line on the screen.

We can draw lines from a location called the current *graphic output position* to a given set of coordinates. In other words, if the current graphic output position is at position x:

we can use the _lineto() function (Turbo C: lineto()) to draw a line from x to a point we pass to _lineto(). If we pass the coordinates of, say, y, to _lineto(), then the screen looks like this:

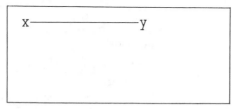

We pass only the coordinates of y to lineto(); the current graphics output position, x, is set with a function named _moveto() (Turbo C: moveto()). That means we have to set x with _moveto(), move around using the cursor keys, and then draw the line when we're at the new location, y.

Let's put this into our program. We have to specify the two points x and y. We can use the program's pixel-setting ability to mark one end of the line, x, then move around and type 'l' to draw a line from the pixel we just set to our present location. In the modified program, when you type 'p' for pixel, it not only sets the pixel to cyan on the screen, but also sets the graphic output position, x, to that location. Then you can move around the screen using the cursor keys. When you type 'l', a (cyan) line is drawn from the pixel you set at location x to the position you moved to, y. Here's the new program with _moveto() and _lineto():

```
#include <stdio.h>
#include <graph.h>

main()
{
   int in;
   int xloc = 0, yloc = 0;

   _setvideomode(_MRES4COLOR);
```

```
_setcolor(1);
while((in = getch()) != 'q')
{
            if (!in) in = getch() + 128;
            switch (in)
            {
              case 208:        /* up */
                      yloc++;
                      break;
              case 203:        /* left */
                      xloc--;
                      break;
              case 205:        /* right */
                      xloc++;
                      break;
              case 200:        /* down */
                      yloc--;
                      break;
              case 'p':
                      _setpixel(xloc,yloc);
→                    _moveto(xloc,yloc);
                      break;
→             case 'l':
→                    _lineto(xloc,yloc);
→                    break;
              default:
                      ;

            }
      }
}
```

However, the C library offers us more than lines. For example, we can draw rectangles almost as easily.

Rectangles

There is a _rectangle() function in the Microsoft C library (Turbo C: rectangle()). This function differs from _lineto() in that it needs two sets of coordinates—the upper left and lower right coordinates of the rectangle:

`x1, y1` →

← `x2, y2`

The call to the function _rectangle() is made in this way:

```
_rectangle(control, x1, y1, x2, y2)
```

(Turbo C: rectangle(x1, y1, x2, y2)). Microsoft C gives you the option of filling in the rectangle: The parameter named control in the previous call is given the value of one of two constants: _GFILLINTERIOR or _GBORDER (both defined in GRAPH.H). If you select _GFILLINTERIOR, the rectangle that is drawn is filled with the current drawing color (in our case, cyan). If you choose _GBORDER, only the border is drawn.

To draw rectangles, we have to establish two pairs of coordinates on the screen, (x1,y1) and (x2,y2). An easy way to do this is to set the first pair when we use the pixel command, 'p', and to add another command, 'r', to draw the rectangle.

To put it to use, move to the upper left corner of the rectangle that you want to draw, and press 'p'. A pixel appears, marking that location (and setting (x1, y1)). Next, move to the lower right corner and press 'r'. Your present position on the screen is taken as (x2, y2), and the rectangle is drawn. We can add these lines to case 'p' to set (x1, y1):

```
case 'p':
        _setpixel(xloc,yloc);
        _moveto(xloc,yloc);
        x1 = xloc;              ←
        y1 = yloc;              ←
        break;
case 'l':
```

Note that the 'p' command now sets both (x1, y1) for drawing rectangles and the current graphics output position for drawing lines.

Then we add the correct lines to the program for the new case, which is 'r':

```
#include <stdio.h>
#include <graph.h>

main()
{
 int in;
 int xloc = 0, yloc = 0, x1 = 0, y1 = 0;

 _setvideomode(_MRES4COLOR);
```

```
_setcolor(1);
 while((in = getch()) != 'q')
 {
            if (!in) in = getch() + 128;
            switch (in)
            {
            case 208:      /* up */
                  yloc++;
                  break;
            case 203:      /* left */
                  xloc--;
                  break;
            case 205:      /* right */
                  xloc++;
                  break;
            case 200:      /* down */
                  yloc--;
                  break;
            case 'p':
                  _setpixel(xloc,yloc);
                  _moveto(xloc,yloc);
                  x1 = xloc;
                  y1 = yloc;
                  break;
            case 'l':
                  _lineto(xloc,yloc);
                  break;
    →       case 'r':
    →             _rectangle(_GBORDER, x1, y1, xloc, yloc);
    →             break;
    →       default:
                  ;
            }
 }
}
```

When you press 'r', a rectangle is drawn from the last pixel you turned on to the current location. The method for drawing ellipses is very similar, so we can add that task immediately to our program.

Ellipses

It's as easy to draw an ellipse as it is to draw a rectangle. All we have to do is to supply the function _ellipse() (Turbo C: ellipse()) with the same coordinates that we might supply to _rectangle(). The pair of coordinates that you pass to _ellipse() define a box, and the ellipse is drawn so that it touches this box at four points. Again, you can use the two constants _GFILLINTERIOR or _GBORDER in Microsoft C. Here's the new addition:

```
#include <stdio.h>
#include <graph.h>

main()
{
int in;
int xloc = 0, yloc = 0, x1 = 0, y1 = 0;

_setvideomode(_MRES4COLOR);

_setcolor(1);
  while((in = getch()) != 'q')
  {
          if (!in) in = getch() + 128;
          switch (in)
          {
          case 208:     /* up */
                  yloc++;
                  break;
          case 203:      /* left */
                  xloc--;
                  break;
          case 205:      /* right */
                  xloc++;
                  break;
          case 200:      /* down */
                  yloc--;
                  break;
          case 'p':
                  _setpixel(xloc,yloc);
                  _moveto(xloc,yloc);
                  x1 = xloc;
                  y1 = yloc;
                  break;
          case 'l':
                  _lineto(xloc,yloc);
                  break;
          case 'r':
                  _rectangle(_GBORDER, x1, y1, xloc, yloc);
                  break;
→         case 'e':
→                 _ellipse(_GBORDER, x1, y1, xloc, yloc);
→                 break;
          default:
                  ;
          }

  }
}
```

In Turbo C, there is a difference here. The call to ellipse() takes these parameters: ellipse(x, y, 0, 360, xradius, yradius), where (x,y) is the location of the exact center of the ellipse. The beginning and ending angles 0 and 360 indicate that we want a closed figure to be drawn. xradius is the radius of the ellipse in the x direction, and yradius is the radius in the y direction. When we rewrite our painting program in Turbo C, we make the call to ellipse() in this way: ellipse((x1 + x2)/2, (y1 + y2)/2, 0, 360, abs(x2 - x1)/2, abs(y2 - y1)/2).

Filling With Color

So far, our program just draws the outline of shapes. We can, however, modify it to fill shapes in. Microsoft C provides the _floodfill() function to do exactly that (Turbo C: floodfill()). You just specify the point on the screen and the color of the border of the area that you want to be filled. The _floodfill() function then fills in the area with the current color, which is cyan for us (set with _setcolor()).

For example, if you draw a rectangle on the screen in cyan, the _floodfill() function can fill it in by coloring until it reaches that boundary color. You simply specify a location on the screen to start filling with color.

To fill an area with color, let's modify our program again to accept the 'x' command. Use the cursor keys to move into a shape that you have already drawn and press 'x'. The area is now colored in solidly. To use _floodfill(), we have to pass it the position on the screen (xloc, yloc), and the boundary color. We are only drawing shapes in cyan (color = 1), so this is how the call to _floodfill() looks:

```
#include <stdio.h>
#include <graph.h>

main()
{
int in;
int xloc = 0, yloc = 0, x1 = 0, y1 = 0;
   FILE *fpointer;
   void  *gpointer;

_setvideomode(_MRES4COLOR);

_setcolor(1);
   while((in = getch()) != 'q')
   {
        if (!in) in = getch() + 128;
```

```
switch (in)
{
case 208:      /* up */
        yloc++;
        break;
case 203:      /* left */
        xloc--;
        break;
case 205:      /* right */
        xloc++;
        break;
case 200:      /* down */
        yloc--;
        break;
case 'p':
        _setpixel(xloc,yloc);
        _moveto(xloc,yloc);
        x1 = xloc;
        y1 = yloc;
        break;
case 'l':
        _lineto(xloc,yloc);
        break;
case 'r':
        _rectangle(_GBORDER, x1, y1, xloc, yloc);
        break;
case 'e':
        _ellipse(_GBORDER, x1, y1, xloc, yloc);
        break;
case 'x':
        _floodfill(xloc, yloc, 1);
        break;
default:
        ;
}


}
}
```

The call is just this: _floodfill(xloc, yloc, 1) (Turbo C: flood-fill(xloc,yloc,1)). The area on the screen bordered by the specified color—cyan—is filled in solidly with the current drawing color (set with _setcolor() or setcolor()). You can experiment with filling in different colors by passing new values to _setcolor() before filling shapes in. In our current four-color CGA mode, _setcolor() can take values from 0 to 3. (We will get a full description of what these values correspond to later.)

Saving Images

We've constructed a useful program to draw various figures on the screen. (You might even add Turbo C's drawpoly() function to draw polygons.) The problem is that when you exit the program, the work on the screen is lost. Is there any way to save it?

Since the screen buffer is just part of memory, there is one way of saving the image—we can simply read the entire screen buffer and write it out to a disk file. When we want to retrieve it, we can just read the file in again and fill the screen buffer with it.

We won't discuss the screen buffer or machine addresses in detail until we talk about assembly language later, but we can get an introduction right now.

The *screen buffer* is the area in memory where the image on the screen is stored. With the CGA, there are 200 pixels vertically and 320 pixels horizontally, so there are 200 x 320, or 64,000 pixels total. Each pixel in this mode can display four colors. To specify four colors, we need two bits (i.e., the four colors correspond to settings 00, 01, 10, 11). This means that there must be 64,000 pixels x 2 bits each, or a total of 128,000 bits. After dividing that by 8, we see that the CGA video buffer must be 16,000 bytes long. In fact, this number is rounded up to 16K (16 x 1,024), and the region of memory starts at address B800:0000.

> If you're not familiar with this type of address, we will discuss it when we talk more about assembly language memory handling. If you don't understand the format used, the actual address is not important for this example. If you wish, you can also skip ahead to Chapter 7 and read about addresses now.

We can reach that memory region. To write and read the screen dump to and from disk, use fwrite() and fread(). Both of these functions need a pointer to the data buffer. Now that we know the address of the video buffer (B800:0000), we can supply that number directly. We'll have to use a two-word pointer.

In C, pointers are just addresses, of course. The standard method of storing a two-word pointer is as a two-word long int; the address B800:0000 would be stored as a long int this way: 0xB8000000. The top word is 0xB800, and the bottom word is 0x0000.

Let's call our pointer gpointer (for graphics pointer). We'll have to use caution when passing gpointer as a parameter to fread() and fwrite(), because different versions of fread() and fwrite() exist, depending upon the memory model that we use. The *memory model* specifies the size of pointers used both for data and code items. In different memory models, the objects that a function expects to receive can change in size. As we'll see in Chapter 5, the large memory model uses two-word pointers for data, and that is what we want.

That means that we'll have to switch C libraries so that the versions of fwrite() and fread() that expect two-word pointers are picked up. The default library in C uses the Small memory model, which supports only one-word pointers. The use of a different library is as easy as giving a command to the compiler. For example, if we call the program ARTIST.C, we can use this command in QuickC:

```
qcl -AL artist.c
```

The -AL (Turbo C: -ml) switch indicates that we want to use the Large memory model, not the default Small model. Here's the program itself, complete with gpointer, which we actually fill with an immediate number:

```
#include <stdio.h>
#include <graph.h>

main()
{
int in;
int xloc = 0, yloc = 0, x1 = 0, y1 = 0;
  FILE *fpointer;
  void  *gpointer;

_setvideomode(_MRES4COLOR);

_setcolor(1);
  while((in = getch()) != 'q')
  {
          if (!in) in = getch() + 128;
          switch (in)
          {
          case 208:      /* up */
                  yloc++;
                  break;
          case 203:      /* left */
                  xloc--;
                  break;
          case 205:      /* right */
                  xloc++;
                  break;
          case 200:      /* down */
                  yloc--;
```

```
                   break;
         case 'p':
                   _setpixel(xloc,yloc);
                   _moveto(xloc,yloc);
                   x1 = xloc;
                   y1 = yloc;
                   break;
         case 'l':
                   _lineto(xloc,yloc);
                   break;
         case 'r':
                   _rectangle(_GBORDER, x1, y1, xloc, yloc);
                   break;
         case 'e':
                   _ellipse(_GBORDER, x1, y1, xloc, yloc);
                   break;
         case 'x':
                   _floodfill(xloc, yloc, 1);
                   break;
→        case 's':
→                 fpointer=fopen("screen.dmp","wb");
→                 gpointer = 0xb8000000;
→                 fwrite(gpointer, 16*1024, 1, fpointer);
→                 fclose(fpointer);
→                 break;
→        case 'f':
→                 fpointer=fopen("screen.dmp","rb");
→                 gpointer = 0xb8000000;
→                 fread(gpointer, 16*1024, 1, fpointer);
→                 fclose(fpointer);
→                 break;
         default:
                   ;
         }


     }
}
```

To save the screen in a file named SCREEN.DMP, type 's' when running the program. To retrieve the saved file, type 'f'. Let's take a look at those two cases:

```
case 's':
          fpointer=fopen("screen.dmp","wb");
          gpointer = 0xb8000000;
          fwrite(gpointer, 16*1024, 1, fpointer);
          fclose(fpointer);
          break;
```

```
case 'f':
    fpointer=fopen("screen.dmp","rb");
    gpointer = 0xb8000000;
    fread(gpointer, 16*1024, 1, fpointer);
    fclose(fpointer);
    break;
```

When you type 's', a file named SCREEN.DMP is opened for writing as a binary file. The call to fopen() returns a file pointer, which we name fpointer. We use that pointer later when we dump the screen data to disk.

Next, we fill gpointer with the address of the beginning of the CGA graphics buffer (keep in mind that gpointer is a far pointer—a normal pointer is only one word long). The use of immediate values for pointers is very machine-dependent, and as such is not very good programming practice; however, it works here.

> Note that this method works also with EGA and VGA monitors when they are in CGA mode. For backwards-compatibility with graphics programs, their screen buffer starts at B800:0000 when in CGA mode.

Now that we can point to the video buffer , we can write it out to disk with this fwrite() command:

```
fwrite(gpointer, 16*1024, 1, fpointer);
```

Of course, reading the file back in is just the opposite. The 16K file SCREEN.DMP is opened for binary reading. (Opening it as an ASCII file would be catastrophic because of the translations that would occur.) Then the file is simply read in and placed in the CGA graphics video buffer, overwriting what was already there. In this way, we can save screens full of images. Later in this chapter, we'll do almost the same thing with the C functions _getimage() and _putimage() (Turbo C: getimag() and putimage()).

It is rare that we actually know the address of the memory location(s) that we want to work with. Far more often, we let C handle those details for us. However, it is good to know that we can reach specific memory if we need to. In assembly language, as we begin to take advantage of the system resources, this will change. There it is more frequently the case that you want to get something from a specific area—such as a DOS or BIOS data area in memory. If you know the correct address, nothing stops you from working with it directly.

> Under OS/2, the situation is different. There, you cannot normally access real, physical memory because the 80x86 chip handles that for you. In restricting memory access, the 80x86 chip offers more protection to other processes.

Now our program can save images on disk and restore them when needed. We'll cover two last topics to complete our drawing program: fill patterns and changing the drawing color.

Fill Patterns

It turns out that we didn't need to fill our shapes with solid color—we could have specified a (single-color) pattern to use. In fact, we can design such a pattern ourselves.

We have to define the pattern first. We use an eight-by-eight pattern of pixels to define our pattern:

```
XXXXXXXX
XXXXXXXX
XXXXXXXX
XXXXXXXX
XXXXXXXX
XXXXXXXX
XXXXXXXX
XXXXXXXX
```

If we want a solid color, we can leave it this way, translating all xs into 1s. Each row is treated as a *byte* (8 bits), which makes our solid pattern into 8 0xFF bytes:

```
11111111   →   0xFF
11111111   →   0xFF
11111111   →   0xFF
11111111   →   0xFF
11111111   →   0xFF
11111111   →   0xFF
11111111   →   0xFF
11111111   →   0xFF
```

Then we set up an 8-element array of unsigned chars:

```
char fillarray[] = {0xFF, 0xFF, 0xFF, 0xFF, 0xFF, 0xFF, 0xFF, 0xFF};
```

To install this pattern as the fill pattern, we then pass this array to the function _setfillmask():

```
_setfillmask(fillarray);
```

(Turbo C: setfillpattern(fillarray, index); where index is the color to use when drawing the pattern). A fill pattern of solid color is not very exciting, however. We can choose a checkerboard pattern:

$$10101010 \rightarrow 0xAA$$
$$01010101 \rightarrow 0x55$$
$$10101010 \rightarrow 0xAA$$
$$01010101 \rightarrow 0x55$$
$$10101010 \rightarrow 0xAA$$
$$01010101 \rightarrow 0x55$$
$$10101010 \rightarrow 0xAA$$
$$01010101 \rightarrow 0x55$$

or stripes:

$$01010101 \rightarrow 0x55$$
$$01010101 \rightarrow 0x55$$
$$01010101 \rightarrow 0x55$$
$$01010101 \rightarrow 0x55$$
$$01010101 \rightarrow 0x55$$
$$01010101 \rightarrow 0x55$$
$$01010101 \rightarrow 0x55$$
$$01010101 \rightarrow 0x55$$

For our example, let's choose stripes. We can set the fill pattern easily with _setfillmask(). Now, when we fill with the 'x' command, we get stripes. Here's the new program:

```c
#include <stdio.h>
#include <graph.h>

main()
{
int in;
int xloc = 0, yloc = 0, x1 = 0, y1 = 0;
FILE *fpointer;
void  *gpointer;
char fillarray[] = {0x55, 0x55, 0x55, 0x55, 0x55, 0x55, 0x55, 0x55};

_setvideomode(_MRES4COLOR);

_setcolor(1);

_setfillmask(fillarray);

while((in = getch()) != 'q')
{
        if (!in) in = getch() + 128;
        switch (in)
        {
        case 208:      /* up */
                yloc++;
```

```
              break;
      case 203:       /* left */
              xloc--;
              break;
      case 205:       /* right */
              xloc++;
              break;
      case 200:       /* down */
              yloc--;
              break;
      case 'p':
              _setpixel(xloc,yloc);
              _moveto(xloc,yloc);
              x1 = xloc;
              y1 = yloc;
              break;
      case 'l':
              _lineto(xloc,yloc);
              break;
      case 'r':
              _rectangle(_GBORDER, x1, y1, xloc, yloc);
              break;
      case 'e':
              _ellipse(_GBORDER, x1, y1, xloc, yloc);
              break;
      case 'x':
              _floodfill(xloc, yloc, 1);
              break;
        case 's':
              fpointer=fopen("screen.dmp","wb");
              gpointer = 0xb8000000;
              fwrite(gpointer, 16*1024, 1, fpointer);
              fclose(fpointer);
              break;
      case 'f':
              fpointer=fopen("screen.dmp","rb");
              gpointer = 0xb8000000;
              fread(gpointer, 16*1024, 1, fpointer);
              fclose(fpointer);
              break;
      default:
              ;
    }

    }
}
```

The only thing that we can't do in the ARTIST.C program now is to change colors. We draw in cyan, and this is a distinct drawback if you want to use another color. Let's add different colors to ARTIST.C.

There are many colors available on the PC. (In the case of the VGA, an enormous number are available.) To learn to work with them, we have to understand how the different PC screen modes work. Some colors that are available under one screen mode, for example, are available under others.

Screen Modes

Screen displays on the PC machines have gotten steadily better over time, and this has been a popular improvement. The original Color Graphics Adapter (CGA) only displayed four colors at a time, with a poor resolution of 320 x 200 (320 vertical columns, 200 horizontal rows), and it flickered badly.

The other option at that time—the Monochrome Display Adapter (MDA)—didn't flicker and had good resolution, but it also didn't do graphics: It only used alphanumeric characters. With the introduction of other computers, it became clear that graphics was an up-and-coming issue in hardware, and IBM eventually followed the lead.

In 1984, IBM introduced what has since become the standard for PC displays: the Enhanced Graphics Adapter (EGA). The EGA selects 16 colors to display at once from a selection of 64 colors, doesn't flicker, and offers good resolution: 640 x 350 (almost as good as the monochrome display, which has a resolution of 720 x 350).

In addition, the EGA can display anything that the CGA (Color Graphics Adapter) or MDA (Monochrome Graphics Adapter) display—it even uses the same character set as the monochrome screen. The improvement can be readily seen in the difference in memory size allocated to the CGA (16K) versus the EGA (up to 256K).

Then, in April 1987, along with the introduction of the PS/2, the Video Graphics Adapter (VGA) was born. The VGA can do everything the EGA can do and more. Specifically, of course, is offers a tremendous expansion in the numbers of colors that can be displayed—in one particular (low-resolution) mode, the VGA displays 256 colors at once, chosen from a selection of 256K possibilities. This immense number is slightly qualified by the poor resolution in this mode: only 320 x 200. Other VGA graphics modes allow higher-resolution display (such as 640 x 480), but with a correspondingly fewer number of available colors.

Here's a list of all of the graphics modes, their resolutions, and number of colors:

Table 3.1   Graphics Modes

Mode	Display Lines	Number of Colors	Adapters
0	40x25	B&W text	CGA, EGA, VGA
1	40x25	Color text	CGA, EGA, VGA
2	80x25	B&W text	CGA, EGA, VGA
3	80x25	Color text	CGA, EGA, VGA
4	320x200	4	CGA, EGA, VGA
5	320x200	B&W	CGA, EGA, VGA
6	640x200	2 (on or off)	CGA, EGA, VGA
7	80x25	Monochrome	MDA, EGA, VGA
8	160x200	16	PCjr
9	320x200	16	PCjr
A	640x200	1	PCjr
B	Reserved for future use.		
C	Reserved for future use.		
D	320x200	16	EGA, VGA
E	640x200	16	EGA, VGA
F	640x350	monochrome	EGA, VGA
10H	640x350	16	EGA, VGA
11H	640x480	2	VGA
12H	640x480	16	VGA
13H	320x200	256	VGA

Some of these modes are *alphanumeric*—that is, they are text modes that don't support graphics (modes 0-3, and 7). You can still use text as usual in graphics modes, however.

| In graphics modes, the cursor does not appear on the screen. |

You can see how the modes are partitioned by adapter—modes 0-6 are used on the CGA (and EGA and VGA, since they're compatible). Mode 7 is for the monochrome display adapter, MDA (and EGA and VGA again, since they can mimic the MDA). Modes 8-0AH are for the PCjr, and modes 0DH-10H are for the EGA and VGA. (Here, the VGA emulates the EGA for compatibility.) Modes 11H-13H are just for the VGA. (Mode 13H is the 256-color mode.)

Mode			
0	CGA	EGA	VGA
1			
2			
3			

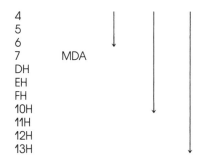

Setting Video Modes in Microsoft C

When you use graphics, the first step is often checking the current video mode. You can do so with Microsoft C by calling the function _getvideoconfig(). This fills a structure of type videoconfig (defined in GRAPH.H). You can declare one of these structures in this way:

```
struct videoconfig myvid;
```

and pass its name to _getvideoconfig():

```
_getvideoconfig(&myvid);
```

All of these fields are filled in the structure myvid (they are all ints):

myvid.numxpixels	=	number of pixels on X axis
myvid.numypixels	=	number of pixels on Y axis
myvid.numtextcols	=	number of text columns available
myvid.numtextrows	=	number of text rows available
myvid.numcolors	=	number of actual colors
myvid.bitsperpixel	=	number of bits per pixel
myvid.numvideopages	=	number of available video pages
myvid.mode	=	current video mode
myvid.adapter	=	active display adapter
myvid.monitor	=	active display monitor
myvid.memory	=	adapter video memory in K bytes

To see what kind of adapter card is in place, check the adapter field of the videoconfig structure, myvid.adapter, against these constants. (The constants are defined in GRAPH.H, and you can use them if you include that file.)

_MDPA	Monochrome Display Adapter
_CGA	Color Graphics Adapter
_EGA	Enhanced Graphics Adapter
_VGA	Video Graphics Array
_MCGA	MultiColor Graphics Array
_HGC	Hercules Graphics Card

To check what kind of monitor is installed, check the monitor field, myvid.monitor, against these constants:

_MONO	Monochrome
_COLOR	Color (or Enhanced emulating color)
_ENHCOLOR	Enhanced Color
_ANALOGMONO	Analog Monochrome only
_ANALOGCOLOR	Analog Color only
_ANALOG	Analog Monochrome and Color modes

After checking these fields, you know what kind of video mode the computer can accept. Here are the choices of possible video modes that you can use:

_DEFAULTMODE	Restore screen to original mode
_TEXTBW40	40-column text, 16-tone grey
_TEXTC40	40-column text, 16/8 color
_TEXTBW80	80-column text, 16-tone grey
_TEXTC80	80-column text, 16/8 color
_MRES4COLOR	320 x 200, 4 color
_MRESNOCOLOR	320 x 200, 4 grey
_HRESBW	640 x 200, BW
_TEXTMONO	80-column text, BW
_HERCMONO	720 x 348, BW for HGC
_MRES16COLOR	320 x 200, 16 color
_HRES16COLOR	640 x 200, 16 color
_ERESNOCOLOR	640 x 350, BW
_ERESCOLOR	640 x 350, 4 or 16 color
_VRES2COLOR	640 x 480, BW
_VRES16COLOR	640 x 480, 16 color
_MRES256COLOR	320 x 200, 256 color

To select one of these modes, pass one of these constants to _setvideomode(). For example, in ARTIST.C we set four-color medium CGA resolution with _setvideomode(_MRES4COLOR).

Selecting Colors in Microsoft C

To draw, you have to select a color, and that is as easy as passing a parameter to _setcolor(). These 16 colors are already set up by default in Microsoft C:

_BLACK	_BLUE	_GREEN	_CYAN	_RED
_MAGENTA	_BROWN	_WHITE	_GRAY	_LIGHTBLUE
_LIGHTGREEN	_LIGHTCYAN	_LIGHTRED	_LIGHTMAGENTA	_LIGHTYELLOW
_BRIGHTWHITE				

When you include GRAPH.H, these constants are already defined. If you have selected an EGA or VGA mode capable of supporting 16 colors, you can select a color as easily as using this instruction:

```
_setcolor(_RED);
```

You can use these predefined constants even if you are using 256-color VGA mode.

> Color mixing is another story—if you want to change the default colors, the EGA is capable of displaying 16 colors at once out of a selection of 64, and the VGA is capable of displaying up to 256 colors out of a selection of 256K. The way that you select colors from those color ranges is complex in both Microsoft C and Turbo C. It's beyond the scope of this book, but it can be done.

Not all screen modes support 16 colors, however. In CGA 4-color mode, you must select a background color and three foreground colors.

Although you can select the background color from the range of 16 possible choices, you are not free to choose any three foreground colors—you must choose between a choice of four *palettes*.

After you select a palette, the palette colors make up color values 1, 2, and 3. (The background color makes up color value 0.) These color values are the values you pass to _setcolor() to select the drawing color. Here are the palettes under Microsoft C:

Table 3.2   Microsoft C Palettes

Palette Number	Color Value		
	1	2	3
0	green	red	brown
1	cyan	magenta	light grey
2	light green	light red	yellow
3	light cyan	light magenta	white

For example, let's say we want to choose palette 1 (cyan, magenta, and light gray). We can do that with a call to _selectpalette():

```
_selectpalette(1);
```

Now we can choose drawing colors with _setcolor(). We have selected the cyan/magenta/light gray palette, so color 1 is cyan, color 2 is magenta, and color 3 is light gray. To draw in magenta, make this call:

```
_setcolor(2);
```

Color values 1 - 3 are the palette colors, and color value 0 is the background color, which you set with _setbkcolor().

You can choose the background color out of 16 choices above. For example, to make the background color blue, use this call:

```
_setbkcolor(_BLUE);
```

It is important to realize that when you select the background color, the whole background changes to that color—in this case, the background is now blue, not black.

Selecting the background color sets color value 0. When you want to draw in the background color, pass a value of 0 to _setcolor().

Setting Video Modes in Turbo C

In Turbo C, the situation is similar. Here, you can detect which graphics equipment and mode are currently installed with detectgraph():

```
detectgraph(&grdriver, &grmode);
```

Both grdriver and grmode are int variables that you declare yourself.

Turbo C requires you to load a graphics driver before using video modes. To determine if a graphics driver has already been loaded, check the returned value of grdriver against this list of constants (they are defined in GRAPHICS.H):

CGA
MCGA
EGA

EGA64
EGAMONO
IBM8514
HERCMONO
ATT400
VGA
PC3270

If the driver for one of these monitors has already been installed, then you can use the video modes of that monitor. If you want to use a different monitor driver, you must load it yourself. (We'll do this shortly.)

You can also check the returned value for grmode against this list to see which mode is current:

CGAC0	320x200	palette 0
CGAC1	320x200	palette 1
CGAC2	320x200	palette 2
CGAC3	320x200	palette 3
CGAHI	640x200	
MCGAC0	320x200	palette 0
MCGAC1	320x200	palette 1
MCGAC2	320x200	palette 2
MCGAC3	320x200	palette 3
MCGAMED	640x200	
MCGAHI	640x480	
EGALO	640x200	16 color
EGAHI	640x350	16 color
EGA64LO	640x200	16 color
EGA64HI	640x350	4 color
EGAMONOHI	640x350	
HERCMONOHI	720x348	
VGALO	640x200	16 color
VGAMED	640x350	16 color
VGAHI	640x480	16 color

If you want to change the video mode, first make sure that the appropriate graphics driver is loaded. To load a graphics driver, call the initgraph() function: initgraph(&grdiver, &grmode, grpath), where grdriver and grmode are ints as defined in the constants above. The grpath variable is a string indicating where the driver software (which comes with Turbo C—these files have the extension .BGI) for the particular monitor is to be found. If the driver software is in the current subdirectory, just set grpath to a NULL string, " ". For example, to load the CGA driver, use this code:

```
int g_driver, g_mode;

g_driver = CGA;
g_mode = CGAC3;

initgraph(&g_driver, &g_mode, "");
```

After the driver software is installed, we do not need to install it again to switch modes. Instead, call setgraphmode() to set a new mode (as long as the driver software supports the requested mode):

```
        int g_driver, g_mode;

        g_driver = CGA;
        g_mode = CGAC3;

        initgraph(&g_driver, &g_mode, "");

→       setgraphmode(CGAC3);
```

Selecting Colors in Turbo C

Just as in Microsoft C, there are 16 predefined constants in Turbo C (in GRAPHICS.H) for the 16 default colors:

```
            BLACK
            BLUE
            GREEN
            CYAN
            RED
            MAGENTA
            BROWN
            LIGHTGRAY
            DARKGRAY
            LIGHTBLUE
            LIGHTGREEN
            LIGHTCYAN
            LIGHTRED
            LIGHTMAGENTA
            YELLOW
            WHITE
```

In 16-color modes, select the current drawing color by using setcolor(). For example, if we want to draw in brown, we make this call:

```
setcolor(BROWN);
```

In the four-color CGA mode, we can select the background color from the full choice of 16. For example, this call makes the background magenta:

```
setbkcolor(MAGENTA);
```

In Turbo C, you can select the CGA palette when you set the mode (because the mode constants are defined for each CGA mode). These four palettes are used in Turbo C:

Table 3.3   Turbo C Palettes

Palette Number	Color Value		
	1	2	3
0	light green	light red	yellow
1	light cyan	light magenta	white
2	green	red	brown
3	cyan	magenta	light grey

To select palette 0, set the mode to CGAC0:

```
setgraphmode(CGAC0);
```

When you select a palette, you've selected colors 1 - 3. If we wanted to draw in light green (color 1 of palette 0) after making this call, we simply make this next call to setcolor:

```
setcolor(1)
```

Adding Color to ARTIST.C

Now that we know a little more about color, we can use the four CGA colors in ARTIST.C. Let's use the spacebar to set colors. Every time we type a space, the color value (1 - 3) is increased by 1 until we get to 3, when it's reset to 1. This way we can cycle through the available colors.

In addition, when we draw in the background color, it's like erasing. This means we can erase images if we add a delete command with, say, 'd'. All that 'd' does is set the color to 0 (the background color). Here's the final program:

```
#include <stdio.h>
#include <graph.h>

main()
{
int in, index = 1;
int xloc = 0, yloc = 0, x1 = 0, y1 = 0;
FILE *fpointer;
void *gpointer;
char fillarray[] = {0x55, 0x55, 0x55, 0x55, 0x55, 0x55, 0x55, 0x55};

_setvideomode(_MRES4COLOR);

_setcolor(1);

_setfillmask(fillarray);

while((in = getch()) != 'q')
  {
        if (!in) in = getch() + 128;
        switch (in)
        {
        case 208:       /* up */
                yloc++;
                break;
        case 203:       /* left */
                xloc--;
                break;
        case 205:       /* right */
                xloc++;
                break;
        case 200:       /* down */
                yloc--;
                break;
        case 'p':       /* put pixel */
                _setpixel(xloc,yloc);
                _moveto(xloc,yloc);
                x1 = xloc;
                y1 = yloc;
                break;
        case 'l':       /* draw line */
                _lineto(xloc,yloc);
                break;
        case 'r':       /* draw rectangle */
                _rectangle(_GBORDER, x1, y1, xloc, yloc);
                break;
        case 'e':       /* draw ellipse */
                _ellipse(_GBORDER, x1, y1, xloc, yloc);
                break;
        case 'x':       /* fill */
                _floodfill(xloc, yloc, 1);
                break;
```

```
→          case ' ':       /* change color */
→                 (index >= 3 ? index = 1 : index++);
→                 _setcolor(index);
→                 break;
→          case 'd':       /* delete */
→                 _setcolor(0);
→                 break;
           case 's':       /* save screen */
                  fpointer=fopen("screen.dmp","wb");
                  gpointer = 0xb8000000;
                  fwrite(gpointer, 16*1024, 1, fpointer);
                  fclose(fpointer);
                  break;
           case 'f':       /* restore from file */
                  fpointer=fopen("screen.dmp","rb");
                  gpointer = 0xb8000000;
                  fread(gpointer, 16*1024, 1, fpointer);
                  fclose(fpointer);
                  break;
           default:
                  ;
      }

  }
}
```

For almost every subject in this book, Microsoft C and Turbo C overlap well enough not to be considered as separate programs. However, graphics is an exception. We have to load a graphics driver, select modes, and make different calls. We can write ARTIST.C in Turbo C:

```
#include <stdio.h>
#include <graphics.h>

main()
{
int in, index = 1;
int xloc = 0, yloc = 0, x1 = 0, y1 = 0;
FILE *fpointer;
void  *gpointer;
char fillarray[] = {0x55, 0x55, 0x55, 0x55, 0x55, 0x55, 0x55, 0x55};
int g_driver, g_mode;

g_driver = CGA;
g_mode = CGAC3;

initgraph(&g_driver, &g_mode, "");

setgraphmode(CGAC3);

setcolor(1);

setfillpattern(fillarray,1);

while((in = getch()) != 'q')
```

```
{
        if (!in) in = getch() + 128;
        switch (in)
        {
        case 208:       /* up */
                yloc++;
                break;
        case 203:       /* left */
                xloc--;
                break;
        case 205:       /* right */
                xloc++;
                break;
        case 200:       /* down */
                yloc--;
                break;
        case 'p':       /* put pixel */
                putpixel(xloc,yloc,1);
                moveto(xloc,yloc);
                x1 = xloc;
                y1 = yloc;
                break;
        case 'l':       /* draw line */
                lineto(xloc,yloc);
                break;
        case 'r':       /* draw a rectangle */
                rectangle(x1, y1, xloc, yloc);
                break;
        case 'e':       /* draw ellipse */
                ellipse((x1 + xloc)/2, (y1 + yloc)/2, 0, 360,\
                    abs(xloc - x1)/2, abs(yloc - y1)/2);
                break;
        case 'x':       /* fill */
                floodfill(xloc, yloc, 1);
                break;
        case ' ':       /* change color */
                (index >= 3 ? index = 1 : index++);
                setcolor(index);
                break;
        case 'd':       /* delete */
                setcolor(0);
                break;
        case 's':       /* save screen */
                fpointer=fopen("screen.dmp","wb");
                gpointer = 0xb8000000;
                fwrite(gpointer, 16*1024, 1, fpointer);
                fclose(fpointer);
                break;
        case 'f':       /* restore from file */
                fpointer=fopen("screen.dmp","rb");
                gpointer = 0xb8000000;
                fread(gpointer, 16*1024, 1, fpointer);
                fclose(fpointer);
```

```
        break;
    default:
        ;
    }

}
}
```

And that's it for ARTIST.C. Now that we've started with graphics,
let's continue with some more advanced work.

Animation With Getimage() and Putimage()

There are many things you can do with graphics images, and surely
one of the most attractive is animation. We can do this in Microsoft C
with _getimage() and _putimage() (Turbo C: getimage() and
putimage()). If we store images and then restore them, we can animate action on the screen.

In order to store an image, pass _getimage() the upper left coordinates, the lower right coordinates, and the address of the area in
memory where the image is to be stored. Once the image is stored in
memory, you can write it out to a disk file and then pop it back on the
screen with _putimage().

In order to store images, we need to set aside memory space. How
much space is required for a graphics image? You can calculate the
space requirement, of course, but you can also use the _imagesize()
(Turbo C: imagesize()) function. Just pass the coordinates of the image
(i.e., four short integers). _imagesize() returns the number of bytes
needed to store the image. We can use this number with malloc() to
reserve memory space.

Let's put animation into action by writing a program that draws a
succession of multicolored rectangles on the screen, stores each
image, and then replays them. Start by setting the graphics mode. We
are drawing in different colors this time, so let's use a 16-color, 640 x
350 mode, such as _ERESCOLOR (in Turbo C, this is EGAHI):

```
        #include <stdio.h>
        #include <graph.h>

    main()
    {

→       _setvideomode(_ERESCOLOR);
                    :
                    :
    }
```

Next, we have to set aside memory space for our images. Let's generate rectangles inside the region (0,0) to (50,50). If we use all available EGA colors, we'll have 16 rectangles. We can get the size requirements from _imagesize and use malloc() at the same time:

```
#define MAXX 50
#define MAXY 50
#include <stdio.h>
#include <graph.h>

main()
{
char *images;

_setvideomode(_ERESCOLOR);

images = malloc(16 * _imagesize(0, 0, MAXX, MAXY));
            :
            :
}
```

Now include a variable to hold the color value (0 - 15), and enter our drawing loop:

```
#define MAXX 50
#define MAXY 50
#include <stdio.h>
#include <graph.h>

main()
{
char *images;
int colorval, x = MAXX/16, y = MAXY/16;

_setvideomode(_ERESCOLOR);

images = malloc(16 * _imagesize(0, 0, MAXX, MAXY));

for(colorval = 0; colorval < 16; colorval++, x+= MAXX/16, y+= MAXY/16)
{
      _setcolor(colorval);
      _rectangle(_GBORDER, 0, 0, x, y);

}
}
```

To save the images, add _getimage():

```
#define MAXX 50
#define MAXY 50
```

```
#include <stdio.h>
#include <graph.h>

main()
{
char *images;
int colorval, x = MAXX/16, y = MAXY/16;

_setvideomode(_ERESCOLOR);

images = malloc(16 * _imagesize(0, 0, MAXX, MAXY));

 for(colorval = 0; colorval < 16; colorval++, x+= MAXX/16, y+= MAXY/16)
 {
        _setcolor(colorval);
        _rectangle(_GBORDER, 0, 0, x, y);
        _getimage(0, 0, MAXX, MAXY, images);
        images += _imagesize(0, 0, MAXX, MAXY);
 }
}
```

Now that the images are stored, blank the screen with _clear-screen(_GCLEARSCREEN) (Turbo C: cleardevice() with no parameters) and then put them back one by one. We have set up a pointer to the memory storage area we set aside earlier. Each time through the retrieval loop, we increment the memory storage area by the size of the image in memory:

```
#define MAXX 50
#define MAXY 50
#include <stdio.h>
#include <graph.h>
#include <malloc.h>

main()
{
char *images;
char *frame;
int colorval, x = MAXX/16, y = MAXY/16;
int size;

_setvideomode(_ERESCOLOR);

images = malloc(16 * _imagesize(0, 0, MAXX, MAXY));
frame = images;

 for(colorval = 0; colorval < 16; colorval++, x+= MAXX/16, y+= MAXY/16)
 {
        _setcolor(colorval);
        _rectangle(_GBORDER, 0, 0, x, y);
        _getimage(0, 0, MAXX, MAXY, frame);
  →      frame += _imagesize(0, 0, MAXX, MAXY);
 }
```

```
_clearscreen(_GCLEARSCREEN);
frame = images;

        for(colorval = 0; colorval < 16; colorval++)
        {
                _putimage(0, 0, frame, 0);
                frame += _imagesize(0, 0, MAXX, MAXY);
        }
}
```

That's it. When the program runs, the rectangles appear, each one larger than the last. After the last colored rectangle appears, the screen is cleared, and the sequence repeats. The second time, however, we retrieve the images from memory and play them back.

Of course, we can animate other images besides rectangles. We will take a look at one last graphics program before leaving the subject.

Viewports

Let's say we want to draw a stick figure on the screen:

```
(0,0)xxxx
        x       x
         xxxx (6,6)
           x
         xx(4,8)
        x  x  x
      x    x    x
  (0,14)x    x      x(8,14)
        x  x
      x       x
    x           x
(0,25)x           x(8,25)
```

Drawing the figure could be done with the _moveto() and _lineto() functions, using these instructions:

```
#include <stdio.h>
#include <graph.h>

main()
{
        _setvideomode(_MRES4COLOR);
        _ellipse(_GFILLINTERIOR, 0, 0, 6, 6);
        _moveto(4,8);
        _lineto(0,14);
        _moveto(4,8);
```

```
        _lineto(8,14);
        _moveto(4,8);
        _lineto(4,14);
        _lineto(0,25);
        _moveto(4,8);
        _lineto(8,25);
}
```

To animate the figure, add the next image:

```
(0,0)xxxx
        x       x
         xxxx (6,6)
           x
         xx(4,8)
        x  x   x
        x  x    x
(2,14)  x  x       x(10,14)
          x  x
          x    x
          x      x
(4,25)  x          x(12,25)
```

In code, that step looks like this:

```
#include <stdio.h>
#include <graph.h>

main()
{
        _setvideomode(_MRES4COLOR);
        _ellipse(_GFILLINTERIOR, 0, 0, 6, 6);
        _moveto(4,8);
        _lineto(0,14);
        _moveto(4,8);
        _lineto(8,14);
        _moveto(4,8);
        _lineto(4,14);
        _lineto(0,25);
        _moveto(4,8);
        _lineto(8,25);

        _moveto(4,8);
        _lineto(2,14);
        _moveto(4,8);
        _lineto(10,14);
        _moveto(4,8);
```

```
_lineto(4,14);
_lineto(4,25);
_moveto(4,8);
_lineto(12,25);
```

```
}
```

Now that we have instructions for drawing two images of the figure, we can store both images and alternate them across the screen (by passing different coordinates to _putimage()) and create the illusion that the figure is walking.

There is another way to do the same thing—we can use *viewports*. In MicroSoft and Turbo C, a viewport can be defined on the screen as an area like this:

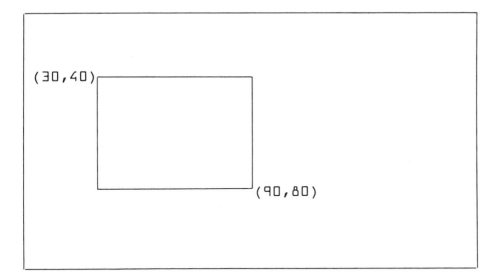

If you pass these coordinates to _setviewport() (Turbo C: setviewport()), this area becomes the only active area on the screen. An attempt to draw outside of this area does nothing. Keep in mind that once you set a viewport, you will not be able to draw outside of it (a viewport is also called a *clip region*). The top left corner of the viewport becomes the new origin (0,0):

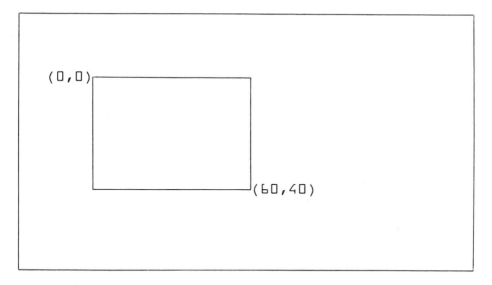

The origin is set every time the viewport is set, so we can easily move our figure across the screen with _setviewport():

```
#include <stdio.h>
#include <graph.h>

main()
{
int i;
        _setvideomode(_MRES4COLOR);

        for (i = 0; i < 100; i++)
                {
        _setviewport(100-i,0,125-i,25);          ←
        _ellipse(_GFILLINTERIOR, 0, 0, 6, 6);
        _moveto(4,8);
        _lineto(0,14);
        _moveto(4,8);
        _lineto(8,14);
        _moveto(4,8);
        _lineto(4,14);
        _lineto(0,25);
        _moveto(4,8);
        _lineto(8,25);

        _clearscreen(_GCLEARSCREEN);

        _moveto(4,8);
```

```
_lineto(2,14);
_moveto(4,8);
_lineto(10,14);
_moveto(4,8);
_lineto(4,14);
_lineto(4,25);
_moveto(4,8);
_lineto(12,25);

_clearscreen(_GCLEARSCREEN);
        }
}
```

When this program runs, a one-inch high figure appears to run across the screen from right to left. As we continue to draw the figure on the screen, we also shift the screen coordinates with _setvieworg(). The origin of the screen moves across the screen, and our figure moves with it.

Viewports are very useful for graphics programs because they allow you to break the screen up into windows. In fact, there are a whole set of window functions in Microsoft C. You can use either viewports or windows in Microsoft C—if you use windows, you can rescale the axes of the window to fit whatever you want, and the new coordinates are referred to as *window coordinates*

The End of Graphics

That's it for graphics. There are topics we didn't cover— graphics itself could make up a book. For example, you can use various graphic fonts under either Microsoft or Turbo C (but they are complex to use, and their use varies between compilers). Nonetheless, we've gotten a good introduction to the subject.

Now that we know something about presenting data, let's take a look at handling it in the next chapter on databasing.

4

Databasing

This chapter has a lot to do with crunching and organizing data. In it, we're going to write a small database program, and upgrade arrays to pointer notation.

From Arrays to Pointers

C, like most computer languages, uses arrays in one form or another. To use an array, we first have to declare it:

```
       main()
       {
  →    int array[10];
       :
       :
       }
```

We can refer to individual elements of this array with an index, which we can call i:

```
       main()
       {
       int array[10], i=3;
       :
  →    array[i] = 7;
       :
       }
```

We mentioned earlier that the name of an array is really a pointer. What does that mean?

It means is that the term "array" is really a constant in our program, and stands for the address at which the array's data begin. That is to say, array[0] is equal to *array.

This is an important fact, and most of this chapter is built on it. In addition to our expression for array[0], we can say this for array[i]:

117

```
array[i] = *(array + i)
```

That is, we can substitute *(array + i) for array[i] in our example program to produce this:

```
     main()
     {
     int array[10], i=3;
     :
→    *(array + i) = 7;
     :
     }
```

At first, this might seem like nothing more than an exercise in making programs more complex and difficult to read. It turns out, however, that there is a good deal more happening here, both in terms of execution speed and memory-storage efficiency.

A Question of Speed

For example, look at this program:

```
main()
{
char array[] = "Hello, world.\r\n";
int i;

for(i = 0; i < 15; i++)
        putch(array[i]);

}
```

It prints out "Hello, world.", one character at a time. Each time through, we increment the index i and print the character array[i]. Each time that we make the reference to array[i], the program is forced to use a memory reference such as this one:

```
&array[0] + i*sizeof(char)
```

In this simple case, sizeof(char) is just one byte in size, and the multiplication is easy—but if you had an array of floats or doubles, it would be different. Each time you reference an item in an array, a multiplication operation is performed, and multiplications are among the most time-consuming instructions in the 80x86.

On the other hand, consider this addition to the program:

```
main()
{
char array[] = "Hello, world.\r\n", *array_pointer = array;  ←
int i;

for(i = 0; i < 15; i++)
        putch(array[i]);

for(i = 0; i < 15; i++)
        putch(*array_pointer++);
}
```
→
→

Now we've added a pointer to the beginning of the array, named array_pointer. Each time through the loop, we increment array_pointer and print out *array_pointer. The result is the same as before—the string "Hello, world." is printed. Although we do the same thing (increment through the elements of an array), however, no multiplications are involved. Hardware multiplications are very slow instructions, so we've saved a good deal of time. Using addition when incrementing through the elements of an array is far faster than generating a complete address for the item array[i]. By using pointer notation, we can take advantage of that fact.

Memory Usage

Pointer notation is frequently faster than array notation. There are other reasons to consider pointer notation instead of array notation. Consider an array of character strings:

array[0][]	h	e	l	l	o	☐					
array[1][]	W	o	r	l	d	.	☐				
array[2][]	M	a	r	s	h	m	a	l	l	o	w	☐
array[3][]	F	l	i	n	g	i	n	g	☐			
array[4][]	r	e	d	☐							
array[5][]	b	u	t	t	o	n	s	☐			
array[6][]	w	i	l	d	l	y	☐				

You can see that much space is wasted—the array has to have as many columns as there are characters in the longest string. With an array of pointers, however, we can do this:

array[0]	→	h	e	l	l	o	□				
array[1]	→	W	o	r	l	d	.	□			
array[2]	→	M	a	r	s	h	m	a	l	l	o	w	□
array[3]	→	F	l	i	n	g	i	n	g	□	
array[4]	→	r	e	d	□						
array[5]	→	b	u	t	t	o	n	s	□		
array[6]	→	w	i	l	d	l	y	□			

Here we have a number of pointers, each pointing to character strings. No space is wasted—the strings can be stored one right after the other. (We will use this technique in our database program developed later in this chapter.) Frequently, memory is at a premium in programs, and the use of pointers rather than arrays can save room. In addition, our database program will be able to support variable-length fields.

Using Pointer Notation

To switch to pointer notation inside a program, just substitute *(array + i) for array[i]. You may understand that array is the name of a pointer pointing to the beginning of the array, but you may wonder about the part where we add i to array. After all, what if array is of a type where all elements are two bytes long?

array[0]

array[1]

array[2]

: 2 bytes

array[3]

Surely if we want array[2], but only add 2 to array, we'll end up get-
ting array[1]? Actually, that is not the case. The compiler is smart
enough to know how pointer addition should work. When you add 2
to array, C will check array's type (let's say it's int) and realize that
each element is two bytes long. It will then add *four* bytes to array, to
end up at the address of array[2].

In other words, when you add values to a pointer, the values are
understood to be in units of elements, not in bytes.

> If you are familiar with the idea of segments (discussed in Chapter 7),
> there is one more thing to add when discussing adding values to
> pointers: You must be careful not to increment the pointer over *seg-*
> *ment boundaries* unless you have made special preparations, as we'll
> see later.

In general, you can add numbers to pointers, and even subtract two
pointers from each other to find a relative offset. If you subtract two
pointers, the result will be presented in units of the array's element
size, not in bytes.

For instance, look at this program:

```
#include <stdio.h>

main()
{
float array[] = {3.14, 2.13, 1.73, 1.44, 2.32}, *begin_ptr, *end_ptr;

begin_ptr = &array[0];
end_ptr = &array[5];

printf("Number of elements from beginning to end: %d", end_ptr - begin_ptr);
}
```

Here we subtract two pointers to find the distance in elements
between end_ptr and begin_ptr. The result of the program is 5, as it
should be because pointer subtraction is done in terms of elements,
not bytes. (If we ask for begin_ptr - end_ptr, the result is -5).

> To find distances in bytes, cast the pointers into integers first. (For far
> pointers, which we'll get to next chapter, use long ints.)

Converting LOOKUP.C

In Chapter 2, we developed a program called LOOKUP.C. It read a file named DEF.TXT and searched for the definition of a given word. This is LOOKUP.C:

```
#include <stdio.h>
#include <string.h>

main(argc,argv)
int argc;
char *argv[];
{
char lword[10][20], ldef[10][80], tofind[20];
int i;
FILE *file_pointer;

strcpy(tofind, argv[1]);

        if( (file_pointer = fopen( "def.txt", "r") ) != NULL)
        {
                fread(lword, sizeof(lword), 1, file_pointer);
                fread(ldef, sizeof(ldef), 1, file_pointer);
        }
else perror("Error reading def.txt\n");

fclose(file_pointer);

        for(i = 0; i <= 10; i++)
        {
                if(strstr(tofind, lword[i]) != NULL && lword[i][0] != '\0')
                printf("\nDefinition: %s", ldef[i]);
        }
}
```

We can easily convert this program to LOOKUP2.C, which uses pointer notation. Simply convert expressions such as array[i] to *(array + i):

```
#include <stdio.h>
#include <string.h>

main(argc,argv)
int argc;
char *argv[];
{
char lword[10][20], ldef[10][80], tofind[20];
int i;
FILE *file_pointer;

→    strcpy(tofind, *(argv +1));

        if( (file_pointer = fopen( "def.txt", "r") ) != NULL)
```

```
        {
                fread(lword, sizeof(lword), 1, file_pointer);
                fread(ldef, sizeof(ldef), 1, file_pointer);
        }
else perror("Error reading def.txt\n");


fclose(file_pointer);


        for(i = 0; i <= 10; i++)
        {
            if(strstr(tofind, *(lword +i)) != NULL && **(lword +i) != '\0')
            printf("\nDefinition: %s", *(ldef + i));
        }
}
```

There was very little to change, and the program functions as
before. You might notice that lword[i][0] became **(lword + i). To
understand more about two-dimensional arrays, especially in more
complicated cases where both of the indices are nonzero, let's take a
look at them.

Two-dimensional Arrays

When the compiler sees this program:

```
main()
{
int array[4][3], i=1, j = 2;
:
array[i][j] = 7;
:
}
```

it makes up a formula to reference data items in array[][]. That type of
formula looks like this:

array[i][j] = *(&array[0][0] + 3*i + j)

In other words, the compiler knows where the array starts in memory
(i.e., the address of array[0][0]). In order to find array[i][j], it sets up
an equation such as the previous one because the array is stored in
this way:

```
array[0][0]  ┌───────┐    · · · · · · · · · ·
             │       │
array[0][1]  │       │        Row  0
             │       │
array[0][2]  │       │
             ├───────┤    · · · · · · · · · ·
array[1][0]  │       │
             │       │
array[1][1]  │       │        Row  1
             │       │
array[1][2]  │       │
             ├───────┤    · · · · · · · · · ·
array[2][0]  │       │
             │       │
array[2][1]  │       │
             │       │        Row  2
array[2][2]  │       │
             ├───────┤    · · · · · · · · · ·
array[3][0]  │       │
             │       │
array[3][1]  │       │        Row  3
             │       │
array[3][2]  │       │
             └───────┘
```

All three columns of Row 0 are stored first, then all three columns of Row 1 are stored next, and so on.

To find array[i][j], C uses this formula: array[i][j] = *(&array[0][0] + 3*i + j). To find an element, we only need the number of columns (in this case, 3), not the number of rows. In fact, this is the reason that you don't have to declare the number of rows when declaring an automatic array. (You do need to declare the number of rows for static arrays, because C needs to know the total memory space that will be used.) For example, in a function, variables are automatic, so this is legal:

```
      main()
      {
      sub();
      }

      sub(array)
  →   int array[][3];
      {
      }
```

This is because C only needs the second index in order to know where to find a particular element. C skips over groups of numbers—three at a time—to get to the right location, so 3 is the only important number here.

> A few tricks used by experienced C programmers are worth mentioning here. C, unlike some other languages, does not normally let you pass a whole array to a function. However, if we do want to pass a copy of the whole array, it is worth knowing that with a very simple trick, you *can* pass an array as a function parameter. That simple trick is to make the array into a structure element—paradoxically, C does let you pass whole structures to functions. If one of the structure elements is an array, the structure element goes too. In this same way, you can make array assignments. The statement array2 = array1; is illegal. However, if you make the arrays into elements of a structure, there is no problem. Struct2 = struct1; works perfectly.

Because two-dimensional arrays are stored row by row, you can initialize them:

```
int array[2][3]=   {{1, 2, 3,}
                    {4, 5, 6,}};
```

Now let's look at two-dimensional arrays in pointer notation. If a one-dimensional array name is just a pointer to the first element of an array, what is a two-dimensional array name? A two-dimensional array name is a pointer to an array of one-dimensional arrays.

Let's take this step by step. We saw earlier how an array declared as int array[4][3] is stored in memory. It turns out that after we make that declaration, expressions such as array[0] or array[1] are legal in our program too. They are just pointers to one-dimensional arrays, each of which makes up a row:

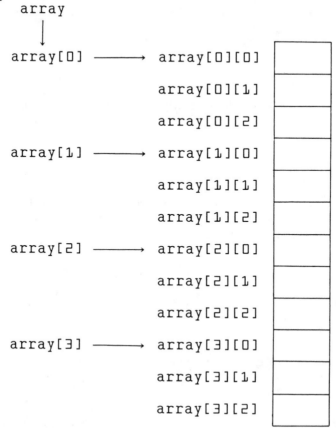

```
array[2]  ─────→  array[2][0]  ┌──────┐
                               │      │
                  array[2][1]  ├──────┤
                               │      │
                  array[2][2]  ├──────┤
                               │      │
array[3]  ─────→  array[3][0]  ├──────┤
                               │      │
                  array[3][1]  ├──────┤
                               │      │
                  array[3][2]  └──────┘
```

The name array is just a pointer to this one-dimensional array of pointers:

```
array
  │
  ↓
array[0]  ─────→  array[0][0]  ┌──────┐
                               │      │
                  array[0][1]  ├──────┤
                               │      │
                  array[0][2]  ├──────┤
                               │      │
array[1]  ─────→  array[1][0]  ├──────┤
                               │      │
                  array[1][1]  ├──────┤
                               │      │
                  array[1][2]  ├──────┤
                               │      │
array[2]  ─────→  array[2][0]  ├──────┤
                               │      │
                  array[2][1]  ├──────┤
                               │      │
                  array[2][2]  ├──────┤
                               │      │
array[3]  ─────→  array[3][0]  ├──────┤
                               │      │
                  array[3][1]  ├──────┤
                               │      │
                  array[3][2]  └──────┘
```

If we make the declaration int array[4][3], then array is a pointer to an array whose elements are array[0], array[1], and array[2]. array[1] is a pointer to an array whose elements are array[1][0], array[1][1], and array[1][2]:

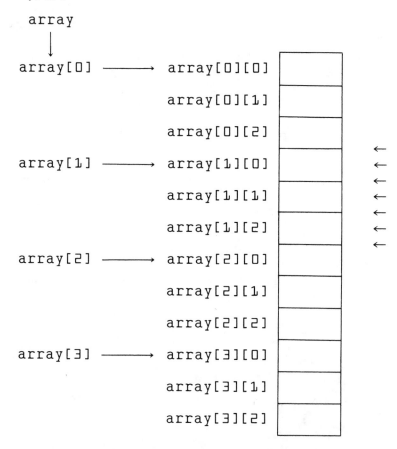

In general, an integer element can be reached in this way:

*(array[m] + n) = array[m][n]

If we expand the expression array[m], we get this:

((array + m) + n) = array[m][n]

In the case of array[0][0], this breaks down to **array. In the case of LOOKUP2.C, lword[i][0] becomes **(lword + i).

The parentheses in the expression *(*(array + m) + n) are important. When we add a value to a pointer, the value is taken to be in units of the pointer's object. The term array is a pointer to an array of pointers; when we add m to array, we are moving down the line by m pointers. On the other hand, *(array + m) is just a pointer to an integer; when we add n to *(array + m), we are moving down the line by n integers.

Each time we increment the m in *(*(array + m) + n), we are moving by one row through array[][]. This means that to move the m in *(*(array + m) + n) outside of its parentheses, we have to multiply by the column size of the array:

*(*array + m*column_size + n) = *(*(array + m) + n)

To sum up our exploration of two-dimensional arrays, take a look at these expressions. They all refer to the same object:

array[m][n]
*(array[m] + n)
((array + m) + n)
*(*array + m*column_size + n)

We can put these ways of looking at two-dimensional arrays together in this program, which prints out 7,7,7:

```
        main()
{
int array[4][3];

array[2][1] = 7;

printf("%d,%d,%d",array[2][1],*(*array + 2*3 + 1),*(*(array + 2) + 1));

}
```

Now we know enough about managing data to put together our own database program. Database programs rely upon *records*, and although database records don't mean exactly the same thing as file records, they are very close.

The DB.C Program

In a real database, you can set up your own record format, but that will not be the case in our program. Writing a complex record-editor would serve no purpose. (We want to look at pointer manipulations, not command parsers.) The record format we use simple, and it will contain three *fields*:

```
Name:
Owes:
Monthly payment:
```

For example, we can have a record that contains this information:

```
Name: Carson
Owes: 712.26
Monthly payment: 23.56
```

The first field is a character string, and the next two fields are stored as doubles. Let's say this is record 0. When we enter a great number of such records, we have a database. In order to profitably use it, we have to be able to manipulate the database in several ways.

For example, we may want to find all records that fit a certain criterion, such as monthly payment under $50.00. Or we may want to sort the records in ascending order of the amount owed. In other words, we want to be able to sort or search a given field of all the records. This means that we'll have to be careful about setting the records up in memory. Of course, we'll want to be able to look at any given record too, so part of our program will have to display records on command.

The Actual Database

Let's consider how we want to store the data in memory. For example, this could be the data that we want to include in our database:

```
"Carson"
712.26
23.26
"Adams"
245.23
29.17
"Banks"
633.90
87.17
```

We can store the character strings of field 0 in an array called field0[], and store the numerical values of the other two fields in arrays named field1[] and field2[]. They might look like this:

field0[0]	C	a	r	s	o	n	0										
field0[1]	A	d	a	m	s	0											
field0[2]	B	a	n	k	s	0											

```
field1[0] 712.26
field1[1] 245.23
field1[2] 633.90

field2[0] 23.26
field2[1] 29.17
field2[2] 87.17
```

We have to provide for long names, so the field1 array is very wasteful of space. On the other hand, we could forget about arrays altogether and just use pointers.

As long as we keep track of each field's data with a pointer:

```
field0ptrs[0]  →   C | a | r | s | o | n | 0

field0ptrs[1]  →   A | d | a | m | s | 0

field0ptrs[2]  →   B | a | n | k | s | 0
```

```
field1ptrs[0]  →  712.26
field1ptrs[1]  →  245.23
field1ptrs[2]  →  633.90

field2ptrs[0]  →  23.26
field2ptrs[1]  →  29.17
field2ptrs[2]  →  87.17
```

then the actual data can be located anywhere in memory.

Let's use pointers in this way. We will have three arrays of pointers: field0ptrs[], field1ptrs[], and field2ptrs[]. Let's say that we want to find out how much Carson owes. That amount is stored somewhere in memory—we need to find the pointer to it. The amount owed is Field 1, so we would use field1ptrs[]. This is an array of pointers to all amounts owed, indexed by record numbers. Carson is record 0, so we use field1ptrs[0]. This is a pointer to the amount Carson owes—the number itself is then just *field1ptrs[0].

Field0ptrs[] is now an array of pointers to strings, so we don't need to set aside the same amount of room in memory for each string. In fact, the whole thing looks like this in memory:

"Carson", "Adams", "Banks", 712.26, 245.23, 633.90, 23.26, 29.17, 87.17

But that's not important. As long as a pointer points to each data item, we don't need to know the details (except that we're saving space).

To sort the database in terms of a certain field (e.g., amount owed), or to find all records where a specified field meets some criterion (e.g., monthly payment under $50.00), we simply pass the name of the field's pointer array to a function. The function then loops through the entries in that field for all records. For example, to sort the database on Field 2 (the amount owed), we make a function call like this:

```
sort(field2ptrs);
```

and sort() checks all values by looping over *field2ptrs[].

A good question here is: Why are we using arrays of pointers to numerical data:

```
field1ptrs[0]  →  712.26
field1ptrs[1]  →  245.23
field1ptrs[2]  →  633.90

field2ptrs[0]  →  23.26
field2ptrs[1]  →  29.17
field2ptrs[2]  →  87.17
```

and not just arrays of data, like this:

```
field1[0]  =  712.26
field1[1]  =  245.23
field1[2]  =  633.90

field2[0]  =  23.26
field2[1]  =  29.17
field2[2]  =  87.17
```

That is, we could keep the data in an array such as field2[], instead of by using pointers, and sort it directly in this way:

```
sort(field2)
```

So why do we need pointers to numerical data elements? If we use pointer notation, we can use variable-length fields, which is especially important with strings:

```
field0ptrs[0]  →  | C | a | r | s | o | n | 0 |

field0ptrs[1]  →  | A | d | a | m | s | 0 |

field0ptrs[2]  →  | B | a | n | k | s | 0 |
```

In other words, it makes sense to store an array of pointers for variable-length data, and field0ptrs[] is set up for just that reason. But what about field1ptrs[] and field2ptrs[]? Numerical data for a specific field is almost always stored with the same length—we don't need variable length here. We've seen that the use of compact pointer expressions such as *array + + in loops, instead of in array[i + +] can save time, but even if we store the numerical data in this way:

```
field1[0]  =  712.26
field1[1]  =  245.23
field1[2]  =  633.90

field2[0]  =  23.26
field2[1]  =  29.17
field2[2]  =  87.17
```

we can still use compact pointer expressions such as *field1 + +. So, why are we using arrays of pointers to numerical data:

```
field1ptrs[0]  →  712.26
field1ptrs[1]  →  245.23
field1ptrs[2]  →  633.90

field2ptrs[0]  →  23.26
field2ptrs[1]  →  29.17
field2ptrs[2]  →  87.17
```

and not just immediate arrays? The answer comes from the way that databases sort records. Database programs need to handle large numbers of records quickly, and each record can be many bytes long. For that reason, good database programs do not sort the records themselves, but instead sort only the pointers to the records.

For example, if a record is 400 bytes long, and we have to sort 3000 records, it takes a long time for all of the memory manipulations to finish. This is especially true when you realize that to sort records, you have to interchange them, which means copying record A to a temporary location, copying record B to record A, and then copying from the temporary location to record A—three moves. Usually, the pointers to the records are sorted instead. The pointers are only a few bytes in size, so sorting them can be extremely quick. That's the way we'll sort our database.

For real speed, you can use only one pointer for the entire record, accessing fields as offsets from the beginning of the record. In this way, you only need to sort one pointer per record. However, doing so makes the programming more involved. Because our program is only a demonstration (and because we're allowing variable-length fields), we'll use three pointers per record, one for each field.

Let's start on the program. We have to fill these three arrays with pointers to data items:

```
field0ptrs[0]
field0ptrs[1]
field0ptrs[2]

field1ptrs[0]
field1ptrs[1]
field1ptrs[2]

field2ptrs[0]
field2ptrs[1]
field2ptrs[2]
```

Whenever we want to reference a data item, we can reach it through *(field#ptrs[Recordnum]). As this is only a demonstration program, we're not going to go through all the details of reading a database file in from disk. Instead, let's just use initializations to set up our data items, one after the other, in memory:

```
#include <stdio.h>

main()
{
char string0[] = "Carson";
double num1 = 712.26;
double num2 = 23.56;
char string1[] = "Adams";
```

```
double num3 = 245.23;
double num4 = 29.17;
char string2[] = "Banks";
double num5 = 633.90;
double num6 = 87.17;
double end1 = -1.;
double end2 = -1.;
```

This initialization of our data area means that the items will be following one after the other in memory. Notice that we also included two -1s at the end. They will be used later to indicate that search or sort has reached the end of the list for the doubles.

Now let's initialize our field pointers:

```
#include <stdio.h>

char    *field0ptrs[10];
double  *field1ptrs[10];
double  *field2ptrs[10];
int thisrec = 3;
char buffer[80];
float buffer2;

main()
{
char string0[] = "Carson";
double num1 = 712.26;
double num2 = 23.56;
char string1[] = "Adams";
double num3 = 245.23;
double num4 = 29.17;
char string2[] = "Banks";
double num5 = 633.90;
double num6 = 87.17;
double end1 = -1.;
double end2 = -1.;
int command;

field0ptrs[0] = string0;       ←
field0ptrs[1] = string1;       ←
field0ptrs[2] = string2;       ←
field1ptrs[0] = &num1;         ←
field1ptrs[1] = &num3;         ←
field1ptrs[2] = &num5;         ←
field1ptrs[3] = &end1;         ←
field2ptrs[0] = &num2;         ←
field2ptrs[1] = &num4;         ←
field2ptrs[2] = &num6;         ←
field2ptrs[3] = &end2;         ←
```

Note that string0, string1, and so forth are already the names of pointers, so we don't have to use the address operator "&" with them. Now our data area is set up.

Let's add a command processor to the program. We'll want to display our records in a minute so we can see what happened, but first let's make it possible to quit the program with a 'q' command:

```
#include <stdio.h>

char    *field0ptrs[10];
double *field1ptrs[10];
double *field2ptrs[10];
int thisrec = 3;
char buffer[80];
float buffer2;

main()
{
char string0[] = "Carson";
double num1 = 712.26;
double num2 = 23.56;
char string1[] = "Adams";
double num3 = 245.23;
double num4 = 29.17;
char string2[] = "Banks";
double num5 = 633.90;
double num6 = 87.17;
double end1 = -1.;
double end2 = -1.;
int command;

field0ptrs[0] = string0;
field0ptrs[1] = string1;
field0ptrs[2] = string2;
field1ptrs[0] = &num1;
field1ptrs[1] = &num3;
field1ptrs[2] = &num5;
field1ptrs[3] = &end1;
field2ptrs[0] = &num2;
field2ptrs[1] = &num4;
field2ptrs[2] = &num6;
field2ptrs[3] = &end2;

while((printf("Command:"), command = getchar()) != 'q')   ←
        {                                                  ←
        }                                                  ←
}
```

This while loop makes it possible to both print out a prompt and read a command. Expressions are evaluated left to right with the comma operator, so the result of

```
(printf("Command:"), command = getchar())
```

is equal to the character that getchar() reads. We check to see if it's 'q', and if it is, we quit.

Even though commercial databases use complex commands, we are going to limit ourselves to single characters to avoid the details of processing input. For example, examining a record is a frequent thing to do when using a database—let's make that particularly easy in DB.C. We can set up the program so that if you type a single-digit number, that record will be typed out. In other words, a single digit will be the command to type out the corresponding record out. Let's add that with our first entry in the while loop:

```
#include <stdio.h>

char    *field0ptrs[10];
double *field1ptrs[10];
double *field2ptrs[10];
int thisrec = 3;
char buffer[80];
float buffer2;

main()
{
char string0[] = "Carson";
double num1 = 712.26;
double num2 = 23.56;
char string1[] = "Adams";
double num3 = 245.23;
double num4 = 29.17;
char string2[] = "Banks";
double num5 = 633.90;
double num6 = 87.17;
double end1 = -1.;
double end2 = -1.;
int command;

field0ptrs[0] = string0;
field0ptrs[1] = string1;
field0ptrs[2] = string2;
field1ptrs[0] = &num1;
field1ptrs[1] = &num3;
field1ptrs[2] = &num5;
```

```
field1ptrs[3] = &end1;
field2ptrs[0] = &num2;
field2ptrs[1] = &num4;
field2ptrs[2] = &num6;
field2ptrs[3] = &end2;

while((printf("Command:"), command = getchar()) != 'q')
        {
→       if(command >= '0' && command <= '9')
→               display(command - '0');
        }
}
```

If a single digit is typed, we pass the number (after converting it from ASCII) to a function we'll call display() to type out that record. All we have to do now is write display().

The Display() Function

The display(recnum) function, where recnum is the record number, is asked to display all of the fields of a record on the screen. We can use printf() to do this. All we have to do is pass the right kind of data.

In array notation, the data we want to print with printf() are field0ptrs[recnum], then *field1ptrs[recnum], then *field2ptrs[recnum]. Note that because field 0 is already an array of pointers to strings (themselves pointers), we don't have to say *field0ptrs[recnum]. We could also convert this to pointer notation, using the array[i] = *(array + i) rule. Then we would simply pass *(field0ptrs + recnum), **(field1ptrs + recnum), and **(field2ptrs + recnum) to printf(). Here's what our display function looks like:

```
display(num)
int num;
{
printf("Name: %s\n",*(field0ptrs + num));
printf("Owes: %.2f\n",**(field1ptrs + num));
printf("Monthly payment: %.2f\n",**(field2ptrs + num));
}
```

Let's put it to work. After compiling DB.C, we can run it:

```
D>db
Command:
```

Our program is waiting for our first command. Let's take a look at the records that we've already stored: 0, 1, and 2:

```
D>db
Command:0       ←
Name: Carson
Owes: 712.26
Monthly payment: 23.56
Command:1       ←
Name: Adams
Owes: 245.23
Monthly payment: 29.17
Command:2       ←
Name: Banks
Owes: 633.90
Monthly payment: 87.17
Command:3       ←
Name: (null)
Owes: -1.00
Monthly payment: -1.00
Command:
```

We can see that the data are all there, and that there is even a fourth record (record number 3) that has the terminating (NULL) string for field 0, and -1.00 for both Fields 1 and 2.

Not bad for a start. Now the data are in a format we can use and display, just like a real database. Let's get to work. Real databases must be able to search through their records to find the ones that meet a certain criterion. For example, we might need the names of all people with monthly payments (Field 2) of less than $50. First, let's add an 'f' (for Find Command) to our while loop. Since we will be adding other commands too, let's put in a switch like this:

```
#include <stdio.h>

char   *field0ptrs[10];
double *field1ptrs[10];
double *field2ptrs[10];
int thisrec = 3;
char buffer[80];
float buffer2;

main()
{
char string0[] = "Carson";
double num1 = 712.26;
double num2 = 23.56;
char string1[] = "Adams";
double num3 = 245.23;
double num4 = 29.17;
char string2[] = "Banks";
```

```
double num5 = 633.90;
double num6 = 87.17;
double end1 = -1.;
double end2 = -1.;
int command;

field0ptrs[0] = string0;
field0ptrs[1] = string1;
field0ptrs[2] = string2;
field1ptrs[0] = &num1;
field1ptrs[1] = &num3;
field1ptrs[2] = &num5;
field1ptrs[3] = &end1;
field2ptrs[0] = &num2;
field2ptrs[1] = &num4;
field2ptrs[2] = &num6;
field2ptrs[3] = &end2;

while((printf("Command:"), command = getchar()) != 'q')
        {
        if(command >= '0' && command <= '9')
                display(command - '0');
   →    switch (command)
   →            {
   →            case 'f':
   →              display(find(field2ptrs));
   →              break;
   →            default:
   →              break;
   →            }
        }
}


display(num)
int num;
{
printf("Name: %s\n",*(field0ptrs + num));
printf("Owes: %.2f\n",**(field1ptrs + num));
printf("Monthly payment: %.2f\n",**(field2ptrs + num)); }
```

What we are writing with our switch is a *function dispatcher*. Depending upon the command read, we will call the appropriate function. (We could, if we wished, even use pointers to functions, and call them that way.)

In the case of the find command 'f', we ask db to display(find(field2ptrs)). What will find(field2ptrs) return? Since this is not a full database, we implement a specific criterion in our find()

function—we will ask it to find the first record where the specified field is less than $50.00. Now we have to tell it which field to search.

We can do so by simply passing the name of the array of field pointers. In this case, that is field2ptrs. The find() function works through this array of pointers. For each pointer, it has to check whether the object pointed at meets the criterion we set.

In this case, that criterion is that Field 2 hold a value less than $50.00. The find() function must search Field 2 of all records to check them. We start in this way:

```
int find(ptr2ptrs);
double **ptr2ptrs;
{
}
```

We pass parameters such as field0ptrs or field1ptrs to the find() function. To search field 1, we pass field1ptrs. To search field 2, we pass field2ptrs. The names field1ptrs or field2ptrs are pointers to pointers, and the array name that is passed is therefore put into ptr2ptprs—the pointer to the field pointers. Inside the function, we need to increment this pointer to loop over every record. In other words, this is what ptr2ptrs points at now:

ptr2ptrs →	field2ptrs[0]	→ Record 0, Field 2
	field2ptrs[1]	→ Record 1, Field 2
	field2ptrs[2]	→ Record 2, Field 2

$$\vdots$$

We have to increment ptr2ptrs, like this:

	field2ptrs[0]	→ Record 0, Field 2
ptr2ptrs →	field2ptrs[1]	→ Record 1, Field 2
	field2ptrs[2]	→ Record 2, Field 2

$$\vdots$$

if we want to examine Field 2 of every record. To increment ptr2ptrs, we need only add 1 to it, or else we can use ptr2ptrs + +.

We will check all the pointers in the array by steadily incrementing ptr2ptrs. But we don't want to look at the pointers—we want to look at the data they point to, so we add another level of indirection. In other words, to look at all field 2s, we just keep looking at **(ptr2ptrs + +).

Since we want to return the record number, we have to track it as we increment. On the other hand, we want to make our find() function as fast as possible. It is better to have a while loop that checks **(ptr2ptrs + +), rather than an if loop that keeps incrementing a record number, determines the new pointer, and then looks at the data. For that reason, let's make a copy of ptr2ptrs called loc, increment only the copy, and return loc - ptr2ptrs as the record number:

```
int find(ptr2ptrs)
double **ptr2ptrs;
{
double **loc;
loc = ptr2ptrs;
while (**loc < 50 && **loc++ != -1.);
return (loc - ptr2ptrs);
}
```

> In addition, it's worth adding that if you search for a match to a variable the size of an int (that is, 16 bits), you should declare the variable you are trying to match as "register int vble", where vble is the variable's name. The register keyword makes C keep the variable in one of the 80x86's registers for fast comparisons, which means it doesn't have to be fetched from memory each time.

Notice also that the way we terminate the search is by checking for the end-of-list marker that we put in, -1. If we find it, we stop looking. For error-checking purposes, and in a real program, find() should return some error code if no match is made.

We can add the find command to our program by including an 'f' case in the function dispatcher switch statement, and by including the find() function:

```
#include <stdio.h>

char    *field0ptrs[10];
double *field1ptrs[10];
double *field2ptrs[10];
```

```
main()
{
char string0[] = "Carson";
double num1 = 712.26;
double num2 = 23.56;
char string1[] = "Adams";
double num3 = 245.23;
double num4 = 29.17;
char string2[] = "Banks";
double num5 = 633.90;
double num6 = 87.17;
double end1 = -1.;
double end2 = -1.;
int command;

field0ptrs[0] = string0;
field0ptrs[1] = string1;
field0ptrs[2] = string2;
field1ptrs[0] = &num1;
field1ptrs[1] = &num3;
field1ptrs[2] = &num5;
field1ptrs[3] = &end1;
field2ptrs[0] = &num2;
field2ptrs[1] = &num4;
field2ptrs[2] = &num6;
field2ptrs[3] = &end2;

while((printf("Command:"), command = getchar()) != 'q')
        {
        if(command >= '0' && command <= '9')
                display(command - '0');
        switch (command)
                {
                case 'f':
                  display(find(field2ptrs));
                  break;
                default:
                  break;
                }
        }
}


display(num)
int num;
{
printf("Name: %s\n",*(field0ptrs + num));
printf("Owes: %.2f\n",**(field1ptrs + num));
printf("Monthly payment: %.2f\n",**(field2ptrs + num));
}
```

```
int find(ptr2ptrs)
double **ptr2ptrs;
{
double **loc;
loc = ptr2ptrs;
while (**loc < 50 && **loc++ != -1.);
return (loc - ptr2ptrs);
}
```

Here we rely upon the fact that, as we set up the data, at least one record does have a value in Field 2 greater than 50. If no such match is made, however, find() returns an impossible record number, 1 greater than the record number that actually exists.

The next step to a real database program is to include a sorting function.

Sorting the Database

Here is where pointers show their utility. Instead of sorting data themselves and moving large numbers of bytes around in memory, we can simply sort the pointers.

In other words, let's say the database looked like this for Field 1:

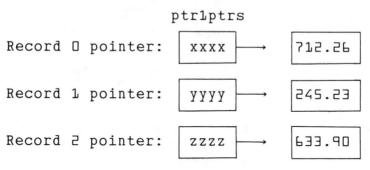

Now we sort the database and get this final result:

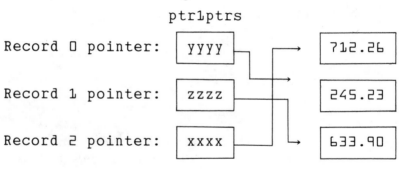

We moved the pointers around so that the Field 1 pointer for Record 0 now points to 245.23, the Field 1 pointer for Record 1 points to 633.90, and the Field 1 pointer for Record 2 points to 245.23. Now that the Field 1 pointers are adjusted, we have to adjust the other pointer arrays (field0ptrs and field1ptrs) and move their pointers around in exactly the same way so that the full records are "moved."

This way, of course, actual data have not been moved. When we are working with only doubles of 8 bytes length, moving only the pointers is not a great time saving. On the other hand, when working with longer records (character strings, or with fields that contain dates and so on), this method is very efficient.

Since our topic here is pointers, we will not use any very fast sorting routines. Such routines exist, but the fastest routines are very long to code, and the algorithm they actually use depends upon the number of items to be sorted. (Various algorithms are the fastest only for specific numbers of elements.) In our case, we will only use a simple exchange sort. Here it is in array terms:

```
for( i = 0; i < n - 1; i++)
        {
    for( j = i + 1; j < n; j++)
            {
        if ( array[i] > array[j] )
                temp = array[i];
                array[i] = array[j];
                array[j] = temp;
                        }
            }
```

Exchanging the array elements is a little more complex, because we have to exchange the corresponding elements in the other two fields to make sure that all of the record's pointers are moved. Here's how we begin:

```
int sorter(ptr2ptrs)
double **ptr2ptrs;
{
int i, j;
char *temp1;
double *temp2;


}
```

Again, we will use the name ptr2ptrs for the name of the passed array of pointers. We'll need the integers i and j as indices in our sort algorithm, and we'll need some temporary variables when we exchange items. We need two temporary variables, one a pointer to type char, and one a pointer to type double.

We need to know the number of records to sort. Let's store that number in a global variable named numrecs. We make it global for two reasons—other functions will need it, and if it's global, other functions can change it. Here's how our loop looks in sorter():

```
int sorter(ptr2ptrs)
double **ptr2ptrs;
{
int i, j;
char *temp1;
double *temp2;

for( i = 0; i < numrecs - 1; i++)
        {
    for( j = i + 1; j < numrecs; j++)
            {


            }
        }
}
```

Now it's up to us to fill in the loop. First, we have to check if *ptr2ptrs[i] is greater than *ptr2ptrs[j] by comparing the two doubles in records i and j. If this is the case, we have to exchange the records. Writing *ptr2ptrs[i] as **(ptr2ptrs + i), we can fill in the loop this way:

```
int sorter(ptr2ptrs)
double **ptr2ptrs;
{
int i, j;
char *temp1;
double *temp2;

for( i = 0; i < numrecs - 1; i++)
        {
    for( j = i + 1; j < numrecs; j++)
            {
→       if (**(ptr2ptrs + i) > **(ptr2ptrs + j))
→               { /* exchange i and j */  }
            }
        }
}
```

This function can also be converted to use compact pointer expressions, such as those used in find() (such as **loc + +).

All that remains is to exchange the pointers for the records i and j. Since there are three different pointer arrays (one for each field), we exchange the ith and jth entry in each of the three arrays. This is the new DB.C:

```
#include <stdio.h>

char   *field0ptrs[10];
double *field1ptrs[10];
double *field2ptrs[10];
int numrecs = 3;   ←

main()
{
char string0[] = "Carson";
double num1 = 712.26;
double num2 = 23.56;
char string1[] = "Adams";
double num3 = 245.23;
double num4 = 29.17;
char string2[] = "Banks";
double num5 = 633.90;
double num6 = 87.17;
double end1 = -1.;
double end2 = -1.;
int command;

field0ptrs[0] = string0;
field0ptrs[1] = string1;
field0ptrs[2] = string2;
field1ptrs[0] = &num1;
field1ptrs[1] = &num3;
field1ptrs[2] = &num5;
field1ptrs[3] = &end1;
field2ptrs[0] = &num2;
field2ptrs[1] = &num4;
field2ptrs[2] = &num6;
field2ptrs[3] = &end2;

while((printf("Command:"), command = getchar()) != 'q')
        {
        if(command >= '0' && command <= '9')
                display(command - '0');
        switch (command)
                {
                case 'f':
```

```
                        display(find(field2ptrs));
                        break;
         →      case 's':
         →        sorter(field1ptrs,3);
         →        break;
                default:
                  break;
                }
            }
}


display(num)
int num;
{
printf("Name: %s\n",*(field0ptrs + num));
printf("Owes: %.2f\n",**(field1ptrs + num));
printf("Monthly payment: %.2f\n",**(field2ptrs + num));
}


int find(ptr2ptrs)
double **ptr2ptrs;
{
double **loc;
loc = ptr2ptrs;
while (**loc < 50 && **loc++ != -1.);
return (loc - ptr2ptrs);
}


int sorter(ptr2ptrs)
double **ptr2ptrs;
{
int i, j;
char *temp1;
double *temp2;

for( i = 0; i < numrecs - 1; i++) {
   for( j = i + 1; j < numrecs; j++) {
        if (**(ptr2ptrs + i) > **(ptr2ptrs + j))
               { /* exchange i and j */
         →        temp1 = *(field0ptrs + i);
         →        *(field0ptrs + i) = *(field0ptrs + j);
         →        *(field0ptrs + j) = temp1;
         →        temp2 = *(field1ptrs + i);
         →        *(field1ptrs + i) = *(field1ptrs + j);
         →        *(field1ptrs + j) = temp2;
         →        temp2 = *(field2ptrs + i);
         →        *(field2ptrs + i) = *(field2ptrs + j);
```

→
```
          *(field2ptrs + j) = temp2; }
          }
                        }
}
```

Notice that we're moving objects around, such as field0ptrs[i] and field0ptrs[j]—which are the pointers to the actual data. Let's put it to the test. We can look at our original database, record by record:

```
Command:0  ←
Name: Carson
Owes: 712.26
Monthly payment: 23.56
Command:1  ←
Name: Adams
Owes: 245.23
Monthly payment: 29.17
Command:2  ←
Name: Banks
Owes: 633.90
Monthly payment: 87.17
```

Note the values of Field 1. We can sort them by Field 1 by typing 's', for this result:

```
Command:0
Name: Carson
Owes: 712.26
Monthly payment: 23.56
Command:1
Name: Adams
Owes: 245.23
Monthly payment: 29.17
Command:2
Name: Banks
Owes: 633.90
Monthly payment: 87.17
Command:s  ←
Command:0  ←
Name: Adams
Owes: 245.23
Monthly payment: 29.17
Command:1  ←
Name: Banks
Owes: 633.90
Monthly payment: 87.17
Command:2  ←
Name: Carson
Owes: 712.26
Monthly payment: 23.56
Command:q
```

The database has been sorted on Field 1. We've been able to manipulate our database, the first step towards writing a useful database program.

We might also wish to give DB.C another feature: the ability to add records.

Adding Records to DB.C

To add a record, we read in the new record's data, field by field, from the keyboard. We have to set aside more memory for the new data items on the fly, which means using malloc(). Let's set up a small function named adder() to add records as required.

Here's how we can start:

```
adder()
{
printf("Name: ");
scanf("%s",buffer);


}
```

We print the name of the first field, then we read the new first field (a character string) into a buffer that we set aside. This buffer is a static character string that we'll declare as char buffer[80];.

After we put the string temporarily into buffer, we store the string in memory to get ready for future strings. If there already are three records, they run 0, 1, and 2. The variable numrecs will be set to 3. The next record that we are going to add will also be 3. That means we can allocate memory space for the new record's Field 0 and fill it from buffer in this way:

```
adder()
{
printf("Name: ");
scanf("%s",buffer);
*(field0ptrs + numrecs) = (char *) malloc(strlen(buffer));    ←
strcpy(*(field0ptrs + numrecs), buffer);                      ←


}
```

Now we have to fill the two double fields, "Owes:" and "Monthly payment:." Here's the new code:

```
adder()
{
printf("Name: ");
scanf("%s",buffer);
```

```
*(field0ptrs + numrecs) = (char *) malloc(strlen(buffer));
strcpy(*(field0ptrs + numrecs), buffer);
printf("Owes: ");
scanf("%f",&buffer2);
**(field1ptrs + numrecs) = (double) buffer2;
printf("Monthly payment: ");
scanf("%f",&buffer2);
**(field2ptrs + numrecs) = (double) buffer2;
}
```

The only remaining thing to do is add the two -1 end-of-list marks for the next record, and update numrecs. The final code for adder() does that. Here's our new DB.C:

```
#include <stdio.h>

char   *field0ptrs[10];
double *field1ptrs[10];
double *field2ptrs[10];
int numrecs = 3;
char buffer[80];      ←
float buffer2;        ←

main()
{
char string0[] = "Carson";
double num1 = 712.26;
double num2 = 23.56;
char string1[] = "Adams";
double num3 = 245.23;
double num4 = 29.17;
char string2[] = "Banks";
double num5 = 633.90;
double num6 = 87.17;
double end1 = -1.;
double end2 = -1.;
int command;

field0ptrs[0] = string0;
field0ptrs[1] = string1;
field0ptrs[2] = string2;
field1ptrs[0] = &num1;
field1ptrs[1] = &num3;
field1ptrs[2] = &num5;
field1ptrs[3] = &end1;
field2ptrs[0] = &num2;
field2ptrs[1] = &num4;
field2ptrs[2] = &num6;
field2ptrs[3] = &end2;

while((printf("Command:"), command = getchar()) != 'q')
        {
        if(command >= '0' && command <= '9')
```

```
                    display(command - '0');
            switch (command)
                    {
                    case 'f':
                      display(find(field2ptrs));
                      break;
                    case 's':
                      sorter(field1ptrs,3);
                      break;
      →             case 'a':
      →               adder();
      →               break;
                    default:
                      break;
                    }
            }
}


display(num)
int num;
{
printf("Name: %s\n",*(field0ptrs + num));
printf("Owes: %.2f\n",**(field1ptrs + num));
printf("Monthly payment: %.2f\n",**(field2ptrs + num));
}


int find(ptr2ptrs)
double **ptr2ptrs;
{
double **loc;
loc = ptr2ptrs;
while (**loc < 50 && **loc++ != -1.);
return (loc - ptr2ptrs);
}


int sorter(ptr2ptrs)
double **ptr2ptrs;
{
int i, j;
char *temp1;
double *temp2;

for( i = 0; i < numrecs - 1; i++) {
   for( j = i + 1; j < numrecs; j++) {
        if (**(ptr2ptrs + i) > **(ptr2ptrs + j))
               { /* exchange i and j */
                temp1 = *(field0ptrs + i);
                *(field0ptrs + i) = *(field0ptrs + j);
                *(field0ptrs + j) = temp1;
                temp2 = *(field1ptrs + i);
                *(field1ptrs + i) = *(field1ptrs + j);
                *(field1ptrs + j) = temp2;
                temp2 = *(field2ptrs + i);
```

```
                        *(field2ptrs + i) = *(field2ptrs + j);
                        *(field2ptrs + j) = temp2; }
                        }
                                }
}


adder()
{
printf("Name: ");
scanf("%s",buffer);
*(field0ptrs + numrecs) = (char *) malloc(strlen(buffer));
strcpy(*(field0ptrs + numrecs), buffer);
printf("Owes: ");
scanf("%f",&buffer2);
**(field1ptrs + numrecs) = (double) buffer2;
printf("Monthly payment: ");
scanf("%f",&buffer2);
**(field2ptrs + numrecs) = (double) buffer2;
numrecs++;
*(field1ptrs + numrecs) = (double *) malloc(sizeof(double));    ←
**(field1ptrs + numrecs) = -1.;                                 ←
*(field2ptrs + numrecs) = (double *) malloc(sizeof(double));    ←
**(field2ptrs + numrecs) = -1.;                                 ←
}
```

Changing Records

The final thing we'll do in DB.C is add the ability to change records.
That process is just like the process of adding a record, except that we
don't actually add another record. Rather than write a new record, we
rewrite an already-existing record.

We can have our record-changing function, changer(), ask for the
number of the record to be changed. The rest is just like adder(). Here,
then, is the final code for DB.C:

```
#include <stdio.h>

char   *field0ptrs[10];
double *field1ptrs[10];
double *field2ptrs[10];
int numrecs = 3;
char buffer[80];
float buffer2;

main()
{
char string0[] = "Carson";
double num1 = 712.26;
double num2 = 23.56;
char string1[] = "Adams";
double num3 = 245.23;
```

```
        double num4 = 29.17;
        char string2[] = "Banks";
        double num5 = 633.90;
        double num6 = 87.17;
        double end1 = -1.;
        double end2 = -1.;
        int command;

        field0ptrs[0] = string0;
        field0ptrs[1] = string1;
        field0ptrs[2] = string2;
        field1ptrs[0] = &num1;
        field1ptrs[1] = &num3;
        field1ptrs[2] = &num5;
        field1ptrs[3] = &end1;
        field2ptrs[0] = &num2;
        field2ptrs[1] = &num4;
        field2ptrs[2] = &num6;
        field2ptrs[3] = &end2;

        while((printf("Command:"), command = getchar()) != 'q')
                {
                if(command >= '0' && command <= '9')
                        display(command - '0');
                switch (command)
                        {
                        case 'f':
                          display(find(field2ptrs));
                          break;
                        case 's':
                          sorter(field1ptrs,3);
                          break;
                        case 'a':
                          adder();
                          break;
                        case 'c':
                          changer();
                          break;
                        default:
                          break;
                        }
                }
        }


display(num)
int num;
{
printf("Name: %s\n",*(field0ptrs + num));
printf("Owes: %.2f\n",**(field1ptrs + num));
printf("Monthly payment: %.2f\n",**(field2ptrs + num));
}


int find(ptr2ptrs)
double **ptr2ptrs;
```

```
{
double **loc;
loc = ptr2ptrs;
while (**loc < 50 && **loc++ != -1.);
return (loc - ptr2ptrs);
}


int sorter(ptr2ptrs)
double **ptr2ptrs;
{
int i, j;
char *temp1;
double *temp2;

for( i = 0; i < numrecs - 1; i++) {
    for( j = i + 1; j < numrecs; j++) {
        if (**(ptr2ptrs + i) > **(ptr2ptrs + j))
                { /* exchange i and j */
                temp1 = *(field0ptrs + i);
                *(field0ptrs + i) = *(field0ptrs + j);
                *(field0ptrs + j) = temp1;
                temp2 = *(field1ptrs + i);
                *(field1ptrs + i) = *(field1ptrs + j);
                *(field1ptrs + j) = temp2;
                temp2 = *(field2ptrs + i);
                *(field2ptrs + i) = *(field2ptrs + j);
                *(field2ptrs + j) = temp2; }
                }
                        }
}


adder()
{
printf("Name: ");
scanf("%s",buffer);
*(field0ptrs + numrecs) = (char *) malloc(strlen(buffer));
strcpy(*(field0ptrs + numrecs), buffer);
printf("Owes: ");
scanf("%f",&buffer2);
**(field1ptrs + numrecs) = (double) buffer2;
printf("Monthly payment: ");
scanf("%f",&buffer2);
**(field2ptrs + numrecs) = (double) buffer2;
numrecs++;
*(field1ptrs + numrecs) = (double *) malloc(sizeof(double));
**(field1ptrs + numrecs) = -1.;
*(field2ptrs + numrecs) = (double *) malloc(sizeof(double));
**(field2ptrs + numrecs) = -1.;
}


changer()
{
int thisrec;
```

```
printf("Change what record:");
scanf("%d",&thisrec);
printf("New Name: ");
scanf("%s",buffer);
*(field0ptrs + thisrec) = (char *) malloc(strlen(buffer));
strcpy(*(field0ptrs + thisrec), buffer);
printf("Owes: ");
scanf("%f",&buffer2);
**(field1ptrs + thisrec) = (double) buffer2;
printf("Monthly payment: ");
scanf("%f",&buffer2);
**(field2ptrs + thisrec) = (double) buffer2;
}
```

Storing Data

Although we're not going to add any further code to DB.C, there is one more point worth talking about. If DB.C is ever to be any good at all, it must be able to write its data out to the disk and then retrieve the data. With its compact data format, DB.C will make a more efficient use of disk space than do most databases. Yet there is a difficulty: How do we write out the pointer information, when we save the data on disk? Pointers are really just addresses, and when the program is loaded into memory again, the addresses of all of the data items may have changed.

To solve this problem, similar programs do not store the pointer itself, but instead store *relative pointers*. We would not store our three arrays of pointers; instead, we would make relative pointers out of them first by subtracting the address of the beginning of the data table from each pointer.

In other words, just before writing the pointers to a file, subtract the address where the data begin. When the data and pointers are read in the next time you start the program, the first thing you should do is find the new address of the beginning of the data table, and add it to all of the pointers to make them correct once again.

The procedure of storing only relative pointers in the file and then converting them back to absolute pointers after the program is loaded again is analogous to the relocation that .EXE files go through when they are loaded. Some of the machine-language jump instructions in the .EXE file need to have the full address of their destination before they can jump to it. The information stored in the .EXE file is only the address relative to the beginning of the file. When the file is loaded in, the new address of the beginning of the file is added to each of these machine-language instructions—this is called *file relocation*.

There are one or two more things that we have to watch out for, which will be discussed in more detail when we get to assembly language. When you add addresses, be careful about segment boundaries. (If you don't know what this means, it will become apparent when we discuss segments). If you work with data areas larger than 64K, this is a consideration when adding values to pointers. For this reason, C cannot work with single data items greater than 64K, even in the Huge model. (See the next chapter.) C can have arrays that are larger than 64K. The address addition is done properly in these arrays.

Finally, be careful if you use malloc() to allocate space for new records (as we have done). When you write all of the data out to the disk, the use of relative pointers assumes that the data were contained in one data table. If you have allocated data space all over memory, you'll have to be careful when reconstructing the pointers.

More Data Handling

There are a few more topics to cover while we're discussing data referencing with pointers. One of these topics is linked lists.

A *linked list* is an ideal way to store data if you don't know in advance how many data items you'll have to store. A linked list works this way: For each data item, there is also a pointer pointing to the next data item. At any time, you can add another data item to the list, as long as you update the last pointer to point to the new data item. The last pointer is usually a NULL pointer (so you know that the list is done when you reach this pointer).

A linked list looks like this:

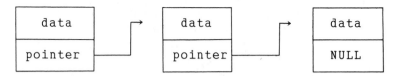

Note that the last pointer is a NULL pointer. Here's how a single element of a linked list might look if we use struct:

```
struct list
{
        char msg[20];
        char *ptr
}
```

This is how we can set it up:

```
#include <stdio.h>

struct list
{
        char msg[20];
        char *ptr;
}

main()
{
        struct list item2 =
        {
        " World.\n",
        "\0"
        };
struct list item1 =
        {
        " there,",
        item2.msg
        };
struct list item0 =
        {
        "Hello",
        item1.msg
        };

printf("%s",item0.msg);
printf("%s",item0.ptr);
printf("%s",item1.ptr);

}
```

Here we can find the next item in the list by referring to the pointer in the present item. We initialize the pointer in each data item in the beginning. (Recall that item2.msg, the name of the character string msg in item2, is a pointer already because it points to a character string. We don't need to initialize the pointer with &item2.msg.)

In addition to this type of linked list, there are also *doubly linked lists*. A doubly linked list contains two pointers: one to the next data item, and one to the last data item.

The most prominent example of a linked list in the PC is the File Allocation Table (FAT) on disks. This is a list of the clusters allocated to files for storage. (A *cluster* is the minimum size of disk storage allocation. On diskettes, a clusters is two sectors long.) The files' sizes can grow, so linked lists are appropriate. Each entry in the FAT represents one cluster on the disk, and holds the location of the next entry. To see in which clusters a file is stored, you work through the FAT until you come to the endmarker at the end of the list.

Circular Buffers

There is one other type of linked list—a list where the last item points to the first one, so that the list forms a circle. This is called a *circular buffer*. The most well-known circular buffer in the PC is the keyboard buffer.

While one part of the PC is putting key codes into the keyboard buffer, another part of the PC is taking them out. The key codes' location in the buffer where they are put in is called the *tail* of the buffer, and the location where the next key code is read from is called the *head*.

When keys are typed in, the tail advances. When they are read, the head advances. As you write to and read from the keyboard buffer, the head and tail march around. Each data location can be the head or the tail. When the buffer is filled, the tail comes up behind the head, and the buffer-full warning beeps.

Use circular buffers when some part of your program is reading data and some part is writing data. Store the location of the head and tail. After you put data into the buffer, advance the tail. After you take data out, advance the head. This way, you can use the same memory space for reading and writing (as long as you keep taking out the data you put in, and the buffer doesn't fill up).

We will say more about the keyboard buffer when we discuss assembly language. Before then, however, we will discuss data storage in the crucial next chapter: C and Memory.

5

C and Memory

Memory is a critical resource, and the C programming language is more memory-conscious than most. In this chapter we'll learn how C uses the Stack, the Heap, and the PC's memory in general. We'll see how to work with large amounts of memory, culminating in a program that juggles two files in memory at once, each of which can be a whopping 128K long.

Memory Models

Memory management on computers that use 80x86 microprocessors is not as simple as it could be. The 80x86 uses 16-bit registers to keep track of data, and 16 bits can express numbers up to 65,535, or 64K - 1. This means that the largest number of memory locations that you can specify with one 16-bit word is 65,536 (if 0 points to the first memory address). The days of 64K computers are long gone, however; the 80x86 has to do better than that. Instead, it uses two 16-bit words to specify a memory address, like this—B800:0000.

The first part of this address, B800H, is referred to as the *segment* address. The second part, 0000H, is called the *offset* address. To find the actual address that B800:0000 represents in memory, multiply the segment address by 16 (10H) and add the result to the offset address:

$$B800H \times 10H = B8000H$$
$$\underline{+\ 0000H}$$
$$B8000H$$

The address 0040:001E (the keyboard buffer in memory) really stands for a linear address of 0041EH:

$$0040H \times 10H = 00400H$$
$$\underline{+\ 001EH}$$
$$0041EH$$

This type of address is the real address that the 80x86s use—20 bits long, which gives the 80x86 an address space of 2^{20}, or = 1MB.

> In protected mode, the 80286 (and the 80386 when it operates as an 80286) use segment *selectors*, which represent 24 address bits and give them an address space of up to 16MB.

Since real addresses use 20 bits, you need two words to specify them. Often, programs set the segment address (the high word) to some value and leave it that way. Since you can address 64K of memory with the same segment address, that gives you a 64K work area.

This method of addressing has consequences for compilers. If you have to call or reference some location with a different segment address, you need both the segment and offset address of the destination. If you are calling or referencing some destination within the 64K space defined by the segment address, you only need one address word—the offset address.

In other words, all objects in memory can be thought of as having a one-word address (if you limit yourself to 64K space total) or a two-word address (if you want to reference any point in memory). That means that library functions that take pointers as parameters have to be written differently in the two cases. In one case, the pointer that is passed to them will be a two-word pointer and in the other case, it's a one-word pointer.

Many functions have to be rewritten, so C places them in different libraries. They can be linked in after you compile your program. The libraries are divided according to *memory model*.

These models set the allowable sizes of the code and data areas. The calls or data references of the functions under the various memory models will have to use one- or two- word addresses, depending upon the model used.

Table 5.1   Memory Model Definitions

Model	Means
Tiny	Code and Data fit into 64K. The program can be made into a .COM file. This model, also called Small Impure, is available only in Turbo C.
Small	All data fit in one 64K segment, all code fits in one 64K segment. Maximum program size is 128K.
Medium	All data fit in one 64K segment, but code may be greater than 64K.

Compact   Data may be greater than 64K (but no single array may be),
           code must be less than 64K. (Turbo C: Static data must be
           less than 64K.)
Large   Both data and code may be greater than 64K, but no single
           array may be. (Turbo C: Static data must be less than 64K.)
Huge   Data, code, and data arrays may be greater than 64K.

Let's sum them up:

Model	DATA vs. 64K	CODE vs. 64K	Arrays vs. 64K
Tiny	<	<	< (Turbo C Only)
Small	<	<	<
Medium	<	>	<
Compact	>	<	<
Large	>	>	<
Huge	>	>	>

When you compile and link, you can specify the model that you
want to use—Small, Medium, or whatever is appropriate. You indicate your choice with a switch such as /AH, which indicates to
Microsoft C that you want to use the Huge model (Turbo C: -mh). If
you don't specify the memory model, the default is Small.

Using memory models, you set the size limits of the code and data
areas for your program. C programs always use different segments for
data and for code (except for the Turbo C Tiny model). Even under the
Small model, your program can be up to 128K long.

If you have more than 64K of data, and so need multiple segments
for data but not for code, use the Compact model. If you have more
code than 64K, and so need multiple segments for code, use the
Medium model. If both parts of your program are greater than 64K,
use the Large memory model.

There is one more option: the Huge memory model. The difference
between Large and Huge is only in pointer arithmetic.

As you move through an array with a pointer, only the offset part of
the pointer is normally incremented. For example, under the Large
model, when you increment the pointer 5000:FFFF, you don't get
6000:0000 as you should—you get 5000:0000. Only the offset part of
the pointer has been incremented, and it wrapped around to the bottom of the segment.

When you increment past the end of one segment while using the
Huge memory model, however, the pointer is handled correctly (that

is, the segment address is updated to point to the next segment). Let's dig into this a little more.

> When arrays get larger than 128K under the Huge model, each element's size must be a multiple of 2, such as 2 bytes, 4 bytes, and so on. If your array is 128K or less, array elements can be any size (up to and including 64K). With assembly language, we don't suffer from such restrictions—all memory is open to us to use.

A Huge Array

Since the biggest thing we can create in C is a huge array of more than 64K, let's do it. Here's a program to make sure that the segment boundary is handled properly—it includes an array of 75,000 bytes:

```
#include <malloc.h>
#include <stdio.h>

main()
{
long i;
int j = 0;
char *array;

array = (char *) halloc(75000, sizeof(char));
for(i= 65535 - 10; i < 65535 + 10; i++)
        printf("address of array[%ld] is %p\n", i, &array[i]);
}
```

> As we'll see, you have to use ALLOC.H in Turbo C, not MALLOC.H, or you can use STDLIB.H, which is portable between Microsoft C and Turbo C.

Note that we did not just declare the array as char array[75000]. That would have made it an automatic variable, and probably would have given us an immediate Stack overflow when the program ran. Instead, we allocate space for the array *after* the program has loaded, with a function named halloc() (Turbo C: farmalloc()). (We'll see this function again in the next section on Heap use—it's the Microsoft C library function that allocates Huge arrays.) You might also notice that in order to handle this array, we had to declare the array index i as a long int.

> Note also the use of the format specifier p. This is the format specifier used when you want to print out the long address of a pointer.

This program will print out the addresses of the array elements as we pass the segment boundary. With Quick C, it has to be compiled under the Huge memory model:

```
qcl /AH huge.c
```

This is the result of running the program:

```
D>huge    ←
address of array[65525] is 0000:FFF5
address of array[65526] is 0000:FFF6
address of array[65527] is 0000:FFF7
address of array[65528] is 0000:FFF8
address of array[65529] is 0000:FFF9
address of array[65530] is 0000:FFFA
address of array[65531] is 0000:FFFB
address of array[65532] is 0000:FFFC
address of array[65533] is 0000:FFFD
address of array[65534] is 0000:FFFE
address of array[65535] is 0000:FFFF
address of array[65536] is 1000:0000
address of array[65537] is 1000:0001
address of array[65538] is 1000:0002
address of array[65539] is 1000:0003
address of array[65540] is 1000:0004
address of array[65541] is 1000:0005
address of array[65542] is 1000:0006
address of array[65543] is 1000:0007
address of array[65544] is 1000:0008
```

As you can see, the array elements go smoothly across the segment boundary (although Quick C gives its own value to the segment address here). Let's try to access some of these array elements. Again, we have to use an array index of type long. This program loads numbers into our array:

```
#include <malloc.h>
#include <stdio.h>

main()
{
long i;
int j = 0;
char *array;

array = (char *) halloc(75000, sizeof(char));
for(i= 65535 − 10; i < 65535 + 10; i++)
→          {array[i] = j++;
            printf("array[%ld]: %d\n", i, array[i]);};
}
```

We can run this program, too; here we fill up the array elements across the segment boundary with the numbers 0 - 19:

```
D>huge2 ←
array[65525]: 0
array[65526]: 1
array[65527]: 2
array[65528]: 3
array[65529]: 4
array[65530]: 5
array[65531]: 6
array[65532]: 7
array[65533]: 8
array[65534]: 9
array[65535]: 10
array[65536]: 11
array[65537]: 12
array[65538]: 13
array[65539]: 14
array[65540]: 15
array[65541]: 16
array[65542]: 17
array[65543]: 18
array[65544]: 19
```

Now that we're using the huge model, *all* pointers in the program become two-word pointers automatically. We have declared array to be a pointer to char—under the Small memory model, it would be a one-word pointer (because data cannot exceed 64K). Under the Huge model, it is two words long.

Mixed-Model Programs

The fact that the size of all memory objects may change at once has its plusses and minuses. If all of your pointers suddenly become two words long, for example (which happens in all memory models that can handle more than 64K of data), your program may slow down. It takes longer to get two words out of memory than to get one word out of memory. Also, when your functions can handle more than 64K of code, longer addresses have to be pushed on the stack for function calls, as well as popped off for function returns.

There is a way to get around all of this. If you just use a few objects with two-word addresses in your program, you should consider using the near, far, or huge keywords when you declare variables. You use these keywords like this:

```
main()
{
char far *farray;
```

```
:
:
:
}
```

For this example, let's say that we use the default Small model. However, we are specifically overriding the type of the character pointer named farray, making it into a far (that is, two-word) pointer.

Note that this does not mean that you can then use normal library functions with farray. Since we will be linking in the Small library functions, they are not changed. If they expected a one-word pointer before, they will have problems with farray. When you link, the types of the memory objects you pass as parameters will be automatically converted to the type that the library function requires—and this may create an error.

However, in this next example:

```
main()
{
char huge *harray;
:
for(i = 0; i < 83000; i++)
        harray[i] = i % 255;
:
}
```

where harray[] is only used internally, the huge keyword is appropriate. We do not call any library functions with harray[], and pointer arithmetic will be done properly even when you pass segment boundaries. We could not use harray[] unless we used the huge keyword, but that does not mean that we have to use the Huge model.

If, however, we *had* used the Huge model, not the Small model, and we had some near data, we could then use the near keyword to make sure the data is addressed only with one-word addresses. The benefit of using one-word pointers is that it speeds access.

It is interesting to note that because you can use keywords and create mixed-model programs, the Compact model is rarely used in practice. The Compact model allows up to 64K of code and more than 64K of data. However, it's normal only to have one or two very large data structures, and the large or huge keywords are usually used for those structures.

> You can also declare functions with the near or far keywords. Keep in mind when you link in locations in other files with extern that you should use the keywords near, far, or huge if appropriate.

Table 5.2   Keywords Summary

Keyword	Data	Code	Pointer Arithmetic
near	16-bit addresses	16-bit addresses	16-bit
far	32-bit addresses	32-bit addresses	16-bit
huge	32-bit addresses	keyword not for code	32-bit

Now that we know what memory models are all about, let's take a new look at the Heap, and how it functions in the light of near or far addresses.

The Heap

The Heap is where we allocate memory at run-time. We've seen the function malloc() at work, and have explored other functions briefly, such as halloc() (Turbo C: farmalloc()). Now we're going to become Heap experts.

Heap Review

In assembly language, there is no such thing as a Heap. All memory is simply there for you to use as you want. In many ways, C is a more attractive programming environment than assembly language is, but there is a price that has to be paid to use C, and that price is separation from the machine. We can't just use memory anywhere we want to in C—we have to ask for it. (In multiuser environments, of course, this type of memory-handling is essential.) The memory from which we take space as needed is called the Heap.

Let's take a look at the memory chart we developed in the beginning of the book:

Code	Program Code
Initialized Data	Initialized Static Variables Initialized Global Variables
Uninitialized Data (BSS)	Uninitialized Static Variables Uninitialized Global Variables

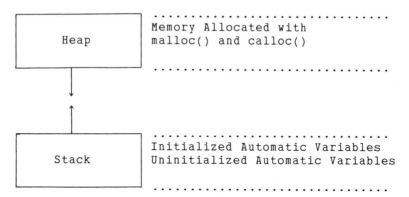

As you can see, the Heap is our responsibility. The C compiler may put automatic variables on the Stack, and may store static variables before the program is loaded, but the Heap is the part of memory that we allocate.

On the other hand, we now know that there are two types of memory—Near and Far. Data objects in Near memory are in the same segment and thus can use the same segment address. Data objects in the Far Heap (beyond our current segment's reach) have to be addressed with two-word addresses.

Let's take a look at the library functions that C provides to manage the Heap. After we do, we can put them to use updating our COPIER program to read and write files in 64K chunks, and then work on the major project of this chapter, a program named COMPARE.C. This program reads in two files and then determines how different they are. If they stop matching at a certain point, COMPARE will check ahead to see where they start matching again.

> In this respect, COMPARE.C is far superior to the DOS COMP utility, which does not compare files if they aren't the same size, and certainly can't check ahead to see where the files start matching again.

Allocating Memory in Microsoft C

Microsoft C uses malloc(), and we're familiar with its use. Under the Small and Medium memory models, a near pointer is returned. Under the Compact, Large, or Huge memory models, a far pointer is returned. (Note that malloc() returns a far, not huge, pointer under the Huge model.) When you use malloc(), include the header file MALLOC.H.

Don't use malloc() when allocating huge arrays—use halloc() instead, because malloc() cannot return Huge pointers, and halloc()

can. The only data object that can explicitly be Huge is an array, so
Microsoft C has a special function for allocating it. Using any function
other than halloc() returns only a near or far pointer.

Allocating Memory in Turbo C

In Turbo C, the situation is different. To allocate memory on the near
Heap, use malloc(); to allocate memory on the far Heap and get a two-
word pointer back, use the farmalloc() function. Under the Compact,
Large, or Huge memory models, just replace malloc() with farmal-
loc(). To use these functions, include the header file ALLOC.H.

   In the large-data models—Compact, Large, and Huge—you can use
farmalloc() to allocate more than 64K of memory. A two-word pointer
is returned. If you want to use the default data segment, use malloc()
instead. A one-word pointer is returned. Either of these functions can
be used in any model—the way the returned pointer ends up depends
upon the memory model used. If you use farmalloc() in a Small model,
the returned far pointer will be made into a near pointer. In the Huge
model, the returned pointer will be huge.

The realloc() Function

There may come a time when we want to readjust our memory allocation. For example, if we are working on a document with a word
processor and we delete a large fraction of it, we no longer need as
much memory as before.

   For such cases, use the realloc() function. Just pass it the pointer
that you got from malloc(). Give realloc() the new size of the object, in
bytes, in this way:

```
array = (char *) realloc(array,newsize);
```

and realloc() will pass back the new address. The newly returned
pointer may not be the same as the old pointer. Both the Turbo and
Microsoft compilers use some form of heap management, so the memory chunks might be moved around when they are resized.

The free(), ffree(), and hfree() Functions

To return a chunk of allocated memory to the unallocated memory
pool, use free(). Under Turbo C, when you are releasing memory on

the far Heap, use farfree(). Just pass the pointer to the section of memory that you want to release.

Microsoft C also provides the means to release Huge arrays. This can be done with hfree() or free(). If you use hfree(), pass the name of the huge array. The entire array is deallocated at one time.

Updating the COPIER.C Program

In a nutshell, Heap management is just the process of deciding how much memory we want (if it is available), and asking for it. If the amount that we want is larger than 64K, we have to consider which memory model we want. There's nothing mysterious here. Let's put this information to work.

We developed a small copying program in Chapter 2. This program read files in 32K chunks and wrote them out again, making a copy of the original file. Why did we use only 32K? One reason was that we were restricted to only one segment of data under the (default) Small model. C puts some information of its own into the data segment, so we didn't have the whole 64K open to us, and 32K was a good round number.

On the other hand, there is no reason why we have to restrict ourselves to just one data segment now. We can compile and link under the Huge memory model and use a 64K data buffer.

You might even think that we could set up a larger memory buffer, such as 128K. Unfortunately, the read() function only takes numbers up to 64K - 2 in any memory model. It returns an int value—the number of bytes read—which already puts a limit of 65,535 on the size of the return value. However, it also returns a value of -1 if an error occurs, and 65,535 = FFFFH = -1, so we couldn't tell if there had been an error if we actually read that many bytes. That means we can make the BUFFSIZE equal to a maximum of 64K - 2.

Even so, that's twice as good as before. Let's adapt COPIER.C into COPIER2.C. The change is very easy to make because we defined the buffer size BUFFSIZE right in the beginning of the program. All we have to do is make these changes and compile under the Huge memory model:

```
#define BUFFSIZE 64*1024 - 2   ←
#include <stdio.h>
#include <fcntl.h>
#include <sys\types.h>
#include <sys\stat.h>
```

```
#include <io.h>
#include <malloc.h>

main()
{
char *buffer;
char source[50];
char target[50];
int s_handle;
int t_handle;
unsigned int num;          ←

if((buffer = halloc((long) BUFFSIZE,1)) == NULL)     ←
                {
                printf("Malloc could not allocate.");
                exit(1);
                }
printf("Source file:");
scanf("%s",source);
printf("Target file:");
scanf("%s",target);

if((s_handle = open(source, O_RDONLY | O_BINARY)) == -1)
                {
                printf("Couldn't open source.");
                exit(1);
                }
if((t_handle = open(target, O_CREAT | O_WRONLY | O_BINARY,
                S_IWRITE )) == -1)
                {
                printf("Couldn't open target.");
                exit(1);
                }
while (num = read(s_handle, buffer, BUFFSIZE))
                write(t_handle, buffer, num);
close(s_handle);
close(t_handle);
}
```

We didn't even have to change the declaration of buffer. Because we are using the Huge memory model, buffer automatically becomes a huge pointer.

It's worth noting that we could also have used the Large memory model here, not the Huge one. However, we chose not to because in Microsoft C, malloc() can't allocate 64K - 2 bytes—it needs to put 20 bytes of header information into an allocated segment, and we would have had to set BUFFSIZE to a maximum of 64K - 20. There is no such restriction in Turbo C. You can allocate memory space up to 65,535 bytes with malloc() (after which you must use farmalloc()).

Note that in our call to halloc(), we used a type cast of long for the buffer size (BUFFSIZE), because halloc() expects a long value. We also changed the number of the bytes-read variable (num) from int to unsigned int (once you get past 32K, the top bit, which is the sign bit, is set):

```
unsigned int num;        ←
if((buffer = halloc((long) BUFFSIZE,1)) == NULL)    ←
            {
                printf("Malloc could not allocate.");
                exit(1);
            }
printf("Source file:");
scanf("%s",source);
printf("Target file:");
scanf("%s",target);
if((s_handle = open(source, O_RDONLY | O_BINARY)) == -1)
            {
                printf("Couldn't open source.");
                exit(1);
            }
if((t_handle = open(target, O_CREAT | O_WRONLY | O_BINARY,
            S_IWRITE )) == -1)
            {
                printf("Couldn't open target.");
                exit(1);
            }
while (num = read(s_handle, buffer, BUFFSIZE))    ←
            write(t_handle, buffer, num);
```

The COMPARE.C Program

Now that we can sling around huge sections of data, let's put together another program: COMPARE.C, which is the comparing program. It will read in files up to 128K long and compare them to see where they differ. This will be a major program for us, and will provide insight into how to handle data under the Huge model.

We can start with the shell of the COPIER2.C program, which already is capable of copying files in 64K chunks. We want to adapt this program to read in up to 128K from each of two files, and then learn how to work with that data in memory.

We start off almost the same way, making only this change:

```
#define BUFFSIZE 128*1024          ←
#include <stdio.h>
#include <fcntl.h>
#include <sys\types.h>
#include <sys\stat.h>
#include <io.h>
#include <malloc.h>
```

Next, we duplicate everything from COPIER2.C so that we can use two files:

```
      #define BUFFSIZE 128*1024
      #include <string.h>
      #include <stdio.h>
      #include <fcntl.h>
      #include <sys\types.h>
      #include <sys\stat.h>
      #include <io.h>
      #include <malloc.h>
  →   char *buffer1;
  →   char *buffer2;
      main()
      {
  →   char file1[50];
  →   char file2[50];
  →   int f1_handle;
  →   int f2_handle;
```

Note that even though buffer1 and buffer2 will be huge pointers, we don't declare them as huge. Since we will be compiling with the Huge memory model, *all* pointers will be huge.

Now we need to get the two file names. Afterwards, we'll try to allocate space for File 1, which could be up to 128K long:

```
#define BUFFSIZE 128*1024
#include <string.h>
#include <stdio.h>
#include <fcntl.h>
#include <sys\types.h>
#include <sys\stat.h>
#include <io.h>
#include <malloc.h>

char *buffer1;
char *buffer2;

main()
{
```

```
char file1[50];
char file2[50];
int f1_handle;
int f2_handle;

printf("File 1:");
scanf("%s",file1);
printf("File 2:");
scanf("%s",file2);
```

→
→
→
→

```
if((buffer1 = halloc((long)BUFFSIZE,1)) == NULL)
            {
                printf("Halloc could not allocate.");
                exit(1);
            }
```

If the memory allocation works, we read in File 1. The whole process is repeated for File 2.

We store the number of bytes actually read in the variables num1 and num2, which we will need to determine how far the files extend in memory:

```
#define BUFFSIZE 128*1024
#include <string.h>
#include <stdio.h>
#include <fcntl.h>
#include <sys\types.h>
#include <sys\stat.h>
#include <io.h>
#include <malloc.h>

char *buffer1;
char *buffer2;

main()
{
char file1[50];
char file2[50];
int f1_handle;
int f2_handle;
```

→
→
→

```
unsigned num = 0;
unsigned long num1 = 0;
unsigned long num2 = 0;

printf("File 1:");
scanf("%s",file1);
printf("File 2:");
scanf("%s",file2);
if((buffer1 = halloc((long)BUFFSIZE,1)) == NULL)
            {
                printf("Halloc could not allocate.");
                exit(1);
```

```
                     }
     if((f1_handle = open(file1, O_RDONLY _ O_BINARY)) == -1)
                     {
                     printf("Couldn't open file 1.");
                     exit(1);
                     }

→    while(num = read(f1_handle, buffer1+num1, 64*1024 - 2))
→              num1 += num;


     if((buffer2 = halloc((long)BUFFSIZE,1)) == NULL)
                          {
                          printf("Halloc could not allocate.");
                          exit(1);
                          }

     if((f2_handle = open(file2, O_RDONLY _ O_BINARY)) == -1)
                          {
                          printf("Couldn't open file 2.");
                          exit(1);
                          }

→    while(num = read(f2_handle, buffer2+num2, 64*1024 - 2))
→              num2 += num;
```

Each time we read from the files, we read the maximum that we can with read()—64K -2 bytes. The read() function returns a short integer, which we place into the variable num. We then add num to the total number of bytes read in so far from the file (num1 or num2).

Notice that the variables num1 and num2 are unsigned long ints. This is an important point—when you work in the Huge model, you will frequently need to use long ints, not just ints. The number returned by read() is a short int, so we leave num as a short. Every time through the reading loop:

```
while(num = read(f1_handle, buffer1+num1, 64*1024 - 2))
           num1 += num;
```

we read in the maximum number of bytes, and track them with num1. The next time through, we don't put the bytes at location buffer1 (where they would write over what's already there), but rather at buffer1 + num1.

Now the two files are in memory, starting at locations buffer1 and buffer2. These two Huge pointers will be our key to reaching the data. Because we are using the Huge memory model, however, we need not concern ourselves that these are Huge pointers. We can just use them as we would normally, forgetting about the size of the data buffers. In addition, the correct library functions will automatically be linked in (i.e., those appropriate to the Huge memory model).

Let's get some more information on the data buffers. What we need are pointers to the end of the data buffers in memory so we know when to stop searching for matches. Let's call those pointers end1 and end2. In addition, since we'll be using string-comparison functions, let's put a '\0' at the end of both files in memory to make them into long character strings:

```
#define BUFFSIZE 128*1024
#include <string.h>
#include <stdio.h>
#include <fcntl.h>
#include <sys\types.h>
#include <sys\stat.h>
#include <io.h>
#include <malloc.h>

char *buffer1;
char *buffer2;
→ char *end1;
→ char *end2;

main()
{
char file1[50];
char file2[50];
int f1_handle;
int f2_handle;
unsigned num = 0;
unsigned long num1 = 0;
unsigned long num2 = 0;

printf("File 1:");
scanf("%s",file1);
printf("File 2:");
scanf("%s",file2);

if((buffer1 = halloc((long)BUFFSIZE,1)) == NULL)
                {
                printf("Halloc could not allocate.");
                exit(1);
                }
if((f1_handle = open(file1, O_RDONLY | O_BINARY)) == -1)
                {
                printf("Couldn't open file 1.");
                exit(1);
                }

while(num = read(f1_handle, buffer1+num1, 64*1024 - 2))
                num1 += num;

if((buffer2 = halloc((long)BUFFSIZE,1)) == NULL)
```

```
               {
               printf("Halloc could not allocate.");
               exit(1);
               }

     if((f2_handle = open(file2, O_RDONLY | O_BINARY)) == -1)
               {
               printf("Couldn't open file 2.");
               exit(1);
               }

     while(num = read(f2_handle, buffer2+num2, 64*1024 - 2))
               num2 += num;
→    end1 = buffer1 + num1;
→    *end1 = 0;
→    end2 = buffer2 + num2;
→    *end2 = 0;
```

Now we're ready to compare. We can make the whole process conceptually easier if we use subroutines. Let's also introduce some new variables, match1 and match2. These will be pointers, one for each data buffer, that indicate where the files start matching. For example, if our two files looked like this:

```
          not a              she
          pig in             gave him
          a poke             a poke
          with...            with...
```

then match1 and match2 would be pointers like this:

```
                  not a                     she
                  pig in                    gave him
match1 →          a poke     match2 →       a poke
                  with...                   with...
```

Next come two more pointers, difference1 and difference2. They indicate where the files start to differ again:

```
                       not a                      she
                       pig in                     gave him
         match1 →      a poke       match2 →      a poke
                       with a                     with a
         difference1 → all          difference2 → laugh
                       that                       and  a
```

Our job will be to set the match and difference pointers correctly, and then print out the different parts. Here's how we can do that with the help of subroutines:

```
#define BUFFSIZE 128*1024
#include <string.h>
#include <stdio.h>
#include <fcntl.h>
```

```
        #include <sys\types.h>
        #include <sys\stat.h>
        #include <io.h>
        #include <malloc.h>

        char *buffer1;
        char *buffer2;
        char *end1;
        char *end2;
→       char *match1;
→       char *match2;
→       char *difference1;
→       char *difference2;
→       int difference_found;

        main()
        {
        char file1[50];
        char file2[50];
        int f1_handle;
        int f2_handle;
        unsigned num = 0;
        unsigned long num1 = 0;
        unsigned long num2 = 0;

        printf("File 1:");
        scanf("%s",file1);
        printf("File 2:");
        scanf("%s",file2);

        if((buffer1 = halloc((long)BUFFSIZE,1)) == NULL)
                    {
                    printf("Halloc could not allocate.");
                    exit(1);
                    }
        if((f1_handle = open(file1, O_RDONLY | O_BINARY)) == -1)
                    {
                    printf("Couldn't open file 1.");
                    exit(1);
                    }

        while(num = read(f1_handle, buffer1+num1, 64*1024 - 2))
                    num1 += num;

        if((buffer2 = halloc((long)BUFFSIZE,1)) == NULL)
                    {
                    printf("Halloc could not allocate.");
                    exit(1);
                    }

        if((f2_handle = open(file2, O_RDONLY | O_BINARY)) == -1)
                    {
                    printf("Couldn't open file 2.");
                    exit(1);
                    }
```

```
        while(num = read(f2_handle, buffer2+num2, 64*1024 - 2))
                    num2 += num;

        end1 = buffer1 + num1;
        *end1 = 0;
        end2 = buffer2 + num2;
        *end2 = 0;
→       match1 = buffer1;
→       match2 = buffer2;

→       while(1){
→               find_next_difference();
→           if(difference_found){
→               find_end_of_difference();
→               print_difference(); }
→           else break;
                }
        }
```

That's all there is to main(). Let's look at the while loop:

```
        while(1){
                find_next_difference();
            if(difference_found){
                find_end_of_difference();
                print_difference(); }
            else break;
                }
```

Inside this while loop, which loops forever, we search ahead for the next place where our files begin to differ:

```
        while(1){
                find_next_difference();
                }
```

→

If a difference is found, we then find the place where the files start matching again:

```
        while(1){
                find_next_difference();
→           if(difference_found){
→               find_end_of_difference();
→           else break;
                }
```

If no difference is found, the remainder of the files match, so we break and quit. Once we find the place in both files where they begin to differ, and then find the place in both files where they begin to match again, we can print out the part we are straddling—that is, the part that is different:

```
while(1){
      find_next_difference();
   if(difference_found){
      find_end_of_difference();
→     print_difference(); }
   else break;
      }
```

That's all there is to it. We keep looping until no more differences are found. Now all we have to do is to write the functions that we call.

The first function, find_next_difference(), is easy. At the beginning, we set match1 and match2 (the places where the files match) to the beginning of the data buffers. Now we have to see how far we can go in both of them before we find a difference (maybe zero bytes). Here's how we do it:

```
find_next_difference()
/*Uses match1, match2. Sets difference1, difference2 */
{
while(*match1++ == *match2++);   ←
}
```

This one-line while loop keeps us going through both files until they stop matching. Note that at the end of the loop, both match1 and match2 point to the bytes *after* the point where the files stopped matching. We have to check why the bytes stopped matching: Did we come to the end of the file? If so, the files matched from our current location all the way to the end, so we want to report no difference. This is done by setting the variable difference_found to 0:

```
find_next_difference()
/*Uses match1, match2. Sets difference1, difference2 */
{
while(*match1++ == *match2++);
if(match1 >= end1 __ match2 >= end2)
→   difference_found = 0;
else{
      }
}
```

If the files do not end, we have found a genuine difference. We set difference_found to 1, and set the two pointers difference1 and difference2 (that's how find_next_difference() reports the location of the difference):

```
find_next_difference()
/*Uses match1, match2. Sets difference1, difference2 */
{
while(*match1++ == *match2++);
if(match1 >= end1 __ match2 >= end2)
     difference_found = 0;
else{
→    difference_found = 1;
→    difference1 = --match1;
→    difference2 = --match2;
     }
}
```

That's all there is to find_next_difference(). It's easy to find where strings stop matching—it's harder to find where they start matching again.

Our next function, find_end_of_difference(), does just that. The two pointers, difference1 and difference2, are already set. Now we have to search ahead and find the places where the files match again, match1 and match2. After we find the locations where the files split and then match again, we can print out the different parts without trouble.

Here's how we'll proceed in find_end_of_difference(). Let's say that the two files look like this:

```
There is a red fox over there...   There is a fox over there...
```

The find_next_difference() function has already set difference1 and difference2:

Now we have to find the point where they start matching again. To start, we will make part of file 1 into a substring by putting a 0 in it, and by copying difference1 into a new pointer, d1temp, for destructive testing:

Now we can try to find the File 1 substring that starts at d1temp in File 2 with strstr(difference2, d1temp). We already know that the files don't match, so this returns NULL. Next we increment our location in File 1 by moving the 0 down one byte, and incrementing d1temp:

We can use strstr(difference2, d1temp), which still returns NULL. Eventually, however, we come to this situation:

Now strstr(difference2, d1temp) does not return NULL, since the strings match. We've found where the files begin matching again.

The same thing works if the difference is in File 2:

In this case, strstr() will find the File 1 substring in File 2 when it skips past the added bytes in File 2. Again we will have found our match.

Now we have to translate the use of d1temp (and the creation of a substring in File 1) into code. Here's how we might begin:

```
find_end_of_difference()
/*Uses difference1, difference2. Sets match1, match2 */
{
char temp_char;
char *temp;
char *d1temp;
int i;

d1temp = difference1;
for(i = 0; i < 1000; i++)
        {
 →      temp = (d1temp + 100 > end1 ? end1 : d1temp + 100);
 →      temp_char = *temp;
 →      *temp = '\0';
        }
}
```

We've established a loop that increments d1temp. We only go up to 1,000, so that will be the extent of the difference that we can tolerate. If the difference in the files is longer than 1,000 bytes, we consider the files too different and quit. (To change this number, just change this 1,000 to whatever value you prefer.)

Next, we make our substring out of the data in buffer1 by establishing a pointer named temp that points to a location 100 bytes down the line from d1temp. If that location turns out to be beyond the end of the buffer, we use the end of the buffer instead. Then we put '\0' in, after saving the character that was already there.

The length of the substring we are going to search for is 100 bytes—in other words, we need at least 100 bytes to have a match. These are the two requirements that we've set up—the differences can't be more than 1,000 bytes, and we need at least 100 bytes to match before we consider the files to be matching again. You may want to change these requirements (for example, to 5,000 and 50).

Now we use strstr() to do the actual work of the program. There are two cases: either strstr() finds a match to our buffer 1 substring in buffer 2, or it doesn't. Here's how we start:

```
        find_end_of_difference()
/*Uses difference1, difference2. Sets match1, match2 */
{
char temp_char;
char *temp;
char *d1temp;
char *d2temp;  ←
int i;

d1temp = difference1;
for(i = 0; i < 1000; i++)
        {
        temp = (d1temp + 100 > end1 ? end1 : d1temp + 100);
        temp_char = *temp;
        *temp = '\0';
   →    if ((d2temp = strstr(difference2, d1temp)) == NULL){

        }
}
```

We place the pointer returned by strstr() into a new pointer, d2temp. Let's first handle the case where a NULL pointer is returned. In this case, we may have reached the end of the file, or we may have just not found a match yet (i.e., we have to use a different substring in File 1). In the latter case, we have to increment d1temp and try again. In either case, we have to restore the zeroed-out byte to temp_char before going on:

```
        find_end_of_difference()
/*Uses difference1, difference2. Sets match1, match2 */
{
char temp_char;
char *temp;
char *d1temp;
char *d2temp;
int i;

d1temp = difference1;
for(i = 0; i < 1000; i++)
        {
        temp = (d1temp + 100 > end1 ? end1 : d1temp + 100);
        temp_char = *temp;
        *temp = '\0';
        if ((d2temp = strstr(difference2, d1temp)) == NULL){
→               *temp = temp_char;
→               if(difference1 >= end1){
→                       mactch1 = end1;
→                       match2 = end2;
→                       break;}
→               else
→                       d1temp++;}
        else{

                }
        }
}
```

If strstr() does not return NULL, then we've found where the files begin matching again, and our job is done—the files begin matching again at d1temp and d2temp. We have to set match1 and match2 from those pointers, and also restore the zeroed-out character from temp_char:

```
find_end_of_difference()
/*Uses difference1, difference2. Sets match1, match2 */
{
char temp_char;
char *temp;
char *d1temp;
char *d2temp;
int i;

d1temp = difference1;
for(i = 0; i < 1000; i++)
        {
        temp = (d1temp + 100 > end1 ? end1 : d1temp + 100);
        temp_char = *temp;
        *temp = '\0';
        if ((d2temp = strstr(difference2, d1temp)) == NULL){
                *temp = temp_char;
                if(d1temp >= end1){
                        match1 = end1;
```

```
                        match2 = end2;
                        break;}
                else
                        d1temp++;}
        else{
→              *temp = temp_char;
→              match1 = d1temp;
→              match2 = d2temp;
→              break;}
        }
}
```

The find_end_of_difference() function is done. Here's how the program looks so far:

```
#define BUFFSIZE 128*1024
#include <string.h>
#include <stdio.h>
#include <fcntl.h>
#include <sys\types.h>
#include <sys\stat.h>
#include <io.h>
#include <malloc.h>

char *buffer1;
char *buffer2;
char *end1;
char *end2;
char *match1;
char *match2;
char *difference1;
char *difference2;
int difference_found;

main()
{
char file1[50];
char file2[50];
int f1_handle;
int f2_handle;
unsigned num = 0;
unsigned long num1 = 0;
unsigned long num2 = 0;

printf("File 1:");
scanf("%s",file1);
printf("File 2:");
scanf("%s",file2);

if((buffer1 = halloc((long)BUFFSIZE,1)) == NULL)
                {
                printf("Halloc could not allocate.");
                exit(1);
                }
if((f1_handle = open(file1, O_RDONLY | O_BINARY)) == -1)
```

```
                        {
                        printf("Couldn't open file 1.");
                        exit(1);
                        }

        while(num = read(f1_handle, buffer1+num1, 64*1024 - 2))
                        num1 += num;

        if((buffer2 = halloc((long)BUFFSIZE,1)) == NULL)
                        {
                        printf("Halloc could not allocate.");
                        exit(1);
                        }

        if((f2_handle = open(file2, O_RDONLY | O_BINARY)) == -1)
                        {
                        printf("Couldn't open file 2.");
                        exit(1);
                        }

        while(num = read(f2_handle, buffer2+num2, 64*1024 - 2))
                        num2 += num;

        end1 = buffer1 + num1;
        *end1 = 0;
        end2 = buffer2 + num2;
        *end2 = 0;
        match1 = buffer1;
        match2 = buffer2;

        while(1){
                find_next_difference();
            if(difference_found){
                find_end_of_difference();
                print_difference(); }
            else break;
                }
}


find_next_difference()
/*Uses match1, match2. Sets difference1, difference2 */
{
while(*match1++ == *match2++);
if(match1 >= end1 __ match2 >= end2)
     difference_found = 0;
else{
     difference_found = 1;
     difference1 = --match1;
     difference2 = --match2;
    }
}


find_end_of_difference()
/*Uses difference1, difference2. Sets match1, match2 */
```

```
{
char temp_char;
char *temp;
char *d2temp;
int i;

for(i = 0; i < 1000; i++)
        {
        temp = (difference1 + 100 > end1 ? end1 : difference1 +
100);
        temp_char = *temp;
        *temp = '\0';
        if ((d2temp = strstr(difference2, difference1)) == NULL){
                *temp = temp_char;
                if(difference1 >= end1){
                        difference1 = end1;
                        difference2 = end2;
                        break;}
                else
                        difference1++;}
        else{
                *temp = temp_char;
                match1 = difference1;
                match2 = d2temp;
                break;}
        }
}
```

The different bytes in the two files have been found—they go from the huge pointers difference1 to match1 in buffer1, and difference2 to match2 in buffer2. The only thing that remains to do is to print out the difference with print_difference(). All we want to do is print out the text from difference1 to match1, and from difference2 to match2. We can do that easily. Here's how we start:

```
print_difference()
{
char *ptr1;
char *ptr2;

    →    printf("\n\n--------------\nFile 1:\n");
    →    for(ptr1=(difference1-20 < buffer1 ? buffer1 : difference1-20);\
    →       ptr1 < (match1+20 > end1 ? end1 : match1 + 20); ptr1++)
    →            putchar(*ptr1);
}
```

We set up ptr1, which points to the character we want to put on the screen as we print from difference1 to match1. After making sure we aren't past the end of the buffer, or before its beginning, we also print out 20 characters around the different text to establish the context. Now we do the same for file 2:

```
print_difference()
{
char *ptr1;
char *ptr2;

        printf("\n\n-------------\nFile 1:\n");
        for(ptr1=(difference1-20 < buffer1 ? buffer1 : difference1-20);\
            ptr1 < (match1+20 > end1 ? end1 : match1 + 20); ptr1++)
                putchar(*ptr1);
  →     printf("\n\nFile 2:\n");
  →     for(ptr2=(difference2-20 < buffer2 ? buffer2 : difference2-20);\
  →        ptr2 < (match2+20 > end2 ? end2 : match2 + 20); ptr2++)
  →             putchar(*ptr2);
}
```

Here's the whole program:

```
#define BUFFSIZE 128*1024
#include <string.h>
#include <stdio.h>
#include <fcntl.h>
#include <sys\types.h>
#include <sys\stat.h>
#include <io.h>
#include <malloc.h>

char *buffer1;
char *buffer2;
char *end1;
char *end2;
char *match1;
char *match2;
char *difference1;
char *difference2;
int difference_found;

main()
{
char file1[50];
char file2[50];
int f1_handle;
int f2_handle;
unsigned num = 0;
unsigned long num1 = 0;
unsigned long num2 = 0;

printf("File 1:");
scanf("%s",file1);
printf("File 2:");
scanf("%s",file2);

if((buffer1 = halloc((long)BUFFSIZE,1)) == NULL)
              {
              printf("Halloc could not allocate.");
              exit(1);
```

```
                           }
          if((f1_handle = open(file1, O_RDONLY | O_BINARY)) == -1)
                           {
                           printf("Couldn't open file 1.");
                           exit(1);
                           }

          while(num = read(f1_handle, buffer1+num1, 64*1024 - 2))
                           num1 += num;

          if((buffer2 = halloc((long)BUFFSIZE,1)) == NULL)
                           {
                           printf("Halloc could not allocate.");
                           exit(1);
                           }

          if((f2_handle = open(file2, O_RDONLY | O_BINARY)) == -1)
                           {
                           printf("Couldn't open file 2.");
                           exit(1);
                           }

          while(num = read(f2_handle, buffer2+num2, 64*1024 - 2))
                           num2 += num;

          end1 = buffer1 + num1;
          *end1 = 0;
          end2 = buffer2 + num2;
          *end2 = 0;
          match1 = buffer1;
          match2 = buffer2;

          while(1){
                find_next_difference();
             if(difference_found){
                 find_end_of_difference();
                 print_difference(); }
             else break;
                 }
}


find_next_difference()
/*Uses match1, match2. Sets difference1, difference2 */
{
while(*match1++ == *match2++);
if(match1 >= end1 __ match2 >= end2)
     difference_found = 0;
else{
     difference_found = 1;
     difference1 = --match1;
     difference2 = --match2;
     }
}
```

```
find_end_of_difference()
/*Uses difference1, difference2. Sets match1, match2 */
{
char temp_char;
char *temp;
char *d2temp;
int i;

for(i = 0; i < 1000; i++)
        {
        temp = (difference1 + 100 > end1 ? end1 : difference1 + 100);
        temp_char = *temp;
        *temp = '\0';
        if ((d2temp = strstr(difference2, difference1)) == NULL){
                *temp = temp_char;
                if(difference1 >= end1){
                        difference1 = end1;
                        difference2 = end2;
                        break;}
                else
                        difference1++;}
        else{
                *temp = temp_char;
                match1 = difference1;
                match2 = d2temp;
                break;}
        }
}

print_difference()
{
char *ptr1;
char *ptr2;

        printf("\n\n-------------\nFile 1:\n");
        for(ptr1=(difference1-20 < buffer1 ? buffer1 : difference1-20);\
           ptr1 < (match1+20 > end1 ? end1 : match1 + 20); ptr1++)
                putchar(*ptr1);
        printf("\n\nFile 2:\n");
        for(ptr2=(difference2-20 < buffer2 ? buffer2 : difference2-20);\
           ptr2 < (match2+20 > end2 ? end2 : match2 + 20); ptr2++)
                putchar(*ptr2);
}
```

It's pretty long—but it would be a lot longer in assembly language. This is a versatile program; it will find differences in files that are up to 128K long each. The differences cannot be longer than 1K, and we need at least 100 bytes to be identical before we consider the files to be matching again. You can change either of these parameters if you wish. (Allowing differences up to 5K can make the program work very slowly.)

This program finishes our use of the Heap in this chapter and has introduced us to some real uses for huge pointers. Let's move on to the Stack.

Stack Review

Here's our memory-use diagram again:

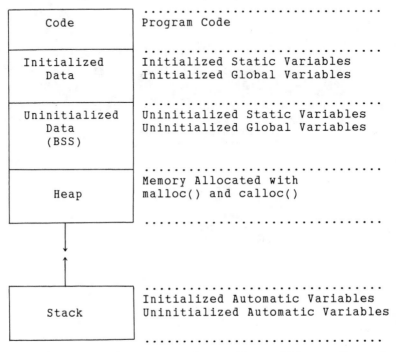

We already know about automatic variables, which are allocated at run-time. If you have more of them than the default stack (2K long in Microsoft C, 4K long in Turbo C) will hold, you'll have to expand the stack. Memory space on the stack is allocated for automatic variables when the program enters the function or *block* in which the variables are defined. For example, look at our earlier program that uses add5():

```
add5();

main()
{
printf("4 + 5 = %d",add5(4));
}

add5(x)
int  x;
{
return x + 5;
}
```

Here, x is an automatic variable. The executable file for this program contains machine code to allocate storage on the Stack for x as soon as add5() is called.

To remind ourselves about Stack and Data Segment use, let's look at this program from Chapter 1:

```
int i;                    [Global → BSS]
int j = 5;                [Global → Initialized Data Area]
static int l = 5;         [Static Global → Initialized Data Area]
static int m = 5;         [Static Global → BSS]

main()
{
int n;                    [Automatic → Stack]
int o = 5;                [Automatic → Stack]
static int p;             [Static → BSS]
static int q = 5;         [Static → Initialized Data Area]
}
```

C does more interesting things than just use the stack for holding automatic variables. C also passes parameters to functions by using the stack.

The C Calling Convention

The C calling convention indicates how parameters are pushed on the stack when a function is called. This convention holds for Microsoft C, Quick C, and Turbo C. It differs from those used in BASIC, FORTRAN, and Pascal in that the language itself removes passed parameters from the Stack after the function call.

Table 5.3   Calling Conventions

Language	Parameters Pushed	Parameters Passed	Return Type
BASIC	In order	As offset addresses	RET #
FORTRAN	In order	As FAR addresses	RET #
C	In REVERSE order	As values	RET
Pascal	In order	As values	RET #

C parameters are always passed by value (not as addresses, as is the case with FORTRAN or BASIC), except for arrays, which are passed by reference (i.e., with a pointer). This reference will be the address of the first element of the array, and will be either two or four bytes long. For near arrays, it will be two bytes; for far arrays, the length is four bytes.

The C calling convention also differs in that it pushes the values to pass in *reverse* order (i.e., right to left). We will see this more clearly when we discuss the stack upon entering assembly language procedures.

As mentioned, C passes parameters as immediate values (except for arrays) and pushes them in reverse order. Let's say we want to link in an external function named summer(). Here is the way it might look:

```
extern int summer(int,int);

main()
{
        printf("3 + 2 = %d\n",summer(3,2));
}
```

In most other languages, the 3 (or its address) is pushed, followed by the 2. However, C pushes parameters in reverse order, so the 2 will be pushed first, followed by the 3. This is how the Stack looks when we start to use it in summer(). (Let's assume that the C program was compiled as small or compact, and that the return address, is, therefore, only one word long.)

```
          High Memory
┌──────────────┐
│      2       │
├──────────────┤
│      3       │
├──────────────┤
│    Return    │
└──────────────┘
          Low Memory
```

In the case of Large, Medium, or Huge memory models, the return address will be four bytes long—which means that the locations of all parameters is shifted up by two bytes:

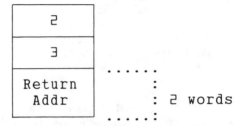

If we were the called function, we could now pick the pushed parameters off the Stack. Usually, C does this for us. (When linking to assembly language, we'll do it ourselves.) However, there is a case where more care than usual must be taken, and that is when we have a function that can take a variable number of arguments.

Using VARARGS.H

Let's suppose that we want to write a function called find_big(). This function takes a variable number of integer parameters and returns the value of the largest one.

A call to find_big() might look like this:

```
big = find_big(2, 3, 4);
```

The leading 2 tells find_big() how many parameters there are to compare. Another call might look like this:

```
big = find_big(5, 23, 89, 44, 91, 7);
```

The C language lets you do this, as we know from our exposure to printf() or scanf(). We have to follow a very careful set of rules, using predefined objects, when we set up find_big(). We start off in this way:

```
→        #include <varargs.h>

→        int find_big(va_alist)
→        va_dcl
         {

         }
```

We have to include the header file VARARGS.H—this header file contains all of the definitions that we will need throughout the program. We also have to supply va_alist as the list of parameters the function will receive. To declare the parameters va_alist, we simply use va_dcl, as shown above (again, va_dcl is defined in VARARGS.H).

To read the passed parameters, we need to define a pointer to the parameter list, and we can call this pointer params. Following the definitions in VARARGS.H, we make this a pointer of type va_list. We also define the local variables temp, biggest, i, and index:

```
#include <varargs.h>

int find_big(va_alist)
va_dcl
{
→    va_list params;
→    int temp, biggest=0;
→    int i, index;

}
```

Next, we have to initialize params to point at the list of parameters on the Stack, with va_start(params):

```
#include <varargs.h>

int find_big(va_alist)
va_dcl
{
va_list params;
int temp, biggest=0;
int i, index;

→    va_start(params);

}
```

Finally, we are free to pick parameters off the Stack with something called va_arg(). Here's how it works:

```
#include <varargs.h>

int find_big(va_alist)
va_dcl
{
va_list params;
int temp, biggest = 0;
int i, index;

va_start(params);

→    index = va_arg(params, int);    /* get number of params */

     for (i = 0; i < index; i++)
     {
→            temp = va_arg(params, int);
              if (temp > biggest) biggest = temp;
     }

return (biggest);

}
```

As we've defined find_big(), the first parameter is the number of parameters that find_big() is supposed to compare—let's call that number index. Each time you call va_arg(), the value that is returned is the next parameter from the Stack. The first time we call it, we put the returned value into index.

We then loop (index times), picking parameters off the Stack with a call to va_arg() each time. As we work through all of the pushed parameters, we keep track of the largest one.

Despite what you may think, va_arg() is not a function—it is a macro. The actual line in VARARGS.H that defines va_arg() looks like this:

```
#define va_arg(ap,t) ((t *)(ap += sizeof(t)))[-1]
```

The pointer ap (which becomes params) has been set to point at va_list in memory (that is, at the place on the Stack where the parameter list starts). C pushes parameters in reverse order, so the last parameters are at highest memory. So each time we pick a parameter off, we have to increment the pointer. That is just what is happening here—when we use va_arg(params, int), the expression looks like this:

```
temp = ((int *)(params += sizeof(int)))[-1]
```

It increments the pointer and picks off a parameter each time it is used. In other words, all the work that we've done to set up our program was actually to set up the pointer params, and now we use it. (Note the negative array index at the end, for positioning purposes. Array indices are translated into pointer references anyway, so negative indices are legal.)

Now we can put find_big() to work in this program:

```
#include <stdio.h>
#include <varargs.h>

main()
{
printf("First biggest: %d\n",find_big(2, 3, 4));
printf("Second biggest: %d\n",find_big(4, 82, 38, 91, 82));
}

int find_big(va_alist)
va_dcl
{
va_list params;
int temp, biggest = 0;
int i, index;
```

```
va_start(params);
index = va_arg(params, int);      /* get number of params */
        for (i = 0; i < index; i++)
        {
                temp = va_arg(params, int);
                if (temp > biggest) biggest = temp;
        }
return (biggest);
}
```

The program sorts through the list 2, 3, and 4, and prints out 4.
Then it sorts through the list 4, 82, 38, 91, and 82, and prints out 91.
We've set up a working function that takes a variable number of
parameters, and learned a few things about the Stack along the way.

That's all the use we have for the stack here. We'll use the Stack
more often towards the end of the book. Until then, we leave C's
memory use behind, and take a look at debugging.

6

Debugging C

Even for the best programmers, errors still occur. This problem becomes more severe as programs become larger—the number of errors can increase, and they can become harder to find. Debugging becomes a fact of life. And because it is, it is a topic we should cover.

Fortunately, we have some excellent debugging tools in C. The first one we'll cover is the assertion statement. Assertions are actually macros—they test statements that you pass to them and, if the statement turns out to be false, halt the program and inform you that the assertion failed.

Assertions

In the case of bugs, assertions can be very valuable. They can check whether certain conditions that you thought were TRUE at some point in a program (e.g., pos_num > 0) are, in fact, TRUE.

Let's see an example is the following buggy program. This program is intended to read in a file named FILE.DAT and print out a character from the file on demand.

```
#include <malloc.h>
#include <stdio.h>

main()
{
FILE *fptr;
char *buffer;
int i;

fptr = fopen("files.dat", "rb");
buffer = malloc(100);
fread(buffer, 1, 100, fptr);
fclose(fptr);

printf("Character number to print:");
```

```
scanf("%d",&i);

putchar(buffer[i]);
}
```

When we run it, however, it generates a run-time error and halts. What's wrong? We start by checking the file pointer fptr with an assertion:

```
#include <malloc.h>
#include <assert.h>
#include <stdio.h>

main()
{
FILE *fptr;
char *buffer;
int i;

fptr = fopen("files.dat", "rb");
assert(fptr != NULL);                  ←
buffer = malloc(100);
fread(buffer, 1, 100, fptr);
fclose(fptr);

printf("Character number to print:");
scanf("%d",&i);

putchar(buffer[i]);
}
```

This new line, assert(fptr != NULL), checks the value of fptr. If there is something wrong with the file printer, the assertion macro ends the program. We can compile this program into ASSERT.EXE and run it:

```
D>ASSERT
Assertion failed: fptr != NULL, file assert.c, line 13

Abnormal program termination
```

It appears that fptr is being left NULL. The assertion tells which assertion failed (fptr != NULL), in which file the failure occurred (ASSERT.C), and in which line (13). This makes debugging easier—you can fill your program with assertions and never see them unless an abnormal condition occurs.

For example, we now know that fopen() can't open FILE.DAT. If we look at the fopen() call, it's easy to see why—there a typo. We have

been trying to open FILES.DAT, not FILE.DAT. We fix that and add
another assertion for error checking:

```
#include <malloc.h>
#include <assert.h>
#include <stdio.h>

main()
{
FILE *fptr;
char *buffer;
int i;

fptr = fopen("file.dat", "rb");      ←
assert(fptr != NULL);
buffer = malloc(100);
fread(buffer, 1, 100, fptr);
fclose(fptr);

printf("Character number to print:");
scanf("%d",&i);
assert(i >= 0);       ←

putchar(buffer[i]);
}
```

This new assertion checks whether the character that we are asked to
print out is always greater than or equal to 0.

   Assertions are frequently used for debugging, but they are usually
left out of the final code. It's hard to see how much help the line:
"Assertion failed: fptr != NULL, file assert.c, line 13" could be to an
unsuspecting user.

   PC versions of C also have a much more powerful debugging tool—
the interactive debugging environment provided by most compilers.
After years of inadequate debuggers, powerful source-level debuggers are now available.

Interactive Debugging

Both Turbo C and Quick C have interactive editors with debugging
features. Both debuggers function similarly: You can set *breakpoints* or
watch given values. In Quick C, you do this by selecting the Debug
menu (press Alt-D), then selecting Breakpoints (Alt-B) or Watch values (Alt-W). In Turbo C, you select the Break/Watch menu (press Alt-

B), then work with Breakpoints or Watch values menu options by pressing the indicated letter. Both menu systems are very easy to use.

In addition to the menu system, there are a number of hotkeys that these debuggers use. Table 6.1 shows some important hotkeys:

Table 6.1   Hotkeys

Debugging Action	Turbo	QuickC
Execute program to cursor line	F4	F7
Trace (go through functions)	F7	F8
Trace (go around functions)	F8	F10
Display output screen	Alt-F5	F4
Select Watch menu	^F7	Alt-D Alt-W
Select Breakpoint menu	^F8	Alt-D Alt-B

More important than particular Alt key combinations or specific hotkeys are debugging concepts. We'll try to make our treatment independent of specific debugger commands We'll use Quick C here. Quick C supports the use of a mouse, so we won't need to use any Alt key combinations or hotkeys except F8 (Turbo C: F7).

Let's start with a program named BUGS.C.

```
#include <stdio.h>
#include <malloc.h>

main()
{
FILE *fptr;
int i, number;
float answer;
char *buffer;

buffer = malloc(1000);
fopen("file.dat", buffer);
fread(buffer, 1, 20, fptr);

for(i = 1; i < 20; i++)
        {
        putchar(buffer[i]);
        if(buffer[i] == 'a') number++;
        }
printf("Number of 'a's: %d",number);

answer = addem(1.2, 3.1);
printf("Answer: .2%f",answer);
```

```
        }

        addem(float param1, float param2)
        {
        return (param1 + param2);
        }
```

This program is intended to read in a small file named FILE.DAT, with these contents:

```
This is a test.<cr>
```

BUGS.C is then supposed to print the file out, find the number of the character 'a's in the file, use a function named addem() to add 1.2 to 3.1, and print that result. However, when we run it, it produces this:

```
i<82t 8P65Number of 'a's: 2416Answer: .24.000000
run-time error R6001
- null-pointer assignment
```

There are obviously a few bugs here, so let's debug it. This is what the Quick C screen looks like:

```
File  Edit  View  Search  Make  Run  Debug  Utility  Options F1 = Help
─────────────────────────────D:\BUGS.C─────────────────────────────
#include <stdio.h>
#include <malloc.h>

main()
{                       ←
FILE *fptr;
int i, number;
float answer;
char *buffer;

buffer = malloc(1000);
fopen("file.dat", buffer);
fread(buffer, 1, 20, fptr);

for(i = 1; i < 20; i++)
        {
        putchar(buffer[i]);
        if(buffer[i] == 'a') number++;
        }

─────────────────────────────────────────────────────────────────
<F1 = Help> <Alt = Menu> <Shift + F5 = Restart>          00001:001
─────────────────────────────────────────────────────────────────
```

We're at the beginning of the program. We can trace through the program line by line. We press F8 (Turbo C: F7) to go to the next executable line:

```
File  Edit  View  Search  Make  Run  Debug  Utility  Options F1 = Help
                                   ─D:\BUGS.C──────────────
#include <stdio.h>
#include <malloc.h>

main()
{
FILE *fptr;
int i, number;
float answer;
char *buffer;

buffer = malloc(1000);        ←
fopen("file.dat", buffer);
fread(buffer, 1, 20, fptr);

for(i = 1; i < 20; i++)
        {
        putchar(buffer[i]);
        if(buffer[i] == 'a') number++;
        }
─────────────────────────────────────────────────────────
<F1 = Help> <Alt = Menu> <Shift + F5 = Restart>         00001:001
```

We are about to read from the file into buffer, so we want to watch
what is going on with the two variables fptr and buffer. We can watch
variables in Quick C with the Debug menu (Turbo C: Break/Watch
menu). If we choose the menu with the mouse, we see these options:

```
File  Edit  View  Search  Make  Run  Debug  Utility  Options F1 = Help
                                   ─D:\B┌──────────────────────┐
#include <stdio.h>                     │ Set Breakpoint...  F9 │
#include <malloc.h>                    │ Watch...              │
                                       └──────────────────────┘
main()
{
FILE *fptr;
int i, number;
float answer;
char *buffer;

buffer = malloc(1000);        ←
fopen("file.dat", buffer);
fread(buffer, 1, 20, fptr);

for(i = 1; i < 20; i++)
        {
        putchar(buffer[i]);
        if(buffer[i] == 'a') number++;
        }
─────────────────────────────────────────────────────────
<F1 = Help> <Alt = Menu> <Shift + F5 = Restart>         00001:001
```

We want to watch a variable, so we select Watch. . . . Quick C asks for the name of the variable to watch, and we type buffer. We can do the same thing for the variable fptr. This is how the screen looks afterwards:

```
File  Edit  View  Search  Make  Run  Debug  Utility  Options  F1 = Help
──────────────────────────────D:\BUGS.C──────────────────────────────
buffer : ""      ←
fptr : 0x51ce:0x0029          ←


#include <malloc.h>

main()
{
FILE *fptr;
int i, number;
float answer;
char *buffer;

buffer = malloc(1000);        ←
fopen("file.dat", buffer);
fread(buffer, 1, 20, fptr);

for(i = 1; i < 20; i++)
        {
        putchar(buffer[i]);
──────────────────────────────────────────────────────────────────────
<F1 = Help>  <Alt = Menu>  <Shift + F5 = Restart>            00001:001
```

Note that two lines have been added. The program displays the values of fptr and buffer, and we watch them change as the program progresses. (Turbo C does the same thing with watched values.)

> Notice that the program is displaying the string pointed to by buffer, not buffer itself (which would be an address). This is very helpful if you want to watch what is going on in the buffer. To see the value of the pointer buffer, and watch it as it changes, watch &(*buffer).

Let's continue tracing through our program. We can trace through two more lines to the fread() command:

```
File  Edit  View  Search  Make  Run  Debug  Utility  Options  F1 = Help
──────────────────────────────D:\BUGS.C──────────────────────────────
buffer : "*%-7 Dge (&JB(U +"   ←
fptr : 0x51ce:0x0029           ←


#include <malloc.h>

main()
{
FILE *fptr;
int i, number;
float answer;
```

```
char *buffer;

buffer = malloc(1000);
fopen("file.dat", buffer);
fread(buffer, 1, 20, fptr);   ←

for(i = 1; i < 20; i++)
        {
        putchar(buffer[i]);
```

`<F1 = Help> <Alt = Menu> <Shift + F5 = Restart>`   `00001:001`

Already, something is wrong. The value of fptr has not changed since the beginning of the program—which means that it hasn't been assigned. Maybe we used fopen() incorrectly. To find the appropriate usage of any C keyword, just position the cursor over the keyword and press F1 (Turbo C: ^F1).

You can use the mouse, too—move the mouse cursor over the keyword and press the right button. A definition appears for fopen(), and shows that we've used it incorrectly like this:

```
fopen("file.dat", buffer);
```

But it should have been used like this:

```
fptr = fopen("file.dat", "rb");
```

We make the change to the program, and try again:

```
#include <stdio.h>
#include <malloc.h>

main()
{
FILE *fptr;
int i, number;
float answer;
char *buffer;

buffer = malloc(1000);
fptr = fopen("file.dat", "rb");     ←
fread(buffer, 1, 20, fptr);

for(i = 1; i < 20; i++)
        {
        putchar(buffer[i]);
        if(buffer[i] == 'a') number++;
        }
```

```
printf("Number of 'a's: %d",number);

answer = addem(1.2, 3.1);
printf("Answer: .2%f",answer);

}

addem(float param1, float param2)
{
return (param1 + param2);
}
```

After compiling and linking, we get this result:

```
D>bugs    ←
his is a test.
g$5Number of 'a's: 144Answer: .24.000000
```

This looks better, but there are still a number of errors. We are missing the first letter of the contents of the file FILE.DAT. Let's debug again. This time, we will watch the character that is to be printed out, buffer[i], directly. Simply use the Watch selection to watch buffer[i], not just buffer. Trace through all the way to the putchar() line:

```
File  Edit  View  Search  Make  Run  Debug  Utility  Options F1 = Help
───────────────────────────────────────D:\BUGS.C──────────────────
buffer : "This is a test\r\n"    ←
buffer[i] : 'h'                  ←
──────────────────────────────────────────────────────────────────

#include <malloc.h>

main()
{
FILE *fptr;
int i, number;
float answer;
char *buffer;

buffer = malloc(1000);
fptr = fopen("file.dat", "rb");
fread(buffer, 1, 20, fptr);

for(i = 1; i < 20; i++)
        {
        putchar(buffer[i]);                       ←
──────────────────────────────────────────────────────────────────
<F1 = Help> <Alt = Menu> <Shift + F5 = Restart>            00001:001
```

It's easy to see that although the whole buffer is there, buffer[i] is "h", not "T". We are about to print out the second character, not the first. The fault lies in the putchar() loop:

```
for(i = 1; i < 20; i++)  ←
{
putchar(buffer[i]);
if(buffer[i] == 'a') number++;
}
```

We start the array index out with 1, not 0. This is an error that is very common in C. We can change that line and our output again:

```
D>bugs  ←
This is a test.
g$5Number of 'a's: 1024Answer: .24.000000
```

The full file is printed out, but some extra characters also appear. That problem is easier to solve. Our printing loop is typing out 20 character, even though the file is only 17 characters long. We can change that by adding a file_length variable:

```
#include <stdio.h>
#include <malloc.h>

main()
{
FILE *fptr;
int i, number, file_length;   ←
float answer;
char *buffer;

buffer = malloc(1000);
fptr = fopen("file.dat", "rb");
file_length = fread(buffer, 1, 20, fptr);  ←

for(i = 0; i < file_length; i++)      ←
        {
        putchar(buffer[i]);
        if(buffer[i] == 'a') number++;
        }
printf("Number of 'a's: %d",number);

answer = addem(1.2, 3.1);
printf("Answer: .2%f",answer);


}

addem(float param1, float param2)
{
return (param1 + param2);
}
```

The output now looks like this:

```
D>bugs    ←
This is a test.
Number of 'a's: 1024Answer: .24.000000
```

The next problem is the number of 'a's. There should be only one 'a' counted in the data from the file, not 1024. We can debug the program again by tracing through it. Let's watch the number of 'a's, which is stored in the variable number:

```
File  Edit  View  Search  Make  Run  Debug  Utility  Options F1 = Help
                              —D:\BUGS.C—
number : 38    ←

#include <malloc.h>

main()
{
FILE *fptr;
int i, number;
float answer;
char *buffer;

buffer = malloc(1000);
fptr = fopen("file.dat", "rb");   ←
fread(buffer, 1, 20, fptr);

for(i = 0; i < 20; i++)
        {
        putchar(buffer[i]);
        if(buffer[i] == 'a') number++;

<F1 = Help> <Alt = Menu> <Shift + F5 = Restart>          00001:001
```

The variable number starts off at 38. When we trace through to the point where it prints out, we can take another look at it:

```
File  Edit  View  Search  Make  Run  Debug  Utility  Options F1 = Help
                              —D:\BUGS.C—
number : 39    ←

main()
{
FILE *fptr;
int i, number;
float answer;
char *buffer;

buffer = malloc(1000);
fptr = fopen("file.dat", "rb");
fread(buffer, 1, 20, fptr);

for(i = 0; i < 20; i++)
        {
```

```
        putchar(buffer[i]);
        if(buffer[i] == 'a') number++;
        }
printf("Number of 'a's: %d",number);    ←
```

```
<F1 = Help> <Alt = Menu> <Shift + F5 = Restart>          00001:001
```

Now it is 39, but it should be 1: We forgot to initialize it to 0. This mistake is of forgetting to initialize counter variables to 0, also very common in C programming.

The next problem in the output is this:

```
D>bugs                                        ──
This is a test.                               V V
g$5Number of 'a's: 1024Answer: .24.000000
```

We've got the format specifier wrong:

```
                    ──
                    V V
printf("Answer: .2%f",answer);
```

It should be %.2f, not .2%f. After fixing it, this is how the output looks:

```
This is a test.
Number of 'a's: 1Answer: 4.00
```

The output has improved considerably. However, there is one last problem. We call addem() with the values 1.2 and 3.1. It should add them together to get 4.3. Instead, we get a result of 4.00. What's wrong?

Here's how addem() looks:

```
addem(float param1, float param2)
{
return (param1 + param2);
}
```

When we debug this time, let's watch the value of param1 + param2:

```
File  Edit  View  Search  Make  Run  Debug  Utility  Options F1 = Help
─────────────────────────────D:\BUGS.C───────────────────────────────
param1 + param2 : <unknown identifier>    ←
```

```
#include <malloc.h>

main()
```

```
{
FILE *fptr;
int i, number;
float answer;
char *buffer;

buffer = malloc(1000);
fptr = fopen("file.dat", "rb");
fread(buffer, 1, 20, fptr);

for(i = 0; i < 20; i++)
        {
        putchar(buffer[i]);
        if(buffer[i] == 'a') number++;
```
```
<F1 = Help> <Alt = Menu> <Shift + F5 = Restart>                00001:001
```

These variables are not filled until we enter the function addem(), because they are automatic variables. However, when we get to the end of addem(), we see that param1 + param2 = 4.3:

```
File  Edit  View  Search  Make  Run  Debug  Utility  Options F1 = Help
──────────────────────────────D:\BUGS.C─────────────────────────────
param1 + param2 : 4.3    ←

for(i = 0; i < file_length; i++)
        {
        putchar(buffer[i]);
        if(buffer[i] == 'a') number++;
        }
printf("Number of 'a's: %d",number);

answer = addem(1.2, 3.1);
printf("Answer: %.2f",answer);

}

addem(float param1, float param2)
{
return (param1 + param2);
}                            ←
```
```
<F1 = Help> <Alt = Menu> <Shift + F5 = Restart>                00001:001
```

In other words, the addition param1 + param2 is being done correctly—the result must be changed when we return to main(). We don't declare a function prototype for addem(), so C assumes that it returns an int (the default). However, addem() doesn't return an int—it returns a floating point number.

The error of omitting the prototype statement is also very common in C. C doesn't complain, it's hard to find this error. If your functions don't return integers, this is a source of possible errors. We fix this last problem by adding a prototype for addem():

```
#include <stdio.h>
#include <malloc.h>
float addem(param1, param2)    ←

main()
{
FILE *fptr;
int i, number, file_length;
float answer;
char *buffer;

buffer = malloc(1000);
fptr = fopen("file.dat", "rb");
file_length = fread(buffer, 1, 20, fptr);
number = 0;

for(i = 0; i < file_length; i++)
        {
        putchar(buffer[i]);
        if(buffer[i] == 'a') number++;
        }
printf("Number of 'a's: %d",number);

answer = addem(1.2, 3.1);
printf("Answer: %.2f",answer);


}

addem(param1, param2)
float param1, param2
{
return (param1 + param2);
}
```

And this is how the output looks now:

```
This is a test.
Number of 'a's: 1Answer: 4.30
```

Except for the minor formatting problems, the output is accurate. The program has been debugged.

Dedicated Debuggers

There is both a Turbo debugger (TD.EXE) and a Microsoft debugger (CodeView—CV.EXE). Both debuggers are dedicated debuggers—

they do not edit your code, nor do they compile it. However, they both are powerful debuggers, and they both function similarly. Most capabilities of either can be found in the other; for example, what CodeView calls breakpoints, watchpoints, and tracepoints, the Turbo Debugger groups into breakpoints and conditional breakpoints.

The Turbo Debugger has some features that CodeView does not. For example, the Turbo Debugger can log debugging sessions, while CodeView cannot. Also, the Turbo Debugger can debug *remotely,* where only a fraction of the whole code (15K) is in memory. The entire CodeView program (about 227K) must be in memory to use it.

Let's put together a program to debug with the Turbo Debbugger, TD.EXE. In this example, we'll present a print formatter—a program to print files on the printer. You can embed special codes in the file to change the format of the printed text. This example will use these codes to turn printing features on or off:

```
@d  →  double spacing
@s  →  single spacing
@u  →  underlining on
@v  →  underlining off
@b  →  bold on
@c  →  bold off
@#  →  indent # spaces
```

For example, if we sent this file (file.dat) to the printer program:

```
This is a test.
This is a test.@d
And this is a test of double spacing.
And this is a test of double spacing.@s
Sometimes, @bbold is better@c. But
not always. Now we can try @5indenting. Is
this working? Let's give it a
few lines to try it out. @0Now we should return
to no indent? Did we? How about a little
@uunderlining@v?
```

Then this is the output we'd expect:

```
This is a test.
This is a test.

And this is a test of double spacing.

And this is a test of double spacing.
Sometimes, (esc)Gbold is better(esc)H. But
not always. Now we can try indenting. Is
        this working? Let's give it a
        few lines to try it out. Now we should return
to no indent? Did we? How about a little
(esc) = 1 underlining(esc) =0?
```

Where (esc) is the escape character, ASCII 27. We want the program to put in certain escape codes that the printer uses (universal printer codes include: (esc)G/(esc)H = turn on/off bold, (esc)-1/(esc)-0 = turn on/off underlining).

In addition, let's make the program able to redirect output to a file, not the printer. For example, if our program was called printer.c, this would print file.dat on the printer:

```
printer file.dat
```

and this would send the output to file.prt instead:

```
printer file.dat file.prt
```

Let's give it a try. Here's the first attempt at printer.c:

```
/* Printer.c formats and prints files. Codes:  */
/*                                              */
/* @d  →  double spacing                        */
/* @s  →  single spacing                        */
/* @u  →  underlining on                        */
/* @v  →  underlining off                       */
/* @b  →  bold on                               */
/* @c  →  bold off                              */

/* @#  →  indent # spaces                       */

#include <stdio.h>

#include <malloc.h>

main(argc, argv)
int argc;
char **argv;
{
FILE *inptr = NULL;
FILE *outptr = NULL;
char *buffer, *endptr, thischar;
int numbytes, spacing = 1, padding = 0, i = 0;

switch (argc)
```

```
            {
            case 0:
                    printf("Usage: printer file.ext [file.prt]");
                    exit(1);
                    break;
            case 1:
                    if((inptr = fopen(*argv, "r")) == NULL)
                            {
                            printf("Could not open input file");
                            exit(1);
                            }
                    else
                        outptr = stdprn;
                        break;
            case 2:
                    if((inptr = fopen(*argv, "r")) == NULL)
                            {
                            printf("Could not open input file");
                            exit(1);
                            }
                    else  if((inptr = fopen(*(argv + 1), "w")) == NULL)
                                {
                                printf("Could not open output file");
                                exit(1);
                                }
                        else break;
            default:
                    break;
            }

    buffer = malloc(20000);
    numbytes = fread(buffer, 1, 20000, inptr);
    endptr = buffer + numbytes;
    *(buffer + numbytes) = '\0';


    while(buffer < endptr){
            if(*buffer != '@' && *buffer != '\n')
                    putc(*buffer++, outptr);
            else if(*buffer == '@')
                    {
                    buffer++;
                    switch (*buffer = thischar)
                            {
                            case 'd':
                                    spacing = 2;
                                    break;
                            case 's':
                                    spacing = 1;
                                    break;
                            case 'u':
                                    putc(27,outptr);
                                    putc('-',outptr);
                                    putc('1',outptr);
                                    break;
                            case 'v':
                                    putc(27,outptr);
                                    putc('-',outptr);
                                    putc('0',outptr);
                                    break;
                            case 'b':
                                    putc(27,outptr);
                                    putc('G',outptr);
```

```
                            case 'c':
                                    putc(27,outptr);
                                    putc('H',outptr);
                                    break;
                            default:
                                    if(thischar <= '9' && thischar >= '1')
                                            padding = thischar - '0';
                                    break;
                                    }
                            buffer++;
                    }
                else
                    {
                    buffer++;
                    putc('\n',outptr);
                    if(spacing == 2)
                            {
                            putc('\r',outptr);
                            putc('\n',outptr);
                            }
                    for(i = 0; i < padding; i++)
                            putc(' ',outptr);
                    }

            }

}
```

The idea is to first use a switch statement to read command-line arguments. The switch statement checks argc. If there were no command-line arguments, printer exits:

```
switch (argc)
        {
→       case 0:
→               printf("Usage: printer file.ext [file.prt]");
→               exit(1);
→               break;
```

If there was one command-line argument, printer.c assumes that it is the name of the file to format and send to the printer. It opens the file and calls the file pointer to this file inptr. We will be writing to the file pointer outptr, and in this case, outptr is set to the predefined pointer stdprn (this is the way you send output to the printer in C):

```
switch (argc)
{
    case 0:
            printf("Usage: printer file.ext [file.prt]");
            exit(1);
            break;
→   case 1:
→           if((inptr = fopen(*argv, "r")) == NULL)
→                   {
→                   printf("Could not open input file");
```

```
→                          exit(1);
→                          }
→             else
→                  outptr = stdprn;
→                  break;
```

Finally, if there were two command-line arguments, we open the input file and the output file:

```
switch (argc)
        {
        case 0:
                printf("Usage: printer file.ext [file.prt]");
                exit(1);
                break;
        case 1:
                if((inptr = fopen(*argv, "r")) == NULL)
                        {
                        printf("Could not open input file");
                        exit(1);
                        }
                else
                     outptr = stdprn;
                     break;
→       case 2:
→                if((inptr = fopen(*argv, "r")) == NULL)
→                        {
→                        printf("Could not open input file");
→                        exit(1);
→                        }
→                else  if((inptr = fopen(*(argv + 1), "w")) == NULL)
→                                {
→                                printf("Could not open output file");
→                                exit(1);
→                                }
→                        else break;
        default:
                break;
        }
```

Now that inptr and outptr are set, we allocate memory, point to it with a pointer called buffer, and read the file—inptr—in. The number of characters we read goes into a variable named numbytes.

```
buffer = malloc(20000);
→ numbytes = fread(buffer, 1, 20000, inptr);
endptr = buffer + numbytes;
*(buffer + numbytes) = '\0';
```

Characters are printed by sending them to outptr with the putc() function. As we print, we check every character, looking for embedded codes that begin with the '@' symbol. If we find one, we examine the next character, which is the format character.

Format characters turn formatting options on or off, and, depending on what the character is, we set or reset a flag. Every time we print a newline character, '\n', we check the flags. If double-spacing is on, for example, we print out a second '\n'. If indenting is on, we print out the required extra characters after the '\n'.

Unfortunately, although it compiles, it doesn't work. This version of the program doesn't even produce an output file. Let's use the Turbo Debugger to debug printer. To do that, we have to compile printer.c with the -v option, like this with TCC.EXE:

```
tcc -v printer.c
```

Using the -v (use -Zi under Microsoft C to prepare a file for CodeView) option makes the compiler keep the symbolic names in the program so they can be used for symbolic debugging.

> It is advisable to also use the -Od switch if you are using the Microsoft C compiler, which turns off optimization—if your code is optimized, Codeview may not be able to match commands in the .EXE file with source code statements.

Now we use the Turbo Debugger, TD.EXE, like this:

```
D:\> TD printer
```

This is what the TD screen looks like this:

```
File    View    Run   Breakpoints    Data    Window    Options    READY
Module:  PRINTER    File: printer.c  1
  /* Printer.c formats and prints files. Codes:    */
  /*                                                */
  /* @d  →  double spacing                          */
  /* @s  →  single spacing                          */
  /* @u  →  underlining on                          */
  /* @v  →  underlining off                         */
  /* @b  →  bold on                                 */
  /* @c  →  bold off                                */
  /* @#  →  indent # spaces                         */
  #include <stdio.h>
  #include <stdlib.h>
  main(argc, argv)
  int argc;
  char **argv;
  {
```

```
Watches ─────────────────────────────────────────────────────────────────┐
│                                                                          │
└──────────────────────────────────────────────────────────────────────────┘
F2-Bkpt F3-Close F4-Here F5-Zoom F6-Next F7-Trace F8-Step F9-Run F10-Menu
```

The commands here are much like those in Quick C or Turbo C—to select a menu option, press Alt and that letter. We can scroll the screen up and down just by using the PgUp, PgDn, up or down arrows.

The area on the bottom of the screen is the watch box, and we will watch certain variables there.

Assembly language programmers familiar with the program DEBUG.COM will be interested to know that you can do everything you can do in DEBUG.COM in TD (except assemble). For example, you can view the registers of the computer by selecting the View menu (press Alt-V) and then choosing Registers in that menu. A window *pane* opens up,and you can see the contents of all the registers:

```
File     View    Run    Breakpoints    Data    Window    Options      READY
Module:  PRINTER    File: printer.c nn ──────────────────────────────────┐
   /* Printer.c formats and prints files. Codes:     */                  │
   /*                                                 */                  │
   /* @d  →  double spacing                           */                  │
   /* @s  →  single spacing                           */                  │
   /* @u  →  underlining on                           */                  │
   /* @v  -Registers--ing off                         */                  │
   /* @b  -_ ax 0000 _                                */                  │
   /* @c  -_ bx 0538 _                                */                  │
                                                                          │
   /* @#  -_ cx 0013 _ spaces                         */                  │
                                                                          │
   #includ_ dx 724D _                                                     │
                                                                          │
   #includ_ si 002A _>                                                    │
   main(ar_ di 052B _                                                     │
   int arg_ bp FFDE _                                                     │
   char **_ sp FFD2 _                                                     │
   {        _ ds 4F6A _                                                   │
   └──────── _ es 4F6A _───────────────────────────────────────────────────┘
Watches──_ ss 4F6A _─────────────────────────────────────────────────────┐
│         _ cs 4D59 _                                                     │
└──────── _ ip 01FA _─────────────────────────────────────────────────────┘
F2-Bkpt F────────────Here F5-Zoom F6-Next F7-Trace F8-Step F9-Run F10-Menu
```

To close a window pane like this one, press Escape. Let's debug printer.c. Press F7 to trace through one command at a time. TD will indicate where you are:

```
File     View    Run   Breakpoints    Data    Window    Options      READY
Module:  PRINTER   File: printer.c nn ─────────────────────────────────
  /* Printer.c formats and prints files. Codes:   */
  /*                                                */
  /* @d  →  double spacing                          */
  /* @s  →  single spacing                          */
  /* @u  →  underlining on                          */
  /* @v  →  underlining off                         */
  /* @b  →  bold on                                 */
  /* @c  →  bold off                                */

  /* @#  →  indent # spaces                         */

  #include <stdio.h>

  #include <stdlib.h>
  main(argc, argv)          ←
  int argc;
  char **argv;
  {
─────────────────────────────────────────────────────────────────────
Watches ─────────────────────────────────────────────────────────────
│
└─────────────────────────────────────────────────────────────────────
F2-Bkpt F3-Close F4-Here F5-Zoom F6-Next F7-Trace F8-Step F9-Run F10-Menu
```

When the program starts, it examines the command-line arguments with the switch statement. Use F7 to trace a few times until you reach line 24 (the line number appears at the top of the screen, right after the file name):

```
File     View    Run   Breakpoints    Data    Window    Options      READY
Module:  PRINTER   File: printer.c 24 ─────────────────────────────────
  int argc;
  char **argv;
  {
  FILE *inptr = NULL;
  FILE *outptr = NULL;
  char *buffer, *endptr, thischar;
  int numbytes, spacing = 1, padding = 0, i = 0;
  switch (argc)   ←
          {
          case 0:
                  printf("Usage: printer file.ext [file.prt]");
                  exit(1);
                  break;
          case 1:
                  if((inptr = fopen(*argv, "r")) == NULL)
                       {
                       printf("Could not open input file");
─────────────────────────────────────────────────────────────────────
Watches ─────────────────────────────────────────────────────────────
│
└─────────────────────────────────────────────────────────────────────
F2-Bkpt F3-Close F4-Here F5-Zoom F6-Next F7-Trace F8-Step F9-Run F10-Menu
```

This is the switch statement. Here, we are checking the value of argc—if it is 0, we exit. If it is one, we read in the file. We can examine the value of argc with by selecting the View menu, and then the Variables option. All the variables yet defined in the program are displayed in two windows. On the left are the internal (Turbo C) variables, and on the right, the ones we have defined. Switch to the set of variables that we have defined by pressing Shift Right Arrow, and it will look something like this:

```
File    View    Run    Breakpoints    Data    Window    Options    READY
Module:  PRINTER    File: printer.c 24 ─────────────────────────────
  int argc;
  char **argv;
  {                       Variables──────
  FILE *inptr = NULL;  │ numbytes            9089 (0x2381)
  FILE *outptr = NULL; │ thischar            '\x03' 3 (0x03)
  char *buffer, *endptr│ endptr   ds:4F6A "            \r\
  int numbytes, spacing│ buffer            ds:052B ""
  switch (argc)        │ outptr            ds:0000
          {            │ inptr             ds:0000
          case 0:      │ argv              ds:FFE6
                  print│ argc                 1 (0x1)  ut]");
                  exit(└──────────────────────────────
                  break;
          case 1:
                  if((inptr = fopen(*argv, "r")) == NULL)
                          {
                          printf("Could not open input file");

Watches ─────────────────────────────────────────────────────────
└─────────────────────────────────────────────────────────────────
F2-Bkpt F3-Close F4-Here F5-Zoom F6-Next F7-Trace F8-Step F9-Run F10-Menu
```

We can scroll through this list, and we see that argc (at the bottom) is 1. Let's examine that command line argument with the watch box. Select the Data menu, and the Watch option in it. TD will prompt you for an expression to examine; simply type *argv and a carriage return. The watch box displays that string, like this (at the bottom of the screen):

```
File    View    Run    Breakpoints    Data    Window    Options    READY
Module:  PRINTER    File: printer.c 24 ─────────────────────────────
  int argc;
  char **argv;
  {
  FILE *inptr = NULL;
  FILE *outptr = NULL;
  char *buffer, *endptr, thischar;
  int numbytes, spacing = 1, padding = 0, i = 0;
  switch (argc)   ←
          {
          case 0:
                  printf("Usage: printer file.ext [file.prt]");
                  exit(1);
                  break;
          case 1:
                  if((inptr = fopen(*argv, "r")) == NULL)
                          {
```

```
                          printf("Could not open input file");
```
```
Watches
  *argv                                char * ds:FFEA "C:\\TC\\PRINTER.EXE"
```
F2-Bkpt F3-Close F4-Here F5-Zoom F6-Next F7-Trace F8-Step F9-Run F10-Menu

As you can see, the string at argv is simply the name of the program, printer.exe. Unfortunately, argc is 1 if there are no command-line arguments—not 0 as we have been assuming. The name of the program itself always counts as one command-line argument. We can see that all the cases in our switch statement are off by one—we should exit if argc is 1, not 0, and so forth. This:

```
switch (argc)
{
case 0:
printf("Usage: printer file.ext [file.prt]");
exit(1);
break;
```

Should become this:

```
switch (argc)
{
case 1:      ←
printf("Usage: printer file.ext [file.prt]");
exit(1);
break;
```

We must add 1 to each case in the switch statement and compile again. This time, we will pass command-line arguments to printer.exe. To do that, we have to invoke TD this way:

```
C:\>TD printer file.dat file.prt
```

When we supply command-line arguments this way, they will be passed correctly to printer.exe when we run. In our case there will be 3 command-line arguments, printer, file.dat, and file.prt. We work through case 3 of the switch statement by tracing a few times with F7. After case 3 is completed, let's check the values of inptr and outptr (inptr is for file.txt and outptr for file.prt) to make sure they were assigned:

```
File    View    Run    Breakpoints    Data    Window    Options    READY
Module:  PRINTER    File: printer.c 50 ───────────────────────────────
                         break;
            case 3:
                    if((inptr = fopen(*(argv+1), "r")) == NULL)
                         {
                         printf("Could not open input file");
                         exit(1);
                         }
                    else  if((inptr = fopen(*(argv+2), "w")) == NULL)
                              {
                              printf("Could not open output file");
                              exit(1);
                              }
                         else break;
            default:
                    break;
           }        ←
───────────────────────────────────────────────────────────────────────
Watches ────────────────────────────────────────────────────────────────
  outptr                              struct  * ds:0000
| inptr                               struct  * ds:02D4
───────────────────────────────────────────────────────────────────────
F2-Bkpt F3-Close F4-Here F5-Zoom F6-Next F7-Trace F8-Step F9-Run F10-Menu
```

The pointer outptr is a null pointer—it was never assigned. Let's look at case 3 of the switch statement, where we open the files:

```
39:        case 3:
40:                if((inptr = fopen(*(argv + 1), "r")) == NULL)
41:                     {16: int argc;
45:        →      else  if((inptr = fopen(*(argv + 2), "w")) == NULL)
46:                          {
47:                          printf("Could not open output file");
48:                          exit(1);
49:                          }
```

Line 45 should open the output file, but we have mistakenly assigned the file pointer to intptr. This line should be changed to this:

```
45:                else  if((outptr = fopen(*(argv + 2), "w")) == NULL)
```

This time, the program does produce an output file. However, it looks like this:

```
This is a test.
This is a test.
And this is a test of double spacing.
And this is a test of double spacing.
Sometimes, bold is better. But
not always. Now we can try indenting. Is
this working? Let's give it a
few lines to try it out. Now we should return
to no indent? Did we? How about a little
underlining?
```

All the control codes have been neatly stripped out, but ignored. Our file isn't formatted at all. What's wrong?

Let's watch as the data in the file is processed. The line after the switch statement is line 55:

```
50:                          else break;
51:         default:
52:                 break;
53:         }
54:
55:         buffer = malloc(20000);                    ←
56:         numbytes = fread(buffer, 1, 20000, inptr);
```

So let's set a *breakpoint* there. Then, when we run the program, execution will automatically stop at that line, that is, right after the switch statement. We can watch as the data is read in and formatted.

Breakpoints

Scroll down to line 55, and press F2. The line turns red to indicate that a breakpoint has been set there. Now simply let the program execute with the Go—F9—key. Execution halts at line 55 automatically, because we set a breakpoint there:

```
File    View    Run    Breakpoints    Data    Window    Options    READY
Module:  PRINTER    File: printer.c 55 ─────────────────────────────────┐
                             printf("Could not open output file");
                             exit(1);
                             }
                     else break;
        default:
                break;
        }
        buffer = malloc(20000);            ←
        numbytes = fread(buffer, 1, 20000, inptr);
        endptr = buffer + numbytes;
        *(buffer + numbytes) = '\0';
        while(buffer < endptr){
                if(*buffer != '@' && *buffer != '\n')
                        putc(*buffer++, outptr);
                else if(*buffer == '@')
                        {
─────────────────────────────────────────────────────────────────────────
Watches ─────────────────────────────────────────────────────────────────

─────────────────────────────────────────────────────────────────────────
F2-Bkpt F3-Close F4-Here F5-Zoom F6-Next F7-Trace F8-Step F9-Run F10-Menu
```

At line 55, we are about to allocate 20000 bytes of memory in the area named buffer, and then read in the data from the file. The number of bytes we read will go into numbytes. Let's trace through a few lines and then check the value of buffer and numbytes:

```
File    View    Run    Breakpoints    Data    Window    Options    READY
Module:  PRINTER    File: printer.c 57 ─────────────────────────────
                   break;
          }
          buffer = malloc(20000);
          numbytes = fread(buffer, 1, 20000, inptr);
          endptr = buffer + numbytes;                        ←
          *(buffer + numbytes) = '\0';
          while(buffer < endptr){
                  if(*buffer != '@' && *buffer != '\n')
                          putc(*buffer++, outptr);
                  else if(*buffer == '@')
                      {
                          buffer++;
                          switch (*buffer = thischar)
                              {
                              case 'd':

Watches ────────────────────────────────────────────────────────────
 buffer   char * ds:0972 "This is a test.\nThis is a test.@d\nAnd this is
 numbytes                     int 328 (0x148)

F2-Bkpt F3-Close F4-Here F5-Zoom F6-Next F7-Trace F8-Step F9-Run F10-Menu
```

As you can see, numbytes, the number of bytes read in, is 148, and the data is in buffer—we have gotten this far without error.

Let's set a watch on the characters in buffer as we step through the program:

```
File    View    Run    Breakpoints    Data    Window    Options    READY
Module:  PRINTER    File: printer.c 60 ─────────────────────────────
                   break;
          }
          buffer = malloc(20000);
          numbytes = fread(buffer, 1, 20000, inptr);
          endptr = buffer + numbytes;
          *(buffer + numbytes) = '\0';
          while(buffer < endptr){
                  if(*buffer != '@' && *buffer != '\n')            ←
                          putc(*buffer++, outptr);
                  else if(*buffer == '@')
                      {
                          buffer++;
                          switch (*buffer = thischar)
                              {
                              case 'd':

Watches ────────────────────────────────────────────────────────────
 buffer   char * ds:0972 "This is a test.\nThis is a test.@d\nAnd this is

F2-Bkpt F3-Close F4-Here F5-Zoom F6-Next F7-Trace F8-Step F9-Run F10-Menu
```

We keep looping over the characters in the buffer until we come to a newline character or a '@'. Let's continue tracing until we can see that the first format code, @d, is about to be interpreted:

```
This is a test.
This is a test.@d   ←
And this is a test of double spacing.
And this is a test of double spacing.@s
Sometimes, @bbold is better@c. But
not always. Now we can try @5indenting. Is
this working? Let's give it a
few lines to try it out. @0Now we should return
to no indent? Did we? How about a little
@uunderlining@v?
```

Here we are in TD—the character at *buffer is now the @ in @d (see the display of buffer at the bottom):

```
File    View    Run    Breakpoints    Data    Window    Options    READY
Module:  PRINTER   File: printer.c 60
                break;
        }
      buffer = malloc(20000);
      numbytes = fread(buffer, 1, 20000, inptr);
      endptr = buffer + numbytes;
      *(buffer + numbytes) = '\0';
      while(buffer < endptr){
            if(*buffer != '@' && *buffer != '\n')
                    putc(*buffer++, outptr);
            else if(*buffer == '@')
                {
                    buffer++;
                    switch (*buffer = thischar)
                        {
                        case 'd':
```
```
Watches
buffer   char * ds:0991 "@d\nAnd this is a test of double spacing.\nAnd
```

F2-Bkpt F3-Close F4-Here F5-Zoom F6-Next F7-Trace F8-Step F9-Run F10-Menu

Since *buffer is '@', the program traces through these lines:

```
63:              else if(*buffer == '@')                     ←
64:                  {
65:                    buffer++;
66:                    switch (*buffer = thischar)
67:                        {
68:                        case 'd':
69:                              spacing = 2;
```

What is happening is that we increment buffer to point to the d in @d:

```
63:                    else if(*buffer == '@')
64:                    {
65:                        buffer++;
66:                        switch (*buffer = thischar)          ←
67:                        {
68:                            case 'd':
69:                                        spacing = 2;
```

and then enter a switch statement designed to check what the format code (now *buffer) is for.

Inside this new switch statement, we interpret the various printing formats and set the necessary flags—you can see the double-spacing case in line 68 above, where spacing is set to 2. We enter the default case of the switch statement if the format code was not a letter, in which case we assume it was a single digit number meant to set indenting.

In that default case, we use a variable named thischar (line 93, below). That variable will hold a copy of the current character in the buffer, *buffer, so we have been assigning it in the beginning of the switch statement, line 66:

```
63:                    else if(*buffer == '@')
64:                    {
65:                        buffer++;
66:                        switch (*buffer = thischar)  ←
67:                        {
68:                            case 'd':
69:                                        spacing = 2;
 :                                         :
 :                                         :
92:                                     default:
93:        →                                if(thischar <= '9' && thischar >=
'1')
94:                                                       padding = thischar -
'0';
95:                                    break;
96:                        }
```

Unfortunately, the assignment in line 66 is backwards. This line in the code:

```
63:                    else if(*buffer == '@')
64:                    {
65:                        buffer++;
66:    →                   switch (*buffer = thischar)
67:                        {
68:                            case 'd':
69:                                        spacing = 2;
```

Should be switch (thischar = *buffer). What the program has been doing so far is overwriting the control code in the buffer with the unitialized variable thischar, and then examining a control code that was meaningless.

We can fix that by making *buffer = thischar into thischar = *buffer. Here's the way the output of the command

```
printer file.dat file.out
```

looks now:

```
This is a test.
This is a test.

And this is a test of double spacing.

And this is a test of double spacing.
Sometimes, (esc)G(esc)Hbold is better(esc)H. But
not always. Now we can try indenting. Is
     this working? Let's give it a
     few lines to try it out. Now we should return
     to no indent? Did we? How about a little
     (esc)underlining(esc)?
```

There has been considerable improvement. However, one thing we see immediately is that instead of turning bold on (with (esc)G), we've turned it both on and off (with (esc)G(esc)H). This type of error is the sure mark of leaving out the break in a case statement. We check our code:

```
case 'b':
        putc(27,outptr);
        putc('G',outptr);
                            ← missing break;
        case 'c':
        putc(27,outptr);
        putc('H',outptr);
        break;
    default:
        if(thischar <= '9' && thischar >= '1')
                padding = thischar - '0';
        break;
```

and see that that is what is happening. Control just passes on to the next case, where we turn bold off. This type of error, also very common in C programming, can cause many problems unless you catch it. We add the missing break, yielding this:

```
This is a test.
This is a test.

And this is a test of double spacing.

And this is a test of double spacing.
Sometimes, (esc)Gbold is better(esc)H. But
not always. Now we can try indenting. Is
      this working? Let's give it a
      few lines to try it out. Now we should return
      to no indent? Did we? How about a little
      (esc)underlining(esc)?
```

This looks much better, but we still have trouble turning off the indent. Let's see what's wrong. The number of spaces to indent is stored in a variable named padding. We can watch when padding is set back to zero with a *watchpoint*.

A watchpoint is a special kind of breakpoint. Unlike a simple breakpoint, a watchpoint is line-independent. A watchpoint is triggered when a certain *condition* becomes true.

First, select the View menu, and the Breakpoints option in it. Next, press Alt-F10 to pop up the Breakpoints local menu. To create a breakpoint, select the option named Global—a breakpoint named Global_1 will be added to the list of breakpoints. Next, in the same local Breakpoints menu, select Condition, and then the Expression True option. TD prompts you for an expression; type 'padding = 0''. The watchpoint is set. Now, when padding is set to 0, the program will terminate.

We run the program with the F9 key—but the watchpoint is never triggered. In other words, padding must never be set to zero. Let's see what's going on with a breakpoint at the line (94) where padding is set, and then go. We stop at line 94:

```
File   View   Run   Breakpoints   Data   Window   Options   READY
Module:  PRINTER   File: printer.c 94 ─────────────────────────────────
                            putc('0',outptr);
                            break;
                  case 'b':
                            putc(27,outptr);
                            putc('G',outptr);
                            break;
                  case 'c':
                            putc(27,outptr);
                            putc('H',outptr);
                            break;
                  default:
                            if(thischar <= '9' && thischar >= '1
                     →             padding = thischar - '0';
                            break;
                            }
            buffer++;
```

```
                         }
                         else
```

```
Watches
```

F2-Bkpt F3-Close F4-Here F5-Zoom F6-Next F7-Trace F8-Step F9-Run F10-Menu

Here, padding is set to the value of thischar - '0'. We can check the value of thischar by watching it:

```
File    View    Run    Breakpoints    Data    Window    Options    READY
Module:  PRINTER    File: printer.c 94
                              putc('0',outptr);
                              break;
                     case 'b':
                              putc(27,outptr);
                              putc('G',outptr);
                              break;
                     case 'c':
                              putc(27,outptr);
                              putc('H',outptr);
                              break;
                     default:
                              if(thischar <= '9' && thischar >= '1
                    →               padding = thischar - '0';
                              break;
                              }
                     buffer++;
                }
                else
```

```
Watches
  thischar                        char '5' 53 (0x35)
```

F2-Bkpt F3-Close F4-Here F5-Zoom F6-Next F7-Trace F8-Step F9-Run F10-Menu

The answer is "5"—this is the point where padding is set to 5 in the test file:

```
This is a test.
This is a test.@d
And this is a test of double spacing.
And this is a test of double spacing.@s
Sometimes, @bbold is better@c. But
not always. Now we can try @5indenting. Is   ←
this working? Let's give it a
few lines to try it out. @0Now we should return
to no indent? Did we? How about a little
@uunderlining@v?
```

Now we want to see it set back to 0. We type F9 to continue—and the program ends. We never reach line 94 again to set padding back to 0. The fault must lie in the test we make on thischar before setting the variable padding. If we look at that test, we can see what's wrong:

```
92:                     default:
93:          →                   if(thischar <= '9' && thischar >= '1')
94:                                    padding = thischar - '0';
95:                          break;
96:                          }
```

When we check to make sure thischar is a single digit, we check whether it is is less than or equal to '9' and greater than or equal to '1'—but the test should be whether it is greater than or equal to '0'. The way the program is now, we can never set padding back to 0.

We change this to: if(thischar <= '9' && thischar >= '0'), and recompile. This time, the output file looks like this:

```
This is a test.
This is a test.

And this is a test of double spacing.

And this is a test of double spacing.
Sometimes, (esc)Gbold is better(esc)H. But
not always. Now we can try indenting. Is
        this working? Let's give it a
        few lines to try it out. Now we should return
to no indent? Did we? How about a little
(esc)underlining(esc)?
```

It is correct. We've gotten all the bugs out (as far as our test file goes, anyway). Here is the debugged version of printer.c:

```
/* Printer.c formats and prints files. Codes:  */
/*                                             */
/* @d  →  double spacing                       */
/* @s  →  single spacing                       */
/* @u  →  underlining on                       */
/* @v  →  underlining off                      */
/* @b  →  bold on                              */
/* @c  →  bold off                             */

/* @#  →  indent # spaces                      */

#include <stdio.h>

#include <malloc.h>

main(argc, argv)
int argc;
char **argv;
{
FILE *inptr = NULL;
FILE *outptr = NULL;
char *buffer, *endptr, thischar;
int numbytes, spacing = 1, padding = 0, i = 0;

switch (argc)
        {
        case 1:
```

```
              printf("Usage: printer file.ext [file.out]");
              exit(1);
              break;
case 2:
              if((inptr = fopen(*(argv + 1), "r")) == NULL)
                      {
                      printf("Could not open input file");
                      exit(1);
                      }
              else
                  outptr = stdprn;
                  break;
case 3:
              if((inptr = fopen(*(argv + 1), "r")) == NULL)
                      {
                      printf("Could not open input file");
                      exit(1);
                      }
              else  if((outptr = fopen(*(argv + 2), "w")) == NULL)
                          {
                          printf("Could not open output file");
                          exit(1);
                          }
                  else break;
default:
              break;
      }

buffer = malloc(20000);
numbytes = fread(buffer, 1, 20000, inptr);
endptr = buffer + numbytes;
*(buffer + numbytes) = '\0';

while(buffer < endptr){
        if(*buffer != '@' && *buffer != '\n')
                putc(*buffer++, outptr);
        else if(*buffer == '@')
                  {
                  buffer++;
                  switch (thischar = *buffer)
                        {
                        case 'd':
                                spacing = 2;
                                break;
                        case 's':
                                spacing = 1;
                                break;
                        case 'u':
                                putc(27,outptr);
                                putc('-',outptr);
                                putc('1',outptr);
                                break;
                        case 'v':
                                putc(27,outptr);
                                putc('-',outptr);
                                putc('0',outptr);
                                break;
                        case 'b':
                                putc(27,outptr);
                                putc('G',outptr);
                                break;
                        case 'c':
                                putc(27,outptr);
```

```
                                putc('H',outptr);
                                break;
                    default:
                                if(thischar <= '9' && thischar >= '0')
                                        padding = thischar - '0';
                                break;
                                }
                buffer++;
            }
        else
            {
            buffer++;
            putc('\n',outptr);
            if(spacing == 2)
                        {
                        putc('\r',outptr);
                        putc('\n',outptr);
                        }
            for(i = 0; i < padding; i++)
                        putc(' ',outptr);
            }
    }
```

That's it for debugging C. The range and power of the options available to you today are impressive. In fact, debugging techniques can make up an entire book by themselves.

Now, though, it's time to turn to assembly language.

7

Welcome to Assembly Language

Machine Language

Now we're going to start working with the machine on the lowest levels. This chapter and the next one cover the basics of assembly language. We'll learn how to write stand-alone assembly language modules, assemble them, and run them. Then, we'll work on interfacing them to C, or using inline assembly code in C programs. The most important thing is to get a good base from which to start.

To get a computer to do something, you have to supply machine language instructions, which are only comprehensible to the processor. Often, only part of the machine language instruction tells the computer what to do. The rest of the instruction is data. For example, you can write an instruction to put the byte FFH into a certain memory location. Part of the instruction tells the microprocessor that you want to store a number, part of the instruction tells at which it the location in memory you want to store the number, and part of it is the number itself, FFH.

Although machine language instructions can be many bytes long, data and the instruction code itself never mix across byte boundaries. For example, one machine language instruction may be all instruction to the microprocessor:

```
01010101
```

Instruction

And another is a mix of both instruction and data:

```
10101010   10111010
```

Instruction   Data used by the instruction.

or even mostly data:

01010101	10111010 10010101 001010100

Instruction   Data used by the instruction.

The data used by the instruction is either memory address(es) or immediate data, such as the FFH we wanted to store in a memory location earlier.

Reading this kind of binary code is extremely difficult. Imagine yourself confronted with a page of numbers, all 0s or 1s. Even if such instructions were converted to hexadecimal, you'd have to look up the meaning of each byte before you could understand what is going on. (Tables in the manuals that accompany assemblers list which binary instructions convey which meanings.) Mostly, what means everything to the microprocessor means nothing to us.

Assembly Language

This is where assembly language enters. It is the direct intermediary between machine language and English. For every machine language instruction, there is one assembly language instruction. Rather than using a byte such as 10101010B, an English-language mneumonic is used, such as : MOV AX,5.

This instruction, MOV AX,5, may be terse, but it is still an improvement on 10101010B, or even 0AAH. This instruction means that the byte 10101010B is directing the machine to move (the MOV part of MOV AX,5) the value of 5 into one of the 80x86's *registers*. A *register* is a place for temporarily storing data in the microprocessor, and we're going to discuss them very shortly.

What an assembler does is simple: It takes the program you've written in assembly language and converts it, instruction by instruction, directly into machine language.

The machine language is then run by the microprocessor. Let's see some assembly language examples. These examples are assembly language instructions that were assembled—converted into machine language—plus the corresponding machine language for each instruction. (All numbers are in hexadecimal.)

Table 7.1   What An Assembler Does

MOV	DI,00B0	→	BF B0 00
MOV	COUNTER,00B0	→	C7 06 C3 01 B0 00
MOV	BX,0080	→	BB 80 00
CMP	INDEX,00	→	80 3F 00
JZ	0670	→	74 12
CMP	[SI],0D	→	80 3C 0D
JZ	0666	→	74 03
MOVSB		→	A4
JMP	065E	→	EB F8

Sometimes assembly language is hard to write, and sometimes it's hard to debug. There is no escaping the fact. It has to follow the microprocessor, and as we'll see, assembly language for the PC and the PS/2 has many quirks.

Registers in the Microprocessor

The 80x86 is built with a number of internal registers, called *general purpose registers*, and we may think of them as predefined variables. Each one of these registers holds exactly one word, 16 bits. There are four general purpose registers: AX, BX, CX, and DX. These registers are always inside the 80x86, and it's hard to think of an assembly language program that could get along without them. They hold our data, one word at a time, while we work with it.

Operations that involve moving data around (except for some options with the 80x86's useful string-moving instructions, which we'll see later) always use these registers in some way. This moving operation is our introduction to assembly language.

The MOV Instruction

The most fundamental assembly language instruction is MOV, which moves data between registers and memory, or between register and registers. The MOV format is: MOV Destination, Source. The data is moved from the source into the destination. If you have something stored in memory and want to work with it, you can use MOV. Here's how it works:

```
MOV     AX,0FFFFH
```

Here we put the number 0FFFFH (65535) into AX. This is the biggest number that any register (all are 16 bits) can hold. Notice the leading 0, which is added to let the assembler know that we intend 0FFFFH to be taken as a number, and not as an English word.

We can take the 0FFFFH in the register AX and move it into the register DX:

```
MOV      DX,AX    (Move the data from AX into DX)
```

Now, DX and AX hold the same value.

Data can also be moved into these registers from memory. Let's say we have a memory location with 0 in it. This can be moved into CX in this way:

```
MOV      CX,[Memory Location]
```

We can move whatever is in DX into the memory location in this way:

```
MOV      [Memory Location],DX
```

However, data cannot be moved from memory to memory. This is one of the peculiarities of the 80x86. Data cannot go directly from memory location to memory location in one instruction. We can move data from memory to general purpose register and then to memory again:

```
MOV AX, COUNTER
MOV INDEX, AX
```

But it cannot be moved in this way:

```
MOV COUNTER, INDEX
```

Seeing It Work

It's always better to see an example. An excellent program comes with all DOS versions, named DEBUG. DEBUG can assemble small programs that you write on the spot—a mini-assembler is built into the program. We'll use this mini-assembler to convert our instruction MOV AX,5 into machine language, and then run it, watching the value stored in AX change from 0 to 5. Start the DEBUG program; it gives you its hyphen prompt:

```
DEBUG
```

The command "R" in DEBUG stands for Register, and lets you see the contents of all the 80x86's registers. You can pick the general purpose registers AX, BX, CX, and DX out readily. (Note: All numbers displayed in DEBUG are in hexadecimal, which is standard for assembly language debuggers.)

```
A>DEBUG
-R
AX=0000  BX=0000  CX=0000  DX=0000  SP=FFEE  BP=0000  SI=0000  DI=0000
DS=0EF1  ES=0EF1  SS=0EF1  CS=0EF1  IP=0100   NV UP EI PL NZ NA PO NC
0EF1:0100 9AEC04020F    CALL    0F02:04EC
```

In addition to the registers shown:

```
A>DEBUG
-R
AX=0000  BX=0000  CX=0000  DX=0000  SP=FFEE  BP=0000  SI=0000  DI=0000
DS=0EF1  ES=0EF1  SS=0EF1  CS=0EF1  IP=0100   NV UP EI PL NZ NA PO NC
0EF1:0100 9AEC04020F    CALL    0F02:04EC
```

The settings of the internal *flags* of the 80x86 are shown (there are 8 flags):

```
A>DEBUG
-R
AX=0000  BX=0000  CX=0000  DX=0000  SP=FFEE  BP=0000  SI=0000  DI=0000
DS=0EF1  ES=0EF1  SS=0EF1  CS=0EF1  IP=0100   NV UP EI PL NZ NA PO NC
0EF1:0100 9AEC04020F    CALL    0F02:04EC
```

Flags are used in conditional jumps, and we'll work with them in the next chapter. When you execute some instruction—a comparison, for example, between two integers—the flags are set in a way that indicates the result. You can then execute a conditional jump, which does different things, depending upon how the flags are set.

DEBUG also tells you the current memory location. Here, we are at memory location 0EF1:0100:

```
A>DEBUG
-R
AX=0000  BX=0000  CX=0000  DX=0000  SP=FFEE  BP=0000  SI=0000  DI=0000
DS=0EF1  ES=0EF1  SS=0EF1  CS=0EF1  IP=0100   NV UP EI PL NZ NA PO NC
0EF1:0100 9AEC04020F    CALL    0F02:04EC
```

The final part of the DEBUG 'R' display indicates what is to be found at the current memory location. In our case, the current memory location holds the bytes following the address in the "R" display.

```
A>DEBUG
-R
AX=0000  BX=0000  CX=0000  DX=0000  SP=FFEE  BP=0000  SI=0000  DI=0000
DS=0EF1  ES=0EF1  SS=0EF1  CS=0EF1  IP=0100    NV UP EI PL NZ NA PO NC
0EF1:0100 _9AEC04020F_    CALL     0F02:04EC
```

DEBUG tries to group bytes together, starting at the current memory location (which only holds 1 byte), into what would be a valid machine-language instruction. It then provides an assembly language translation of the machine-language instruction that begins at our present location.

When in reality no machine language instruction is there, as is frequently the case, the translation is meaningless. This is the case here: Having just started DEBUG up, there is as yet no program to look at. DEBUG is just taking left-over bytes in the computer's memory and trying to make sense out of them. In fact, DEBUG's supplied translation means nothing:

```
A>DEBUG
-R
AX=0000  BX=0000  CX=0000  DX=0000  SP=FFEE  BP=0000  SI=0000  DI=0000
DS=0EF1  ES=0EF1  SS=0EF1  CS=0EF1  IP=0100    NV UP EI PL NZ NA PO NC
0EF1:0100 9AEC04020F→ CALL     0F02:04EC
```

We'll use the "A" command (for Assemble) to put in our own program, consisting of only one line: MOV AX,5. The "A" command needs an address at which to start depositing the machine-language instructions it will generate in memory. Our current address is 0EF1:0100, and we tell it to assemble the machine language right there, by using the shorthand A100:

```
A>DEBUG
-R
AX=0000  BX=0000  CX=0000  DX=0000  SP=FFEE  BP=0000  SI=0000  DI=0000
DS=0EF1  ES=0EF1  SS=0EF1  CS=0EF1  IP=0100    NV UP EI PL NZ NA PO NC
0EF1:0100 9AEC04020F    CALL     0F02:04EC
-A100                        ← Here is the A100 command.
0EF1:0100                    ← DEBUG's response.
```

Following the A100 command, DEBUG returns with the line 0EF1:0100, showing the current address at which it will deposit assembled code. We simply type MOV AX,5 and then a carriage return.

```
A>DEBUG
-R
AX=0000  BX=0000  CX=0000  DX=0000  SP=FFEE  BP=0000  SI=0000  DI=0000
DS=0EF1  ES=0EF1  SS=0EF1  CS=0EF1  IP=0100    NV UP EI PL NZ NA PO NC
```

```
0EF1:0100 9AEC04020F      CALL     0F02:04EC
-A100
0EF1:0100 MOV        AX,5              ← Type "MOV AX,5<cr>"
0EF1:0103
```

DEBUG then prompts for the next instruction with the address 0EF1:0103. There are no more instructions to assemble at this time, so we give DEBUG a carriage return. DEBUG interprets the blank line to mean that we are through assembling, and returns to its normal prompt.

That's all there is to it. We've just assembled our first line of assembly language. To see what occurred, remember that the "R" command displays the current memory location and instruction. We assembled MOV AX,5 at the current memory location, so let's give the "R" command and take a look:

```
A>DEBUG
-R
AX=0000  BX=0000  CX=0000  DX=0000  SP=FFEE  BP=0000  SI=0000  DI=0000
DS=0EF1  ES=0EF1  SS=0EF1  CS=0EF1  IP=0100   NV UP EI PL NZ NA PO NC
0EF1:0100 9AEC04020F      CALL     0F02:04EC
-A100
0EF1:0100 MOV        AX,5
0EF1:0103
-R                                           ←
AX=0000  BX=0000  CX=0000  DX=0000  SP=FFEE  BP=0000  SI=0000  DI=0000
DS=0EF1  ES=0EF1  SS=0EF1  CS=0EF1  IP=0100   NV UP EI PL NZ NA PO NC
0EF1:0100 B80500          MOV      AX,0005
```

We can see the instruction. (Note the machine language instruction B8 05 00 that corresponds to MOV AX,5 in DEBUG's display.) Executing the instruction is simple; DEBUG has a trace command. Typing "T" once executes the current instruction and increments us to the next memory location:

```
A>DEBUG
-R
AX=0000  BX=0000  CX=0000  DX=0000  SP=FFEE  BP=0000  SI=0000  DI=0000
DS=0EF1  ES=0EF1  SS=0EF1  CS=0EF1  IP=0100   NV UP EI PL NZ NA PO NC
0EF1:0100 9AEC04020F      CALL     0F02:04EC
-A100
0EF1:0100 MOV        AX,5
0EF1:0103 -R
AX=0000  BX=0000  CX=0000  DX=0000  SP=FFEE  BP=0000  SI=0000  DI=0000
DS=0EF1  ES=0EF1  SS=0EF1  CS=0EF1  IP=0100   NV UP EI PL NZ NA PO NC
0EF1:0100 B80500          MOV      AX,0005
-T                                   ←    This will execute our MOV instruction.

AX=0005  BX=0000  CX=0000  DX=0000  SP=FFEE  BP=0000  SI=0000  DI=0000
DS=0EF1  ES=0EF1  SS=0EF1  CS=0EF1  IP=0103   NV UP EI PL NZ NA PO NC
0EF1:0103 020F            ADD      CL,[BX]                        DS:0000=CD
```

After the "T" command, DEBUG gives its usual display to indicate the register contents and flags. AX now holds 5.

All of the flags remain unchanged. On the other hand, the memory location HAS changed, from 0EF1:0100 to 0EF1:0103. This is because the machine language instruction corresponding to MOV AX,5 is 3 bytes long in memory (B8H 05H 00H). The instruction following it begins 3 bytes later: Therefore, the 100 has changed to 103.

A Program

DEBUG not only allows you to assemble programs, but it lets you write them out to the disk as well. Let's use DEBUG to assemble our first assembly language progam. This program will simply type out the letter "Z" and exit.

We'll start with the "A" command. We start our machine language code at location 0100H:

```
A>DEBUG
-A100                              ←
0EF1:0100
```

Just type in the following assembly language instructions verbatim. Follow them with a carriage return after the prompt 0EF1:010A to stop assembling:

```
A>DEBUG
-A100
0EF1:0100 MOV     AX,0200          ←
0EF1:0103 MOV     DX,005A          ←
0EF1:0106 INT     21               ←
0EF1:0108 INT     20               ←
0EF1:010A              ← Just type a <cr> here.
-
```

What our progam is doing is loading the registers AX and DX with the MOV instruction. This is the preparation for having the program print out the character "Z".

What happens next is that two INT instructions are given, INT 21H, and INT 20H. These instructions will be important ones for us—they are the way programs can interface with DOS and BIOS. We'll discuss the exact nature of these instructions in our program later. The way we have loaded the registers AX and DX here will make the instruction INT 21H print out a "Z"; at the end we use the INT 20H instruction to end the program. We will write our program out to the disk by naming the program first with the N (for Name) command. Let's call the program PRINTZ.COM, following its function. We name it this way:

```
A>DEBUG
-A100
0EF1:0100 MOV      AX,0200
0EF1:0103 MOV      DX,005A
0EF1:0106 INT      21
0EF1:0108 INT      20
0EF1:010A
-NPRINTZ.COM       ←
```

Now we can write it out. (DEBUG will write this file in the current directory.) DEBUG needs the number of bytes to write out, and in our case, the program goes from locations 0100H to 0109H. Each memory location holds a byte, so that makes 10 bytes. DEBUG is expecting hexadecimal format, so we will give it a value of 0AH.

The DEBUG "W" command, Write, reads the number of bytes to write as a file directly out of the CX register. This means that to write our 10-byte program PRINTZ.COM, we load the CX register with 0AH and then give the "W" command.

To move 0AH into CX, we can use the R (Register) command again. If you use the "R" command without any arguments, DEBUG gives you its standard display. On the other hand, giving the command RCX indicates to DEBUG that you wish to change the value in CX. (This will work with any register.) DEBUG displays the current value in CX (which is 0000) and gives a colon prompt, after which we will type our new value for CX, A (for 0AH), and a carriage return. Then we can write PRINTZ.COM by giving the "W" command:

```
A>DEBUG
-A100
0EF1:0100 MOV      AX,0200
0EF1:0103 MOV      DX,005A
0EF1:0106 INT      21
0EF1:0108 INT      20
0EF1:010A
-U100 109
0EF1:0100 B80002          MOV      AX,0200
0EF1:0103 BA5A00          MOV      DX,005A
0EF1:0106 CD21            INT      21
0EF1:0108 CD20            INT      20
-NPRINTZ.COM
-RCX              ←
CX 0000           ←
:A               ←
-W               ←  The W command
Writing 000A bytes
-Q
```

Let's run PRINTZ.COM:

```
F:\>printz
Z
F:\>
```

And PRINTZ.COM does what it's supposed to do: It types out "Z" and exits.

The High and Low Bytes of General Purpose Registers

In the 80x86 microprocessors, there is a way to split the general purpose registers—AX, BX, CX, and DX—into their high and low bytes, and then use them independently. Only the general purpose registers can be split up. For example, the top half of AX can be referred to as AH (H for High byte), and the bottom byte can be referred to as AL (L for low byte). For instance, we could say:

```
MOV       AH,5
```

or

```
MOV       AL,3AH
```

> Notice that the single instruction MOV AX,053AH does the same thing as using both instructions MOV AH,5 and MOV AL,3AH.

The high and low registers that can be used as separate registers are AH, AL, BH, BL, CH, CL, DH, and DL. Very often, when we pass information to DOS or BIOS, we use these one-byte registers.

The INT 21H instruction, which we can use to print out our character and to do many more things, needs information to be passed to it in the AH and DL registers. Our program could have been shortened to this:

```
MOV       AH,02H    ←
MOV       DL,5AH    ←
INT       21H
INT       20H
```

This version of PRINTZ.COM works just as our old one did, because this printing service of INT 21H only requires information in the one-byte registers AH and DL. Let's take a closer look at the INT instruction now.

Interrupts

When you execute an INT instruction, some prewritten program is run. For example, one of these programs prints out characters on the screen. The programs that are run are parts of DOS or BIOS, and the instructions are stored in reserved parts of memory.

These prewritten programs were written in assembly language. They do all of the hard work of actually handling the disk drive controllers, or the screen controller chips, by having the microprocessor send signals to them. That's not something we should have to do in our programs—every time we want to print on the screen, we don't want to have to check the video controller rescan register and the dozens of other necessary things. With software *interrupts*, all of the work can be condensed into one instruction.

The 80x86 has the ability to use 256 possible interrupts, from INT 00 to INT FFH. Some of these interrupts are used by DOS, some by BIOS, and some by BASIC. Here are all the interrupts that the PC or PS/2 is capable of using, and which part of the operating system:

Table 7.2   PS/2, PC Interrupts

Interrupt Number (Hex)	Used By
00 - 1F	BIOS
18	Starts ROM BASIC
19	BOOTSTRAP (Boots PC)
1A - 1F	BIOS
20 - 3F	DOS
40 - 5F	BIOS (PC XT and Later)
60 - 67	Free
68 - 7F	BIOS (PC XT and Later)
80 - F0	BASIC
F0 - FF	Free

A group of interrupts, INTs 20H-3FH, has been set aside for DOS. The DOS interrupts do many things, from printing on the screen, to opening and closing files, to putting keyboard input into a buffer in memory for you to printing out many characters at once. Among the DOS interrupts is a giant that we will come to know well, INT 21H.

INT 21H

IBM decided to group almost all of DOS' capabilities into INT 21H.
(See the listing of all the interrupts in the appendix of this book.) If a
program wants to work with files on the PS/2 or PC, it calls INT 21H at
a low level. These capabilities of DOS are open to us because we are
programming in its home language, assembly language. For example,
our program PRINTZ.COM has been typing characters on the screen
in the same way that DOS itself does, by using INT 21H, service 2.

INT 21H is divided into numerous services. The number of services
grow with each DOS version. The INT 21H printing service is service 2.
To select an INT 21H service, we have to load its number in the AH register before our INT 21H instruction, as we have done in PRINTZ.COM:

```
MOV     AH,02H    ←
MOV     DL,5AH
INT     21H
INT     20H
```

In addition, Service 2 expects us to supply it with the ASCII code of the
letter it is to type out. In this case, "Z" is equal to ASCII 90, or 5AH. We
can execute the INT 21H instruction, and "Z" appears on the screen.

Here are some possible services that can be used in INT 21H. (This
list is just to get us started, and we will add more services later.) To
use these INT 21H services, just load the registers as shown and execute an INT 21H instruction.

Table 7.3 INT 21H Services   Service #

Name	Set These	What Happens	
1	Keyboard Input	AH = 1	ASCII code of typed key returned in AL
2	Character Output	AH = 2 DL = ASCII CODE	The character corresponding to the in DL is put on the screen
9	String Output	AH = 9 DS:DX = Address of string of characters to print	Prints a string of bytes from memory on the screen (we will use this service in this chapter)

Other INT 21H services create files or subdirectories, delete files, load programs, allocate memory, and many other things.

INT 20H, the last instruction in PRINTZ.COM, lets DOS know that we are done. DOS exits from the program and returns us to the command prompt like C:\>. Most of the programs we write will end with INT 20H, the standard last instruction for assembly language programs.

Now that we have some experience, we can start putting together assembly language programs without using DEBUG. To do so, we have to review the way memory is accessed by the 80x86 chips—memory usage is even more important in assembly language than it is in C.

A Review of Segmentation

The address 0EF1:0100 is made up of two hexadecimal numbers, each 16 bits long. As we know, this is usual for addresses—two words are involved for a full address. The 0EF1H in 0EF1:0100 is the segment address of that particular memory location, and 0100H is the offset address:

```
A Typical Address

0EF1:0100
  |    |_____Offset Address
  |_____Segment Address
```

Using these 20-bit addresses, we can refer to 1 megabyte, 1024K:

```
Segmented Address              Real Address
-----------------              ------------


            F000:FFFF  |1 Byte|  FFFFFH  ← The top of memory
                                            (FFFFFH = 1 MByte - 1)
            F000:FFFE  |1 Byte|  FFFFEH

            F000:FFFD  |1 Byte|  FFFFDH

            F000:FFFC  |1 Byte|  FFFFCH

                          :

            C000:AAAA  |1 Byte|  CAAAAH

            C000:AAA9  |1 Byte|  CAAA9H

1 Megabyte
```

Address		Linear
C000:AAA8	1 Byte	CAAA8H
C000:AAA7	1 Byte	CAAA7H
:		
0000:0003	1 Byte	00003H
0000:0002	1 Byte	00002H
0000:0001	1 Byte	00001H
0000:0000	1 Byte	00000H ← The bottom of memory

Segments In Memory

We are already familiar with the idea of segments: A segment is the memory space that can be addressed with one particular segment address. A segment can go from xxxx:0000 to xxxx:FFFF—64K. For example, the segment that starts at the bottom of memory, segment 0000, can extend from 0000:0000 to 0000:FFFF (keeping the segment address, 0000, unchanged). Once you choose a segment address you have a 64K workspace to use without having to change the segment address again.

On the other hand, even though segments can describe such a large area, they can overlap. The next possible segment is segment 0001. This segment extends from 0001:0000 to 0001:FFFF. Converting these numbers to 20-bit addresses gives 00010 to 1000F.

Segment 0001 starts just 16 bytes (called a *paragraph*) after segment 0000. Segment 0002 starts just 16 bytes after segment 0001. Choosing a segment gives you a 64K work space, but that 64K work space overlaps with many other segments.

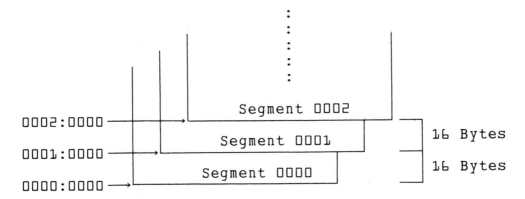

To let you set the segment that you want to choose as your work area, the 80x86 provides four *segment registers*. You set these segment registers at the beginning of a program, or let them be set automatically for you. Keep in mind, however, that they only define a 64K area. If you want something outside that area, you'll have to of set them as required.

The four segment registers are CS, DS, ES, and SS. They stand for Code Segment, Data Segment, Extra Segment, and Stack Segment.

Segment Register	Means	Used With
CS	Code Segment	Your program's Instructions.
DS	Data Segment	The data you want to work on.
ES	Extra Segment	Auxilary data segment register.
SS	Stack Segment	Set by DOS; holds the "stack".

The Code Segment is where the instructions of your program are stored. When your program is loaded, the Code Segment is chosen for it by the program loader. You will not have to set this segment register, CS, for the things we are going to do in this book. If, however, a program wants to know where it was placed in memory (i.e., what the segment address of the code is), it can read the value in CS at any time.

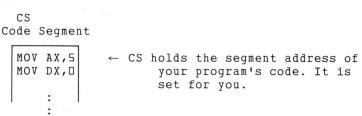

```
       CS
Code Segment

  MOV AX,5      ← CS holds the segment address of
  MOV DX,0            your program's code. It is
                      set for you.
      :
      :
```

The DS register holds the value of the Data Segment. Anything that you want to store as data and do not the computer to execute (such as cell entries in a spreadsheet, or text in a word processor), can be stored here.

You usually set DS, the Data Segment register, at the beginning of the program and then leave it alone. To read bytes from far-away places in memory—to examine the screen buffer, or the keyboard buffer, for example—we'll have to set DS before we can address them. Using DS as the high word of our addresses, we can reach and read (or write) any byte in memory.

Let's say that our program code is in the segment 2000H, and data is in the segment at 3000H:

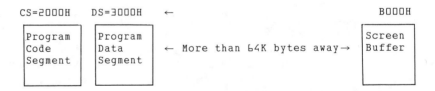

Now let's say that we want to change data in the video buffer (i.e., the letters that appear on the screen), which is at segment B000H for a monochrome monitor. We have to change the data segment that we're using in DS to B000H:

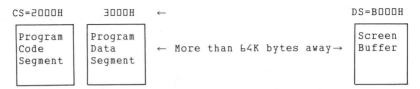

We can reference any data there with our instructions.

Whenever we read from (or write to) memory using labels such as VALUE, the 80x86 checks the value of DS for the segment part of the address. Instructions that reference memory locations (such as the MOV) automatically mean that DS is used as the segment address.

ES can be used as another data segment. For example, the 80x86 has a number of fast string instructions, which can move strings of bytes from one location in memory to another location extremely quickly. If the location we are sending bytes to is far away, we cannot point to both the source and the destination with the same segment register, DS. Instead, we can use ES as a second segment register for the far destination. The string instructions in the 80x86 require that you use ES as well as DS (although they may be set to the same segment).

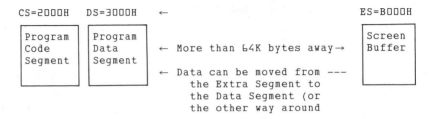

Finally, DOS stores the address for function calls on the Stack, an area of memory put aside for this purpose. Since DOS maintains it, we will pay little attention to the Stack until later.

Segment Registers in Use: .COM Files

The first programs we write will be .COM files. The default for .COM files is to set all four segment registers to the same value—CS. This is the same use of memory that the Tiny memory model (under Turbo C) makes. We will do this so that we do not have to worry about the segment registers in our first programs.

Everything that occurs in a .COM file is limited to one 64K workspace. When the program is loaded, DOS sets that segment address for us. That means in practice that we do not have to be careful about how the segment registers are set for .COM files until later. Here, CS = DS = ES = SS.

A .COM file is the simplest working program that you can write on the PC or PS/2 (although the .COM format is no longer supported under OS/2). This file is, quite literally, just machine language instructions, ready to be executed.

In the other available format, .EXE files, all kinds of things have been added on by the linker or macro assembler.

Pseudo-Ops

When you write a .ASM file that will be turned into a .COM file, you have to specify where you want the code to be placed in the code segment, what the name of the code segment will be, whether you will have a separate Data Segment, and so forth. You set up your segments with Pseudo-Ops.

In addition to our simple assembly language instructions, we are going to have to add a number of directions for the assembler. These directions—read only by the macro assembler—are called Pseudo-Ops. The Pseudo-Ops do not generate any code. What they do is give directions to the assembler, (and only that).

You can set up either Code or Data Segments when you are write a program, and you use Pseudo-Ops to do so. If you set up a code segment, your program instructions go there. If you set up a Data Segment, you predefine some variables or constants that your program will later use—or you just set aside some blank space that the program will use. The asembler makes sure that this information is loaded into the correct segments in memory, if you specify the segments with Pseudo-Ops.

The SEGMENT *and* ENDS *Pseudo-Ops*

We can switch segments by moving a new value (a 16-bit word) into a segment register. The macro assembler has no idea about how your program will run, so we have to tell it what the various segment registers will be holding—at all times.

In practice, this means that everything we put into our .ASM files is enclosed inside a segment definition, giving a name to the segment (because we don't have the segment register's actual value, which is set only when the program runs). Then we can tell the assembler to assume, for example, that CS holds the value for what we have in CODE_SEG, and so on. We can add SEGMENT definitions to PRINTZ.COM immediately:

```
CODE_SEG          SEGMENT              ←

          MOV     AH,2
          MOV     DL,5AH        INT      21H
          INT     20H

CODE_SEG          ENDS                 ←
```

When we define a segment name, we use the SEGMENT Pseudo-Op. At the end of the segment definition, you must use the ENDS Pseudo-Op.

The ASSUME *Pseudo-Op*

Enclosing all of our code inside CODE_SEG means that we can refer to the value that *will* be in CS when the program is loaded. We tell the assembler to *assume* that CS will be set to CODE_SEG by using the ASSUME Pseudo-Op:

```
CODE_SEG          SEGMENT

          ASSUME  CS:CODE_SEG,DS:CODE_SEG,ES:CODE_SEG      ←
          MOV     AH,2
          MOV     DL,5AH
          INT     21H
          INT     20H

CODE_SEG          ENDS
```

Notice here that we use the Pseudo-Op ASSUME CS:CODE_SEG,DS:CODE_SEG,ES:CODE_SEG. Here we tell the assembler that CS, DS, and ES will all use the same segment, which we call CODE_SEG. Since we are building a .COM file, this is correct.

Whenever your program changes the value of a segment register, immediately precede the value with an ASSUME so that the assembler knows the new value of the segment register.

Labelling

Labels are also Pseudo-Ops. We can label our data byte by byte or word by word. Similarly, we can label an instruction in our program itself so that we can jump from the current instruction to the labeled one, which may be some distance away.

When MOV AH,2 is translated into machine language, it is three bytes in size. We can give a label to that instruction: Let's call it START. We can also give a label to the last instruction (INT 20H): let's call it EXIT.

```
CODE_SEG          SEGMENT

          ASSUME  CS:CODE_SEG,DS:CODE_SEG,ES:CODE_SEG
START:    MOV     AH,2      ←
          MOV     DL,5AH
          INT     21H
EXIT:     INT     20H       ←

CODE_SEG          ENDS
```

A label is just a name followed by a colon. If, during our program, we wanted to leave quickly, we could just go the label EXIT, and the INT 20H instruction would be executed, causing us to finish and quit. If we did decide to go there, the assembler would have to know the address of the EXIT instruction, and it finds this by counting the number of machine language bytes it has produced from the beginning of the code segment (what we have labelled START).

The assembler translates all of these labels into *offsets*—that is, 16-bit words holding the distance in bytes of the label from the beginning of the appropriate segment. If we are dealing with a data label, the label is translated into the offset—in other words, into a pointer—from the beginning of what we called the Data Segment. (The segment address of the Data Segment will be in DS at run-time.)

For labels given to instructions, the assembler uses the offset from the beginning of the code segment. This is the offset of a label that is actually stored in the machine language program, not the label itself. Labels come in very handy when we write programs: anything that gets more English into the program helps.

> You may make labels as long as you want. However, only the first 31 characters count—that's all that the assembler reads.

Positioning Our Code in the Code Segment

When .EXE files are loaded, they are put at the beginning of the Code Segment that they have been given, at CS:0000. Their first instruction can start right there. .COM files, on the other hand, are supplied with a header that is loaded in before they are loaded. The header is actually the header that is put at CS:0000, not the first instruction of the .COM file. This header is 100H (256 decimal— bytes long. The header thus runs from CS:0000 to CS:00FF, and the .COM file, now loaded into memory, starts exactly at CS:0100:

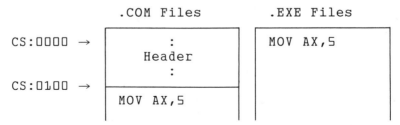

This means that we have to start the code in PRINTZ.ASM at offset 0100H in the Code Segment. This is why we start assembling at 0100H in our DEBUG example (using A100): In a .COM file, machine language instructions must start at offset 0100H inside the program.

The ORG Pseudo-Op

We set our location in the Code Segment with the Pseudo-Op ORG:

```
CODE_SEG          SEGMENT

        ASSUME    CS:CODE_SEG,DS:CODE_SEG,ES:CODE_SEG
        ORG       100H      ←
START:  MOV       AH,2
        MOV       DL,5AH
```

```
            INT     21H
EXIT:       INT     20H

CODE_SEG            ENDS
            END     START
```

This tells the assembler to make the offset of START (the line immediately after the ORG Pseudo-Op) into 0100H. The assembler now treats the instruction MOV AH,2 as though it will be placed at CS:0100, and not at CS:0000 (and everything to follow is treated as though it were placed after this instruction). Now we have made the correct allowance for the .COM file header that is automatically loaded.

The END *Pseudo-Op*

The final step is to set an entry point for the program. In C, the entry point is set when you define the function main()—control is always passed to main(). In assembly language, you can set the entry point anywhere in your program. Here we set the sentence entry point with the Pseudo-Op END. Every .ASM file needs to end with END so the assembler knows when to stop. At the same time, you can set the entry point by adding its label after END.

In this case, we want the entry point to be at 0100H in the Code Segment. We have labeled that instruction already and called it START. Our final Pseudo-Op END START:

```
CODE_SEG            SEGMENT

            ASSUME  CS:CODE_SEG,DS:CODE_SEG,ES:CODE_SEG
            ORG     100H
START:      MOV     AH,2
            MOV     DL,5AH
            INT     21H
EXIT:       INT     20H

CODE_SEG            ENDS
            END     START   ←
```

The Instruction Pointer

When the .COM file is loaded into memory for the first time, we know that the value chosen by DOS for the Code Segment is placed into CS. But there is also a special register to hold the offset address in the

Code Segment of the instruction about to be executed. This register is called IP, the Instruction Pointer.

When the program is loaded and CS is set, IP is loaded with 0100H (for a .COM file). The next instruction about to be executed is always at CS:IP; here, it's CS:0100. When .COM files begin, IP is automatically given a value of 0100H. (In .EXE files, however, the offset address of the first instruction to execute can be anywhere in the code segment.) IP is loaded from a value stored in the .EXE file's header.

Assembling PRINTZ.ASM

If you have a word processor or an editor, use it to type our program into a file named PRINTZ.ASM. (Assembly language source file names usually end with .ASM, just as C source file names usually end with .C.)

We are ready to use an assembler. If you have the Microsoft assembler (we use Microsoft MASM version 5.1), type this command:

```
A>masm printz;   ←
```

The macro assembler does this:

```
A>masm printz;
Microsoft (R) Macro Assembler Version 5.10
Copyright (C) Microsoft Corp 1981, 1988.  All rights reserved.

  50144 + 31277 Bytes symbol space free

    0 Warning Errors
    0 Severe  Errors
```

If you use the Turbo Assembler (we use TASM version 1.0), type this:

```
A>tasm printz;
```

TASM prints this:

```
Turbo Assembler  Version 1.0  Copyright (c) 1988 by Borland International
Assembling file:   PRINTZ.ASM
Error messages:    None
Warning messages:  None
Remaining memory:  381k
```

We've assembled the program, but, all we have is an .OBJ file. The next step is to strip off some information left by the assembler in the

.OBJ file. Although the linker is normally used for combining .OBJ files into big executable files, even single .OBJ files have to go through the linker before becoming .COM files.

The linker checks all segments (among other things). This is going to be a .COM file, so there is only one segment—CODE_SEG. Programs that are not .COM files need all segments to be explicitly spelled out—and the linker will give us a warning that we have no STACK segment. This is the normal warning you recieve when you produce .COM files. With the Microsoft assembler, use LINK:

```
A>link printz;          ←
Microsoft (R) Overlay Linker  Version 3.64
Copyright (C) Microsoft Corp 1983-1988.  All rights reserved.

LINK : warning L4021: no stack segment
```

With the Turbo Assembler, use TLINK:

```
A>tlink printz;         ←
Turbo Link  Version 2.0  Copyright (c) 1987, 1988 Borland International
Warning: no stack
```

The warning is there, and we are now almost ready. The linker has taken the .OBJ file, PRINTZ.OBJ, and produced an .EXE file, PRINTZ.EXE. However, we did not set this up as a .EXE file—it is a .COM file. For the final step of stripping off the header that the linker left in the .EXE file, we run a DOS program called EXE2BIN. Run this on output from either LINK or TLINK.

This is the last program that we need to run. It converts the .EXE file to .COM format:

```
exe2bin printz printz.com
```

Finally, our .COM file is there, ready to go. Try running it to confirm that it prints out the "Z". Give PRINTZ.COM a try. You will see that it prints out "Z", just as our DEBUG version did. Now we've got a working .ASM file.

On the other hand, this is really only half the story. As it stands, PRINTZ.ASM is a working program, but it is not very representative. In almost all .COM files, some data is stored.

Every variable used in a program is data, like the variable VALUE. We might want to read in a file from the disk and store it in the data area, treating it as data. Or we might have program messages such as "Hello, world." in the data area.

Let's look at an example that shows how you can use variables in assembly language, just like higher-level languages. We use the DB, or Define Byte, Pseudo-Op.

The DB Pseudo-Op

The way that we define bytes such as VALUE in the data segment is with special instructions in the part of your program that you set aside as the Data Segment. To define a byte named VALUE, use DB in a Data Segment definition:

```
VALUE DB 5
```

In your program, the code might look like this:

```
CODE_SEG          SEGMENT
ASSUME CS:CODE_SEG, DS:DATA_SEG
MOV     AX,VALUE
        :
CODE_SEG ENDS

DATA_SEG          SEGMENT
VALUE    DB 5
        :
DATA_SEG ENDS
```

Note that just defining a Data Segment doesn't load the DS register with that segment's address when the program runs. We have to do that explicitly. However, CS is loaded with the Code Segment's address automatically.

In memory, the Code Segment and the Data Segment might look like this:

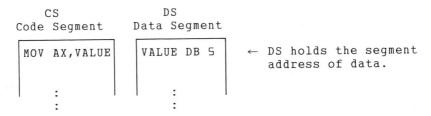

Now we are free to read the data in VALUE in the program:

```
MOV AX, VALUE
```

This is the way to use memory in the PC or PS/2: Set up storage for it in the part of your program that you label the Data Segment (or the Common Segment in the case of a .COM file). Give names of variables to all of the bytes you set aside (with DB or, as we will see, similar Pseudo-Ops). You can then use these names just like variables in a high-level language.

Let's add some data to PRINTZ.ASM. About the only data we have is the character we're going to print out, ''Z''. Let's store it in memory:

```
CODE_SEG          SEGMENT

          ASSUME  CS:CODE_SEG,DS:CODE_SEG,ES:CODE_SEG
          ORG     100H
          Our_Character    DB "Z"   ←
START:    MOV     AH,2
          MOV     DL,5AH
          INT     21H
EXIT:     INT     20H

CODE_SEG          ENDS
          END     START
```

DB tells the assembler that the data that follows is to be put into the program without interpretation: It is data. We set aside a location. (1 byte) that we call Our_Character, and initialize it by putting the character ''Z'' in it. The assembler translates the ''Z'' into the ASCII code that the machine needs: 5AH. (We can have alternatively use Our_Character DB 5AH—it is the same thing to the assembler.) Here are some DB examples:

```
Flag    DB 0
  Char_Z  DB "Z"
  Numbers DB 1,2,3,4,5,0   ← 6 bytes are put aside.
  Prompt  DB "How long has it been since you called "
          DB "your mother?"
```

When we refer to the names Flag, Char_Z, Numbers or Prompt, we are actually referring to the first byte in whatever follows DB. Labels such as these are actually pointers. For example, we can use this code:

```
MOV     AH,Numbers
```

The 1 (that is, the first number after DB) is the loaded into AH.

In PRINTZ.ASM, this is how we load our character into DL just before printing it out:

```
CODE_SEG            SEGMENT

        ASSUME  CS:CODE_SEG,DS:CODE_SEG,ES:CODE_SEG
        ORG     100H
        Our_Character   DB "Z"
START:  MOV     AH,2
        MOV     DL,Our_Character   ←
        INT     21H
EXIT:   INT     20H

CODE_SEG            ENDS
        END     START
```

That is the way to define and use variables in assembly language. We've labeled and used a memory location.

On the other hand, we've left ourselves with a problem. The label START is supposed to be at 100H in the Code Segment. Now that we've added 1 byte of memory space just before it, it is at the wrong location (specifically, at 101H). To solve this problem, we do what most .COM files that use data do. We set aside a data area at the beginning of the program and add a *jump* command. When things start up at 100H, the microprocessor first jumps *over* the data area and to the first instruction. It looks like this:

```
CODE_SEG            SEGMENT

        ASSUME  CS:CODE_SEG,DS:CODE_SEG,ES:CODE_SEG
        ORG     100H
START:  JMP     PRINTZ   ←
        Our_Character   DB "Z"
PRINTZ: MOV     AH,2
        MOV     DL,Our_Character
        INT     21H
EXIT:   INT     20H

CODE_SEG            ENDS
        END     START
```

We move the label START to point to an instruction that is at 100H. That command says JMP PRINTZ, which means that the microprocessor jumps to the label PRINTZ and then continues.

JMP is an assembly language command—it is similar to a goto in C. The computer jumps to wherever you tell it, and starts executing code there. To use JMP, just provide a label to jump to, as we have done here (JMP PRINTZ).

A .COM File Shell

In general, this is how a .COM file shell looks:

```
CODE_SEG          SEGMENT

        ASSUME    CS:CODE_SEG,DS:CODE_SEG,ES:CODE_SEG
        ORG       100H
START:  JMP       PROG
        -------------------
                     :
            This the data area. Use DB here.
        -------------------
PROG:                :
            And this is where the program goes.
        -------------------
EXIT:   INT       20H

CODE_SEG          ENDS
        END       START
```

There is an area set aside for data (using DB) and a part for the program (use this shell for your own programs). Now we've updated PRINTZ.ASM to include data and a data area.

Strings in Memory

We still have not resolved how to store character strings in memory, or for that matter, how to store whole 16-bit words. (DB only stores byte-by-byte). A character string, as in C (or Pascal or BASIC) is just a series of letters, one after the other, that makes sense to us but not to the computer. We want to keep them together: The computer only sees a number of bytes with no apparent relation.

Strings in assembly language are just stored as bytes, as they are in C. Like strings in C, they have a terminator. Although strings usually end with 0 (in what is called ASCIIZ format), this is not always the case. Strings are stored as is the PROMPT string. If you want the string to end with a 0 byte, it is your responsibilty to put it in:

```
Prompt  DB "How long has it been since you called "
        DB "your mother?", 0
```

The assembler lets you store strings in this way, using the quotation marks as shorthand (otherwise, you'd have to use DB for each letter.)

INT 21H Service 9—Print a String

The string printing service, service 9, of INT 21H prints out strings. Service 9 has no way to know when it comes to the end of the string. To terminate the string for this service, a '$' (not a 0 byte) is added as the last character. This is an indication to service 9 to stop printing, and is one of the times when strings are not terminated with 0. Let's change our program to PRINTXYZ.COM:

```
CODE_SEG          SEGMENT

        ASSUME  CS:CODE_SEG,DS:CODE_SEG,ES:CODE_SEG
        ORG     100H
START:  JMP     PRINTZ
        Our_Characters  DB 'XYZ$'  ←
PRINTZ: MOV     AH,2
        MOV     DL,Our_Character
        INT     21H
EXIT:   INT     20H

CODE_SEG          ENDS
        END     START
```

Notice the "$" character is the last byte in the string. We have to tell service 9 where to find the string it should print, and change the call from service 2 to service 9. Service 9 requires the address at which the string to be printed begins in memory—a pointer to the string, just as printf() might require. It also requires this address to be in DS:DX. If the address is 0EF1:0105, for example, we have to load 0EF1H into DS, and 0105H into DX.

Since we are dealing with a .COM file, the value of DS never changes, so DS is already set for service 9. When the program runs, DS points at the Data Segment, which is the only segment. To get the offset address of Our_Characters, we use the OFFSET Pseudo-Op:

```
CODE_SEG          SEGMENT

        ASSUME  CS:CODE_SEG,DS:CODE_SEG,ES:CODE_SEG
        ORG     100H
START:  JMP     PRINTZ
        Our_Characters  DB 'XYZ$'
PRINTZ: MOV     AH,9
```

```
        MOV     DX, OFFSET Our_Characters              ←
        INT     21H
EXIT:   INT     20H

CODE_SEG        ENDS
        END     START
```

The OFFSET Pseudo-Op gives you a label's offset value from the beginning of the Data Segment. You can think of it as returning a pointer to that object (but only a near pointer). For example, the line:

```
MOV     DX, OFFSET Our_Characters
```

loads the offset of Our_Characters into DX. OFFSET is a handy Pseudo-Op that we'll use often because many interrupt services require that we pass them the address of data.

That's all there is to it. We now have a new working .ASM file that prints out 'XYZ' instead of just "Z".

Using Comments

The final topic of this chapter is the use of comments. Comments can be added in assembly language by preceding them with a semi-colon, ";", such as in PRINTXYZ:

```
CODE_SEG        SEGMENT         ;This will be the code segment.

        ASSUME  CS:CODE_SEG,DS:CODE_SEG,ES:CODE_SEG
        ORG     100H            ;Set up for a .COM file.
START:  JMP     PRINTZ          ;JMP over data area.
        Our_Characters  DB 'XYZ$'      ;We will print out this string.
PRINTZ: MOV     AH,9            ;Request INT 21H service 9.
        MOV     DX, OFFSET Our_Characters       ;Point to our string.
        INT     21H             ;And print it out here.
EXIT:   INT     20H             ;End the program.

CODE_SEG        ENDS            ;End the code segment.
        END     START           ;Set entry point to label START.
```

By reading down the side of the program, you can see what was intended by each line. Now that we've mastered the fundamentals of writing programs, let's broaden our library of instructions.

8

An Assembly Language Primer

Accepting Input

Now we start using assembly language in earnest. First, we have to learn how to write a program that accepts input.

The most basic of the DOS services is service 1, which reads keyboard input. This is really the primary input service. You request service 1 from INT 21H by setting AH to 1 and executing an INT 21H instruction. When a key is typed, it is echoed on the screen and its ASCII code is returned in the AL register.

Not all character input services echo the typed character—there is more than one way to read a single character. Besides INT 21H service 1, there are also services 6, 7, and 8. They all return the ASCII code of the key that is typed in AL. Only service 1 echoes the typed character on the screen. Some of them quit when a Control-Break is typed. Service 6 does not wait until a key is struck—it returns a character immediately if one is in the keyboard buffer. Here is a list of how DOS single-character input services work:

INT 21H Service	Will Wait	^Break Seen	Will Echo
1	X	X	X
6			
7	X		
8	X	X	

In addition to these single-character services, we'll see a program in this chapter that accepts buffered input and can read a character string. Let's start with an example that accepts character input.

The Program CAP.COM

The following example program accepts a letter that you type, capitalizes it, and prints it on the screen. For the first time, we will get our assembly language program to accept input from us. Let's start with the .COM file shell:

```
CODE_SEG        SEGMENT
        ASSUME  CS:CODE_SEG,DS:CODE_SEG,ES:CODE_SEG,SS:CODE_SEG

        ORG 100H
START:  JMP CAP
        ;Data Area
CAP:
        ;Program will go here.

EXIT:   INT     20H

CODE_SEG        ENDS
        END START
```

Add the instructions that let the program accept input:

```
CODE_SEG        SEGMENT

        ORG 100H
START:  JMP CAP
        ;Data Area
CAP:    MOV     AH,1    ;Request keyboard input   ←
        INT     21H     ;From INT 21H             ←

EXIT:   INT     20H

CODE_SEG        ENDS
        END START
```

After the INT 21H instruction is executed, the ASCII code of the typed character is in AL. The program's job is to capitalize the letter and print it out. There is an easy way to capitalize letters—ASCII codes for the small letters, (e.g., "a") have higher values than the ASCII codes for the small letters (e.g., "A"). The ASCII codes for "A" to "Z" run from 65 to 90; for "a" to "z" from 97 to 122. To capitalize a letter, we just subtract a number from its ASCII code in order to move the code from its place in the a…z part of the table to its corresponding place in the A…Z part:

Table 8.1   Capitalizing

Capitals	Code		Smalls	Code
A	65←subtract 32——		a	97
B	66←subtract 32——		b	98
C	67←subtract 32——		c	99
	:			:
	:			:
Z	90←subtract 32—		z	122

The number we have to subtract is just equal to ASCII("a") - ASCII("A"), which is 97 - 65 = 32, the distance between the two parts of the table. Here's how we capitalize the ASCII value in AL, introducing the new instruction, SUB, for subtract:

```
CODE_SEG          SEGMENT
        ASSUME    CS:CODE_SEG,DS:CODE_SEG,ES:CODE_SEG,SS:CODE_SEG

        ORG 100H
START:  JMP CAP
        ;Data Area
CAP:    MOV    AH,1     ;Request keyboard input
        INT    21H      ;From INT 21H
→       SUB    AL,"a"-"A"       ;Capitalize the typed key

EXIT:   INT    20H

CODE_SEG          ENDS
        END START
```

The SUB and ADD Instructions

The SUB instruction is used this way:

```
SUB       AL,5
```

Here 5 is subtracted from the contents of AL; AL is changed. Similarly, you can execute this instruction:

```
SUB       AX,DX
```

and subtract the contents of DX from AX. AX is changed, but DX is not. Besides the SUB instruction, there is ADD, the built-in add instruction. We will use ADD and SUB frequently.

The assembler has a preprocessor, just as C does, and it lets you use expressions such as 'a' - 'A'. For instance, we can use a line like this one:

```
SUB     AL,'a'-'A'
```

which makes what we are doing much clearer than if we simply said:

```
SUB     AL,32
```

Similarly, expressions such as 'a' + 'A' are allowed. The assembler understands expressions that include operators such as +,-,/, and *, so it's often a good idea to use them to make your code clearer. For example, to read data from a file in 1K sections, where each section is prefaced by a header of 256 bytes, this line:

```
MOV     DX, 256 + 1024
```

can make it a lot clearer that you want to use a header and one data section than this line does:

```
MOV     DX, 1280
```

In our program, all that is left to do is to type the newly capitalized letter on the screen. We can do that with INT 21H service 2, as we've already seen.

Printing Out Capital Letters

INT 21H service 2, which prints a character on the screen, expects the ASCII code of the character that it is to print in DL. In CAP.ASM so far, the ASCII code is still in the AL register because service 1 returned it there. We have to move the code from AL to DL and then print the character:

```
CODE_SEG        SEGMENT
        ASSUME  CS:CODE_SEG,DS:CODE_SEG,ES:CODE_SEG,SS:CODE_SEG

        ORG 100H
START:  JMP CAP
        ;Data Area
CAP:    MOV     AH,1        ;Request keyboard input
        INT     21H         ;From INT 21H
        SUB     AL,"a"-"A"      ;Capitalize the typed key
        MOV     DL,AL       ;Set up for service 2.
```

```
          MOV     AH,2     ;Request character output  ←
          INT     21H      ;Type out character.       ←
EXIT:     INT     20H

CODE_SEG          ENDS
          END START
```

CAP.ASM is complete. We read in a typed letter with INT 21H service 1, capitalize it ourselves, and then print it out with INT 21H service 2. Type in the letter, assemble, and produce CAP.COM.

When you run it, you see this:

```
A>cap
```

The program waits for a key to be typed. As soon as you type a letter, such as s, it echoes the letter and prints out a capital S. Then it simply exits:

```
A>cap
sS
A>
```

If we had wanted to rewrite CAP so that the "s" wasn't echoed on the screen, we could have used service 8, for example, instead of service 1:

```
CODE_SEG          SEGMENT
          ASSUME  CS:CODE_SEG,DS:CODE_SEG,ES:CODE_SEG,SS:CODE_SEG

          ORG 100H
START:    JMP CAP
          ;Data Area
CAP:      MOV     AH,8     ;Request keyboard input  ←
          INT     21H      ;From INT 21H
          CMP     AL,"a"   ;Compare the incoming ASCII code to "a".
          JB      EXIT     ;If the letter is not lower case, exit.
          CMP     AL,"z"   ;Compare the incoming ASCII code to "z".
          JA      EXIT     ;If the letter is not lower case, exit.
          SUB     AL,"a"-"A"       ;Capitalize the typed key
          MOV     DL,AL    ;Set up for service 2.
          MOV     AH,2     ;Request character output
          INT     21H      ;Type out character.
EXIT:     INT     20H

CODE_SEG          ENDS
          END START
```

This new CAP.COM waits for your typed-in letter, capitalizes it, and prints only the result on the screen.

Although it is gratifying to get the result we expected, there are a number of problems with this program. Perhaps the most serious one is: What happens if you type in some character other than a lowercase letter? Odd characters will be printed, because we are only ready to handle small letters.

This problem may be fixed if we check the incoming ASCII code to make sure that it actually represents a lowercase letter. We have to check to make sure that the ASCII code is between the values for "a" and "z." This type of checking brings us to the topic of conditional jumps, which are extremely important in assembly language because they are almost the only branch instruction available.

Conditional Jumps

We want to check that the incoming ASCII code is between "a" and "z". If it is not, the program exits. We have to divide the process into two steps: The first step is to check whether AL is greater than or equal to "a," the second step is to check if AL is less than or equal to "z." If both tests pass, we capitalize the letter, type it, and exit.

The CMP Instruction

Checking a value against some known comparison value is done with the assembly language instruction, CMP (for compare). To branch on the results of the comparison, we then use a *conditional jump* immediately after the CMP instruction. Unlike C, comparisons are a two-step process in assembly language. For example, this code checks whether AL is above or equal to "a" (JB means jump if below):

```
CODE_SEG        SEGMENT
        ASSUME  CS:CODE_SEG,DS:CODE_SEG,ES:CODE_SEG,SS:CODE_SEG

        ORG 100H
START:  JMP CAP
        ;Data Area
CAP:    MOV     AH,1    ;Request keyboard input
        INT     21H     ;From INT 21H
→       CMP     AL,"a"  ;Compare the incoming ASCII code to "a".
→       JB      EXIT    ;If the letter is not lower case, exit.

        SUB     AL,"a"-"A"      ;Capitalize the typed key
        MOV     DL,AL   ;Set up for service 2.
        MOV     AH,2    ;Request character output
        INT     21H     ;Type out character.
EXIT:   INT     20H

CODE_SEG        ENDS
        END START
```

We compare AL to the ASCII value for "a," and then immediately followed this with a JB instruction:

```
CMP     AL,"a"   ;Compare the incoming ASCII code to "a".
B       EXIT     ;If the letter is not lower case, exit.
```

If the comparison shows that the value in AL (the first item in the CMP instruction) is below "a," we jump to the label EXIT at the end of the program, and leave without capitalizing the ASCII code.

The process works like this: First, the microprocessor's flags are set by the CMP instruction. The JB instruction checks these internal flags and acts accordingly:

```
CMP     AL,"a"   ← Sets Flags
JB      EXIT     ← Reads Flags
```

Now we check that the ASCII code is below or equal to "z." This is done with the JA (Jump if Above) instruction:

```
CODE_SEG          SEGMENT
         ASSUME   CS:CODE_SEG,DS:CODE_SEG,ES:CODE_SEG,SS:CODE_SEG
         ORG 100H
START:   JMP CAP
         ;Data Area
CAP:     MOV    AH,1     ;Request keyboard input
         INT    21H      ;From INT 21H
         CMP    AL,"a"   ;Compare the incoming ASCII code to "a".
         JB     EXIT     ;If the letter is not lower case, exit.
→        CMP    AL,"z"   ;Compare the incoming ASCII code to "z".
→        JA     EXIT     ;If the letter is not lower case, exit.
         SUB    AL,"a"-"A"        ;Capitalize the typed key
         MOV    DL,AL    ;Set up for service 2.
         MOV    AH,2     ;Request character output
         INT    21H      ;Type out character.
EXIT:    INT    20H
CODE_SEG          ENDS
         END START
```

That completes the program CAP.ASM, our first assembly language program. It accepts input and generates output; and it even checks for errors.

More Conditional Jumps

We have used the two instructions, JA and JB. These follow a CMP instruction, and, depending upon the result, a jump may be made. There are many conditional jumps. In fact, there are even those variations of JA and JB: JAE (Jump if Above or Equal), JBE (Jump if Below or Equal), JNA (Jump if Not Above), JNB (Jump if Not Below), JNAE (Jump if Not Above or Equal), and JNBE (Jump if Not Below or Equal). All of these are used after a CMP instruction.

Probably the two most common conditional jumps are JE, (Jump if Equal) and JNE (Jump if Not Equal), and we will use them soon. Here are a number of conditional jumps and their meanings:

Conditional Jump	Meaning
JA/JG	Jump if Above/Greater
JB/JL	Jump if Below/Less
JAE/JGE	Jump if Above/Greater or Equal
JBE/JLE	Jump if Below/Less or Equal
JNA/JNG	Jump if Not Above/Not Greater
JNB/JNL	Jump if Not Below/Not Less
JNAE/JNGE	Jump if Not Above/Greater or Equal
JNBE/JNLE	Jump if Not Below/Less or Equal
JE	Jump if Equal
JNE	Jump if Not Equal
JZ	Jump if result was Zero
JNZ	Jump if result was Not Zero
JCXZ	Jump if CX = 0 (Used at end of loops)

You can see that there is a rich selection of jump instructions. Without such a selection of conditional jumps, assembly language would be very difficult to use. As it is, there are conditional jumps that meet most needs. If you are new to assembly language, it might take you a while to become practived in their use.

You can see that for a number of jumps there are two variations—Jump if Above (JA) or Jump if Greater (JG), for example. The difference has to do with signed and unsigned numbers, and the way the computer treats them. So far, we have been dealing with only unsigned numbers but, of course, that's only half the story. And, as it turns out, only half the conditional jumps (the ones like JA or JB)—to learn how to use the others (like JG or JL), we will have to understand signed numbers at the lowest level.

Signed Numbers

The 80x86 instructions only work with integer arithmetic—no floating point calculations. In addition, we've used unsigned integers so far and a number held in one register can range only from 0000H to FFFFH. However, any modern computer has to be able to use signed numbers.

In *signed numbers*, the highest bit—the leftmost bit—in a byte or word is regarded as the sign bit. When you pay attention to this bit, the number is signed. In unsigned bytes or words, this bit was always there, but it was only the highest bit, and had no other significance. In other words, to make a number signed, you just treat it as signed by giving the sign bit a special significance.

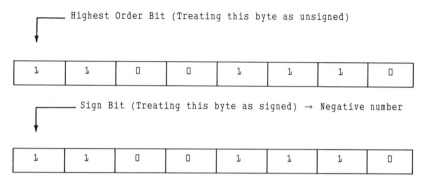

Highest Order Bit (Treating this byte as unsigned)

| 1 | 1 | 0 | 0 | 1 | 1 | 1 | 0 |

Sign Bit (Treating this byte as signed) → Negative number

| 1 | 1 | 0 | 0 | 1 | 1 | 1 | 0 |

The method used to represent signed numbers inside the microprocessor can be derived from the simple fact that $1 + (-1) = 0$. If we want to do any calculations with negative numbers, the number we choose to be -1, when added to 1, has to yield 0. Yet this seems impossible. Can you think of an eight-bit number that, when added to 1, gives a result of 0? It seems as though the result must always be 1 or greater.

In fact, if we limit ourselves to the 8 bits of the byte, there is an answer. If we add 255 (11111111B) and 1:

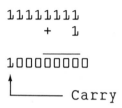

```
 11111111
+       1
─────────
100000000
```

Carry

it yields 100000000B; that is, the eight-bit register is left holding 00000000, or 0. There is a carry, because the 1 is in the 2^8 place (256), more than the register's capacity to hold. This carry means that the *carry flag* is set. This flag is set when the results of an addition yield a number that is beyond the capacity of the register that holds the result. (Similarly, if a borrow is required during a subtraction, the carry flag is set.)

In unsigned arithmetic, you can check if a carry was generated with the JC (Jump on Carry) instruction:

```
ADD     AX, DX
JC      RESULT_TOO_BIG
```

> The ADC (Add with Carry) and SBB (Subtract with Borrow) instructions were developed to help chain small additions and subtractions into larger ones. We will work with them later.

In this case, however, if we ignore the carry and only keep the 8 bits that fit into the byte, we are left with 00000000B; in other words, FFH + 1 = 0.

This is exactly what we want, and that is how it works: When we work with negative numbers, we use instructions that ignore the carry flag. The only way the carry flag is used is if we explicitly check it (with, for example, the conditional jump JC). With signed calculations, we ignore the way it is set. Therefore, to us, 11111111B + 1 = 0. In this scheme, called *two's complement notation*, 11111111B = -1, and 10000000B = -128. In other words, the two's complement of 1 is 11111111B, and the two's complement of 128 is 10000000B.

We can find the two's complement of any number easily. Begin by noting that if you take a number such as 5 (00000101B), flip all of its bits (11111010B = FAH), and add the two together, you get FFH:

```
  00000101  ← 5
+ 11111010  ← 5 with bits flipped [ FAH ]
  11111111  = FF
```

That is, 5 + FAH = 11111111B. This is close to what we want—adding 1 to this sum gives us 0 with a carry. If we ignore the carry, we can see that 5 + FAH + 1 = 0. In other words, adding 5 to (FAH + 1) yields 0 with the (ignored) carry:

```
        5
+ (FAH + 1)
        0
```

That means that -5 must equal (FAH + 1), or FBH. This is how negative numbers are found. The rule is simple: To find any number's two's complement (and thus to change its sign), just flip the bits and add 1. As an example, we can see that -1 = Flip(1) + 1 = 11111110B + 1 = 11111111B = FFH (in byte form). We'll need to know this information later when we start dealing with the internal representation of negative numbers in C.

The NOT and NEG Instructions

To flip the bits in a word or byte, use the NOT instruction. For example, if AL equals 00000000, then NOT AL makes AL equal to 11111111. If BL equals 01010101, then NOT BL makes it 10101010. If you apply NOT to a word or a byte and add 1 to the result, you get that word or byte's two's complement.

There is a special 80x86 instruction, called NEG, that changes signs. NEG is the same as NOT, except that it adds 1 at the end to make a two's complement of the number. If AX holds 1, then NEG AX would make it 1111111111111111B, or FFFFH. NEG flips signs; it does not always make signs negative. For example, NEG -1 = 1.

The ranges of signed numbers are important, too. An unsigned byte can hold numbers from 0 to 255; a signed byte can hold numbers from -128 (10000000B = 80H) to 127 (01111111 = 7FH). The unsigned range for a word goes from 0 to 65535; a signed word can go from -32768 (8000H) to 32767 (7FFFFH).

> Note that the range of positive numbers in a word or byte is one less than the range of negative numbers, because 0 is treated as part of the positive range.

New Jumps, Not New Numbers

When we use signed numbers, the registers in the microprocessor do not change. We use signed numbers by using instructions that pay attention to the sign bit and ignore the carry flag. Those instructions are the Greater/Less conditional jumps. If we use unsigned numbers, we use the Above/Below conditional jumps. We can compare two numbers, such as FFH (11111111B) and 7FH (01111111B), was with conditional jumps like JA or JB. For example, look at this:

```
MOV     AX,11111111B    [FF]
CMP     AX,01111111B    [7F]
JA      AX_BIG
```

If this jump is made, we assume that the value in AX, which is 11111111B, is bigger than the value it is being compared to, which is 01111111B. That is true if we use unsigned numbers—FFH is bigger than 7FH. On the other hand, if we use signed numbers, we use a new set of conditional jumps that watch the sign bit. Here, we use JG (Jump if Greater):

```
MOV       AX,11111111B     [ -1  ]
CMP       AX,01111111B     [ 127 ]
JG        AX_BIG
```

The JG instruction knows that 127 is greater than -1, and the jump to AX_BIG is not made. For the numerical conditional jumps, there is both an unsigned and a signed version. "Above" becomes "Greater" and "Below" becomes "Less." We can regroup our earlier table of conditional jumps into signed and unsigned jumps. Here they are:

Table 8.2   Corresponding Jumps for Unsigned And Signed Numbers

Unsigned		Signed	
JA	Jump if Above	JG	Jump if Greater
JNA	Jump if Not Above	JNG	Jump if Not Greater
JB	Jump if Below	JL	Jump if Less
JNB	Jump if Not Below	JNL	Jump if Not Less
JAE	Jump if Above or Equal	JGE	Jump if Greater or Equal
JNAE	Jump if Not Above or Equal	JNGE	Jump if Not Greater or Equal
JBE	Jump if Below or Equal	JGE	Jump if Greater or Equal
JNBE	Jump if Not Below or Equal	JNLE	Jump if Not Less or Equal

Let's put all this to work and see a signed arithmetic example in action. Say we want a program to take the number stored at the memory location NUMBER and put its absolute value at ABS_VAL. This is how it would look. (Notice the use of NEG AX.)

```
CODE_SEG          SEGMENT
        ASSUME    CS:CODE_SEG,DS:CODE_SEG
        ORG       100H
ENTRY:  JMP       PROG
        NUMBER    DW -10
        ABS_VAL   DW ?
PROG    PROC
        MOV       AX,NUMBER          ←
        CMP       AX,0               ←
        JG        LOAD_ABS_VAL       ←
```

```
          NEG      AX                      ←
LOAD_ABS_VAL:                              ←
          MOV      ABS_VAL,AX              ←
          INT      20H
PROG      ENDP
CODE_SEG           ENDS
          END      ENTRY
```

This program leaves 10 in ABS_VAL. In cases like this, we have to use the signed conditional jump JG, and not the unsigned version, JA. It's that easy—when using signed numbers, just use the Greater/Less jumps, not the Above/Below jumps.

The JC and JO Conditional Jumps

There is one more conditional jump to explore—the JC (Jump on Carry) conditional jump. Now that we neglect the carry flag, we've left ourselves without a means of checking for possible overflows when we do calculations. For instance, if we add -1 and -128:

```
    11111111
  + 10000000
   101111111
```

the result is -129, and that is too negative to hold in one byte because the minimum is -128. In this calculation, the byte-long result is left as 01111111B, which looks like a positive number, not -129. A new flag is set when a number's sign is inadvertantly changed—that is, when some math operation gives a result that can't be held in the byte's or the word's two's complement capacity.

This flag is the *overflow flag*. When we are concerned about the possible size of a result, we can use the carry flag:

```
ADD     AX,BX
JC      TOO_BIG
```

Now, when dealing with signed numbers, the overflow flag is used in the same way, with JO (Jump if Overflow) and JNO (Jump if No Overflow):

```
ADD     AX,BX
JO      SIGN_CHANGED
```

If we are worried that the result of a calculation may exceed the register's size, we can check the overflow flag.

That completes our introduction to signed numbers in the PS/2 and PC, although we'll have more to say about them later. In the meantime, let's put our expertise to work.

DEHEXER.ASM

In the beginning of this book, we developed a small program to change numbers from decimal to hexadecimal. We can do the reverse here in assembly language, developing a program that changes four-digit hexadecimal numbers to decimal. We start with the .COM file shell:

```
CODE_SEG         SEGMENT
        ASSUME   CS:CODE_SEG, DS:CODE_SEG, ES:CODE_SEG, SS:CODE_SEG

        ORG 100H
ENTRY:  JMP DEHEXER

        ;Data will go here.

DEHEXER:

        ;Program will go here.


        INT     20H
CODE_SEG         ENDS

        END     ENTRY
```

First, we have to read the hexadecimal number in from the keyboard. DOS provides buffer input services to read strings. We can use DOS if we set up a buffer in memory with the DB Pseudo-Op:

```
BUFFER DB #, 0, 0, 0, 0, 0, 0, 0, 0, 0, 0, 0
```

To fill the buffer, we use DOS INT 21H, service 0AH (get string). We set the number (# above) in the beginning of the buffer. INT 21H service 0AH needs that number—the buffer length—so it won't overfill the buffer. Service 0AH always sets the last byte of the buffer to ASCII 13 (a carriage return) as an end-of-string marker, so we set # to one more than the number of characters we expect as input.

The second byte in the buffer is filled by service 0AH with the number of bytes actually typed. If we're careful, we can set up our buffer with some foresight by giving names to the important bytes in it:

```
CODE_SEG           SEGMENT
        ASSUME  CS:CODE_SEG, DS:CODE_SEG, ES:CODE_SEG, SS:CODE_SEG

        ORG 100H
ENTRY:  JMP DEHEXER
        PROMPT            DB 'Type in a 4 digit hex number:$'
   →    BUFFER            DB 5
   →    NUM_TYPED         DB 0
   →    ASCII_NUM         DB 3 DUP (0)
   →    END_NUM           DB 0
   →    CRLF              DB 0
DEHEXER:MOV     AH,9
        MOV     DX,OFFSET PROMPT
        INT     21H
        MOV     AH,0AH
        MOV     DX,OFFSET BUFFER
        INT     21H

        INT     20H
CODE_SEG           ENDS
```

Notice that we also add a prompt to be typed out, named PROMPT. Service 9, the string-printing service, is the printf() of DOS. In order to print out our prompt, we have to pass service 9 a pointer to the string to print. Service 9 expects an offset address in DX, and expects the string terminate with "$":

```
CODE_SEG           SEGMENT
        ASSUME  CS:CODE_SEG, DS:CODE_SEG, ES:CODE_SEG, SS:CODE_SEG

        ORG 100H
ENTRY:  JMP DEHEXER
        PROMPT            DB 'Type in a 4 digit hex number:$'
        BUFFER            DB 5
        NUM_TYPED         DB 0
        ASCII_NUM         DB 3 DUP (0)
        END_NUM           DB 0
        CRLF              DB 0
DEHEXER:MOV     AH,9
   →    MOV     DX,OFFSET PROMPT
   →    INT     21H
```

After printing out the prompt:

```
Type in a 4 digit hex number:
```

we use service 0AH to read the four-digit hexadecimal number from the keyboard. This is the number we will convert to decimal and print out. We have to pass a pointer (in DX) to the beginning of the buffer for service 0AH to use, so we move the offset of BUFFER into that register:

```
CODE_SEG        SEGMENT
        ASSUME  CS:CODE_SEG, DS:CODE_SEG, ES:CODE_SEG, SS:CODE_SEG

        ORG 100H
ENTRY:  JMP DEHEXER
        PROMPT          DB 'Type in a 4 digit hex number:$'
        BUFFER          DB 5
        NUM_TYPED       DB 0
        ASCII_NUM       DB 3 DUP (0)
        END_NUM         DB 0
        CRLF            DB 0
DEHEXER:MOV     AH,9
        MOV     DX,OFFSET PROMPT
        INT     21H
        MOV     AH,0AH
→       MOV     DX,OFFSET BUFFER
→       INT     21H

        INT     20H
CODE_SEG        ENDS
```

Next we issue an INT 21H command and accept the hexadecimal number.

> If you try to type more than the number of characters that the buffer can accept, the computer beeps. This is the same beep that DOS uses and, for that matter, the same internal service (0AH) that it uses to accept keyboard input at the DOS prompt.

The <cr> at the end of the returned string will go into the byte marked CRLF, and we can ignore it.

Notice the use of the Pseudo-Op DUP:

```
ASCII_NUM       DB 3 DUP (0)
```

This Pseudo-Op saves us time. This expression is equal to ASCII_NUM DB 0, 0, 0; not such a big saving for 3 bytes, but what if you needed to reserve space for 32,000?

> You can also allocate space on the Heap (although assembly language doesn't call it the Heap—it's simply available memory) in assembly language by using the assembly language equivalents of malloc() and realloc(), which are the DOS INT 21H services referred to as GET-BLOCK and SETBLOCK. See the appendix on DOS and BIOS interrupts at the end of this book for more information.

Pointers in Assembly Language

After the buffer has been filled with input from the keyboard, the ASCII string extends from the pointers ASCII_NUM to END_NUM in memory. We have to convert that string into a number.

If this was the number:

1234H

we just point to the last number (4), convert it from ASCII to binary, then point to the next number (3), convert it to binary, multiply by 16 and add it to the 4 we already have. In this way, we loop over all characters.

That is the method we will use. We have labeled the last ASCII digit in memory as END_NUM:

```
END NUM

   |
   |
   ▼

1234H
```

We are familiar with data labels—to get the ASCII character from that location, we can just say MOV AL, END_NUM. But how do we point to the previous digits?

We use a register as a pointer. In assembly language, the BX register was designed explicitly to be used as a pointer. (The only other registers that can function as pointers are the SI and DI registers, which we'll cover soon.) Let's examine how that's done.

We need a loop to read all four digits, so we load BX with the address of END_NUM:

```
CODE_SEG          SEGMENT
        ASSUME  CS:CODE_SEG, DS:CODE_SEG, ES:CODE_SEG, SS:CODE_SEG

        ORG 100H
ENTRY:  JMP DEHEXER
        PROMPT          DB 'Type in a 4 digit hex number:$'
        BUFFER          DB 5
        NUM_TYPED       DB 0
        ASCII_NUM       DB 3 DUP (0)
        END_NUM         DB 0
        CRLF            DB 0
DEHEXER:MOV     AH,9
        MOV     DX,OFFSET PROMPT
        INT     21H
        MOV     AH,0AH
        MOV     DX,OFFSET BUFFER
```

```
           INT      21H

           MOV      CX, 0
           MOV      AX,0
    →      MOV      BX, OFFSET END_NUM
LOOP1:
           :
           :
           :
           JL       LOOP1


           INT      20H
CODE_SEG            ENDS

           END      ENTRY
```

Now we load the ASCII character into the DL register:

```
CODE_SEG           SEGMENT
       ASSUME  CS:CODE_SEG, DS:CODE_SEG, ES:CODE_SEG, SS:CODE_SEG

           ORG 100H
ENTRY:  JMP DEHEXER
           PROMPT           DB 'Type in a 4 digit hex number:$'
           BUFFER           DB 5
           NUM_TYPED        DB 0
           ASCII_NUM        DB 3 DUP (0)
           END_NUM          DB 0
           CRLF             DB 0
DEHEXER:MOV      AH,9
           MOV      DX,OFFSET PROMPT
           INT      21H
           MOV      AH,0AH
           MOV      DX,OFFSET BUFFER
           INT      21H

           MOV      BX, OFFSET END_NUM
LOOP1:  MOV      DL, BYTE PTR [BX]            ←
           DEC      BX                          ←
           :
           :

           JL       LOOP1


           INT      20H
CODE_SEG           ENDS

           END      ENTRY
```

Putting BX inside square brackets—[BX]—means that the microprocessor uses the address stored in BX to reference memory.

The expression BYTE PTR:

```
                MOV     BX, OFFSET END_NUM
        LOOP1:  MOV     DL, BYTE PTR [BX]            ←
                DEC     BX
                :
                :
```

means "byte pointer." It is frequently used with [BX] and is analogous to (char *). Here we indicate to the assembler that the value we want to put into DL is a byte. The type cast is not actually needed here because the DL register is one byte long, which means that [BX] must be taken as a one-byte expression. On the other hand, the expression MOV [BX], 0 is not clear. We might want to overwrite the byte pointed to by BX, or we might want to overwrite the word starting at that location. Here we would use one of the two type cast Pseudo-Ops available, BYTE PTR or WORD PTR, to indicate what we want.

After moving the byte into DL, we decrement the pointer BX with DEC (like – –). Also available is INC (like + +). This points us to the previous ASCII character in preparation for the next time through the loop. Now the ASCII character is in DL, and we must convert it into binary. We do so in this way:

```
CODE_SEG        SEGMENT
        ASSUME  CS:CODE_SEG, DS:CODE_SEG, ES:CODE_SEG, SS:CODE_SEG


        ORG 100H
ENTRY:  JMP DEHEXER
        PROMPT          DB 'Type in a 4 digit hex number:$'
        BUFFER          DB 5
        NUM_TYPED       DB 0
        ASCII_NUM       DB 3 DUP (0)
        END_NUM         DB 0
        CRLF            DB 0
DEHEXER:MOV     AH,9
        MOV     DX,OFFSET PROMPT
        INT     21H
        MOV     AH,0AH
        MOV     DX,OFFSET BUFFER
        INT     21H


        MOV     BX, OFFSET END_NUM
LOOP1:  MOV     DX,0
        MOV     DL, BYTE PTR [BX]
        DEC     BX
        CMP     DL,'9'                      ←
        JLE     UNDER_A                     ←
        SUB     DL, 'A' – '0' – 10          ←
UNDER_A:SUB     DL, '0'                     ←
```

```
          :
          JL        LOOP1


          INT       20H
CODE_SEG            ENDS

          END       ENTRY
```

DL now holds the numerical value of the hexadecimal digit. To convert the entire four-digit number to decimal, we multiply each digit by the appropriate power of 16 and add it to the running total. We can *shift* the value in DL left—shifting left by four places is the same as multiplying by 16.

When we shift DL left by more than two hexadecimal places, however, the result is bigger than a byte can hold. Instead, we use the whole DX register, not just DL. After it is shifted, we add this current hexadecimal digit to the running total.

Let's keep the running total in AX, and add DX to it each time we loop through. The way it looks is this:

```
CODE_SEG            SEGMENT
          ASSUME    CS:CODE_SEG, DS:CODE_SEG, ES:CODE_SEG, SS:CODE_SEG

          ORG 100H
ENTRY:    JMP DEHEXER
          PROMPT              DB 'Type in a 4 digit hex number:$'
          BUFFER              DB 5
          NUM_TYPED           DB 0
          ASCII_NUM           DB 3 DUP (0)
          END_NUM             DB 0
          CRLF                DB 0
DEHEXER:MOV       AH,9
          MOV       DX,OFFSET PROMPT
          INT       21H
          MOV       AH,0AH
          MOV       DX,OFFSET BUFFER
          INT       21H

→         MOV       CX, 0
→         MOV       AX,0
          MOV       BX, OFFSET END_NUM
LOOP1:    MOV       DX,0    ←
          MOV       DL, BYTE PTR [BX]
          DEC       BX
          CMP       DL,'9'
          JLE       UNDER_A
          SUB       DL, 'A' - '0' - 10
UNDER_A:SUB       DL, '0'
→         SHL       DX, CL
→         ADD       AX, DX
→         ADD       CX,4
```

```
  →         CMP       CX,16
            JL        LOOP1


            INT       20H
CODE_SEG              ENDS

            END       ENTRY
```

Note that we load DX with 0 at the top of the loop to make sure their DH is clear (so we don't add leftover data into AX after we shift DX). Now, every time through the loop, we load the ASCII value into DL, make it into a binary number, shift it to the left, and add it to the running total in AX.

We use the SHL instruction, which can either shift left by the number in the CL register:

```
SHL       DX,CL
```

or with an immediate value: SHL AX,4. If we want to shift to the right, we can use SHR DX, CL.

> One quirk of the 80x86 is evident here—you can't store the number of places for shift instructions in any register other than CL. For example, we can't say SHL DX,AL. In addition, the 8088 does not support immediate values for SHL and SHR greater than 1.

We only loop four times, one time for each digit. Now the ASCII string has been converted into binary, and we still have to convert it back to (decimal) ASCII.

The way to do so is to successively peel off the decimal digits by dividing the number in AX by 10. Each time we divide by 10, the remainder is a decimal digit.

The DIV and MUL Instructions

There is a divide instruction in assembly language called DIV. If you load the number to be divided into AX, and divide by a byte-long register like this:

```
DIV BL
```

then the instruction divides AX by BL. AX is assumed to hold the number to be divided when you divide by a byte. The quotient is returned in AL and the remainder is returned in AH.

On the other hand, if you give the command DIV BX, the microprocessor assumes that you are dividing the double-word number in DX:AX by the specifed general-purpose register (here, BX). The terminology DX:AX is an unfortunate way to specifying double words, because addresses are also specified with a colon—however, when segment registers are used, you can be sure it's an address.

Similarly, MUL BL multiplies AL by BL and leaves the result in AX. MUL BX multiplies BX by AX and leaves the result in DX:AX.

If we use the DIV BX command, the number in DX:AX is divided by BX. Let's load DX with 0, and BX with 10. AX already holds the number to be converted. After the division is through, AX holds the quotient (ready to be divided by 10 again in the next pass to peel the next decimal digit off) and DX holds the remainder. The remainder is what we want—it's the current decimal digit. Note that we peel the digits off in backwards order. For example, if we have the number 4321 (decimal) in AX, the first time we divide by 10 we get a remainder of 1; the next time, a remainder of 2; and so on.

To store these decimal digits, we push them on the stack using the command PUSH DX. We also keep track of how many numbers we've pushed in the CX register so we can POP them later. (A four-digit hexadecimal number may give from 1 to 5 decimal digits.) PUSHing and POPping these digits does more than just store them, however—it reverses their order as well. Here's the way it looks:

```
CODE_SEG        SEGMENT
        ASSUME  CS:CODE_SEG, DS:CODE_SEG, ES:CODE_SEG, SS:CODE_SEG

        ORG 100H
ENTRY:  JMP DEHEXER
        PROMPT          DB 'Type in a 4 digit hex number:$'
        BUFFER          DB 5
        NUM_TYPED       DB 0
        ASCII_NUM       DB 3 DUP (0)
        END_NUM         DB 0
        CRLF            DB 0
DEHEXER:MOV     AH,9
        MOV     DX,OFFSET PROMPT
        INT     21H
        MOV     AH,0AH
        MOV     DX,OFFSET BUFFER
        INT     21H

        MOV     CX, 0
        MOV     AX,0
        MOV     BX, OFFSET END_NUM
LOOP1:  MOV     DX,0
        MOV     DL, BYTE PTR [BX]
```

```
            DEC     BX
            CMP     DL,'9'
            JLE     UNDER_A
            SUB     DL, 'A' - '0' - 10
UNDER_A:SUB     DL, '0'
            SHL     DX, CL
            ADD     AX, DX
            ADD     CX,4
            CMP     CX,16
            JL      LOOP1

            MOV     CX,0                ←
            MOV     BX, 10              ←
LOOP2:      MOV     DX,0                ←
            DIV     BX                  ←
            PUSH    DX                  ←
            INC     CX                  ←
            CMP     AX,0                ←
            JA      LOOP2               ←


            INT     20H
CODE_SEG            ENDS

            END     ENTRY
```

At this point, we're almost done. The decimal digits are on the stack, and the number of digits is in CX. Let's print out a message saying "That number in decimal is: " with service 9 of INT 21H:

```
CODE_SEG            SEGMENT
            ASSUME  CS:CODE_SEG, DS:CODE_SEG, ES:CODE_SEG, SS:CODE_SEG

            ORG 100H
ENTRY:  JMP DEHEXER
            PROMPT              DB 'Type in a 4 digit hex number:$'
            BUFFER              DB 5
            NUM_TYPED           DB 0
            ASCII_NUM           DB 3 DUP (0)
            END_NUM             DB 0
            CRLF                DB 0
→           ANS_STRING          DB 13, 10, 'That number in decimal is: $'
DEHEXER:MOV     AH,9
            MOV     DX,OFFSET PROMPT
            INT     21H
            MOV     AH,0AH
            MOV     DX,OFFSET BUFFER
            INT     21H

            MOV     CX, 0
            MOV     AX,0
            MOV     BX, OFFSET END_NUM
LOOP1:  MOV     DX,0
            MOV     DL, BYTE PTR [BX]
```

```
            DEC     BX
            CMP     DL,'9'
            JLE     UNDER_A
            SUB     DL, 'A' - '0' - 10
UNDER_A:SUB         DL, '0'
            SHL     DX, CL
            ADD     AX, DX
            ADD     CX,4
            CMP     CX,16
            JL      LOOP1

            MOV     CX,0
            MOV     BX, 10
LOOP2:  MOV         DX,0
            DIV     BX
            PUSH    DX
            INC     CX
            CMP     AX,0
            JA      LOOP2

    →       MOV     AH,9
    →       MOV     DX,OFFSET ANS_STRING
    →       INT     21H

            INT     20H
CODE_SEG            ENDS

            END     ENTRY
```

Now, just print out the digits using service 2 of INT 21H and POP DX.
(We POP the digits back into DX because service 2 expects the ASCII
character that is to be printed to be in DL):

```
CODE_SEG            SEGMENT
        ASSUME  CS:CODE_SEG, DS:CODE_SEG, ES:CODE_SEG, SS:CODE_SEG

        ORG 100H
ENTRY:  JMP DEHEXER
        PROMPT          DB 'Type in a 4 digit hex number:$'
        BUFFER          DB 5
        NUM_TYPED       DB 0
        ASCII_NUM       DB 3 DUP (0)
        END_NUM         DB 0
        CRLF            DB 0
        ANS_STRING      DB 13, 10, 'That number in decimal is: $'
DEHEXER:MOV     AH,9
        MOV     DX,OFFSET PROMPT
        INT     21H
        MOV     AH,0AH
        MOV     DX,OFFSET BUFFER
        INT     21H

        MOV     CX, 0
        MOV     AX,0
        MOV     BX, OFFSET END_NUM
```

```
LOOP1:     MOV      DX,0
           MOV      DL, BYTE PTR [BX]
           DEC      BX
           CMP      DL,'9'
           JLE      UNDER_A
           SUB      DL, 'A' - '0' - 10
UNDER_A:SUB         DL, '0'
           SHL      DX, CL
           ADD      AX, DX
           ADD      CX,4
           CMP      CX,16
           JL       LOOP1

           MOV      CX,0
           MOV      BX, 10
LOOP2:     MOV      DX,0
           DIV      BX
           PUSH     DX
           INC      CX
           CMP      AX,0
           JA       LOOP2

           MOV      AH,9
           MOV      DX,OFFSET ANS_STRING
           INT      21H

           MOV      AH,2              ←
LOOP3:     POP      DX               ←
           ADD      DX,'0'           ←
           INT      21H              ←
           LOOP     LOOP3            ←

           INT      20H
CODE_SEG            ENDS

           END      ENTRY
```

This introduces us to the LOOP command, which we use to loop over the pushed digits, pop them, and print them out.

The LOOP Instruction

In order to use LOOP, just fill CX with the number of times you want to loop, define a label, and loop:

```
           MOV      CX,5
LOOP_1:
             :
             :
           LOOP     LOOP_1
```

Here, the body of LOOP_1 will be executed five times. The LOOP instruction functions much like a do while loop in C (where the loop condition is checked at the end).

In DEHEXER (and with a little foresight), the previous loop leaves the number of digits in CX already, so the loop index CX is all set. All we have to do is use LOOP.

The program now works—give it a try. It accepts four-digit hexadecimal numbers and prints out the correct decimal version. On the other hand, there is still one difference between this program and most .ASM files—most .ASM files have at least one procedure defined inside them.

Procedures

We can make DEHEXER into a single procedure:

```
CODE_SEG        SEGMENT
        ASSUME  CS:CODE_SEG, DS:CODE_SEG, ES:CODE_SEG, SS:CODE_SEG

        ORG 100H
ENTRY:  JMP DEHEXER
        PROMPT          DB 'Type in a 4 digit hex number:$'
        BUFFER          DB 5
        NUM_TYPED       DB 0
        ASCII_NUM       DB 3 DUP (0)
        END_NUM         DB 0
        CRLF            DB 0
        ANS_STRING      DB 13, 10, 'That number in decimal is: $'
DEHEXER PROC
        MOV     AH,9
        MOV     DX,OFFSET PROMPT
        INT     21H
        MOV     AH,0AH
        MOV     DX,OFFSET BUFFER
        INT     21H

        MOV     CX, 0
        MOV     AX,0
        MOV     BX, OFFSET END_NUM
LOOP1:  MOV     DX,0
        MOV     DL, BYTE PTR [BX]
        DEC     BX
        CMP     DL,'9'
        JLE     UNDER_A
        SUB     DL, 'A' - '0' - 10
UNDER_A:SUB     DL, '0'
        SHL     DX, CL
        ADD     AX, DX
        ADD     CX,4
```

```
            CMP     CX,16
            JL      LOOP1

            MOV     CX,0
            MOV     BX, 10
LOOP2:      MOV     DX,0
            DIV     BX
            PUSH    DX
            INC     CX
            CMP     AX,0
            JA      LOOP2

            MOV     AH,9
            MOV     DX,OFFSET ANS_STRING
            INT     21H

            MOV     AH,2
LOOP3:      POP     DX
            ADD     DX,'0'
            INT     21H
            LOOP    LOOP3

            INT     20H
DEHEXER ENDP                              ←
CODE_SEG        ENDS

        END     ENTRY
```

We add the PROC and ENDP Pseudo-Ops, which define procedures. Usually, code is enclosed inside procedures. (However, if you only have one procedure in your program, you don't have to use the PROC and ENDP Pseudo-Ops to define it.)

When you have more than one procedure, you must use these Pseudo-Ops. The PROC Pseudo-Op tells the assembler that you want to define a procedure, and the ENDP Pseudo-Op indicates that the procedure definition is finished.

You can declare procedures NEAR or FAR, like this:

```
DEHEXER PROC NEAR
DEHEXER PROC FAR
```

The reason for this declaration is the same as the reason for memory models in C: The assembler needs to know the size of addresses used for code. FAR procedures may be called from another code segment, but NEAR procedures may not.

As in C, you can use the keywords NEAR and FAR to set up mixed-model programs. As we have done in C, however, we will use the standard memory models, and omit keywords such as NEAR and FAR. When you define a memory model (which we do in the next chapter with the .MODEL directive), all of the details are taken care of for you.

| The default memory model is SMALL, and that's how our programs have been assembled so far. |

Unless you are in the main procedure, you have to end the procedure with a return, or RET, instruction. Let's break up DEHEXER to see how this is done:

```
CODE_SEG        SEGMENT
        ASSUME  CS:CODE_SEG, DS:CODE_SEG, ES:CODE_SEG, SS:CODE_SEG

        ORG 100H
ENTRY:  JMP DEHEXER
        PROMPT          DB 'Type in a 4 digit hex number:$'
        BUFFER          DB 5
        NUM_TYPED       DB 0
        ASCII_NUM       DB 3 DUP (0)
        END_NUM         DB 0
        CRLF            DB 0
        ANS_STRING      DB 13, 10, 'That number in decimal is: $'
DEHEXER PROC
        MOV     AH,9
        MOV     DX,OFFSET PROMPT
        INT     21H
        MOV     AH,0AH
        MOV     DX,OFFSET BUFFER
        INT     21H

        MOV     CX, 0
        MOV     AX,0
        MOV     BX, OFFSET END_NUM
LOOP1:  MOV     DX,0
        MOV     DL, BYTE PTR [BX]
        DEC     BX
        CMP     DL,'9'
        JLE     UNDER_A
        SUB     DL, 'A' - '0' - 10
UNDER_A:SUB     DL, '0'
        SHL     DX, CL
        ADD     AX, DX
        ADD     CX,4
        CMP     CX,16
        JL      LOOP1

        CALL    PRINT_NUM               ←

        INT     20H
DEHEXER ENDP

PRINT_NUM       PROC                    ←
        MOV     CX,0
        MOV     BX, 10
LOOP2:  MOV     DX,0
        DIV     BX
        PUSH    DX
```

```
            INC     CX
            CMP     AX,0
            JA      LOOP2

            MOV     AH,9
            MOV     DX,OFFSET ANS_STRING
            INT     21H

            MOV     AH,2
LOOP3:      POP     DX
            ADD     DX,'0'
            INT     21H
            LOOP    LOOP3
            RET                                        ←
PRINT_NUM           ENDP                               ←


CODE_SEG            ENDS          END     ENTRY
```

Here we break DEHEXER up into two procedures, DEHEXER itself and PRINT_NUM:

```
CODE_SEG            SEGMENT
        ASSUME  CS:CODE_SEG, DS:CODE_SEG, ES:CODE_SEG, SS:CODE_SEG

        ORG 100H
ENTRY:  JMP DEHEXER
        ;Data
DEHEXER PROC
           :
           :
        CALL    PRINT_NUM               ←
        INT     20H
DEHEXER ENDP


PRINT_NUM          PROC                 ←
           :
           :
        RET
PRINT_NUM          ENDP

CODE_SEG           ENDS
        END        ENTRY
```

It works as you'd expect—when you call PRINT_NUM, control is transferred to the first line there. Execution continues until the return instruction, RET, is reached. Control returns to the line just after the CALL PRINT_NUM instruction in the main procedure.

Procedures in assembly language don't specifically return any values, as they can in C. Instead, information is returned in the registers, or, in some cases, in the flags. For example, a procedure may set the carry flag to indicate an error, and you can check for that condition by following the call to the procedure immediately with a JC instruction. Also, there is no such thing as a formal local variable in assembly language, unless the variable is in another file.

Let's make one more refinement to DEHEXER.ASM. We know that in C, you can pass command-line arguments to a program with argc and argv[]. The same is true in assembly language.

Command-Line Arguments

If you've ever wondered what happens to the characters you type after a file's name, such as "FILE.TXT" here:

```
A>EDIT FILE.TXT
```

then here's the answer: They go into the Program Segment Prefix, the header installed for the program, ready to be read. Every program, from huge editors to the small programs we've been writing, can read what was typed on the command line. All of the command-line characters are placed in the header that DOS sets up for the program in memory—this is the header we referred to when we first discussed .COM files. The characters are stored there in a way much like the way we've set up our buffer BUFFER in DEHEXER.ASM, so we can easily convert DEHEXER.ASM to use this information. You use DEHEXER.ASM like this:

```
A>DEHEXER 12AF
```

The characters typed after the program's name on the command line can be found in a .COM file's Program Segment Prefix (PSP), starting at location CS:0080H. This first byte holds the number of characters that were typed, including the space that separated them from the program's name. In other words, for this command:

```
A>PROG abcxdef
```

PROG finds the string in the PSP at CS:0080:

```
CS:0000  →  ┌─────────────────────────────────────┐
            │                                     │
            │                                     │
CS:0080  →  │ 8 abcxdef                           │
            │                                     │
            │                                     │
            │                                     │
CS:0100  →  ├─────────────────────────────────────┤
            │         JMP    START                │
            │         -- Data Area --             │
            │ START:  The Program                 │
            │         MOV    DX,5                  │
            │                :                    │
            │                :                    │
            └─────────────────────────────────────┘
```

The area at CS:0080H looks like this:

```
CS:80H  81H  82H  83H  84H  85H  86H  87H  88H  89H
   8    ' '  'a'  'b'  'c'  'x'  'd'  'e'  'f'  0DH
```

where 'a' means the ASCII code for "a" and so on. The first byte contains the number of bytes typed (8 including the leading space) At the end is the byte 0DH, which is the ASCII code for a carriage return. This buffer always ends with the 0DH carriage return byte, and this final byte is not included in the byte count.

This information is very similar to what we have in DEHEXER.ASM, so we can easily change DEHEXER.ASM to use this buffer instead of the one we have set aside. Using this default buffer allows us to accept input without using INT 21H service 0AH.

Here's the new program:

```
CODE_SEG          SEGMENT
        ASSUME  CS:CODE_SEG, DS:CODE_SEG, ES:CODE_SEG, SS:CODE_SEG

        ORG 100H
ENTRY:  JMP DEHEXER
        ANS_STRING      DB 13, 10, 'That number in decimal is: $'
DEHEXER PROC

        MOV     CX,0
        MOV     AX,0
        MOV     BX, 85H          ←
LOOP1:  MOV     DX,0
        MOV     DL, BYTE PTR [BX]
        DEC     BX
        CMP     DL,'9'
        JLE     UNDER_A
        SUB     DL, 'A' - '0' - 10
```

```
UNDER_A:SUB     DL, '0'
        SHL     DX, CL
        ADD     AX, DX
        ADD     CX,4
        CMP     CX,16
        JL      LOOP1

        CALL    PRINT_NUM

        INT     20H
DEHEXER ENDP

PRINT_NUM       PROC
        MOV     CX,0
        MOV     BX, 10
LOOP2:  MOV     DX,0
        DIV     BX
        PUSH    DX
        INC     CX
        CMP     AX,0
        JA      LOOP2

        MOV     AH,9
        MOV     DX,OFFSET ANS_STRING
        INT     21H

        MOV     AH,2
LOOP3:  POP     DX
        ADD     DX,'0'
        INT     21H
        LOOP    LOOP3
        RET
PRINT_NUM       ENDP

CODE_SEG        ENDS

        END     ENTRY
```

Nothing's changed except that we've removed BUFFER, the prompt, and the code to type it out. Instead, we know that we will find the number of characters typed at CS:0080. At CS:0081, there is a space, and following that, the number to be converted, which must therefore end at CS:0085. In order to read that number, we load BX with 85H, not with the offset of END_NUM. From then on, the process is just the same as with the original version of DEHEXER.ASM.

We've been dealing with character strings in a limited way—by decrementing a pointer through a four-digit hexadecimal number. There are many more-sophisticated methods of working with strings in assembly language, and because of their speed and power, they are very important. We should take a look at them before we start using assembly language inside C.

The String Instructions

What a programmer regards as a string of bytes in memory is just unconnected bytes to the microprocessor. Working with such strings was a weak point in assembly language with the original Intel chips, until the string instructions were added. These instructions are as follows:

Instruction	Action	Explanation
SCASB	Scans	Scan byte string at ES:DI for byte in AL
CMPSB	Compares	Compare byte string at ES:DI to one at DS:SI
MOVSB	Moves	Move byte string byte by byte from DS:SI to ES:DI
STOSB	Stores	Store byte in AL to string at ES:DI

> Starting with the 80286, two more string instructions were added, INS (Input String from a Port) and OUTS (Output String to a Port). A port is how I/O devices are connected to the PS/2 or PC: port 60H is where data comes in from the keyboard, for example.

Each of these string instructions has two forms. One to use if your string is made up of bytes, and the other to use if your string is made up of words. For example, SCASB can be used as either SCASB or SCASW. Simply by changing the final letter—B for byte or W for word—you can tell the string instructions what type of string to operate on. Here are the word versions of the string commands:

Instruction	Action	Explanation
SCASW	Scans	Scan word string at ES:DI for word in AX
CMPSW	Compares	Compare word string at ES:DI to one at DS:SI
MOVSW	Moves	Move word string word by word from DS:SI to ES:DI
STOSW	Stores	Store word in AX to string at ES:DI

The idea of word strings is new to us. In them, each element is one word long, not just one byte long. We can store words in memory in a way similar to the method used to store bytes, except that instead of DB, we use the Pseudo-Op DW. The use of DW is close to DB, but with word-length items. Here are two examples:

```
ALL_FULL  DW 0FFFFH
 NUMBERS   DW 1234H, 5678H, 9ABCDH
```

When the assembler sees the definition of ALL_FULL, for instance, it sets aside one word (two bytes) for it. We can work with ALL_FULL in this way:

```
MOV     AX,ALL_FULL
   MOV       ALL_FULL,DX
```

But we can't do the following:

```
MOV     AL,ALL_FULL
```

ALL_FULL is defined with DW (Define Word), and AL is only an 8-bit register, so there is a type mismatch. The data types must match inside an instruction. The assembler does not place a value that is defined as byte-length (or that comes in a byte-length register) into one that is defined as word-length (or a word-length register). If you try to do so, the assembler gives you an error.

Byte and Word Strings in Memory

Storing a byte is easy with DB. Here we can do it in DEBUG:

```
-A100
0EF1:0100 DB      5
0EF1:0101
```

By dumping memory with the DEBUG D command, we can see the 5 in memory at location CS:0100:

```
-D100
          _
          v
0EF1:0100  05 EC 04 02 0F 8B E5 5D-CB 00 00 00 00 00 00 00   .......].........
0EF1:0110  00 00 2E F6 06 00 00 01-74 0E BA DA 03 EC A8 08   ........t........
0EF1:0120  74 FB BA D8 03 B0 21 EE-C3 2E F6 06 00 00 01 74   t.....!........t
0EF1:0130  06 BA D8 03 B0 29 EE C3-8C D8 8E C0 8B 3E 4C F6   .....).......>L.
0EF1:0140  8B 0E 96 F6 B0 0A FC C3-E8 ED FF 8B 1E 48 F6 2B   .............H.+
0EF1:0150  1E 58 F6 74 0D FD 4F 4F-F2 AE 83 EB 50 75 F9 47   .X.t..OO....Pu.G
0EF1:0160  47 FC C3 E8 E2 FF 89 3E-4C F6 CB E8 CA FF 2B CF   G......>L.....+.
0EF1:0170  F2 AE E3 03 EB 16 90 B8-00 00 CB E8 BA FF 3B 3E   ..............;>
```

Things are not so straightforward with DW. Here we can use DW 0102H, for example:

```
-A100
0EF1:0100 DW      0102
0EF1:0102
```

And also dump it:

```
-D100
           _  _
           V  V
OEF1:0100  02 01 04 02 0F 8B E5 5D-CB 00 00 00 00 00 00 00    .......].........
OEF1:0110  00 00 2E F6 06 00 00 01-74 0E BA DA 03 EC A8 08    ........t.........
OEF1:0120  74 FB BA D8 03 B0 21 EE-C3 2E F6 06 00 00 01 74    t.....!........t
OEF1:0130  06 BA D8 03 B0 29 EE C3-8C D8 8E C0 8B 3E 4C F6    .....)........>L.
OEF1:0140  8B 0E 96 F6 B0 0A FC C3-E8 ED FF 8B 1E 48 F6 2B    .............H.+
OEF1:0150  1E 58 F6 74 0D FD 4F 4F-F2 AE 83 EB 50 75 F9 47    .X.t..OO....Pu.G
OEF1:0160  47 FC C3 E8 E2 FF 89 3E-4C F6 CB E8 CA FF 2B CF    G......>L.....+.
OEF1:0170  F2 AE E3 03 EB 16 90 B8-00 00 CB E8 BA FF 3B 3E    ..............;>
```

You might have expected to see 01 02 in memory, not 02 01. However, 0102H is stored as 02 01 because the 80x86 *reverses* the order of the bytes in a word that it stores in memory. The high byte (01) is stored at a higher memory location. This does not affect the way you store or read words, however. If you define:

```
WORD_VARIABLE     DW          0
```

And then use the word like this:

```
MOV      WORD_VARIABLE,0102H     ← Storing
MOV      AX,WORD_VARIABLE        ← Reading
```

then AX is left with 0102H, as you'd expect. The way that the bytes of a word are stored is important only if you examine the individual bytes of a stored word in memory. We'll run into this again when we look at the internal representation of floating point numbers in C.

Now that we can set up strings in memory, we can use the string instructions with them. Those instructions assume the use of two new registers, DI and SI.

The DI and SI registers

SI and DI are two registers put aside for string operations. String manipulation is so important that both of these registers were designed to be used with them exclusively. DI stands for Destination Index, and SI stands for Source Index.

String instructions *assume* that the address of the source string is in the SI register, and that the address of the target s tring is already loaded into the DI.

> To be exact, the string instructions assume that DS:SI is set up as a pointer to the beginning of the source string, and that ES:DI is set up as a pointer to the beginning of the target string. In the 80386, string instructions can be used with *double words*; the instruction SCASB can become SCASD.

Every time you execute the instruction MOVSB, one byte is taken from the location DS:SI and copied to ES:DI. DS:SI is the *source* pointer, and ES:DI is the *destination* pointer. Also, as with all string instructions, MOVSB automatically increments the string registers it uses. In this case, the string registers are both SI and DI:

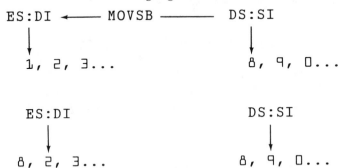

SI and DI can automatically be set to *decrement*, instead of increment, by setting the *direction flag*. Just use the instruction STD (Set Direction Flag) to do this. To clear the flag, use CLD (Clear Direction Flag). We will not use the direction flag ourselves—when programs are loaded, string commands are set to increment as the default.

Just using MOVSB by itself, however, only moves 1 byte. If you have this line in your program:

```
          MOV      AH,2
LOOP3:    POP      DX
          ADD      DX,'0'
          INT      21H
          MOVSB
          LOOP     LOOP3
          RET
```

every time the line is executed, the microprocessor would read the byte at DS:SI, makes a copy of it, places the copy at ES:DI, and then increments both DI and SI. However, MOVSB alone (as with any string instruction alone) only works on one byte or word every time it is executed. To do more, you have to use REP.

The REP Prefix

The REP Prefix can augment any string command so that it is performed a number of times. This is very useful if you want to copy a whole string of data, for example, or search a string for a matching byte.

REP stands for repeat: It repeats a string operation a number of times. This number is set by the value in the CX register. For example,

```
        MOV     CX,5
REP     MOVSB
```

copies 5 bytes, in order, from DS:SI to ES:DI. If the bytes at those locations look like this to begin with:

```
DS:SI                           ES:DI
|                               |
↓                               ↓
0, 1, 2, 3, 4, 5, 6...  9, 9, 9, 9, 9, 9...
```

they look this way after REP MOVSB (where CX is 5 to start):

```
            DS:SI                           ES:DI
            |                               |
            ↓                               ↓
0, 1, 2, 3, 4, 5, 6...  0, 1, 2, 3, 4, 9...
```

There are three forms of REP: REP, REPE, and REPNE. REP repeats the string instruction CX times, REPE means Repeat While Equal (up to CX times), and REPNE means Repeat While Not Equal (also up to CX times). For example, a popular string instruction is REPNE SCASB—Repeat While Not Equal, Scan for Byte. It scans a string at ES:DI up to CX bytes for a match to the byte in AL. It keeps scanning while the bytes do not equal the byte in AL; if a match is found, the instruction terminates.

To use REPNE SCASB to find a byte, load ES:DI with the address of the string to be scanned, put the byte to be found in AL, and set CX to the number of bytes in the string. Then just give the instruction REPNE SCASB:

```
ZEBRA_STRING        DB "There is a zebra over there."
                    :
        MOV         DI, OFFSET ZEBRA_STRING
        MOV         CX,28   ;The number of bytes in the string.
        MOV         AL,"z"  ;The byte we want to find.
REPNE   SCASB       ←
```

When the instruction finishes, one of two things happens: either a match is found to the byte in AL, or we run out of bytes to compare

(CX becomes 0). In order to check if we found a match or reached the end, REPNE SCASB is often followed by the JCXZ instruction, which stands for Jump if CX is Zero:

> JCXZ is designed for just such cases—there is no JBXZ instruction, for example.]

```
ZEBRA_STRING      DB "There is a zebra over there."
                  :
        MOV       DI, OFFSET ZEBRA_STRING
        MOV       CX,28    ;The number of bytes in the string.
        MOV       AL,"z"   ;The byte we want to find.
REPNE   SCASB
        JCXZ REACHED_END
FOUND_MATCH:               ;We found z.
```

If we do not jump to the label REACHED_END in this example, we've found a match to the byte we were looking for, "z". In this case, ES:DI points at the byte just *after* the match.

We've seen how SCASB and MOVSB work. The STOSB instruction, Store Byte, just makes duplicates of the byte in AL and stores them at location ES:DI, and then increments DI. STOSW does the same thing with the word in AX, and DI is incremented by 2 to point to the next word in memory. You can use both forms with the REP prefixes.

The CMPSB string instruction is more interesting. With it, you can compare two strings to see where they start matching (using REPNE CMPSB) or where they start differing (using REPE CMPSB). Here's an example:

```
CODE_SEG        SEGMENT
        ASSUME  CS:CODE_SEG, DS:CODE_SEG, SS:CODE_SEG, ES:CODE_SEG
ORG     100H
ENTRY:  JMP     START
DATA_1  DB      "A rose by any other name would smell as sweet."
DATA_2  DB      "A nose by any other name would smell as sweetly."
MSG     DB      "The strings started differing at character $"
START:  MOV     DI,OFFSET DATA_1
        MOV     SI,OFFSET DATA_2
        MOV     CX,47   ;The length of DATA_1.
REPE    CMPSB
        JCXZ    EXIT    ;If we ran out of bytes to compare, strings matched.
        MOV     DX,OFFSET MSG   ;Mismatch must have been found -- print MSG.
        MOV     AH,9
        INT     21H
        SUB     DI,OFFSET DATA_1        ;Like subtracting pointers.
        ADD     DI,'0'
        MOV     DX,DI   ;Get ASCII place number in DL for INT 21H service 2.
```

```
        MOV     AH,2
        INT     21H      ;Print place number out.
EXIT:   INT     20H

CODE_SEG        ENDS
        END     ENTRY
```

We use REPE CMPSB (Repeat While Equal, Compare String Byte) to compare two strings, DATA_1 and DATA_2. This instruction keeps comparing bytes until two bytes are unequal. Depending upon how the instruction stopped (i.e., did we run out of bytes to compare?), we know where the mismatch starts, and can print that location out. The result of this program is:

```
The strings started differing at character 3
```

The 80x86's string instructions are fast. If you're a programmer, they represent a great asset of the machine—when you want to use them, just drop into assembly language and pick up some speed. To learn how to do that, we have to learn how to interface assembly language to C.

9

Interfacing Assembly Language to C

Now we put C and assembly language together for the first time. There are two main ways to do this—using inline assembly language, and linking assembly language modules into your program. Both have their uses. We'll explore both of them in this chapter, beginning with inline assembly language.

Inline Assembly Language

Using inline assembly language used to be very primitive. In fact, in some languages, you had to type in the actual bytes of machine code (this was called *inline code*). However, as speed became more important, languages started to improve their support of inline assembly language. Now, in the Microsoft C or Turbo C series, you can do practically anything that you can do in normal assembly language.

There is one notable exception: You can't use the data Pseudo-Ops (like DB or DW) in Microsoft C. (You can in Turbo C.) Besides that, however, you are free to do most things.

In Turbo C, you have to include this line in your program before you can use assembly language:

```
#pragma inline
```

In addition, you have to use TASM, Turbo Assembler. The Turbo C compiler actually creates a file out of your assembly language instructions, assembles it with TASM.EXE, and links the .OBJ file in. When writing inline assembly language with Turbo C, you have to preface every assembly language line with the letters asm, like this:

```
#pragma inline
main()
```

```
{
asm mov dl, 90
asm mov ah, 2
asm int 21h
}
```

This is our earlier program PRINTZ.EXE—that's all there is to it. You can create the file PRINTZ.EXE with the command:

```
F:\>tcc printz.c
```

When you run it, PRINTZ.EXE prints "Z", just as the straight assembly language version did. Using inline assembly language is easy—just put the assembly code into your C source file and mark it appropriately.

Under Microsoft C, you can preface a whole block with the keyword _asm, like this:

```
main()
{
_asm{
mov dl, 90
mov ah, 2
int 21h
    }
}
```

Then, just use the C compiler as usual. For example, to create PRINTZ.EXE, you might use Quick C this way:

```
F:\>qcl printz.c
```

Turbo C and Microsoft C are very close when it comes to inline code, except that Microsoft C doesn't let you use the define-data Pseudo-Ops. Instead, you define data in the normal C fashion (as C variables) and then reference it in the assembly language code. Let's see exactly how that's done.

Using Data in Inline Assembly Language

Here we write an example program to print out the line "Hello, world.\n" using inline assembly language.

We start this way:

```
main()
```

```
{
char *MSG "Hello, world.\n$";


}
```

We are setting up a string of type char in memory. Notice that we end it with $ so that we can use it with the string-printing DOS service, service 9. Even though the actual string is terminated with a null byte, we only print out characters to the $.

Now we can set up our inline code (under Microsoft C):

```
main()
{
char *MSG "Hello, world.\n$";

_asm{
mov dx,MSG
mov ah,9
int 21h
      }
}
```

That's it. MSG is a pointer—that is, the address of the beginning of string MSG in memory—so we omit the Pseudo-Op OFFSET when using it. We do not use the instruction mov dx, offset MSG, as we would in an assembly language program. The normal assembly language program looks like this:

```
CODE_SEG           SEGMENT
          ORG 100H
ENTRY:    JMP HELLO
          MSG DB "Hello, world.",13,10,"$"
HELLO     PROC NEAR
          MOV DX,OFFSET MSG  ←
          MOV AH,9
          INT 21H
          INT 20H
HELLO     ENDP

CODE_SEG ENDS
          END ENTRY
```

With that understanding, the use of character strings is easy. Here, for example, is our entire DEHEXER.ASM (which doesn't use any data except for character strings), written as DEHEXER.C under Microsoft C:

```c
main()
{
char *PROMPT = "Type in a 4 digit hex number:$";
char *BUFFER = "\5       ";
char *ANS_STRING = "\nThat number in decimal is: $";
char *END_NUM = BUFFER + 5;

_asm{
DEHEXER:MOV      AH,9
        MOV      DX, PROMPT
        INT      21H
        MOV      AH,0AH
        MOV      DX, BUFFER
        INT      21H

        MOV      CX, 0
        MOV      AX,0
        MOV      BX, END_NUM
LOOP1:  MOV      DX,0
        MOV      DL, [BX]
        DEC      BX
        CMP      DL,'9'
        JLE      UNDER_A
        SUB      DL, 'A' - '0' - 10
UNDER_A:SUB      DL, '0'
        SHL      DX, CL
        ADD      AX, DX
        ADD      CX,4
        CMP      CX,16
        JL       LOOP1

        MOV      CX,0
        MOV      BX, 10
LOOP2:  MOV      DX,0
        DIV      BX
        PUSH     DX
        INC      CX
        CMP      AX,0
        JA       LOOP2

        MOV      AH,9
        MOV      DX, ANS_STRING
        INT      21H

        MOV      AH,2
LOOP3:  POP      DX
        ADD      DX,'0'
        INT      21H
        LOOP     LOOP3

        }

}
```

You can compile this as you would compile any normal C program. Here's the same program written in Turbo C. (Notice that you must define the labels in the code as normal C labels.)

```
main()
{
char *PROMPT = "Type in a 4 digit hex number:$";
char *BUFFER = "\5        ";
char *END_NUM = BUFFER + 5;
char *ANS_STRING = "\n\rThat number in decimal is: $";
#pragma inline
asm         MOV      AH,9
asm         MOV      DX, PROMPT
asm         INT      21H
asm         MOV      AH,0AH
asm         MOV      DX, BUFFER
asm         INT      21H
asm
asm         MOV      CX, 0
asm         MOV      AX,0
asm         MOV      BX, END_NUM
LOOP1:
asm         MOV      DX,0
asm         MOV      DL, [BX]
asm         DEC      BX
asm         CMP      DL,'9'
asm         JLE      UNDER_A
asm         SUB      DL, 'A' - '0' - 10
UNDER_A:
asm         SUB      DL, '0'
asm         SHL      DX, CL
asm         ADD      AX, DX
asm         ADD      CX,4
asm         CMP      CX,16
asm         JL       LOOP1
asm
asm         MOV      CX,0
asm         MOV      BX, 10
LOOP2:
asm         MOV      DX,0
asm         DIV      BX
asm         PUSH     DX
asm         INC      CX
asm         CMP      AX,0
asm         JA       LOOP2
asm
asm         MOV      AH,9
asm         MOV      DX, ANS_STRING
asm         INT      21H
```

```
asm
asm             MOV       AH,2
LOOP3:
asm             POP       DX
asm             ADD       DX,'0'
asm             INT       21H
asm             LOOP      LOOP3
asm
}
```

The way you use other types of data is similar. The usual method is to simply declare the data in C format so the C part of the code can use it as well, and then refer to it in your inline assembly language as you would if you had declared it with DB or DW.

C Data Formats

However, you must know the data format that C uses for its variables. A short int, for example, is simply a 16-bit word, so we can write the following program:

```
main()
{
int apples = 5;               ←
int oranges = 3;              ←
char *msg2 = "Total fruit: $";
_asm{
mov       dx,msg2
mov       ah,9
int       21h
mov       dx,apples
add       dx,oranges
add       dx,'0'
mov       ah,2
int       21h
    }
}
```

Here we define two ints: apples and oranges. They are just two one-word variables, so those declarations are just the same as they would be if we used the DW Pseudo-Op. We can read the value in apples like this: mov dx,apples. We add this value to the value in the variable oranges and print out the sum.

The result of the program is the output "Total fruit: 8". Our inline assembly language code can use the variables just as the C part of the code can—if we know the data format.

We can also use byte-long values, instead of word-long ones (note the use of DL, not DX):

```
main()
{
char apples = 5;            ←
char oranges = 3;           ←
char *msg2 = "Total fruit: $";
_asm{
mov     dx,msg2
mov     ah,9
int     21h
mov     dl,apples          ←
add     dl,oranges         ←
add     dl,'0'             ←
mov     ah,2
int     21h
        }
}
```

Here we declare apples and oranges as variables of type char, which is the same as declaring them with DB.

We can also look at unsigned long int format. We already know that long (two-word) numbers (such as 12345678H are stored with high and low words reversed *and* with high and low bytes reversed. In other words, 12345678H is stored as 78H 56H 34H 12H.

This means that our number for apples, if stored as a long double, looks like this: 05 00 00 00. Since that's the case, we can just load apples into dx again, because 05 00 (the low word) is the word that we are interested in, and that is the first word in memory. (If we want the high word, we can use a pointer to it.)

```
main()
{
long apples = 5;           ←
long oranges = 3;          ←
char *msg2 = "Total fruit: $";
_asm{
mov     dx,msg2
mov     ah,9
int     21h
mov     dx,apples          ←
add     dx,oranges         ←
```

```
add       dx,'0'
mov       ah,2
int       21h
      }
}
```

For signed integers, two's complement notation is used. For example, in this program:

```
main()
{
int apples = -1;                    ←
int oranges = 3;
char *msg2 = "Total fruit: $";
_asm{
mov       dx,msg2
mov       ah,9
int       21h
mov       dx,apples
add       dx,oranges
add       dx,'0'
mov       ah,2
int       21h
      }
}
```

the number in apples, -1, is stored as FFFFH. Since we already know how to use two's complement, we are prepared for this format.

As you can see, working with integer formats is not difficult. We can read from memory and write to it without difficulty. Floating point formats, however, are more difficult to decipher.

We can store a floating point number like this:

```
main()
{
float val = 10.5;                   ←
          :
          :
}
```

That looks easy enough—but what is the internal representation of such a floating point number?

If we dig into the .EXE file, we find that our number 10.5 is stored as 41280000H. Where did it come from? The format for floating point numbers is complex. A number such as 32.1 is just $3 \times 10^1 + 2 \times 10^0 + 1 \times 10^{-1}$. On the other hand, the computer is a binary machine, which means that it uses base 2, so a number such as 10.5 must be stored as

$1x2^3 + 1x2^1 + 1x2^{-1}$, which is 1010.1, where the point is a binary point. It is possible to store any number in binary that can be stored in decimal, but it takes more places. For instance, 0.75 can be broken down into 1/2 + 1/4, or $2^{-1} + 2^{-2}$, so .75 = .11B.

The numbers stored as floats are all *normalized*, which means they appear with the binary point near the beginning; so 1010.1 appears as: $1.0101x2^3$. To expand this, just move the binary point three places to the right, resulting in 1010.1 again. You can see that the first digit in any normalized binary number is always 1. Under C floating point format, the leading 1 is *implicit*. In other words, all that is stored of the *significand* is 0101. The exponent is still 3—but to make matters even more complex, all exponents are stored after being added to some offset or *bias*.

For a float, this bias is 7FH, or 127. For doubles, this number is 3FFH, or 1023. In other words, if the number 1010.1B is going to be stored as a float, the exponent is 3 + 127 = 130 = 82H. Finally, the first bit of any floating point number is the *sign* bit. Floating point numbers are NOT stored in two's complement notation. If the sign bit is 1, the number is negative; if it is 0, the number is positive—that's the only distinction between positive and negative numbers. The float format looks like this:

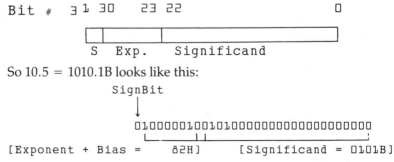

So 10.5 = 1010.1B looks like this:

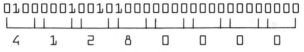

This can be made into hexadecimal by grouping every four binary digits together:

```
01000001001010000000000000000000
L_ll_ll_ll_ll_ll_ll_ll_l
 4  1  2  8  0  0  0  0
```

So 10.5 is stored as 41280000H. In fact, due to the the 80x86's method of storing low bytes first inside a word and then storing low words first, 10.5 actually shows up in memory as 00H 00H 28H 41H. These bytes are a far cry from 10.5. If you are going to work with floating point numbers, the first thing you should do is write a function to translate floating point format into something you can use.

The format for doubles is this:

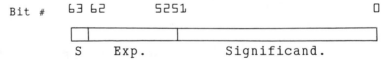

To use this format, you have to write a translating function as well. It's worth noting that this floating point format is the same format used by the 80x87 co-processors, so you can interface with them easily. Also, a number of library functions are provided with the Microsoft assembler (in the IBMUTIL library) that translate to and from floating point format.

Working directly with variables provides one way to communicate with the C program, but often you don't know the names of the specific variables used in the program. For example, you might be writing some speedy assembly language code to replace a ponderous standard C library function. In that case, all you'll have are the parameters passed to you. And now we'll pick them right off the Stack.

Passing Parameters

Let's say we want to write a C function in inline assembly language without passing any parameters. We could write this program:

```
char *MSG "Hello, world.\n$";

main()
{
print_msg();      ←
}

print_msg()      ←
{
_asm{
mov dx,MSG
mov ah,9
int 21h
    }
}
```

That is easy enough. (Notice that we make MSG a global variable so print_msg() can have access to it.) In this way, we can write specialized functions in assembly language—nothing can beat assembly language for tight code.

But what if we want to pass a parameter to that function? What if, for example, we want to change our PRINTZ function to print_char()? In this case, we call print_char() with an argument, like this: print_char('Z');. The question becomes: What happens to the function's argument?

To answer this question, we have to understand C's *calling convention*.

Calling Conventions

High-level languages pass parameters to subroutines and functions on the Stack. To interact with high-level languages, we have to pick these parameters off the Stack. If we have a function named summer(), which just sums two numbers (summer(3,2) returns 5, for example), then the high-level language places the parameters 3 and 2 onto the Stack before calling the address it has for summer().

Different languages do this differently. A calling convention indicates the way that a higher-level language passes parameters to routines that it calls. It specifies these things: the order parameters are pushed in, how they are pushed (as addresses or as immediate values), and how to reset the Stack afterwards. To successfully interface to C, we have to mimic what it might expect from its own library of routines.

Some languages push parameters in the order you see them, and some in reverse order. Some languages (such as FORTRAN) don't push the values 3 and 2 at all but, rather, push their addresses. Also, at the end of the call, when we are about to return, some languages demand that the Stack be reset in the proper way. In BASIC, FORTRAN, and Pascal, this means that after returning to the high-level language, the Stack should be set the way it was before the parameters were pushed for the call.

The C language, however, takes care of this for us. When linking to C programs, we just end our function with the assembly language instruction RET, for return. This information all comes together in the calling convention table. (As you can see, no calling convention matches any other.)

Language	Parameters Pushed	Parameters Passed	Return Type
BASIC	In order	As offset addresses	RET #
FORTRAN	In order	As FAR addresses	RET #
C	In REVERSE order	As values	RET
Pascal	In order	As values	RET #

[Note: Where RET # is used, # equals the total size in bytes of all pushed parameters.]

Similarly, this table indicates how the process of parameter passing works—whether parameters are passed by address or by their actual value.

Language	Near References	Far References	By Value
BASIC	Everything		
FORTRAN		Everything	
C	Near Arrays	Far Arrays	Everything else
Pascal	VAR, CONST	VARS, CONSTS	Everything else

C parameters are always passed by value (not as addresses, as is the case with FORTRAN or BASIC), except for arrays, which are passed by reference (i.e., with a pointer). The array reference is the address of the first element of the array. It's either 2 or 4 bytes long, depending upon the pointer size in the memory model used. Even structures are passed by value—the last word is pushed first, and so on, down to the first word. (The C calling convention also differs in that it pushes the values to pass in *reverse* order.)

Let's give this a try. In our program with the print_msg() function:

```
char *MSG "Hello, world.\n$";

main()
{
print_msg();      ←
}

print_msg()       ←
{
_asm{
mov dx,MSG
mov ah,9
int 21h
    }
}
```

there are no parameters to be passed. That means that the Stack when we arrive at print_msg() looks like this:

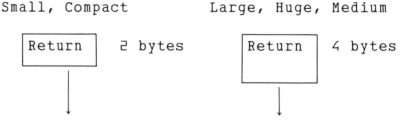

Small, Compact   Large, Huge, Medium

Return   2 bytes   Return   4 bytes

The size of the return address pushed on the Stack depends upon the memory model used in the C program. In the Large, Huge, and

Medium models, code can be more that one segment long, so the return address is 4 bytes (2 words). The downward-pointing arrows are there to remind us that the Stack grows downwards in memory.

Passing Char or Int Parameters

Let's change our example so that we pass two char parameters:

```
main()
{
print_2char('A','Z');     ←
}

print_2char(a,b)     ←
char a,b;
{
_asm{
    :
    :
    }
}
```

This time, we pass the two parameters ASCII 65 ('A') and 90 ('Z'). The Stack arrives at print_2char() like this:

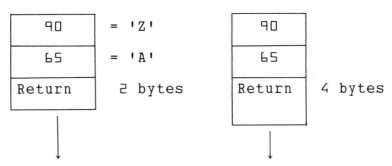

Note that C pushes the parameters in reverse order—first, the "Z" was pushed, then 'A'. Notice also that each parameter takes up a full word—you cannot push byte values.

In order to pick these parameters from the stack, our strategy is the same one that library routines normally use. Instead of actually popping parameters off the Stack, we make a copy of the Stack Pointer register (SP) in the BP register, and set up a *stack frame*.

The SP register is set aside for use exclusively with the Stack. The Stack has a segment register too, named SS. At all times, SS:SP points to the current word on the Stack. BP, an alternate Stack pointer, can be used as a pointer like this: MOV AX,[BP]. We are using the BP register, so the segment register is taken to be the SS register. We can even use instructions such as : MOV AX,[BP + 8].

When we make a copy of SP in BP and refer to the Stack with expressions such as [BP + 8], we are setting up a *Stack frame*. We can refer to any location on the stack. As the program executes, the Stack may be used and SP changes, but our original copy, in BP, does not change. It is be safe to read from the stack with BP until we return to the calling function.

When control is passed to a function, the first thing Microsoft C does is to set up a stack frame. If we just have this much code:

```
main()
{
print_2char('A','Z');
}

print_2char(a,b)
char a,b;
{
_asm{
}
}
```

we can already compile it and unassemble it to give this for the (seemingly empty) function print_2char():

```
_print_2char
5AA1:0037 55              PUSH    BP
5AA1:0038 8BEC            MOV     BP,SP
5AA1:003B B80000          MOV     AX,0000
5AA1:003D E87602          CALL    __chkstk (02B6)
5AA1:0040 56              PUSH    SI
5AA1:0041 57              PUSH    DI
                          ← function body normally goes here.
5AA1:0042 5F              POP     DI
5AA1:0043 5E              POP     SI
5AA1:0044 8BE5            MOV     SP,BP
5AA1:0046 5D              POP     BP
5AA1:0047 C3              RET
```

This is not code that we wrote; this is code that Microsoft C has already put in. Before the function body is even entered, as you can see, Microsoft C pushes BP, SI, and DI. These three registers are pushed because if the function we are about to enter changes their values, the calling function might be disrupted when we return. In general, a function should preserve the values it finds in the registers, unless it is returning data in some specific register.

Of course, these three pushes add more layers to the Stack. Before we get control in the inline assembly language for print_2char(), the Stack looks like this:

`Small, Compact`   `Large, Huge, Medium`

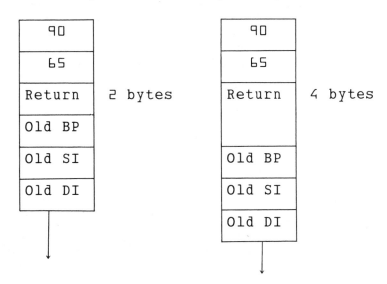

Now we can take over. We load BP with the value of SP:

```
main()
{
print_2char('A','Z');
}

print_2char(a,b)
char a,b;
{
_asm{
mov      bp,sp     ←


    }
}
```

Now we can refer to parameters on the Stack. Even if more items are pushed, the value in BP does not change—it still points to a particular location on the Stack. We have established our Stack frame, and we can pick off our parameters from the Stack like this:

Small, Compact   Large, Huge, Medium

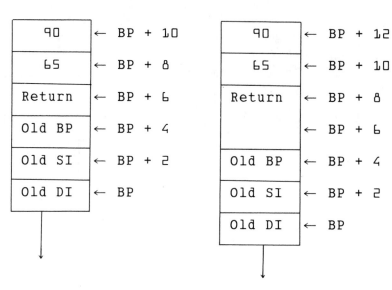

Here we assume that the program was compiled under the Small model. When we get control, parameter 1 is referred to as [BP + 8], and parameter 2 as [BP + 10]. Now we can easily pick the parameters off the Stack and complete our program:

```
main()
{
print_2char('A','Z');
}

print_2char(a,b)
char a,b;
{
_asm{
mov      bp,sp
mov      ah,2
mov      dx,[bp+8]          ←
int      21h
mov      dx,[bp+10]         ←
int      21h
        }
}
```

We just read the two parameters, [bp + 8] and [bp + 10], and print them out.

The Turbo C version is close, but not exactly the same. The difference is that before giving you control in a function, Turbo C does not push DI and SI. This means that the Stack looks like this:

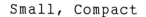

`Small, Compact`   `Large, Huge, Medium`

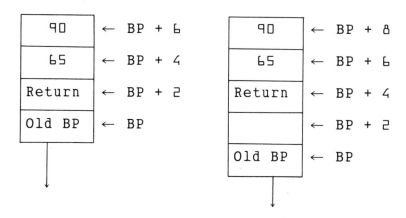

All of our previous Stack locations have to be adjusted by 4 bytes. Here is the Turbo C version of the same program:

```
                main()
            {
            print_2char('A','Z');
            }

            print_2char(a,b)
            char a,b;
            {
            #pragma inline
asm         mov     bp,sp
asm         mov     ah,2
asm         mov     dx,[bp+4]    ←
asm         int     21h
asm         mov     dx,[bp+6]    ←
asm         int     21h
            }
```

It's the same for passing integers as for chars. In fact, when you pass a char, it is upgraded to an int because you can't push just a byte. We pick parameters off the Stack one word at a time, and it is the same for integers.

A Better Way

Many times, programmers will want to pick values off the Stack, as we have done. However, sometimes you don't have to go to that length. For example, since we use word-length variables here, we can refer to them as a C function would:

```
main()
{
print_2char('A','Z');
}

print_2char(a,b)
char a,b;
{
_asm{
mov      ah,2
mov      dx,0
mov      dl,a      ←
int      21h
mov      dx,0
mov      dl,b      ←
int      21h
}
}
```

| Note that we zero DX first, to make sure that DL is loaded properly. |

Here, we don't need to pick parameters off the Stack. We just move a or b into DL. Here's the same program in Turbo C:

```
              main()
              {
print_2char('A','Z');
}

print_2char(a,b)
char a,b;
{
▽pragma inline
asm          mov      bp,sp
asm          mov      ah,2
asm          mov      dx,0
asm          mov      dl,a      ←
asm          int      21h
asm          mov      dx,0
asm          mov      dl,b      ←
asm          int      21h
}
```

Even though you should know how to use the Stack for more complex arguments, it's good to know that you can also find the arguments this way as well. If you're not doing anything very complex, this way is much easier.

Passing Longs

It makes sense that we can pass one-byte or one-word parameters easily by pushing them. But what if we need to push more than one word? For example, what happens in this dum() function:

```
main()
{
long numb = 0xaaaabbbb;
dum(numb);
}
dum(long a)
{
}
```

when we enter it? This time, C has to push a long value (two words) onto the Stack. It pushes the high word first, followed by the low word. Then it pushes the return address.

In Microsoft C, BP, SI, and DI are all pushed before you get control in the inline function. Here's how the Stack looks, by memory model:

Small, Compact   Large, Huge, Medium

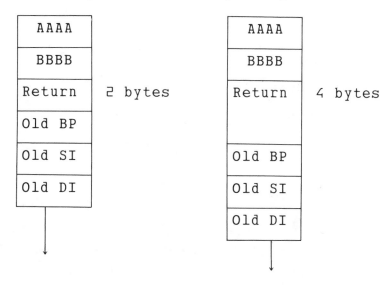

The top word of the long variable numb is highest in memory, and the low word is just below it. Here are the offsets we can use for Microsoft C:

`Small, Compact`   `Large, Huge, Medium`

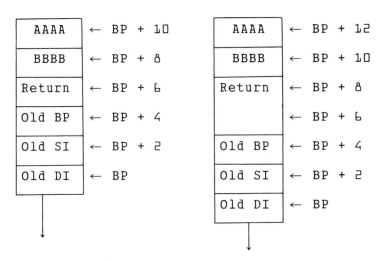

To put the long integer passed into the DX:AX register pair, all we do is this (in the Small or Compact models):

```
main()
{
long numb = 0xaaaabbbb;

dum(numb);
}

dum(long a)
{
_asm{
        mov     bp,sp
        mov     dx,[bp+10]          ←
        mov     ax,[bp+12]          ←
        :
        :
        :

    }
}
```

In Turbo C, we don't have to worry about having SI and DI already pushed. Here is the corresponding program:

```
main()
{
long numb = Oxaaaabbbb;

dum(numb);
}

dum(long a)
{
#pragma inline
asm          mov          bp,sp
asm          mov          dx,[bp+6]        ←
asm          mov          ax,[bp+8]        ←
                          :
                          :
}
```

It turns out that we can read long parameters the easy way here, too. The number passed to our function is a long value—however, we can convert it to two one-word values for use in our assembly language code:

```
main()
{
long numb = Oxaaaabbbb;

dum(numb);
}

dum(long a)
{
int ahigh, alow;

alow = (int) a;                    ←
ahigh = (int) a >> 16;             ←

_asm{
        mov          dx,ahigh         ←
        mov          ax,alow          ←
                     :
                     :
     }
}
```

We put the low word into the variable alow by using a typecast of int, and then load the high word by first shifting the long variable a down by 16 places (so the high word becomes the low word). Then we refer to those variables in our inline code. We can do the same in Turbo C:

```
main()
{
long numb = 0xaaaabbbb;
dum(numb);
}
dum(long a)
{
int ahigh, alow;
alow = (int) a;
ahigh = (int) a >> 16;

#pragma inline
asm          mov       bp,sp
asm          mov       dx,ahigh
asm          mov       ax,alow
                :
                :
                :
      }
}
```

Again, we should let C handle the details of manipulating the Stack if we can.

Passing Arrays, Pointers, and Structures

With arrays and pointers, things become a little more complex, depending upon the memory model. Array names are passed as pointers, of course, but the size of a pointer depends on the model in which the C program is compiled. Here is the data pointer size and return address size (in words) by memory model:

Table 9.1   Data Pointer and Return Address Size (Words)

	Small	Medium	Compact	Large	Huge
Data Pointer Size:	1	1	2	2	2
Return Address Size:	1	2	1	2	2

This means that our Stack frame looks different for all models when we pass a pointer. Let's look at this example:

```
main()
{
char array[5];
   :
```

```
sort5(array);
    :
}
```

When we reach the inline code in function sort5(), how does the Stack look after we set up our stack frame and are ready to take off the pointer array? Depending upon the model, it looks like this in Microsoft C. (Neglect the SI and DI pushes for Turbo C.)

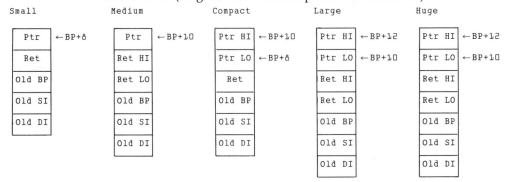

As before, we can pick the parameters off as needed.

C has a very easy method of working with structures—the whole structure is passed. C starts by pushing the last word, and keeps working backwards until it reaches the first. If your function expects a structure as a parameter, you have to know exactly how long the structure is. Then you have to read the structure, word by word, from the Stack. Because the last word is pushed first, the word order of the structure is inverted on the Stack. Often, it's easier to make the structure global than to pass it to a function yourself.

If you want to let C handle the details of Stack manipulation, you are responsible for isolating the high word of the pointer, as well as the low word. This can be done before you enter the inline assembly language. In the inline code, you have to load those words into the appropriate segment and offset registers.

Passing Floats and Doubles

Floating point format is a little trickier. First of all, all floats are upgraded to doubles before being passed to functions. Secondly, as we have seen, floating point and double-precision numbers are stored in a complex format. When your function is called with a floating point parameter, you have to pick 8 bytes off the Stack (because doubles are 8 bytes long). After that, you still have to convert them to a usable format. Or, you can convert them in the C program, and then use inline code. It's usually easier to work with integers.

Now that we've gained some expertise with passing parameters, how about returning values? We can read the parameters that the calling function passes to us; but we know that real functions can return values as well. That's something we can do, too—and it's much easier than reading passed parameters.

Returning Values Using Functions

Returning values is unexpectedly easy. The convention (Microsoft C, Turbo C, etc.) is to use these registers to return values from functions:

Returning	Use
char	AL
short	AL
int	AX
long	DX:AX (high word in DX, low in AX)
float	AX = Address (DX:AX for far)
double	AX = Address (DX:AX for far)
struct	AX = Address (DX:AX for far)
near pointer	AX
far pointer	DX:AX

It's very simple: Depending upon the return value expected from the function (set with the function prototype), C reads values from AL, AX, or DX:AX.

To return a byte-long value, leave the value in AL when you exit the function. If the calling function is expecting a byte-long return value, it reads that byte from AL. Word values (such as short integers) are returned in AX. Doubleword values are simply returned in DX:AX (DX = high word, AX = low word).

Let's put this to use by writing the function we referred to earlier, named summer(). This function will add two integers. We'll accept two ints, and return an int value (in AX). Here's how it looks under the Small model:

```
main()
{
printf("3 + 2 = %d",summer(3,2));
}

int summer(int a, int b)
```

```
{
_asm{
mov        ax,a
add        ax,b
      }
}
```

This program leaves the result in AX, and the result therefore becomes the function's return value. When we return to the calling function, we type out a message and the return value of summer(). Here, the program types out "3 + 2 = 5". Here's the same program under Turbo C:

```
main()
{
printf("3 + 2 = %d",summer(3,2));
}

int summer(int a, int b)
{
#pragma inline
asm mov        ax,a
asm add        ax,b
}
```

If we add two integers together, the result could be a long integer. We should adjust summer() to allow for such a result. We can return a long integer in DX:AX like this under Microsoft C:

```
unsigned long summer(int a, int b);

main()
{
unsigned int x = 50000, y = 60000;
printf("%u + %u = %lu", x, y, summer(x,y));
}

unsigned long summer(int a, int b)
{
_asm{
mov        dx,0
mov        ax,a
add        ax,b
adc        dx,0
}
}
```

and like this under Turbo C:

```
        unsigned long summer(int a, int b);

        main()
        {
        unsigned int x = 50000, y = 60000;
        printf("%u + %u = %lu", x, y, summer(x,y));
        }

        unsigned long summer(int a, int b)
        {
        #pragma inline
asm         mov     dx,0
asm         mov     ax,a
asm         add     ax,b
asm         adc     dx,0
        }
```

Here we anticipate the next chapter with the use of the instruction adc dx,0. This command makes dx equal to 1 if there is a carry from the addition, and equal to 0 otherwise. The output of this program is "50000 + 60000 = 110000".

Now we have considerable expertise in writing inline assembly language. We can use data that have been declared in C format. We can read parameters passed to us in a function. And now we can even return values. This means that we can write whole functions in pure assembly language, taking advantage of the improved speed and shortened size that such functions offer.

There is much more to interfacing assembly language to C than the use of inline assembly language. The second half of this chapter covers the other, more common technique: writing files in assembly language and linking them in as modules. This is the first step in the process of building your own library of assembly language C functions to link in your C progress.

Linking in External Files

We have to learn about linking under assembly language before we can link our own streamlined code into C. We will use a simple example—a small program that uses INT 21H service 9 (the string printer) to print out the message "Hello, world."

Just to make sure we are on solid ground, the first method used to print out "Hello, world." will be familiar. We already know how to write a program this way:

```
CODE_SEG        SEGMENT
        ASSUME  CS:CODE_SEG,DS:CODE_SEG,ES:CODE_SEG,SS:CODE_SEG
        ORG     100H
ENTER:  JMP     PRINT
        ALL_OK  DB "Hello, world.$"
PRINT   PROC    NEAR
        MOV     DX,OFFSET ALL_OK
        MOV     AH,9
        INT     21H
        INT     20H
PRINT   ENDP
CODE_SEG        ENDS
        END     ENTER
```

This works well, and it's a method we're familiar with. If we had more to do, we might want to call a subprocedure. We've also seen how this works: Both procedures are in the same file, and one calls the other. We can even put the data into the subprocedure:

```
CODE_SEG        SEGMENT
        ASSUME  CS:CODE_SEG,DS:CODE_SEG,ES:CODE_SEG,SS:CODE_SEG
        ORG     100H

ENTER:  PRINT   PROC    NEAR
        CALL    SUB_PRINT
        INT     20H
PRINT   ENDP

SUB_PRINT       PROC NEAR
        JMP     GO
        ALL_OK  DB "Hello, world.$"          ←
GO:     MOV     DX,OFFSET ALL_OK
        MOV     AH,9
        INT     21H
        RET
SUB_PRINT       ENDP
CODE_SEG        ENDS
        END     ENTER
```

When we call SUB_PRINT, the first instruction we encounter is JMP GO, which means that we pass over the data and move on to the next instructions. Putting purely local data into the procedure that uses it makes sense. If you have a lot of procedures, it's a good idea.

Linking

Now we're going to work with two files and link them together. Let's break our example up into separate files:

File 1

```
CODE_SEG        SEGMENT
        ASSUME  CS:CODE_SEG,DS:CODE_SEG,ES:CODE_SEG,SS:CODE_SEG
        ORG     100H
ENTER:
PRINT   PROC    NEAR
        CALL    SUB_PRINT
        INT     20H
PRINT   ENDP
CODE_SEG        ENDS
        END     ENTER
```

File 2

```
CODE_SEG        SEGMENT
        ASSUME  CS:CODE_SEG,DS:CODE_SEG,ES:CODE_SEG,SS:CODE_SEG
SUB_PRINT       PROC NEAR
        JMP     GO
        ALL_OK  DB "Hello, world.$"
GO:     MOV     DX,OFFSET ALL_OK
        MOV     AH,9
        INT     21H
        RET
SUB_PRINT       ENDP
CODE_SEG        ENDS
        END
```

Notice that while the code in both files is enclosed inside CODE_SEG definitions, the END ENTER statement and the ORG 100H statement are only in the first file. This is because the whole program can only have one entry point, which we call ENTER in File 1. In addition, it is clear that since we want the files to end up one after the other in memory, like this:

```
        ORG     100H
ENTER:
PRINT   PROC    NEAR
        CALL    SUB_PRINT
        INT     20H
PRINT   ENDP

SUB_PRINT       PROC NEAR
        JMP     GO
        ALL_OK  DB "Hello, world.$"
GO:     MOV     DX,OFFSET ALL_OK
        MOV     AH,9
        INT     21H
```

```
                RET
SUB_PRINT        ENDP
```

we cannot have ORG 100H in the second file.

We are not ready to link yet. The code segment in both of our files is named CODE_SEG. This is correct because we want the code from both files to end up in the same segment. On the other hand, we could not link in to a C program this way—the default name for the Code Segment there is _TEXT.

To write assembly language functions that we can link into C programs, we have to use the same segment names. Both Turbo C and Microsoft use practically the same names for segments. Here's a list of the segment names used in the standard C library functions by memory model:

Small
```
        _TEXT               SEGMENT WORD PUBLIC 'CODE'
        _DATA               SEGMENT WORD PUBLIC 'DATA'
        _BSS                SEGMENT WORD PUBLIC 'BSS'
        DGROUP              GROUP _DATA, _BSS
        ASSUME              CS:_TEXT, DS:DGROUP, ES:DGROUP
                Code pointers:      DW _TEXT:zzzz
                Data pointers:      DW DGROUP:zzzz
```

Medium
```
        module_TEXT         SEGMENT WORD PUBLIC 'CODE'
        _DATA               SEGMENT WORD PUBLIC 'DATA'
        _BSS                SEGMENT WORD PUBLIC 'BSS'
        DGROUP              GROUP _DATA, _BSS
        ASSUME              CS:_TEXT, DS:DGROUP, ES:DGROUP
                Code pointers:      DD yyyy:zzzz
                Data pointers:      DW DGROUP:zzzz
                "module" can vary since multiple code segments
                                are allowed
```

Compact
```
        _TEXT               SEGMENT WORD PUBLIC 'CODE'
        _DATA               SEGMENT WORD PUBLIC 'DATA'
        _BSS                SEGMENT WORD PUBLIC 'BSS'
        module_DATA         SEGMENT WORD PRIVATE 'DATA' (MS Only)
        DGROUP              GROUP _DATA, _BSS
        ASSUME              CS:_TEXT, DS:DGROUP, ES:DGROUP
                Code pointers:      DW _TEXT:zzzz
                Data pointers:      DD DGROUP:zzzz (Turbo)
                                    DD yyyy:zzzz   (MS)
                "module" can vary since multiple data segments
                                are allowed
```

Large
```
        module_TEXT         SEGMENT WORD PUBLIC 'CODE'
        _DATA               SEGMENT WORD PUBLIC 'DATA'
        _BSS                SEGMENT WORD PUBLIC 'BSS'
        module_DATA         SEGMENT WORD PRIVATE 'DATA' (MS Only)
        DGROUP              GROUP _DATA, _BSS
```

```
ASSUME                   CS:module_TEXT, DS:DGROUP,
                         ES:DGROUP
       Code pointers:        DD yyyy:zzzz
       Data pointers:        DD DGROUP:zzzz (Turbo)
                             DD yyyy:zzzz   (MS)
          "module" can vary since multiple code and data segments
                    are allowed
```

Huge
```
       module_TEXT       SEGMENT WORD PUBLIC 'CODE'
       module_DATA       SEGMENT WORD PUBLIC 'DATA'
       module_BSS        SEGMENT WORD PUBLIC 'BSS'
       ASSUME            CS:module_TEXT, DS:module_DATA,
                         ES:module_DATA
          Code pointers:     DD yyyy:zzzz
          Data pointers:     DD yyyy:zzzz
          "module" can vary since multiple code and data segments
                       are allowed
```

These are the actual segment declarations from the C libraries. There is a tremendous amount of information here. Program code goes into the segment of type CODE, initialized static data goes into the segment of type DATA, and unitialized static code go into the segment of type BSS (Block Started Segment).

Just keeping track of all these names, model by model, would be a difficult task. Recently, however, Microsoft introduced—and Turbo C now supports—*simplified segment directives*, which makes the whole process very simple.

Simplified Segment Directives

We can simply use these keywords to define our segments in place of the above declarations:

```
.CODE          Code
.DATA          Initialized data
.DATA?         Uninitialized data
.FARDATA       Initialized non-DGROUP data (Compact/Large/Huge)
.FARDATA?      Uninitialized non-DGROUP data (Compact/Large/Huge)
```

They are not model-dependent. The correct segment names are substituted for them when you use a particular memory model. Let's get back to our example to see how this works.

We can switch from our own segment name (CODE_SEG) to the more standard names by introducing simplified segment directives:

File 1

```
.MODEL SMALL    ←
.CODE           ←
       ORG      100H
ENTER:
```

```
PRINT     PROC     NEAR
          CALL     SUB_PRINT
          INT      20H
PRINT     ENDP
          END      ENTER
```

File 2

```
.MODEL SMALL      ←
.CODE             ←
SUB_PRINT         PROC NEAR
          JMP     GO
          ALL_OK  DB "Hello, world.$"
GO:       MOV     DX,OFFSET ALL_OK
          MOV     AH,9
          INT     21H
          RET
SUB_PRINT         ENDP
          END
```

You declare the model in an assembly language program with the
.MODEL directive. After we've declared the model to be Small with
.MODEL SMALL, the standard segment names are substituted for the
.CODE, .DATA, and .DATA? directives in our program. Since we are
making a .COM file here, we only use the Code Segment. We start
that with the directive .CODE.

You may notice that there is no corresponding .ENDCODE directive. When the end of the file is reached, the assembler terminates the
Code Segment. We don't need to include an ENDS (end segment)
Pseudo-Op. In addition, if we start to define another segment such as
.DATA (and we will later), the Code Segment is automatically ended
and the Data Segment is begun. In this way, we do not have to worry
about what the real name of these segments are. We can use our code
under any memory model, and the assembler puts in the correct code
names for us.

> If you ever want to find out the real segment address when using sim-
> plified segment directives, use the @code, @data, and @fardata
> keywords. For example, if you have use the .DATA directive, your
> data go into the data segment. If you want to load the segment ad-
> dress of the data into the AX register, use this instruction in your pro-
> gram: mov ax,@data.

In order to link the files, we have to inform the assembler that the
procedure SUB_PRINT will not be found in File 1—it will be linked in

later. We can do this with an EXTRN Pseudo-Op (much like the corresponding EXTERN instruction in C). To declare a label as EXTRN, you have to tell the assembler what kind of label it is, NEAR or FAR. This way, it can leave the proper length in the code for the address (one word or two), which the linker fills in later. An EXTRN statement might look like this:

```
EXTRN   LABEL_1:NEAR, LABEL_2:FAR
```

In addition, we have to do something we would not have to do in C—we have to declare SUB_PRINT as PUBLIC in File 2. The assembler does not save actual labels used in the program (as C does). If we want to save a label for the linker's use later, we have to explicitly do so. Here is how our new files look:

File 1

```
EXTRN   SUB_PRINT:NEAR     ←
.MODEL SMALL
.CODE
        ORG     100H
ENTER:
PRINT   PROC    NEAR
        CALL    SUB_PRINT
        INT     20H
PRINT   ENDP
        END     ENTER
```

File 2

```
PUBLIC  SUB_PRINT   ←
.MODEL SMALL
.CODE
SUB_PRINT       PROC NEAR
        JMP     GO
        ALL_OK  DB "Hello, world.$"
GO:     MOV     DX,OFFSET ALL_OK
        MOV     AH,9
        INT     21H
        RET
SUB_PRINT       ENDP
        END
```

They are all set to be linked. We can link them into one .COM file. First, we assemble FILE1.ASM and FILE2.ASM, like this:

```
C>MASM FILE1;
```

```
Microsoft (R) Macro Assembler Version 5.10
Copyright (C) Microsoft Corp 1981, 1988.  All rights reserved.

  50106 + 31315 Bytes symbol space free

      0 Warning Errors
      0 Severe  Errors

C>MASM FILE2;

Microsoft (R) Macro Assembler Version 5.10
Copyright (C) Microsoft Corp 1981, 1988.  All rights reserved.

  50260 + 31161 Bytes symbol space free

      0 Warning Errors
      0 Severe  Errors
```

Then we link them together with the program LINK:

```
C>LINK FILE1+FILE2;

Microsoft (R) Overlay Linker  Version 3.64
Copyright (C) Microsoft Corp 1983-1988.  All rights reserved.

LINK : warning L4021: no stack segment
```

This generates an .EXE file named FILE1.EXE. We can run FILE1.EXE through EXE2BIN to create the .COM file, and run the .COM file:

```
C>EXE2BIN FILE1 FILE1.COM

C>FILE1
Hello, world.
```

We've linked two files together. Using Turbo Assembler, the process is identical, except for one small detail: The label ENTER, which we use in File 1, is a reserved keyword in TASM. Instead of ENTER, we rename the label ENTER_1:

File 1

```
EXTRN    SUB_PRINT:NEAR
.MODEL SMALL
.CODE
        ORG     100H
ENTER_1:                        ←
PRINT   PROC    NEAR
        CALL    SUB_PRINT
        INT     20H
PRINT   ENDP
        END     ENTER_1         ←
```

File 2

```
PUBLIC   SUB_PRINT
.MODEL SMALL
.CODE
SUB_PRINT        PROC NEAR
        JMP      GO
        ALL_OK   DB "Hello, world.$"
GO:     MOV      DX,OFFSET ALL_OK
        MOV      AH,9
        INT      21H
        RET
SUB_PRINT        ENDP
        END
```

And we're all set. We just use TASM on both files:

```
C>TASM FILE1;
Turbo Assembler  Version 1.0  Copyright (c) 1988 by Borland International

Assembling file:    FILE1.ASM
Error messages:     None
Warning messages:   None
Remaining memory:   381k


C>TASM FILE2;
Turbo Assembler  Version 1.0  Copyright (c) 1988 by Borland International

Assembling file:    FILE2.ASM
Error messages:     None
Warning messages:   None
Remaining memory:   381k
```

And then TLINK with the same syntax that we used with LINK:

```
C>TLINK FILE1+FILE2;

Turbo Link  Version 2.0  Copyright (c) 1987, 1988 Borland International
Warning: no stack
```

Finally, we use EXE2BIN and run the program:

```
C>EXE2BIN FILE1 FILE1.COM

C>FILE1
Hello, world.
```

Now that we've seen how to link assembly language to assembly language, let's look at the process of linking assembly language to C.

Linking Assembly Language Functions to C

This program calls a function named vidmode(), which we are going to write in assembly language:

```
extern int vidmode();

main()
{
printf("The video mode is: %d\n", vidmode());
}
```

The vidmode() function is declared as external with the line extern int vidmode(). (vidmode() returns an integer value.) We will pass no parameters to vidmode().

Let's assume that the C program was compiled under the Small or Compact model (and therefore the call to vidmode() is a near call). Here's how the Stack looks when we get into vidmode() (after the initial PUSH BP that we put in to set up our Stack frame):

```
┌──────────┐
│  Return  │   ←  BP+2
├──────────┤
│  Old BP  │   ←  BP
└──────────┘
```

Since this is a near call, there is only one word (the return offset address) pushed onto the stack by the C call instruction.

We can't just write an assembly language procedure for vidmode(). The C naming convention for library functions is to use an underscore before the name of the procedure to be linked in, like this: _vidmode. Our function returns the current video mode in AX, and this is the way the assembly language program might look. (Keep in mind that we have to use _vidmode, not vidmode()). We can use the simplified directives to make everything easy:

```
.MODEL   SMALL
.CODE
         PUBLIC   _vidmode          ;For C Interface
_vidmode         PROC
         PUSH     BP
         MOV      BP,SP

         PUSH     SI
```

```
            PUSH    DI
            PUSH    DS

            MOV     AH,0FH   ←
            INT     10H      ←
            MOV     AH,0     ←

            POP     DS
            POP     DI
            POP     SI

            POP     BP
            RET
_vidmode    ENDP
            END
```

We find the video mode with service 0FH of BIOS INT 10H (described in the Appendix). The details of this service are unimportant here—it just returns the video mode information in AX, and we can return that information in the same register. Notice that we are very careful to preserve and restore the value in all other registers so as not to disturb the calling program. This is a procedure you should follow—if your function is going to change a value in a register, you should restore the register when you return (unless you return a value in the register, of course).

Also notice that we have left the word _vidmode in small letters. This is because C is case sensitive, and from our C source code, it will expect to find the _vidmode label in small letters. The assembler, however, makes all PUBLIC labels into capital letters by default, unless we use the -mx switch (with both the Microsoft Assembler and Turbo Assembler). If you use this switch, the assembler does not change the case of PUBLIC labels.

We can link VIDMODE.OBJ into our C program. For example, under Microsoft Quick C and MASM, the process would look like this:

```
F:\>qcl -c vid.c;
Microsoft (R) Quick C Compiler Version 2.00
Copyright (c) Microsoft Corp 1987-1989. All rights reserved.


F:\>masm -mx vidmode;
Microsoft (R) Macro Assembler Version 5.10
Copyright (C) Microsoft Corp 1981, 1988.  All rights reserved.

  50020 + 336953 Bytes symbol space free

    0 Warning Errors
    0 Severe  Errors
```

We have given our files different names—VID.C and
VIDMODE.ASM—so the .OBJ files do not have the same name. First,
we compile with the -c option so that Quick C does not call the linker.
Next, we assemble VIDMODE with the -mx option. Now we can link
to create the .EXE file:

```
F:\>link vid+vidmode;
Microsoft (R) QuickC Linker  Version 4.06
Copyright (C) Microsoft Corp 1984-1989.  All rights reserved.
```

That's all we need to do. The linker fills the CALL instruction in VID.C
with the address of _vidmode in VIDMODE.ASM. When run, the
program calls _vidmode, which returns the video mode, and the program prints it out.

Under Turbo C, the process is the same. Let's combine the compila-
tion and linking into one step with TCC.EXE. First, we assemble
VIDMODE:

```
F:\>tasm -mx vidmode;
Turbo Assembler  Version 1.0  Copyright (c) 1988 by Borland International

Assembling file:    VIDMODE.ASM
Error messages:     None
Warning messages:   None
Remaining memory:   381k
```

Then we compile VID.C and link VIDMODE.OBJ in at the same time:

```
F:\>tcc vid.c vidmode.obj
Turbo C  Version 2.0  Copyright (c) 1987, 1988 Borland International
vid.c:
Turbo Link  Version 2.0  Copyright (c) 1987, 1988 Borland International

        Available memory 330906
```

And that's all there is to it. VID.EXE works as before.

Passing Parameters

The VIDMODE example is less than realistic—usually, we will want to
pass some parameters. To link in our function SUMMER() to add two
integers, this is the way it might look:

```
extern int SUMMER(int,int);

main()
{
```

```
        printf("3 + 2 = %d\n",SUMMER(3,2));
}
```

We leave the function name in capital letters to show that you don't have to use the -mx option when assembling. When assembling, the label _summer is capitalized by the assembler by default, and that is what we want if C is looking for _SUMMER, not _summer.

C pushes parameters in reverse order, so the 2 is pushed first, followed by the 3. This is how the stack looks when we start to use it in SUMMER(). (We assume that the C program was compiled as Small or Compact, so the return address is only one word long.)

2	← BP+6
3	← BP+4
Return	← BP+2
Old BP	← BP

In the case of Large, Medium, or Huge memory models, the return address is 4 bytes long—which means that the locations of all parameters are shifted up by 2 bytes:

2	← BP+8
3	← BP+6
Return	← BP+4
Addr	← BP+2
Old BP	← BP

Here is SUMMER.ASM (Small model):

```
.MODEL  SMALL
.CODE
        PUBLIC   _SUMMER                ;For C Interface
_SUMMER PROC
        PUSH     BP
        MOV      BP,SP

        PUSH     SI
        PUSH     DI
```

```
            PUSH      DS

            MOV       AX,[BP+4]
            MOV       BX,[BP+6]

            ADD       AX,BX

            POP       DS
            POP       DI
            POP       SI

            POP       BP
            RET
_SUMMER     ENDP
            END
```

Notice that we start the procedure name with an underscore (_SUMMER). SUMMER() is now ready to use with C. Under Quick C and MASM, it looks like this:

```
F:\>masm summer;          ←
Microsoft (R) Macro Assembler Version 5.10
Copyright (C) Microsoft Corp 1981, 1988.  All rights reserved.

  49868 + 337105 Bytes symbol space free
        0 Warning Errors
        0 Severe  Errors
sum.c

F:\>qcl sum.c summer.obj  ←
Microsoft (R) QuickC Linker   Version 4.06
Copyright (C) Microsoft Corp 1984-1989.  All rights reserved.

Object Modules [.OBJ]: SUM.OBJ +
Object Modules [.OBJ]: SUMMER.OBJ
Run File [SUM.EXE]: SUM.EXE /NOI
List File [NUL.MAP]: NUL
Libraries [.LIB]:

F:\>sum
3 + 2 = 5
```

The process is identical for Turbo C if you substitute tasm for masm, and tcc for qcl.

A Better Way

In fact, we can go even farther with the new MODEL and the newly extended (under MASM 5.1 or TASM 1.0) PROC Pseudo-Op. There has been a significant effort to make linking in assembly language even easier. Let's take a look at our program SUMMER.ASM. First, we start by specifying that not only is the model Small, but also that we are using the C calling convention:

```
.MODEL   SMALL, C  ←
         :
         :
```

Other languages that you could use here include PASCAL, FOR-TRAN, and BASIC. Using the C keyword does more than just set us up to use the C calling convention—in addition, all names declared EXTRN or PUBLIC now *automatically* have the underscore put in front of them. The next line looks like this:

```
.MODEL   SMALL, C

.CODE
PUBLIC   SUMMER   ←      ;For C Interface
         :
         :
```

with no underscore. Now we declare the procedure with PROC. It looks like this under the new PROC specifications:

```
.MODEL   SMALL, C

.CODE
         PUBLIC   SUMMER           ;For C Interface
SUMMER PROC NEAR USES DI SI, VALUE1:WORD, VALUE2:WORD   ←
         :
         :
```

This will save us a lot of time: We are saying that PROC is a NEAR procedure that uses the registers DI and SI (note that there are no commas separating them above). MASM or TASM will automatically add the needed pushes and pops to our function to save and restore those registers. Finally, we list the arguments passed to us, in the order they appear in the C call, and with the names we will refer to them in our assembly-language program. We specify that two arguments are passed, which we will refer to as VALUE1 and VALUE2, both words. Other variable types you could use instead of WORD include BYTE, DWORD, and QWORD (for quad word). The assembler will generate the correct [bp + n] expression whenever we refer to those names from now on. Here, then, is the rest of our program:

```
.MODEL   SMALL, C

.CODE
        PUBLIC   SUMMER          ;For C Interface
SUMMER PROC NEAR USES DI SI, VALUE1:WORD, VALUE2:WORD

        MOV      AX,VALUE1
        ADD      AX,VALUE2

        RET
SUMMER ENDP
        END
```

That's it—that's all there is to it. You can see that this new method of using PROC and MODEL saves a lot of time. (Note that although we specify that we are using SI and DI, that is for demonstration purposes only. We do not, in fact, use them in our program, so we do not have to save them.)

How About Data?

That approach is fine if, like SUMMER(), we don't have any data in our linked-in functions. If we do, however, we can use one of two approaches. We can bury the data in the Code Segment, as we did in File 2:

File 2

```
PUBLIC  SUB_PRINT
.MODEL SMALL
.CODE
SUB_PRINT          PROC NEAR
        JMP        GO
        ALL_OK     DB "Hello, world.$"   ←
GO:     MOV        DX,OFFSET ALL_OK
        MOV        AH,9
        INT        21H
        RET
SUB_PRINT          ENDP
        END
```

where we jump over the data. However, that is a little clumsy, and it limits us to the use of the Code Segment for our data. On the other hand, the Microsoft Quick C or Turbo C programs use a Data Segment, and we can put our data into their Data Segment with the .DATA directive. When linked this way, all of the data go into the same area.

Let's assume that we want to link in a function written in assembly language, which we call PRINT(). This function prints "Hello, world." Here's how the C code looks:

```
extern PRINT();

main()
{
PRINT();
}
```

And this is how the assembly language function PRINT looks:

```
PUBLIC   _PRINT
.MODEL SMALL
.DATA
          ALL_OK  DB "Hello, world.$"

.CODE
_PRINT  PROC    NEAR
        MOV     DX, OFFSET ALL_OK
        MOV     AH,9
        INT     21H
        RET
_PRINT  ENDP
        END
```

You can see that there are now two segments being used—one for data and one for code. Beyond that, nothing special is required; we just assemble, compile, and link as before (under both Microsoft or Turbo C), and the program runs correctly. That's the way we can set aside storage space for data—just use a simplified segment directive for a data area, such as .DATA, and then refer to the data as normal.

Let's try another example. Here we set up a function named MAX(), which returns the maximum of two integers. Here's how the C code might look:

```
extern MAX(int x, int y);

main()
{
int a = 12, b = 27;

printf("The larger of %d and %d is %d", a, b, MAX(a,b));
}
```

And the corresponding assembly language program might look like this (note that we are using the extended PROC and MODEL directives):

```
.MODEL    SMALL, C

.DATA
INT1      DW        0          ←
INT2      DW        0          ←

.CODE
          PUBLIC    MAX
          MAX       PROC NEAR USES BX, PARAM1:WORD, PARAM2:WORD

          MOV       AX,PARAM1
          MOV       INT1,AX
          MOV       AX,PARAM2
          MOV       INT2,AX

          MOV       AX,INT1
          CMP       AX,INT2
          JA        OVER
          MOV       AX,INT2

OVER:     RET
MAX       ENDP
          END
```

Here we move integers in and out of the Data Segment. We refer to INT1 and INT2 as PARAM1 and PARAM2, load them into memory, compare them, and return the larger one in AX.

As we can see, using data is easy—just put it into the Data Segment, and use it as we use the Data Segment in our assembly language programs. That's all there is to linking our assembly language procedures in as C functions.

| In the next chapter, we will see how to create libraries out of assembly language modules. |

Linking C into Assembly Language

Besides linking assembly language subroutines into C, we can go the other way, too. Let's develop an example to print out our phrase "Hello, world." by using printf()—but calling it from an assembly language program.

As it turns out, most C functions expect some initialization to have been done before they are called. This means that we will have to make a preliminary call to C before taking over in our assembly language program. We'll set up a dummy main routine:

```
main()
{
real_main();
}
```

that just calls real_main(), the assembly language program that makes up the real main module. Here's how REALMAIN.ASM looks:

```
.MODEL SMALL
PUBLIC _real_main
EXTRN  _printf:NEAR

.DATA
MSG DB "Hello, world.",0
FORMAT_STRING DB "%s",0

.CODE
_real_main PROC NEAR
MOV        AX,OFFSET MSG
PUSH       AX
MOV        AX,OFFSET FORMAT_STRING
PUSH       AX
CALL       _printf              ←
ADD        SP,4                 ←

RET
_real_main ENDP

END
```

We do something very important after the call to _printf: We reset the Stack pointer SP by adding 4 to it. In C, the calling procedure is responsible for resetting the Stack after the call is complete. We push two words—pointers to MSG and FORMAT_STRING—as required for printf(). After the call, we reset the Stack by adding 4 bytes to SP. Adding numbers directly to SP hasn't been necessary before because we've never called a C function—however, if you unassemble the C library, you'll see pages of such instructions.

Notice also that the procedure ends with a RET, even though it is the real main module. This returns control to the dummy C main module, where the stack is cleared, and the program exits. Also, notice that we don't include an entry point in the .ASM file.

In order to use printf(), we first have to link it in. Because C is case-sensitive, we use lowercase characters and precede the name with an underscore, as well as declaring it EXTRN:

```
.MODEL SMALL
PUBLIC _real_main
EXTRN  _printf:NEAR                            ←

.DATA
MSG DB "Hello, world.",0
FORMAT_STRING DB "%s",0

.CODE
_real_main PROC NEAR
MOV       AX,OFFSET MSG
PUSH      AX
MOV       AX,OFFSET FORMAT_STRING
PUSH      AX
CALL      _printf                              ←
ADD       SP,4

RET
_real_main ENDP

END
```

As mentioned, the assembler normally converts all labels to capital letters. If we did nothing else, we wouldn't find printf() in the C library when we linked. However, you can tell the assembler not to convert the labels with the -mx switch:

```
E>masm -mx realmain;
```

After we compile the C module, DUM.C, we can link the files together. To pick up the function printf(), we link in the library of Small model C functions. (Under Microsoft C, it's called SLIBCE.LIB):

```
E>link dum+realmain

Microsoft (R) QuickC Linker  Version 4.06
Copyright (C) Microsoft Corp 1984-1989.  All rights reserved.

Run File [DUM.EXE]:
List File [NUL.MAP]:
Libraries [.LIB]:slibce.lib   ←
```

And now we can run it:

```
E>dum
Hello, world.
```

It works. Now we can go both ways. Not only can we write C library functions in assembly language, but we can use C library functions in our assembly langauge programs. These techniques, of course, take practice, if speed and size are an issue, they can be invaluable.

In the next chapter, we start augmenting our assembly language knowledge in preparation for working with libraries of assembly language routines.

10

Assembly Language
Expertise

In this chapter, we're going to explore more about assembly language. We'll see what assembly language is good for. You can also build libraries of your assembly language routines, and we'll see how to do that here. We'll wind up by looking at the .EXE format of assembly language programs.

Some Fast Math

The largest capacity of any register in the PC is 16 bits, which can hold numbers (unsigned) up to 65535. In other words, 16 bits only gives us mathematical accuracy to 4 decimal places reliably. This level of accuracy is far too low for most programs. On the other hand, if we use two words—32 bits—for each operand, we can handle numbers up to 4,294,967,299. Since this is the degree of accuracy that makes computers useful, we'll work with 32-bit math in this chapter.

The 80x86 has provisions for handling 32 bits in both addition and subtraction. Even multiplication can be handled by breaking the number into partial products. Division, though, is more difficult—there is no easy way to break a division up into smaller sections. Instead, when we come to high-precision division, we'll develop a fast bit-by-bit algorithm.

Adding

If we want to add the number held in DX:AX to the number held in BX:CX, and if both are unsigned (or can be made so by finding their two's complements), we can use these instructions:

```
ADD   AX,CX        [Add DX:AX + BX:CX]
ADC   DX,BX
JC    ERROR
```

We first add the lower 16 bits of both numbers, held respectively in AX and CX. The result is stored in AX. If this answer is too large to hold in 16 bits, there is a carry, and the carry flag is set. To include that carry in the subsequent addition of the top 16 bits, we use the *Add with Carry instruction*, ADC:

```
      ADD     AX,CX          [Add DX:AX + BX:CX]
  →   ADC     DX,BX
      JC      ERROR
```

ADC includes the carry (if there is one) in this addition. The final result is stored in DX:AX. In this calculation, we are not prepared for answers longer than 32 bits (although they can be handled with an additional ADC to as many stages as you desire). If there was a carry after the second addition, we jump to a location marked ERROR.

Subtracting

Subtraction follows this plan as well. If we subtract a big number from a small one, we have to borrow from higher order places. The 80x86's designers included the SBB (Subtract with Borrow) command expressly for this use:

```
      SUB     AX,CX          [Sub DX:AX - BX:CX]
  →   SBB     DX,BX
      JC      ERROR
```

Here we determine the result of DX:AX - BX:CX. Again, if there is a carry, we consider it an error and jump to ERROR.

Multiplying

The MUL command requires that we start out with the AX register. If we execute the instruction MUL BX, then the 80x86 multiplies AX by BX and leaves the 32-bit result in DX:AX. If we want to multiply AX:DX by BX:CX, we must be prepared for a 64-bit result, using up all our registers.

Much more common is the use of memory locations. We can multiply the number Y1:Y0 (held in 16-bit words we've named Y1 and Y0) by the number Z1:Z0 (locations Z1 and Z0). We have to be prepared to store our result in four memory locations as a number such as A:B:C:D. We can use this code:

```
MOV     B,0
MOV     A,0
MOV     AX,Z0
MUL     Y0
MOV     D,AX
MOV     C,DX
MOV     AX,Z0
MUL     Y1
ADD     C,AX
ADC     B,DX
ADC     A,0
MOV     AX,Z1
MUL     Y0
ADD     C,AX
ADC     B,DX
ADC     A,0
MOV     AX,Z1
MUL     Y1
ADD     B,AX
ADC     A,DX
```

It performs this calculation:

```
                          Y1   :   Y0
                      x   Z1   :   Z0
                      ----------
                              Z0xY0
                    +    Z0xY1
                    +    Z1xY0
                  +  Z1xY1
                  ------------------
```

$$2^{32} \quad Z1xY1 + 2^{16} \quad Z0xY1 + 2^{16} \quad Z1xY0 + Z0xY0$$

This algorithm is nothing more than long multiplication. On occasions, however, multiplying with this kind of accuracy is necessary. To use this algorithm, set aside space for your data:

```
Y1      DW 0
Y0      DW 0
Z1      DW 0
Z0      DW 0
A       DW 0
B       DW 0
C       DW 0
D       DW 0
```

Load your 32-bit multiplicands into Y1:Y0 (i.e., high word in Y1, low word in Y0) and into Z1:Z0, and execute the algorithm. The result of Y1:Y0 x Z1:Z0 is left in A:B:C:D.

Dividing

In division, our path is less smooth. In all three of the previous cases, we divide our calculations into subparts and then join the results together from those parts. Unfortunately, division cannot be dissected that way. We are reduced to dividing on a bit-by-bit level if we want 32-bit accuracy. Here we will use an actual hardware divide algorithm. This algorithm, usually expressed in cryptic computer-design language, is not the fastest available, but it is at least intelligible using the model of long division. It also expresses a wonderful economy in the use of registers that is something of an art in itself.

As we have seen, the 80x86 has an internal DIV command that divides 32 bits (held in the two registers DX:AX) by a 16-bit number (for example, DIV BX divides DX:AX by BX) to return a 16-bit result and a 16-bit remainder. However, we want to maintain our 32-bit accuracy, so here we develop a bit-by-bit divide algorithm that divides a 64-bit number by a 32-bit number, giving powerful 32-bit results and remainders.

As a quick refresher course on long division, especially in binary, let's work through a short example where we divide 14 by 6. As with all division in the PC, our answer come out in whole numbers as an answer and a remainder. 14/6 yields an answer of 2 and a remainder of 2. We start here:

$$A \overline{)B} \quad \rightarrow \quad 6 \overline{)14} \quad \rightarrow \quad 0110 \overline{)1110}$$

To keep the example short, we only use 4 bits and leave the use of 64 bits up to the imagination. Our first move is to compare 0110 against progressively more of the number being divided (B above):

$$0110 \qquad \overline{)1\ 110}$$
$$\qquad \qquad \qquad \wedge$$

Since 0110 is bigger than 1, we place a 0 above it, and subtract 0 from it:

$$\qquad \qquad 0 \leftarrow$$
$$0110 \overline{)1110}$$
$$\qquad -\ 0$$
$$\qquad \overline{\ \ 1}$$

We bring down the next digit of B:

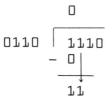

```
         0
0110 | 1110
   -  0 |
      ───┼──
          ↓
        11
```

We're now comparing A, 0110, against the first two digits of B, 11. Since 0110 is also bigger than 11 we put in another 0 up on top, subtract 0 from 11, and bring down another digit, a 1:

```
        00   ←
0110 | 1110
   -  0 |
      ──────┤
        11  │
   -  00    │
      ──────┼──
              ↓
        111
```

Now we are comparing A to the first three digits of B, 111, and 0110 goes smoothly into 111 once, so we put a 1 on top, subtract 0110 from 111, and bring down another digit:

```
         001   ←
0110 | 1110
   -  0
      ─────
        11   │
   -  00     │
      ─────  │
        111  │
   -  110    │
      ───────┼──
               ↓
        0010
```

Now we have to compare 0110 to what is left on the bottom, 0010. Since 0110 is greater than 0010, another 0 goes on top:

```
         0010   Answer
0110 | 1110
   -  0
      ─────
        11
   -  00
```

```
      ___
      111
  -   110
      _____

      0010
  -   0000
      _____

      0010    Remainder
```

This leaves us with a 4-bit answer, 0010 (2) and a 4-bit remainder, 0010 (also 2). To make an algorithm out of this, we have to decide just what it is that we do at each stage. If the problem looks like this:

```
    ___
  A _ B
```

then we compare A to progressively more and more of B, the number being divided. If A is bigger than B, we enter a 0 in the answer, but if A is smaller than B, we enter a 1 and subtract A. We keep going until we have done this four times, once for every bit in B.

Computerizing Our Example

Since we compare registers easily we can make a leap and say that to compare A to progressively more of B, we can just compare two registers using CMP. All we have to do is to use CMP AX,BX where AX holds A and BX holds B.

To get more and more of B into BX, we can simply shift B into it, one bit at a time. Progressively, then, we can compare A to more and more of B, as more and more of B appears in BX. If A is bigger than what we have of B, we put 0 in the answer. If A is smaller, then we subtract B - A and put a 1 into the answer.

In other words, if we start off with AX, BX, and CX loaded like this for 14/6 (treating them as only 4-bit registers):

```
  AX=6    BX     CX=14
  0110    0000   1110
```

then we shift the first digit into BX in this way:

```
  AX=6    BX           CX=14
  0110    0001   ←     110
```

We've got a new BX, so we compare AX to it and see immediately that AX > BX. This means that the first bit of the answer is 0.

This algorithm does not waste any space. It immediately slips this first bit into the newly vacated rightmost bit of CX. When we are done, the answer is fully in CX:

```
AX=6    BX    CX=14
0110    0001  110 0  <
               ^
```

With the first bit of the answer secure, we shift CX again to the left:

```
AX=6    BX           CX=14
0110    0011   ←   10 0
                    ^
```

and again compare AX to the new part of B we have in BX. Again, AX
> BX, so another 0 goes into the answer in CX:

```
AX=6    BX    CX=14
0110    0011  10 00   ←
               ^
```

Now we have to get a new value in BX, and so we shift CX left again:

```
AX=6    BX           CX=14
0110    0111   ←   0 00
                    ^
```

When we compare AX to BX, we have enough bits in BX to make AX <
BX. Just as in our long division example, this means that we subtract A
(in AX) from what we have of B (in BX) and put a 1 into the answer:

```
AX=6        BX       CX=14
0110        0111   0 001  ←
          - 0110      ^
            0001
```

This leaves a 1 in BX:

```
AX=6    BX    CX=14
0110    0001  0 001
               ^
```

We shift the final 0 from CX into BX;

```
AX=6    BX           CX=14
0110    0010   ←   001
                    ^
```

Since 0110 > 10, we finish by putting a 0 into CX:

```
AX=6        BX       CX=14
0110        0010     0010   ←
          Remainder  Answer
```

We've now done our comparison four times, so we're finished. The
leftover bits of B that A didn't divide evenly are the remainder, left in BX.
The final answer that we built bit-by-bit is in CX. In a direct (although
maybe not self-evident) way, this algorithm provides a clever translation
of long division into the language of registers and left shifts.

How Does it Look in Code?

To get this into code that you can use, let us suppose that we want to divide A:B:C:D by Z1:Z0, 64 bits by 32. The actual divison code is relatively small:

```
;64 Bit By 32 Bit Division (memory locations A:B:C:D by Z1:Z0)

            MOV       COUNT,64
            XOR       AX,AX          ;Going to divide A:B:C:D by BX:CX
            XOR       DX,DX          ; End up with quotient in A:B:C:D
            MOV       BX,Z1
            MOV       CX,Z0
SHIF:
        ...CALL       SHLA           ;SHL DX:AX:A:B:C:D by 1 place (96 bits !)
        :   CMP       DX,BX
        :   JB        NOT_YET
        :   JA        HIT
        :   CMP       AX,CX          ;DX = BX, Check AX,CX
        :   JB        NOT_YET
HIT:    :   SUB       AX,CX
        :   SBB       DX,BX
        :   ADD       D,1      ;Put in a 1 since divisor went into dividend once
NOT_YET:
        :   DEC       COUNT
        :   CMP       COUNT,0
        :..JNE        SHIF     ;Keep going all 64 times
```

The variable COUNT serves as a loop index. We clear the registers AX and DX, and load BX:CX with Z1:Z0:

```
MOV       COUNT,64
XOR       AX,AX          ;Going to divide A:B:C:D by BX:CX
XOR       DX,DX          ; End up with quotient in A:B:C:D
MOV       BX,Z1
MOV       CX,Z0
```

XOR AX,AX is a method used by professional programmers to clear the AX register. You can often find it in the BIOS listing. No matter what was in AX before, XOR AX,AX leaves it as 0.

AX may be set to 0 with MOV AX,0, but you often see the instruction XOR AX,AX instead. This instruction is commonly found in the beginning of .EXE files, so let's introduce XOR here.

XOR is the Exclusive Or instruction. It takes two words and matches them up, bit by bit. If a 0 meets a 0, the result is 0. If a 1 meets a 0, the result is 1. But if a 1 meets a 1, the result is 0:

```
XOR  |  0   1
      0  |  0   1
      1  |  1   0
```

When you XOR a number with itself, all 1, are sure to meet 1s and all
0s sure to meet 0s, so the result is 0. XOR AX,AX is sure to make the
contents of AX 0.

We gradually shift more and more of A:B:C:D into DX:AX and compare it to BX:CX. As we shift A:B:C:D into DX:AX, we gradually leave
0s behind in D. Every time that DX:AX is greater than BX:CX, however, we put in a 1 in instead.

The whole process begins by shifting a bit from A:B:C:D into
DX:AX. In other words, we want to execute a command such as SHL
DX:AX:A:B:C:D,1. In the absence of such a handy command, we have
to make one for ourselves, called SHLA:

```
;SHLA, a subroutine to shift 96 bits at once

SHLA      PROC    NEAR
          ;Shifts left 96 (!!) bits of DX:AX:A:B:C:D by 1
          PUSH    BX
          PUSH    CX
          MOV     BX,0
          MOV     CX,0
          SHL     D,1              ;Start with rightmost
          ADC     BX,0             ;Overflow in BX
          SHL     C,1
          ADC     CX,0             ;New overflow in CX, old in BX
          ADD     C,BX
          MOV     BX,0
          SHL     B,1
          ADC     BX,0     ;BX has new overflow, old in CX
          ADD     B,CX
          MOV     CX,0
          SHL     A,1
          ADC     CX,0     ;CX has new overflow, old in BX
          ADD     A,BX
          MOV     BX,0
          SHL     AX,1
          ADC     BX,0     ;BX has new overflow, old in CX
          ADD     AX,CX
          SHL     DX,1     ;Disregard overflow here
          ADD     DX,BX
          POP     CX
          POP     BX
          RET
SHLA      ENDP
```

When we shift a 16-bit word to the left one place, and end up shifting a
1 out to the left, the carry bit is set. SHLA follows all of those carries up

the line with ADC (Add with Carry) into successive words, and that accounts for the majority of its length.

Comparing DX:AX and BX:CX

After we shifted the first part of A:B:C:D into DX:AX, we compare it to the number we divide by, which is BX:CX. We could use a CMP DX:AX,BX:CX command here. Instead, we'll have to do the same thing 16 bits at a time, starting with the highest bits.

```
CMP DX:AX, BX:CX
```

DX>BX: If DX is greater than BX, then DX:AX is definitely greater than BX:CX, and we have a "hit." We move 1 into A:B:C:D.

DX<BX: If DX is less than BX, then DX:AX is less than BX:CX. We will leave the 0 that is shifted into the end.

DX = BX: If, though, DX = BX, then we must check AX and CX. The entire process goes this way:

```
SHIF:     CALL    SHLA                ;SHL DX:AX:A:B:C:D by 1 place (96 bits !)
     →    CMP     DX,BX
          JB      NOT_YET
          JA      HIT
     →    CMP     AX,CX               ;DX = BX, Check AX,CX
          JB      NOT_YET
HIT:      SUB     AX,CX
          SBB     DX,BX
          ADD     D,1     ;Put in a 1 since divisor went into dividend once
NOT_YET: [Shift more of A:B:C:D into DX:AX]
```

Notice the use of two conditional jumps, one right after the other. Conditional jumps do not affect the flags that are set, so this works. (Check your assembler's documentation to learn which commands affect which flags.)

If the part we have of A:B:C:D is bigger than what we're dividing by, we want to subtract it by subtracting DX:AX - BX:CX. This is done at the label HIT:

```
HIT:      SUB     AX,CX
          SBB     DX,BX
          ADD     D,1     ;Put in a 1 since divisor went into dividend once
```

We also put a 1 into the end of A:B:C:D. After we either let the shifted-in 0 stand or put in a 1, we shift more of the number we're dividing into DX:AX, and decrement the count.

```
SHIF:
     ...[Shift to the left and compare]
     :       :
     :       :
     : DEC     COUNT
     : CMP     COUNT,0
     :..JNE    SHIF      ;Keep going all 64 times
```

When you use this algorithm, load the 64-bit number to be divided into A:B:C:D, load the number to divide it by into Z1:Z0, and execute the algorithm. The quotient is left in A:B:C:D, and the remainder in Z1:Z0.

That's it for heavy math—we've gone through addition, subtraction, multiplication, and division. Let's look at some low-level graphics now—setting pixels on the screen.

Turning Pixels On

Regrettably, there is no real graphics support in assembly language—you cannot draw ellipses with an easy call, for example. The services that are available are under BIOS INT 10H (see the Appendix), and all they do is turn a screen pixel on. However, they can do that much faster than C can. We can even do it ourselves much faster than INT 10H can, if we know about the way the video buffer is set up. If you do all your graphics work on such a low level, it can save you a lot of time. Let's look at the way the CGA buffer is set up as an example.

In high-resolution CGA mode (640x200 pixels) you can choose only to turn a pixel on or off (0 or 1). The computer needs to save 1 bit per pixel in this case. There are 200 lines down on the screen. (On graphics monitors, characters are 8 scan lines high, and 8 x 25 lines = 200.) There are 640 columns across, so the total is 640 x 200, or 128,000 bits needed. This makes 16,000 bytes, rounded up in the PC's graphics video buffer to 16K.

In medium resolution (320x200) we can specify one of four colors for each pixel, so we need two bits to hold the possible values for each pixel. There are only half as many pixels (320 across versus 640 across), but each needs twice as many bits, so we use the same size video buffer (16K).

In high-resolution mode, it seems natural that if you want to turn the pixel on at location (0,0), which is the top left corner of the screen, you set the first bit in the video buffer to 1. That is actually how it works. To turn on the next pixel in the top row (row 0) on, you set the next bit to 1, and so forth to the end of the first line on the screen for the first 640 pixels (numbers 0-639).

It also seems natural that to turn on the first pixel of the second row (row 1), you set bit 640 in the video buffer to 1 because the first line goes from 0 to 639. Unfortunately, that is not how it works.

IBM decided to separate the graphics video buffer into two blocks of 8K each. The first block, starting at location B800:0000, holds the even scan lines on the screen. The second block, starting at B800:2000, holds the odd scan lines. The video controller scans over all of the even lines on the screen first, and then over all of the odd lines. To facilitate its operation, IBM gives it the bits in the order needed. This is an added complication for any program; now it has to split up its image between two blocks in memory. In practice, this is not very hard if you have a subroutine that puts pixels on the screen and keeps track of which block they go into, or if you use INT 10H, Service 12.

The scheme in medium resolution is similar, but here there can be four colors, not just two. Four colors requires two bits, so every two bits in the screen buffer can be grouped together into one pixel. There are only one-half as many pixels on a line, but twice as many bits per pixel, so the same number of memory bits correspond to each screen line (640).

The Program PUT_PIXEL

As an example of fairly tight code, here's a small program, PUT_PIXEL, that turns high-resolution CGA pixels on:

```
PUT_PIXEL        PROC    NEAR
        ;SUPPLY DX=ROW,CX=COLUMN. ASSUMES ES=B800H and screen in High
        ; Resolution mode (Use BIOS INT 10H Service 0).
        XOR     BX,BX
        SHR     DX,1
        JNC     CALC
        ADD     BX,8*1024
CALC:   MOV     AX,DX               ;GET 80*DX
        SHL     DX,1
        SHL     DX,1
        ADD     DX,AX
        MOV     AX,CX
        MOV     CL,4
        SHL     DX,CL               ;DX NOW MULTIPLIED BY 80 (16*5)
        ADD     BX,DX               ;ADD TO INDEX
        MOV     DX,AX
        AND     DX,7                ;GET X3 INTO DX
        MOV     CL,3
        SHR     AX,CL               ;CX/8
```

```
        ADD     BX,AX           ;FIND BYTE ALONG ROW
        NEG     DL
        ADD     DL,7
        MOV     CL,DL           ;GET BIT TO TURN ON
        MOV     AL,1
        SHL     AL,CL
        OR      ES:[BX],AL           RET
PUT_PIXEL       ENDP
```

PUT_PIXEL is about three times as fast as the equivalent BIOS service call. If you ever want to work in graphics on the PC, you should know how to address individual pixels on the screen. For that reason, we work through PUT_PIXEL in a little detail. It also gives us experience with code written expressly for speed.

PUT_PIXEL first determines whether the pixel is to be put in an even row or an odd row. The pixel's coordinates are given to PUT_PIXEL in DX (row, 0-199) and CX (column, 0-639). We check whether DX is odd or even. The first 8K of the screen buffer holds lines 0,2,4,6,8, and so forth; the second 8K holds lines 1,3,5,7,9, and so forth:

Screen Row #	1st or 2nd 8K	Line inside 8K Block
0	1	0
1	2	0
2	1	1
3	2	1
4	1	2

For each even line across the screen, there is a row of 640 bits in the first 8K block. For each odd line, there is a row of 640 bits in the second 8K block. To find in which line of 640 bits a particular pixel is located, divide the row number by 2 and disregard the remainder. (See the above table.) This is the same as shifting to the right. We check the low bit of DX (the block number) anyway, so we can shift that bit into the carry bit and use JNC (Jump if No Carry):

```
PUT_PIXEL       PROC    NEAR
        ;SUPPLY DX=ROW,CX=COLUMN. ASSUMES ES=B800H
        XOR     BX,BX
    →   SHR     DX,1
    →   JNC     CALC
    →   ADD     BX,8*1024
CALC:   MOV     AX,DX                   ;GET 80*DX
```

[BX] is used to point to the byte in the screen buffer we have to change. If the pixel is in an odd row, we add 8K to BX so that it points to the second 8K block.

These commands check which block the pixel is in and set DX to that pixel's row of 640 bits. To determine which offset from the beginning of the 8K block that makes in bytes, we multiply the number in DX by 640 bits and divide by 8 bits per byte to yield 80 bytes per row on the screen. Multiplying DX by 80 gives us the byte offset of the pixel's line from the beginning of its block.

The 80x86 has a multiply command, of course, but it is very slow. We should try to avoid using it when speed is of the essence, as it is here. To multiply by 80, we can multiply by 5 and then by 16, or— even better—we can multiply DX by 4, add DX to it again to make 5 times, and then multiply by 16. Multiplying by powers of 2, of course, is done by shifting to the left. The 80x86 can shift registers to the left like this:

```
MOV     CL,3
SHL     DX,CL
```

Here's our multiplication by 80:

```
PUT_PIXEL       PROC    NEAR
        ;SUPPLY DX=ROW,CX=COLUMN. ASSUMES ES=B800H and screen in High
        ; Resolution mode (Use BIOS INT 10H Service 0).
        XOR     BX,BX
        SHR     DX,1
        JNC     CALC
        ADD     BX,8*1024
CALC:   MOV     AX,DX   ←       ;GET 80*DX
        SHL     DX,1    ←
        SHL     DX,1    ←
        ADD     DX,AX   ←
        MOV     AX,CX   ←
        MOV     CL,4    ←
        SHL     DX,CL   ←       ;DX NOW MULTIPLIED BY 80 (16*5)
        ADD     BX,DX           ;ADD TO INDEX
```

Using the two instructions SHL DX,1 SHL DX,1 is marginally faster than using MOV CL,2 SHL DX,CL. We could have used an immediate shift such as SHL DX,2, except that the 8088 doesn't support immediate shifts greater than 1. This code was written to be used on any PC compatible, including those that use 8088s.

DX now holds the byte offset, inside the 8K block, of the line in which our pixel lies. To point to the correct line that holds the pixel that we want to change with [BX], we add (SHR DX,1) x 80 to BX. Once we're in the right row, we still have to find which byte to work on, and that depends upon the column required, 0-639. Each of these

640 places is a bit, so to find the correct byte, we divide CX by 8 and add that total to BX:

```
PUT_PIXEL          PROC    NEAR
        ;SUPPLY DX=ROW,CX=COLUMN. ASSUMES ES=B800H and screen in High
        ; Resolution mode (Use BIOS INT 10H Service 0).
        XOR     BX,BX
        SHR     DX,1
        JNC     CALC
        ADD     BX,8*1024
CALC:   MOV     AX,DX               ;GET 80*DX
        SHL     DX,1
        SHL     DX,1
        ADD     DX,AX
        MOV     AX,CX
        MOV     CL,4
        SHL     DX,CL               ;DX NOW MULTIPLIED BY 80 (16*5)
        ADD     BX,DX               ;ADD TO INDEX
    →   MOV     DX,AX
        AND     DX,7                ;GET X3 INTO DX
    →   MOV     CL,3
    →   SHR     AX,CL               ;CX/8
    →   ADD     BX,AX               ;FIND BYTE ALONG ROW
```

At the same time, we calculate which bit in that byte to turn on. If CX (which can range from 0 to 639) is 0, we want to turn on the left-most bit of the 0th byte of that line, bit 7. In general, the bit we want to turn on is 7 - (CX Mod 8), where CX Mod 8 is the remainder of dividing CX by 8. CX Mod 8 is just AND CX,7, where AND is a logical AND, and works just like the C version. We end up with these instructions:

```
PUT_PIXEL          PROC    NEAR
        ;SUPPLY DX=ROW,CX=COLUMN. ASSUMES ES=B800H and screen in High
        ; Resolution mode (Use BIOS INT 10H Service 0).
        XOR     BX,BX
        SHR     DX,1
        JNC     CALC
        ADD     BX,8*1024
CALC:   MOV     AX,DX               ;GET 80*DX
        SHL     DX,1
        SHL     DX,1
        ADD     DX,AX
        MOV     AX,CX
        MOV     CL,4
        SHL     DX,CL               ;DX NOW MULTIPLIED BY 80 (16*5)
        ADD     BX,DX               ;ADD TO INDEX
        MOV     DX,AX
    →   AND     DX,7                ;GET X3 INTO DX
        MOV     CL,3
        SHR     AX,CL               ;CX/8
        ADD     BX,AX               ;FIND BYTE ALONG ROW
    →   NEG     DL
```

```
    →  ADD     DL,7
    →  MOV     CL,DL            ;GET BIT TO TURN ON
       MOV     AL,1
       SHL     AL,CL
       OR      ES:[BX],AL
       RET
PUT_PIXEL      ENDP
```

At the end, we put a 1 into AL and shift it DL (= 7 - AND(CL,7)) times, then OR the result with whatever byte is in the screen buffer at location [BX]. And that, finally, turns the pixel on. It's pretty clear that working with graphics directly in the PC is not a job that's especially easy.

Note that PUT_PIXEL requires ES to already have a value of B800H. This is because PUT_PIXEL uses the ES segment, and it would slow the program down to load ES with B800H (the segment address of the CGA video buffer) every time it was called to turn a pixel on.

However, to load segment registers, we cannot simply say:

```
MOV     ES,B800H
```

Instead, we have to go through an intermediate step of loading a direct value first into a general-purpose register, such as AX:

```
MOV     AX,B800H
MOV     ES,AX
```

This is just a fact of the 80x86's internal architecture—the same is true of any segment register. Simply use these two lines in your program, and leave ES set to that value while you work with PUT_PIXEL. (Also, of course, you have to include a new ASSUME to inform the assembler about ES's new value.)

PUT_PIXEL provides us with a prime example of the various ways to save time and write code for speed. As you can see, writing in assembly language can become complex quickly. Sometimes, though, it is certainly worth it.

Let's move now from turning pixels on to a way of making our assembly language routines easier to use and easier to link into our C programs: the use of libraries.

Libraries

If you work with many files, there comes a point where the use of libraries is almost necessary. Once you develop routines, you want to forget them and have them automatically linked in.

This is the idea of a library. When we link .OBJ files, the whole thing becomes part of the code (stripped of the .OBJ file header). When we link in a library, the linker looks for *unresolved externals*—labels that have been declared EXTRN but are not yet found in an .OBJ file—and takes only those it needs. Although the library can contain a thousand commonly used procedures, only the ones that the linker needs to complete your file are taken from it.

We can create such libraries with the program LIB.EXE. If we take these two files:

```
——————————— File 1 ———————————
.MODEL    SMALL
          EXTRN     PRINT:NEAR
.CODE
          ORG       100H

PROG      PROC      NEAR
          CALL      PRINT
          INT       20H
PROG      ENDP

          END       PROG
```

```
——————————— File 2 ———————————
.MODEL SMALL
.CODE
          PUBLIC    PRINT
          HELLO_MSG  DB "Hello, world.$"

PRINT     PROC      NEAR
          MOV       DX,OFFSET HELLO_MSG
          MOV       AH,9
          INT       21H
          RET
PRINT     ENDP

          END
```

we can start by making a library out of the second file. Let's call this library PRINT.LIB. Whenever we want to use the procedure PRINT after creating this library, all we have to do is tell the linker to search PRINT.LIB. LINK then finds PRINT in this library and links it in.

Here's how to make FILE2.ASM (which contains the procedure PRINT) into a library, PRINT.LIB:

```
C>MASM FILE2;
Microsoft (R) Macro Assembler Version 5.10
Copyright (C) Microsoft Corp 1981, 1988.  All rights reserved.

   50192 + 31229 Bytes symbol space free

        0 Warning Errors
        0 Severe  Errors

C>LIB PRINT.LIB+FILE2.OBJ;
Microsoft (R) Library Manager  Version 3.10
Copyright (C) Microsoft Corp 1983-1988.  All rights reserved.
```

The LIB command LIB PRINT.LIB + FILE2.OBJ; creates a library file named PRINT.LIB, whose only contents is File 2's object code. (We could have equally as well said LIB PRINT + FILE2.) The .LIB extension is assumed for the first file, and .OBJ is assumed for the second file and any following ones (such as LIB PRINT + FILE2 + FILE3).

If PRINT.LIB already existed, this command would not create it, but would add FILE2.OBJ to it. We'll see this when we add a new routine to PRINT.LIB. Now that we have PRINT.LIB, let's use it. First, assemble FILE1.ASM and then link it, including PRINT.LIB:

```
C>LINK
Microsoft (R) Overlay Linker  Version 3.64
Copyright (C) Microsoft Corp 1983-1988.  All rights reserved.
Object Modules [.OBJ]:FILE1   ← Type this.
Run File [TA.EXE]:
List File [NUL.MAP]:
Libraries [.LIB]:PRINT        ← And this.
LINK : warning L4021: no stack segment
```

Now we can use EXE2BIN on the created file, FILE1.EXE, and run it:

```
C>EXE2BIN FILE1 FILE1.COM

C>FILE1
Hello, world.
C>
```

Adding A Second Module

So far, there has been no advantage to using the library file PRINT.LIB—we could just as well have linked in FILE1.OBJ. On the other hand, we can now add a second procedure to PRINT.LIB. Everything that comes from an .OBJ file and goes into a library is referred to as a *module*. So far, all we have is the FILE2 module. But we can write another .ASM file, identical to FILE2.ASM except for the message, and call this File 3:

```
.MODEL SMALL
.CODE
        PUBLIC  PRINT2
        HOW_MSG      DB "How are you?$"   ←

PRINT2  PROC    NEAR
        MOV     DX,OFFSET HOW_MSG           ←
        MOV     AH,9
        INT     21H
        RET
PRINT2  ENDP

        END
```

Here we define the procedure PRINT2, which prints out "How are you?". We can assemble this file and add it to the already-existing library file PRINT.LIB:

```
C>MASM FILE3;
Microsoft (R) Macro Assembler Version 5.10
Copyright (C) Microsoft Corp 1981, 1988.  All rights reserved.

  50192 + 31229 Bytes symbol space free

     0 Warning Errors
     0 Severe  Errors


C>LIB PRINT.LIB+FILE3.OBJ;       ← This adds PRINT2 to PRINT.LIB
Microsoft (R) Library Manager  Version 3.10
Copyright (C) Microsoft Corp 1983-1988.  All rights reserved.
```

This time, PRINT.LIB is not created because it already exists, but FILE3.OBJ is added to it. Now the PRINT library holds both PRINT ("Hello, world.") and PRINT2 ("How are you?").

We can still link FILE1.OBJ with PRINT.LIB:

```
C>LINK
Microsoft (R) Overlay Linker  Version 3.64
Copyright (C) Microsoft Corp 1983-1988.  All rights reserved.

Object Modules [.OBJ]:FILE1  ← Type this.
```

```
Run File [TA.EXE]:
List File [NUL.MAP]:
Libraries [.LIB]:PRINT        ← And this again.

LINK : warning L4021: no stack segment
```

It *only* takes PRINT from PRINT.LIB because there is no call to PRINT2. Theoretically, there could be hundreds of procedures in PRINT.LIB, and we'd only take those that are needed.

Of course, we can add a call to PRINT2 (in addition to PRINT) in our main file, FILE1:

```
.MODEL    SMALL
          EXTRN    PRINT:NEAR,PRINT2:NEAR
.CODE
          ORG      100H

PROG      PROC     NEAR
          CALL     PRINT
          CALL     PRINT2                          ←
          INT      20H
PROG      ENDP

          END      PROG
```

As long as we add PRINT2 to our declaration of which labels are external:

```
.MODEL    SMALL
          EXTRN    PRINT:NEAR,PRINT2:NEAR
.CODE
          ORG      100H

PROG      PROC     NEAR
          CALL     PRINT
          CALL     PRINT2
          INT      20H
PROG      ENDP

          END      PROG
```

FILE1 can then be assembled, linked, and run:

```
C>MASM FILE1;
Microsoft (R) Macro Assembler Version 5.10
Copyright (C) Microsoft Corp 1981, 1988.  All rights reserved.

  50202 + 31219 Bytes symbol space free

      0 Warning Errors
      0 Severe  Errors
```

```
C>LINK
Microsoft (R) Overlay Linker  Version 3.64
Copyright (C) Microsoft Corp 1983-1988.  All rights reserved.
Object Modules [.OBJ]:FILE1   ←
Run File [TA.EXE]:
List File [NUL.MAP]:
Libraries [.LIB]:PRINT       ←

LINK : warning L4021: no stack segment

C>EXE2BIN FILE1 FILE1.COM

C>FILE1
Hello, world.How are you?
```

As you can see, both calls are made—both PRINT and PRINT2 are found in the library PRINT.LIB. (We don't provide a space in our strings between messages, so they come out right next to each other.)

> Notice that LINK only asks for the names of library files after you give it a full list of .OBJ files to include. If a version of PRINT is in one of them, it is not taken from the file PRINT.LIB, because the EXTRN has already been satisfied.

Deleting Modules

If you wanted to delete a module from a library file such as PRINT.LIB, you use the "-" sign instead of "+". This is done easily enough. Let's delete PRINT2 from PRINT.LIB:

```
C>LIB PRINT-FILE3;
Microsoft (R) Library Manager  Version 3.10
Copyright (C) Microsoft Corp 1983-1988.  All rights reserved.
```

PRINT.LIB now doesn't include PRINT2. When you subtract modules this way, you have to supply the name of the original .OBJ file (FILE3.OBJ), not the name of the procedure that you want to subtract (PRINT2). You cannot subtract individual procedures—only entire .OBJ modules.

Extracting Modules

There is also a provision for extracting modules, and not just deleting them from a library. This is useful if you want to reorganize your libraries. For example, you can *extract* FILE3.OBJ from PRINT.LIB and then add it to another library file, BADNEWS.LIB.

Extraction is done with the "*" symbol. For example, this is how we can move PRINT2 (that is, FILE3.OBJ) from PRINT.LIB and install it into BADNEWS.LIB:

```
C>LIB PRINT*FILE3;
Microsoft (R) Library Manager  Version 3.10
Copyright (C) Microsoft Corp 1983-1988.  All rights reserved.
C>LIB BADNEWS+FILE3;
Microsoft (R) Library Manager  Version 3.10
Copyright (C) Microsoft Corp 1983-1988.  All rights reserved.
```

Once again, you have to extract the entire .OBJ file—not just individual procedures. After you become used to it, using and managing libraries may become an everyday task for you.

Linking to Something That Isn't There

Let's see what happens if we link FILE1 with PRINT.LIB now that we've extracted PRINT2 from PRINT.LIB:

```
C>LINK
Microsoft (R) Overlay Linker  Version 3.64
Copyright (C) Microsoft Corp 1983-1988.  All rights reserved.
Object Modules [.OBJ]:FILE1
Run File [TA.EXE]:
List File [NUL.MAP]:
Libraries [.LIB]:PRINT

LINK : warning L4021: no stack segment

/2 LINK : error L2029: Unresolved externals:

PRINT2 in file(s):
 FILE1.OBJ(FILE1.ASM)

There was 1 error detected
```

LINK is unable to satisfy the call to PRINT2, and gives an error message that calls PRINT2 an Unresolved external.

Replacing Modules

Frequently, newer versions of some modules may be produced. You may debug some code, or there may be changes in what the program is supposed to do. To handle these changes, you can subtract the module and then add a new one. For example, if the .OBJ module put into a library is ALERT.OBJ, and you want to change it to a new version that is now ready on the disk, you can do this:

```
C>LIB PRINT-ALERT;
Microsoft (R) Library Manager  Version 3.10
Copyright (C) Microsoft Corp 1983-1988.  All rights reserved.

C>LIB PRINT+ALERT;
Microsoft (R) Library Manager  Version 3.10
Copyright (C) Microsoft Corp 1983-1988.  All rights reserved.
```

Or, if you wish, the library manager lets you perform both operations at once with the combined operation "-+", which stands for "replace." If there is an .OBJ file on the disk, then -+ deletes the current module in the specified library and add the new one from the disk file. For example, to update ALERT in PRINT.LIB in one step, type:

```
C>LIB PRINT-+ALERT;
Microsoft (R) Library Manager  Version 3.10
Copyright (C) Microsoft Corp 1983-1988.  All rights reserved.
```

> Keep in mind that if a procedure in one of your .LIB files calls a procedure in some other .LIB file, link the one with the call first. LINK won't know that it is supposed to include a particular procedure until that procedure is called. If it has already searched the correct library before you make the call, it won't be able to find the called procedure when you finally do call it.

Libraries can be very useful at helping you to manage your programs, especially when programs become very large. On the other hand, you should keep your library up-to-date. If the library contains old versions of particular modules, they will be linked in.

We will cover one more topic before we are through with assembly language—the .EXE format.

The .EXE Format

When we started linking assembly language into our programs, we put the data into a new segment, the Data Segment. In .COM files, we only have one segment, but DOS supports two kinds of files that you can run: .COM files and .EXE files. The .COM file form we know by now—even with the restriction that you have to start it at 100H, instead of just anywhere, it's pretty easy to use. There is no code in a .COM file that the programmer doesn't put there—we are responsible for everything there.

On the other hand, there are times when you are writing assembly language programs and you need something bigger than .COM format. Sometimes, you just can't squeeze everything into 64K or less. Or perhaps you want the freedom to define segments wherever you want them. In these cases, you can use the .EXE file format. Also, OS/2 *only* supports .EXE files—it does NOT support .COM files.

The .EXE Difference

The big change between .COM files and .EXE files when using assembly language is that we have to become very aware of the segment registers and how they're set. We didn't need to worry about them so much in .COM files, where there was only one segment, but now, with multiple segments involved, we do. You can use any segment name when programming in pure assembly language, so we won't limit ourselves here to the simplified segment directives.

With .COM files, the one segment is usually divided up this way:

```
          ORG      100H
ENTER: JMP         PROG
          :
      Data Goes Here
          :
PROG     PROC NEAR
          :
      Program Goes Here
          :
PROG     ENDP


          :
          :

      Stack Goes Here.
```

The Stack is at the very end of the 64K segment, put there by DOS. If CS is set to 1111H, then the .COM file has free use of 1111:0000 to 1111:FFFF, although the first 100H bytes are taken up by the PSP.

In an .EXE file, the segments can go where you want them, as can the entry point (no longer restricted to 100H):

```
DATA_SEG           SEGMENT
          :
```

```
        Data Goes Here
          :
DATA_SEG              ENDS

CODE_SEG              SEGMENT
          :
     Program Code Goes Here
          :
CODE_SEG              ENDS

STACK                 SEGMENT
          :
     The Stack Goes Here.
          :
STACK                 ENDS
```

This now means that we are responsible for defining the Stack—DOS no longer does it automatically.

In a .COM file, the Stack Segment register, SS, holds the Common Segment, of course; and SP starts off pointing at the very last word in that segment, FFFEH. (The very last byte is CS:FFFFH, and the very last *word* is CS:FFFE.) In .EXE files, you define your own Stack Segment:

```
    DATA_SEG              SEGMENT
              :
         Data Goes Here
              :
    DATA_SEG              ENDS

    CODE_SEG              SEGMENT
              :
         Program Code Goes Here
              :
    CODE_SEG              ENDS

→   STACK                 SEGMENT  STACK
→       DB        30 DUP("STACK ")
→   STACK                 ENDS
```

SP starts off pointing to the very last word in the segment you've defined. Usually it's a good idea to use a Stack that is at least 100 words long (longer in OS/2).

We have to tell the assembler that we intend this segment to be used as the Stack. We define it as a Stack type with the STACK Pseudo-Op (or by using the simplified directive .STACK):

```
STACK        SEGMENT   STACK
```

When the .EXE file is loaded into memory, SS holds the segment address of the beginning of the Stack, and SP points to the last defined word. Next we set aside space for the Stack, filling it with the characters STACK over and over again.

```
STACK        SEGMENT   STACK
DB           30 DUP("STACK ")
```

This is a debugging aid. Can you tell where the Stack starts in this DEBUG dump of an .EXE file?

```
-D
0F16:0000   1E 33 C0 50 B8 16 0F 8E-D8 CB 00 00 00 00 00 00   .3.P...........
0F16:0010   53 54 41 43 4B 20 53 54-41 43 4B 20 53 54 41 43   STACK STACK STAC
0F16:0020   4B 20 53 54 41 43 4B 20-53 54 41 43 4B 20 53 54   K STACK STACK ST
0F16:0030   41 43 4B 20 53 54 41 43-4B 20 53 54 41 43 4B 20   ACK STACK STACK
0F16:0040   53 54 41 43 4B 20 53 54-41 43 4B 20 53 54 41 43   STACK STACK STAC
0F16:0050   4B 20 53 54 41 43 4B 20-53 54 41 43 4B 20 53 54   K STACK STACK ST
0F16:0060   41 43 4B 20 53 54 41 43-4B 20 53 54 41 43 4B 20   ACK STACK STACK
0F16:0070   53 54 41 43 4B 20 53 54-41 43 4B 20 53 54 41 43   STACK STACK STAC
-Q
```

Finally, we end the Stack Segment with a normal ENDS:

```
STACK        SEGMENT   STACK
DB           30 DUP("STACK ")
STACK        ENDS   ←
```

We are now responsible for the Stack that the program uses, so we have to include a Stack Segment in *every* .EXE file we produce. (But only include one Stack Segment—don't define multiple Stacks if you're going to link files together to make your .EXE file.)

The Data Segment

We also have the option to have a Data Segment separate from the Code Segment:

```
→   DATA_SEG        SEGMENT
→          :
→       Data Goes Here
→          :
→   DATA_SEG        ENDS

    CODE_SEG        SEGMENT
           :
        Program Code Goes Here
           :
    CODE_SEG        ENDS

    STACK           SEGMENT  STACK
        DB          30 DUP("STACK ")
    STACK           ENDS
```

In order to use this Data Segment, we have to set DS ourselves. This can be done easily:

```
MOV     AX,DATA_SEG
MOV     DS,AX
ASSUME  DS:DATA_SEG
```

We should not forget to do it whenever we write .EXE files. We'll include these lines in our .EXE file shell in a moment. This sets up DS for us so that whenever we use a label that refers to data, the assembler knows where we mean.

Loading .EXE Files

Before we develop an .EXE file shell that can be used, we have to know how .EXE files are loaded into memory. The very first instructions in every DOS .EXE file are necessary because of this loading process.

Here's the way that process works: At the A> prompt, you type the name of an .EXE file that you want to run. DOS (actually the resident part of COMMAND.COM) reads your keystrokes, checks whether your command is an internal DOS command, finds that it isn't, and then locates the .EXE file on the disk.

A program segment prefix (PSP) for the .EXE file is set up at the lowest available memory location, just as it is for a .COM file. On the other hand, the PSP is not as visible in .EXE file format. In .COM files, the first 100H bytes are set aside for the PSP because everything must fit inside the Common Segment. This is not the case for an .EXE file.

Only ES and DS are set to the same segment as the program segment prefix. The PSP starts at DS:0000 (or ES:0000, which is the same thing). CS, on the other hand, is set to the Code Segment—the first instruction is at CS:0000. SS is set to the location of the stack in the file when it's loaded.

So far, the program segment prefix has been set up in memory. Next, DOS reads in the beginning of the .EXE file—the part called the ".EXE file header." There is no comparable thing in .COM files to the .EXE file header. We will encounter it again in OS/2, so let's give it some attention.

As you know, .EXE files differ from .COM files in that .EXE files can use multiple segments. In .COM files, all addresses are in offset form—that is, one word only, indicating a distance from the beginning of the segment.

For .EXE files, addresses must be able to hold both segment and offset values, because we can reach multiple segments. This means that in a typical .EXE file, a great number of the instructions must hold both segment and offset values. For example, a JMP instruction that is to jump more than 64K must have both segment and offset addresses to jump to.

However, until the program is loaded in to run, the segment value is not known. In other words, we have defined a Segment such as CODE_SEG, and we know the offsets of addresses from that point, but actual value of CODE_SEG is not known until you load your program in. (This is not a problem in one-segment .COM files, where everything is measured from the beginning of the common segment.)

> The segment at which the .EXE file is loaded in varies according to the size of the operating system that fits into memory before it, and according to the number and the size of the memory-resident programs.

This means that many locations in the .EXE file cannot be filled in until the program is loaded. The .EXE file header was created for this purpose, and holds the position of *every* such location in the .EXE file. When the file is loaded in to run, the .EXE file header tells DOS which locations must be filled with the segment address. (This process is called *relocation*.)

The .EXE file header is the reason that .EXE files are larger than corresponding .COM files.

Following the header is the table that holds the positions of the locations that need to be fixed up with the segment address. For each location, there is a two-word address in this table that gives the location's distance from the beginning of the load module. DOS loads in the load module, and sets these locations correctly.

After that, CS:IP is set to the entry point, which you can set to anywhere in the program. You set it using the same method we used in .COM files: with the END Pseudo-Op. For example, END START sets the entry point to the label START, and you can put START wherever you want it. ES and DS are set to the segment address of the PSP. SS:SP is set to the location of the Stack. And the program is ready to run.

A .EXE File Shell

Everything we've discussed so far is necessary in order to understand the environment that we working in inside an .EXE file. Now we've come to the point where we can introduce .EXE file shell. Let's start with what we know so far:

```
        DATA_SEG          SEGMENT
        :                           ;Put data here.
        DATA_SEG          ENDS

        CODE_SEG          SEGMENT
        :                           ;Put code here
        PROG_NAME         ENDP
        CODE_SEG          ENDS

STACK        SEGMENT   STACK
     DB     30 DUP("STACK ")
STACK        ENDS
        END       PROG_NAME
```

While CS is set to CODE_SEG, we have to be careful to let the assembler know that SS will be set to the Stack Segment, STACK. By declaring our Stack of type "STACK", we indicate that SS should point there when the file is loaded. Now, we have to tell the assembler the same thing. Notice that there is no ASSUME yet for DS—we have not set a value for it yet.

```
        DATA_SEG          SEGMENT
                                    ;Put data here.
        DATA_SEG          ENDS

        CODE_SEG          SEGMENT
```

```
  →                       ASSUME   CS:CODE_SEG,SS:STACK
            CODE_SEG              ENDS
STACK         SEGMENT   STACK
    DB          30 DUP("STACK ")
STACK         ENDS
            END       PROG_NAME
```

Next comes the actual program itself, which we call PROG_NAME.
Note that it is declared as FAR:

```
          DATA_SEG             SEGMENT
                                    ;Put data here.
          DATA_SEG             ENDS

          CODE_SEG             SEGMENT
                    ASSUME    CS:CODE_SEG,SS:STACK
  →       PROG_NAME           PROC    FAR
                    :
                    RET
  →       PROG_NAME           ENDP
          CODE_SEG            ENDS

STACK         SEGMENT   STACK
    DB          30 DUP("STACK ")
STACK         ENDS
            END       PROG_NAME
```

Until now, we have let the simplified segment directives take care of
NEAR and FAR declarations for us. Here, however, we are not linking
to C, so we can use our own segment names—which means that we
have to specify NEAR and FAR labels. Now that we've got multiseg-
ment abilities, we have to think about using the FAR keyword. There
are two types of return instructions (RET). When we define a procedure as NEAR:

```
PROG      PROC NEAR
          MOV     AX,5
          MOV     DX,32001
          RET
PROG      ENDP
```

this procedure is only called from within the same segment. Only one
word—the offset address—is put onto the stack when this procedure
is called. At the end of the procedure, only one word has to be popped. The assembler puts in this type of RET instruction (a short
return) because the procedure is declared NEAR. In other words, the

RET at the end is matched to the way that the procedure is defined, (NEAR or FAR).

If we declare something FAR, the RET is made into a FAR return, which pops off two words (both the segment and offset addresses). This kind of procedure can be called across segments, if needed.

How does the assembler know to push one or two words when something is called? How does it know that this CALL will be to a FAR item or to a NEAR item? The type of CALL, after all, has to match the type of return that will be waiting at the end of the called procedure.

Again, the assembler can simply look to see how the procedure is declared (with NEAR or FAR), and set up the type of machine-language CALL instruction accordingly. If the item being called isn't in the present file, we have to use an EXTRN Pseudo-Op and specify whether the label is a NEAR or FAR item so that the assembler can set up the CALL accordingly.

The main procedure in an .EXE file is always FAR. This means that the RET at the end is a FAR RET, which is standard in .EXE files. When this FAR RET is reached, two words are popped off the stack: What are they? It turns out that they are the address of the very first byte in the PSP.

When the FAR RET at the end of the program is encountered, the location we return to is this very first byte in the PSP. The reason this is done is because the first two bytes in the PSP are CDH 20H, the machine-language instruction for INT 20H, which is our normal way of ending a program. .EXE files are ended by returning to this first byte of the PSP, not by explicitly including an INT 20H instruction.

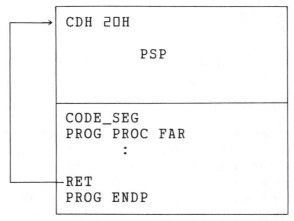

It is usual to jump to this CDH 20H instruction instead of placing an INT 20H at the end of the .EXE file program. CS should be set to the segment that holds the PSP when an INT 20H is executed (as required by DOS). By setting CS:IP to the first location in the PSP, we make sure CS is set correctly. Otherwise, in an .EXE file, CS can set anywhere when the program ends.

> CDH 20H are the first two bytes in any PSP, even in the PSP used for .COM files.

Priming the Stack

We have to push this return address onto the Stack ourselves. This is done at the beginning of every DOS .EXE file (not in OS/2 ones, however). The two words to push form the address of the very first byte of the program segment prefix, This address is DS:0000. (Recall that DS is set to the segment of the PSP upon entering an .EXE file.)

When a FAR call is executed, first a segment address is pushed onto the stack, then an offset address. To set up a return from a FAR call, we push DS first:

```
        DATA_SEG        SEGMENT
                                ;Put data here.
        DATA_SEG        ENDS

        CODE_SEG        SEGMENT
                ASSUME  CS:CODE_SEG,SS:STACK
        PROG_NAME       PROC    FAR
→               PUSH    DS
                :                       ;Prog starts here.
                :
                RET
        PROG_NAME       ENDP
        CODE_SEG        ENDS
STACK      SEGMENT  STACK
     DB      30 DUP("STACK ")
STACK      ENDS
        END     PROG_NAME
```

Note that DS is pushed immediately upon entering the program, before we set it to our own Data Segment. This is to make sure that we push the PSP's segment address, and not the segment address of the Data Segment.

Next we push a word of 0s. To do so, we make the contents of AX equal to 0 with XOR AX,AX 0, and push AX. When the FAR return is reached, DS:0000 is popped off and we go to the correct location. Now that the Stack is set up for the FAR return to the beginning of the PSP, we can change the value in DS. We want to set DS to our own Data Segment. That is accomplished in the usual way by including an ASSUME Pseudo-Op to let the assembler know what's going on:

```
DATA_SEG           SEGMENT
                         ;Put data here.
DATA_SEG           ENDS
CODE_SEG           SEGMENT
       ASSUME      CS:CODE_SEG,SS:STACK
PROG_NAME          PROC    FAR
       PUSH        DS
       XOR         AX,AX
       PUSH        AX
→      MOV         AX,DATA_SEG
→      MOV         DS,AX
→      ASSUME      DS:DATA_SEG
       :                           ;Your Program starts here.
       :
       RET
PROG_NAME          ENDP
CODE_SEG           ENDS
STACK     SEGMENT  STACK
    DB       30 DUP("STACK ")
STACK     ENDS
    END       PROG_NAME
```

The whole thing is ready to run. Note that these first instructions will be the same in almost any .EXE file, so they are included in our .EXE file shell.

We can easily convert our "Hello, world." program to .EXE file format. We just put the data (ALL_OK DB 'Hello, world.$') into the Data Segment, and put the code that prints out the string (using INT 21H service 9) into the program area:

```
DATA_SEG           SEGMENT
ALL_OK  DB "Hello, world.$"            ←
DATA_SEG           ENDS
CODE_SEG           SEGMENT
       ASSUME      CS:CODE_SEG,SS:STACK
PROG_NAME          PROC    FAR
       PUSH        DS
       XOR         AX,AX
       PUSH        AX
       MOV         AX,DATA_SEG
       MOV         DS,AX
       ASSUME      DS:DATA_SEG
→      LEA         DX,ALL_OK        ;Prog starts here.
→      MOV         AH,9
→      INT         21H
```

```
                    RET
          PROG_NAME      ENDP
          CODE_SEG       ENDS

STACK        SEGMENT  STACK
     DB       30 DUP("STACK ")
STACK      ENDS
          END      PROG_NAME
```

The program is about double the length of a similar program set up to use .COM format. We can assemble the program, link it, and run it (no EXE2BIN required!):

```
C>MASM ALLOK;
Microsoft (R) Macro Assembler Version 5.10
Copyright (C) Microsoft Corp 1981, 1988.  All rights reserved.

  50152 + 31269 Bytes symbol space free

     0 Warning Errors
     0 Severe  Errors

C>LINK ALLOK;
Microsoft (R) Overlay Linker  Version 3.64
Copyright (C) Microsoft Corp 1983-1988.  All rights reserved.

C>ALLOK
Hello, world.
C>
```

Now we're going to do something surprising: Something that could not be done in a .COM file. We are going to make sure that ALL_OK is more than 64K away from the instruction LEA DX,ALL_OK, and still have a working program. This can be done easily with the insertion of just one line in the Data Segment:

```
DATA_SEG          SEGMENT
ALL_OK  DB "Hello, world.$"
FILLER  DB 65524 DUP(0)
DATA_SEG          ENDS
```

FILLER represents 65524 bytes of zeroes. This fills up the Data Segment. (There are 12 characters in "Hello, world.$", and 12 + 65524 = 65536, the maximum number of bytes in a segment.) Assemble and link the new program ALLOK.ASM. When run, it gives the same result as before:

```
C>ALLOK
Hello, world.
C>
```

That's all for .EXE files and our exploration of assembly language.

Appendix

BIOS and DOS Reference

This Appendix is intended for use as a reference to all of the interrupts that are available, from 0 to FFH.

Interrupt 0—Divide By 0

This is the first of the BIOS interrupts. BIOS uses interrupts 0 to 1FH, and DOS continues from 20H upward. Interrupt 0 is the divide by 0 routine; if a divide by 0 occurs, this interrupt is called. It prints out the message "Divide Overflow," and usually stops program execution.

Interrupt 1—Single Step

No one, except a debugger, uses this interrupt. It is used to single-step through code, with a call to this interrupt between executed instructions.

Interrupt 2—Non-Maskable Interrupt (NMI)

This is a hardware interrupt. This interrupt cannot be blocked; it always is executed when called.

Interrupt 3—Breakpoint

This is another debugger interrupt. DEBUG uses this interrupt with the Go command. If you want to execute all code up to a particular address and then stop, DEBUG inserts an INT 3 into the code at that point and then gives control to the program. When the INT 3 is reached, DEBUG can take control again.

Interrupt 4—Overflow

This is similar to INT 0. If there is an overflow condition, this interrupt is called. Usually, though, no action is called for, and BIOS simply returns.

Interrupt 5—Print Screen

This interrupt was chosen by BIOS to print the screen out. If you use the PrtSc key on the keyboard, this interrupt is called. Needless to say, your program can also issue an INT 5 by just including that instruction in the program. There are no arguments to be passed.

Interrupts 6 and 7—Reserved

Interrupt 8—Time of Day

This is another hardware interrupt. This interrupt is called to update the internal time of day (stored in the BIOS data area) 18.2 times a second. If the date needs to be changed, this interrupt handles that also.

This interrupt calls INT 1CH as well. If you want to intercept the timer and do something at the rate of 18.2 times a second, it is recommended that you intercept INT 1CH, instead of this one.

Interrupt 9—Keyboard

This hardware interrupt may be intercepted by memory-resident programs.

Interrupt 0AH—Reserved

Interrupts 0BH–0FH

These interrupts point to the BIOS routine D_EOI, which is BIOS' End of Interrupt routine. This routine resets the interrupt handler at port 20H and then returns.

INT 10H Service 0—Set Screen Mode

Input

AH = 0
AL = Mode

Mode (in AL)	Display Lines	Number of Colors	Adapters	Maximum Pages
0	40x25	B&W text	CGA, EGA, VGA	8
1	40x25	Color text	CGA, EGA, VGA	8
2	80x25	B&W text	CGA, EGA, VGA	4 (CGA) 8 (EGA, VGA)
3	80x25	Color text	CGA, EGA, VGA	4 (CGA) 8 (EGA, VGA)
4	320x200	4	CGA, EGA, VGA	1
5	320x200	B&W	CGA, EGA, VGA	1
6	640x200	2 (on or off)	CGA, EGA, VGA	1
7	80x25	Monochrome	MDA, EGA, VGA	1 (MDA) 8 (EGA, VGA)
8	160x200	16	PCjr	1
9	320x200	16	PCjr	1
A	640x200	1	PCjr	1
B	Reserved for future use.			
C	Reserved for future use.			
D	320x200	16	EGA, VGA	8
E	640x200	16	EGA, VGA	4
F	640x350	monochrome	EGA, VGA	2
10H	640x350	16	EGA, VGA	2
11H	640x480	2	VGA	1
12H	640x480	16	VGA	1
13H	320x200	256	VGA	1

INT 10H Service 1—Set Cursor Type

Input	Output
AH = 1	New Cursor
CH = Cursor Start Line	
CL = Cursor End Line	

INT 10H Service 2—Set Cursor Position

Input	Output
DH,DL = Row, Column	Cursor position changed.
BH = Page Number	
AH = 2	

Note DH,DL = 0,0 = Upper Left

INT 10H Service 3—Find Cursor Position

Input

BH = Page Number
AH = 3

Output

DH,DL = Row, Column of Cursor.
CH,CL = Cursor Mode currently Set.

INT 10H Service 4—Read Light Pen Position

Input

AH = 4

Output

AH = 0→Light pen switch not down
AL = 1→ DH,DL = Row, Column of Light Pen position
CH Raster line (Vertical) 0–199
BX Pixel Column (Horizontal) 0–319,639

INT 10H Service 5—Set Active Display Page

Input

AL = 0-7 (Screen Modes 0,1)
0-3 (Screen modes 2,3)
AH = 5

Output

Active Page Changed.

Note: Pages Available in Alphanumeric Modes Only
(Graphics Adapters)

INT 10H Service 6—Scroll Active Page Up

Input

AL = #Lines blanked at bottom (0→Blank whole area)
CH,CL = Upper Left Row,Column of area to scroll
DH,DL = Lower Right Row,Column of area to scroll
BH = Attribute used on blank line
AH = 6

INT 10H Service 7—Scroll Active Page Down

Input

AL = #Lines blanked at bottom (0→Blank whole area)
CH,CL = Upper Left Row,Column of area to scroll
DH,DL = Lower Right Row,Column of area to scroll
BH = Attribute used on blank line
AH = 7

INT 10H Service 8—Read Attribute and Character at Cursor Position

Input   *Output*

BH = Page Number   AL = Character read (ASCII)
AH = 8   AH = Attribute of character (Alphanumerics only)

INT 10H Service 9—Write Attribute and Character at Cursor Position

Input   *Output*

BH = Page Number   Character written on screen at Cursor Position
BL→Alpha Modes = Attribute
     Graphics Modes = Color
CX = Count of characters to write
AL = IBM ASCII code
AH = 9

INT 10H Service A—Write Character ONLY at Cursor Position

Input   *Output*

BH = Page Number   Character written on screen at Cursor Position
CX = Count of characters to write
AL = IBM ASCII code.
AH = 0AH

INT 10H Service B—Set Color Palette

Input

BH = Palette   Color ID
BL   BH = 0→   BL = Background Color
         BH = 1→   BL = Palette Number
                      (0 = Green/Red/Yellow)
                      (1 = Cyan/Magenta/White)
AH = 11

INT 10H Service C—Write Dot

Input

DX = Row Number(0-199)   [0,0] is upper left.
CX = Column Number(0-319,639)
AL = Color Value (0-3)
AH = 12

Note: If bit 7 of AL is 1, the color value is XORed with the current value of the dot.

INT 10H Service D—Read Dot

Input   *Output*

DX = Row Number(0-199)   AL = Color Value (0-3)
CX = Column Number(0-319,639)
AH = 13

[0,0] is upper left.
Note: If bit 7 of AL is 1, the color value is XORed with the current
value of the dot.

INT 10H Service E—Teletype Write to Active Page

Input   *Output*

AL = IBM ASCII code
BL = Foreground Color
          (Graphics mode)
AH = 14

INT 10H Service FH—Return Video State

Input   *Output*

AH = 15   AH = Number of alphanumeric columns on screen
              AL = Current mode (See INT 10H Service 0.)
              BH = Active display page.

INT 10H Service 10H—Set Palette Registers

Default Palette Colors (0-15) on EGA.

Color Value	Color	rgbRGB
0	Black	000000
1	Blue	000001
2	Green	000010
3	Cyan	000011
4	Red	000100
5	Magenta	000101
6	Brown	010100
7	White	000111
8	Dark Gray	111000
9	Light Blue	111001
10	Light Green	111010
11	Light Cyan	111011
12	Light Red	111100
13	Light Magenta	111101
14	Yellow	111110
15	Intense White	111111

INT 10H Service 10H Function 0—Set Individual Palette Register

Input

```
AH = 10H
AL = 0
BL = Palette register to set (0-15)
BH = Value to set (0-63)
```

INT 10H Service 10H Function 1—Set Overscan (Border) Register

Input

```
AH = 10H
BH = Value to set (0-63)
```

INT 10H Service 10H Function 2—Set All Palette Registers

Input

AH = 10H
AL = 2
ES:BX = Address of a 17-byte table holding color selections (0-63)
        Bytes 0 - 15 Hold color selections for palette
                      registers 0 - 15
        Byte 16   Holds the new overscan (border) color

INT 10H Service 10H Function 7—Read Individual Palette Register

Input   *Output*

AH = 10H   BH = Register setting
AL = 7
BL = Register to read (color value)

INT 10H Service 10H Function 8—Read Overscan (Border) Register

Input   *Output*

AH = 10H   BH = Overscan setting
AL = 8

INT 10H Service 10H Function 10H—Set DAC Register

Input

AH = 10H
AL = 10H
BX = Register to set (0 - 255)
CH = Green Intensity
CL = Blue Intensity
DH = Red Intensity

INT 10H Service 10H Function 12H—Set DAC Registers

Input

AH = 10H
AL = 12H
BX = First register to set (0 - 255)
CX = Number of registers to set (1 - 256)
ES:DX = Address of a table of color intensities. Three bytes are used for each DAC register (use only lower 6 bits of each byte).
Table is set up: red, green, blue, red, green, blue...

INT 10H Service 10H Function 13H—Select Color Page Mode

Input

AH = 10H
AL = 13H
BL = 0 Select Color Paging Mode
      BH = 0 Selects 4 DAC register pages of 64 registers each.
      BH = 1 Selects 16 DAC register pages of 16 registers each.
BL = 1 Select Active Color Page
    For use with 4 page mode:
      BH = 0 Selects the first block of 64 DAC registers
      BH = 1 Selects the second block of 64 DAC registers
      BH = 2 Selects the third block of 64 DAC registers
      BH = 3 Selects the fourth block of 64 DAC registers
    For use with 16 page setting:
      BH = 0 Selects the first block of 16 DAC registers
      BH = 1 Selects the second block of 16 DAC registers
                        :
                        :
      BH = 2 Selects the 15th block of 16 DAC registers
      BH = 3 Selects the 16th block of 16 DAC registers

INT 10H Service 11H—Character Generator

INT 10H Service 12H—Alternate Select

Input

AH = 12H
BL = 30H

AL = 0 → 200 screen scan lines
    = 1 → 350 screen scan lines
    = 2 → 400 screen scan lines

INT 11H Equipment Determination

Input   *Output*

Bits of AX
15,14 = Number of Printers
13 Not used
12 Game Adapter attached
11,10,9 Number of RS232 cards installed
8 Unused.
7,6 Number of Diskette drives
    (00→1;01→2;10→3;11→4 If Bit 0 = 1)
5,4 Video Mode
    (00 Unused, 01 = 40x25 Color Card
     10 = 80x25 Color Card, 11 = 80x25 Monochrome)
3,2 Motherboard RAM
    (00 = 16K,01 = 32K,10 = 48K,11 = 64K)
1 Not used
0 = 1 If there are diskette drives attached

INT 12H—Determine Memory Size

Input   *Output*

AX = Number of Contiguous 1K Memory Blocks

INT 13H Service 0—Reset Disk

Input   *Output*

AH = 0   No Carry → AH = 0, Success
           Carry → AH = Error Code (See Service 1.)

Note: Hard disk systems: DL = 80H→reset diskette(s)
                         DL = 81H→reset hard disk.

INT 13H Service 1—Read Status of Last Operation

Input	Output

Input   *Output*

AH = 1   Disk Error
          Codes:
          AL = 00H   No Error.
          AL = 01H   Bad Command passed to controller.
          AL = 02H   Address Mark not found.
          AL = 03H   Diskette is Write Protected.
          AL = 04H   Sector not found.
          AL = 05H   Reset failed.
          AL = 07H   Drive parameters wrong.
          AL = 09H   DMA across segment end.
          AL = 0BH   Bad track flag seen.
          AL = 10H   Bad error check seen.
          AL = 11H   Data is error corrected.
          AL = 20H   Controller failure.
          AL = 40H   Seek operation has failed.
          AL = 80H   No response from disk.
          AL = 0BBH   Undefined error.
          AL = 0FFH   Sense operation failed.

Note: DL = Drive number; set bit 7 to 1 for hard disks
For hard disks, drive number in DL can range from 80H to 87H.

INT 13H Service 2—Read Sectors into Memory

Input   *Output*

AH = 2   No Carry→ AL = no. sectors read (diskette)
DL = Drive Number   Carry→AH = Disk Error Code (See Service 1)
DH = Head Number
CH = Cylinder or Track (Floppies) Number
CL = Bits 7,6 high 2 bits of 10-bit cylinder number
CL = Sector Number (bit 0-5)
AL = Number of Sectors to Read (Floppies 1-8
                        Hard Disks 1-80H
                        Hard Disks Read/Write Long 1-79H).
ES:BX = Address of buffer for reads and writes

Note: DL = Drive number; set bit 7 to 1 for hard disks.
For hard disks, drive number in DL can range from 80H to 87H.

INT 13H Service 3—Write Sectors to Disk

Input   *Output*

AH = 3   No Carry→AL = no. sectors written (diskette)
DL = Drive Number   Carry→AH = Disk Error Code (See Service 1)
DH = Head Number
CH = Cylinder or Track (Floppies) Number
CL = Bits 7,6 high 2 bits of 10-bit cylinder number
CL = Sector Number (bits 0-5)
AL = Number of Sectors to Write (Floppies 1-8
                                           Hard Disks 1-80H
                                           Hard Disks Read/Write Long 1-79H)
ES:BX = Address of buffer for reads and writes

Note: DL = Drive number; set bit 7 to 1 for hard disks.
For hard disks, drive number in DL can range from 80H to 87H.

INT 13H Service 4—Verify Sectors

Input   *Output*

AH = 4   No Carry→AH = 0, Success
DL = Drive Number   Carry→AH = Disk Error Code (See Service 1)
DH = Head
Number
CH = Cylinder or Track (Floppies) Number
CL = Bits 7,6 high 2 bits of 10-bit cylinder number
CL = Sector Number (bits 0-5)
AL = Number of Sectors   (Floppies 1-8
                             Hard Disks 1-80H
                             Hard Disks Read/Write Long 1-79H)

Note: DL = Drive number; set bit 7 to 1 for hard disks.
For hard disks, Drive number in DL can range from 80H to 87H.

INT 13H Service 8—Return Drive Parameters

This service works ONLY on hard disks and PS/2s

Input   *Output*

AH = 8   DL = Number of drives attached to controller
DL = Drive No. (0 based)   DH = Maximum value for Head Number
                           CH = Maximum cylinder value
                           CL = Bits 7,6 high 2 bits of 10-bit cylinder number

CL = Maximum value for sector number (bits 0-5)
BL (For PS/2 diskettes only)
= 1 → 360K drive
= 2 → 1.2 Mbyte drive
= 3 → 720K drive
= 4 → 1.44 Mbyte drive

Note: DL = Drive number; set bit 7 to 1 for hard disks.
For hard disks, drive number in DL can range from 80H to 87H.

INT 13H Services 0AH and 0BH—Reserved

INT 13H Service 0CH—Seek

This service works ONLY on hard disks.

Input	Output
AH = 0CH	No Carry→AH = 0, Success
DH = Head Number	Carry→AH = Disk Error Code (See Service 1.)
DL = Drive Number (80H-87H allowed)	
CH = Cylinder Number	
CL = Sector Number; bits 7,6 of CL = high 2 bits of 10-bit cylinder number	

Note: DL = Drive number; set bit 7 to 1 for hard disks.
For hard disks, Drive number in DL can range from 80H to 87H.

INT 13H Service 0DH—Alternate Disk Reset

INT 13H Services 0EH and 0FH—Reserved

INT 13H Service 10H—Test Drive Ready

INT 13H Service 11H—Recalibrate Hard Drive

This service works ONLY on hard disks.

Input	Output
AH = 11H (Read)	No Carry→AH = 0, Success
	Carry→AH = Disk Error Code (See Service 1.)
DL = Drive Number (80H-87H allowed)	

Note: DL = Drive number; set bit 7 to 1 for hard disks.
For hard disks, drive number in DL can range from 80H to 87H.

INT 13H—Diagnostic Services

These services work ONLY on hard disks.

Input   *Output*

AH = 12H (RAM Diagnostic)   No Carry→AH = 0, Success.
AH = 13H (Drive Diagnostic)   Carry→AH = Disk Error Code (See Service 1.)
AH = 14H (Controller Diagnostic)
DL = Drive Number (80H-87H allowed)

Note: DL = Drive number; set bit 7 to 1 for hard disks.
For hard disks, drive number in DL can range from 80H to 87H.

INT 13H, Service 19H—Park Heads (PS/2 Only)

Input (PS/2)   *Output*

DL = Drive Number   Carry = 1 → Error, AH = Error Code
                                       = 0 → Success

Note: DL = Drive number; set bit 7 to 1 for hard disks.
For hard disks, drive number in DL can range from 80H to 87H.

INT 14H, AH = 0—Initialize RS232 Port

Input

AH = 0
Bits of AL: 0,1 Word Length 01→7 Bits, 11→8 Bits
            2   Stop Bits 0→1, 1→2 stop bits
            3,4 Parity 00→None, 01→Odd, 11→Even
            5,6,7 Baud Rate 000→110
                            001→150
                            010→300
                            011→600
                            100→1200
                            101→2400
                            110→4800
                            111→9600

INT 14H, AH = 1—Send Character Through Serial Port

Input	*Output*
AH = 1	If Bit 7 of AH is set, failure.
AL = Character to send	If Bit 7 is not set, bits 0-6 hold status (see INT 14H, AH = 3).

INT 14H, AH = 2—Receive Character From Serial Port

Input	*Output*
AH = 2	AL = Character Received
	AH = 0, success
	Otherwise, AH holds an error code (see INT 14H, AH = 3).

INT 14H, AH = 3 Return Serial Port's Status

Input   *Output*

AH = 3   AH Bits Set:
    7→Time Out
    6→Shift Register Empty
    5→Holding Register Empty
    4→Break detected
    3→Framing Error
    2→Parity Error
    1→Overrun Error
    0→Data Ready
    AL Bits Set:
    7→Received Line Signal Detect
    6→Ring Indicator
    5→Data Set Ready
    4→Clear to Send
    3→Delta Receive Line Signal Detect
    2→Trailing Edge Ring Detector
    1→Delta Data Set Ready
    0→Delta Clear to Send

INT 15H, Cassette I/O

Input

AH = 0 → Turn Cassette Motor On.
AH = 1 → Turn Cassette Motor Off.
AH = 2 → Read one or more 256 byte
            blocks. Store data at
            ES:BX. CX = Count of Bytes
            to read.
AH = 3 → Write one or more 256 byte
            blocks from ES:BX. Count
            of bytes to write in CX.

Output

DX = Number of bytes actually
        read
Carry flag set if error
If Carry, AH = 01→CRC Error.
         = 02→Data
                transitions lost
         = 04→No Data Found

[In recent BIOS versions, new items have been added to this interrupt, such as joystick support, the ability to switch processor mode (protected or not), mouse support, and some BIOS parameters.

INT 16H, Service 0—Read Key from Keyboard

Input

AH = 0

Output

AH = Scan Code AL = ASCII code

INT 16H, Service 1—Check if Key is Ready to be Read

Input

AH = 1

Output

Zero Flag = 1 → Buffer Empty
Zero Flag = 0 → AH = Scan Code
                AL = ASCII Code

INT 16H, Service 2—Find Keyboard Status

Input

AH = 2

Output

AL = Keyboard Status byte

INT 17H Service 0—Print character in AL

Input

AH = 0
AL = Character to be printed
DX = Printer Number (0,1,2)

Output

AH = 1→ Printer Time Out

INT 17H Service 1—Initialize Printer Port

Input

AH = 1
DX = Printer Number (0,1,2)

Output

AH = Printer Status:
Bits Set of AH:
7→Printer Not Busy
6→Acknowledge
5→Out of Paper
4→Selected
3→I/O Error
2→Unused
1→Also Unused
0→Time Out

INT 17H Service 2—Read Printer Status into AH

Input

AH = 2
DX = Printer Number (0,1,2)

Output

AH Set to Status Byte as in
INT 17H, AH = 1

INT 18H—Resident BASIC

This interrupt starts up ROM-resident BASIC in the PC.

INT 19H—Bootstrap

This interrupt boots the machine (try it with DEBUG).

INT 1AH Service 0—Read Time of Day

Input

AH = 0

Output

CX = High Word of Timer Count
DX = Low Word of Timer Count
AL = 0 If Timer has not passed 24 hours
since last read

Note: Timer count increments by 65536 in one hour.

INT 1AH Service 1—Set Time of Day

Input

AH = 1
CX = High Word of Timer Count
DX = Low Word of Timer Count

Note: Timer count increments by 65536 in one hour.

INT 1BH—Keyboard Break Address

INT 1CH—Timer Tick Interrupt

INT 1DH—Video Parameter Tables

INT 1EH—Diskette Parameters

INT 1FH—Graphics Character Definitions

DOS Interrupts

Interrupt 1FH is the last BIOS Interrupt. DOS starts with INT 20H.

INT 20H—Terminate

Programs are usually ended with an INT 20H.

Interrupt 21H

Interrupt 21H is the DOS service interrupt. To call one of these services, load AH with the service number, and load the other registers
as shown.

INT 21H Service 0—Program Terminate

Input

AH = 0

INT 21H Service 1—Keyboard Input

Input   *Output*

AH = 1   AL = ASCII code of struck key
                                           Does Echo on screen
                   Checks for ^C or ^Break

INT 21H Service 2—Character Output on Screen

Input

DL = IBM ASCII character
AH = 2

INT 21H Service 3—Standard Auxiliary Device Input

Input

AH = 3   Character in AL

INT 21H Service 4—Standard Auxiliary Device Output

Input

AH = 4
DL = Character to output

INT 21H Service 5—Printer Output

Input

AH = 5
DL = Character to output

INT 21H Service 6—Console I/O

Input   *Output*

AH = 6

DL = FF   →   AL holds character if one ready
DL < FF   →   Type ASCII code in DL out
                                    Does NOT Echo on screen
                Does NOT check for ∧C or ∧Break

INT 21H Service 7—Console Input Without Echo

Input   Output

AH = 7   AL = ASCII code of struck key
                                    NO Echo on screen.
                Does NOT Check for ∧C or ∧Break

INT 21H Service 8—Console Input w/o Echo with ∧C Check

Input   Output

AH = 7   AL = ASCII code of struck key
                                    Does NOT Echo on screen
                Checks for ∧C or ∧Break

DOS INT 21H Service 9—String Print

Input

AH = 9
DS:DX point to a string that ends in '$'

INT 21H Service A—String Input

Input   Output

AH = 0AH   Buffer at DS:DX filled
[DS:DX] = Length of buffer   Echo the typed keys
                Checks for ∧C or ∧Break

INT 21H Service 0BH—Check Input Status

Input	*Output*
AH = 0BH	AL = FF → Character ready
	AL = 00 → Nothing to read in

^Break is checked for

INT 21H Service 0CH—Clear Keyboard Buffer and Invoke Service

Input	*Output*
AH = 0CH	Standard Output from the
AL = Keyboard Function #	selected Service

^Break is checked for

INT 21H—Service 0DH Disk Reset

Input

AH = 0DH

INT 21H—Service 0EH Select Disk

Input

AH = 0EH
DL = Drive Number
(DL = 0→A
DL = 1→B
and so on).

INT 21H Service 0FH—Open Preexisting File

Input	*Output*
DS:DX points to an FCB	AL = 0 → Success
AH = 0FH	AL = FF → Failure

INT 21H Service 10H—Close File

Input	Output	
DS:DX points to an FCB	AL = 0	→ Success
AH = 10H	AL = FF	→ Failure

INT 21H Service 11H—Search for First Matching File

Input	Output	
DS:DX points to an unopened FCB	AL = FF	→ Failure
AH = 11H	AL = FF	→ Success
		DTA holds FCB for match

Note: DTA is at CS:0080 in .COM files on startup.

INT 21H Service 12H—Search for Next Matching File

Input	Output	
DS:DX points to an unopened FCB	AL = FF	→ Failure
AH = 12H	AL = 0	→ Success
		DTA holds FCB for match

[Use this Service after Service 11H.]

INT 21H Service 13H—Delete Files

Input	Output	
DS:DX points to an unopened FCB	AL = FF	→ Failure
AH = 13H	AL = 0	→ Success

INT 21H Service 14H—Sequential Read

Input	Output
DS:DX points to an opened FCB.	Requested Record put in DTA
AH = 14H	AL = 0 Success.

Current Block and Record Set in FCB. 1 End of File, no data in record.
2 DTA Segment too small for record.
3 End of File; record padded with 0

[Record address incremented.]

INT 21H Service 15H—Sequential Write

Input   *Output*

DS:DX points to an opened FCB.   One record read from DTA and written.
AH = 15H   AL = 0 Success
Current Block & Record Set in FCB.   1 Disk full
                                                           2 DTA Segment too small for record.
                                                           Record Address Incremented.

INT 21H Service 16H—Create File

Input   *Output*

DS:DX points to an unopened FCB.   AL = 0 Success
AH = 16H   = FF Directory Full

INT 21H Service 17H—Rename File

Input   *Output*

DS:DX points to a MODIFIED FCB.   AL = 0 Success
AH = 17H   = FF Failure

[Modified FCB → Second file name starts six bytes after the
end of the first file name, at DS:DX + 11H.]

INT 21H Service 18H—Internal to DOS

INT 21H Service 19H—Find Current Disk

Input   *Output*

AH = 19H   AL = Current Disk (0 = A, 1 = B, and so on).

INT 21H Service 1AH—Set the DTA Location

Input   *Output*

DS:DX points to new DTA address.   None
AH = 1AH

Note: DTA = Disk Transfer Address, the data area used with FCB
services.
Default DTA is 128 bytes long, starting at CS:0080 in the PSP.

INT 21H Service 1BH—FAT Information for Default Drive

Input   *Output*

AH = 1BH   DS:BX points to the "FAT Byte"
                         DX = Number of Clusters
                         AL = Number of Sectors/Cluster
                         CX = Size of a Sector (512 bytes)
Note: Files are stored in clusters—the smallest allocatable
unit on a disk.

INT 21H Service 1CH—FAT Information for Specified Drive

Input   *Output*

AH = 1CH   DS:BX points to the "FAT Byte"
DL = Drive Number (0 = Default   DX = Number of Clusters
            1 = A...)   AL = Number of Sectors/Cluster
                                 CX = Size of a Sector (512)

Note: Files are stored in clusters, the smallest allocatable unit on a disk.

INT 21H Services 1DH - 20H—Internal to DOS

INT 21H Service 21H—Random Read

Input   *Output*

DS:DX points to an opened FCB.   AL = 00 Success

Set FCB's Random Record field
at DS:DX + 33 and DS:DX + 35
AH = 21H

= 01 end of file, no more data
= 02 not enough space in DTA segment
= 03 end of file, partial record
        padded with 0s

INT 21H Service 22H—Random Write

Input

DS:DX points to an opened FCB.
Set FCB's Random Record field
at DS:DX + 33 and DS:DX + 35
AH = 21H

Output

AL = 00 Success
   = 01 Disk is full
   = 02 not enough space in DTA segment

INT 21H Service 23H—File Size

Input

DS:DX points to an unopened FCB.
AH = 23H

Output

AL = 00 Success
   = FF No file found that matched FCB
Random Record Field set to file length
   in records, rounded up.

INT 21H Service 24H—Set Random Record Field

Input

DS:DX points to an opened FCB.
AH = 24H

Output

Random Record Field set to match
   Current Record and Current Block.

INT 21H Service 25H—Set Interrupt Vector

Input

AH = 25H
AL = Interrupt Number
DS:DX = New Address

Note: This service can help you intercept an interrupt vector.

INT 21H Service 26H—Create a New Program Segment (PSP)

INT 21H Service 27H—Random Block Read

Input

DS:DX points to an opened FCB
Set FCB's Random Record field
   at DS:DX + 33 and DS:DX + 35
AH = 27H

Output

AL = 00 Success
   = 01 end of file, no more data
   = 02 not enough space in DTA segment
   = 03 end of file, partial record
        padded with 0s
CX = Number of records read
Random Record Fields set to access
   next record

Note: The data buffer used in FCB services is the DTA, or Disk Transfer Area.

INT 21H Service 28H—Random Block Write

Input

DS:DX points to an opened FCB.
Set FCB's Random Record field
   at DS:DX + 33 and DS:DX + 35
CX = number of records to write
AH = 28H

Output

AL = 00 Success
   = 01 Disk is full
   = 02 not enough space in DTA segment

Random Record Fields set to access
   next record.

CX = 0 → file set to the size indicated by the Random Record field.
Note: The data buffer used in FCB services is the DTA, or Disk Transfer Area.

INT 21H Service 29H—Parse File Name

Input

DS:SI = Command line to parse.
ES:DI = Address to put FCB at.
AL = Bit 0 = 1 → Leading separators are scanned off command line.
     Bit 1 = 1 → Drive ID in final FCB will be changed ONLY if a
            drive was specified.
     Bit 2 = 1 → File name in FCB changed ONLY if command line includes
            file name.
     Bit 3 = 1 → File name extension in FCB will be changed ONLY if
            command line contains a file name extension.

Output

DS:SI = 1st character after filename.
ES:DI = Valid FCB

AH = 29H

Note: If the command line does not contain a valid file name, ES:[DI + 1] will be a blank.

INT 21H Service 2AH—Get Date

Input	Output
AH = 2AH	CX = Year - 1980
	DH = Month (1 = January, etc.)
	DL = Day of the month

INT 21H Service 2BH—Set Date

Input	Output
CX = Year - 1980	AL = 0 Success
DH = Month	
(1 = January, etc.)	AL = FF Date not valid
DL = Day of the month	
AH = 2BH	

INT 21H Service 2CH—Get Time

Input	Output
AH = 2CH	CH = Hours (0-23)
	CL = Minutes (0-59)
	DH = Seconds (0-59)
	DL = Hundredths of Seconds (0-99)

INT 21H Service 2DH—Set Time

Input	Output
AH = 2DH	AL = 00 Success
CH = Hours (0-23)	AL = FF Time is Invalid
CL = Minutes (0-59)	
DH = Seconds (0-59)	
DL = Hundreds of Seconds (0-99)	

INT 21H Service 2EH—Set or Reset Verify Switch

Input

AH = 2EH
DL = 0
AL = 1 → Turn Verify On.
   = 0 → Turn Verify Off.

INT 21H Service 2FH—Get Current DTA

Input   *Output*

AH = 2FH   ES:BX = Current DTA address

Note: The data buffer used in FCB services is the DTA, or Disk Transfer Area.

INT 21H Service 30H—Get DOS Version Number

Input   *Output*

AH = 30H   AL = Major Version Number (3 in DOS 3.10)
                 AH = Minor Version Number (10 in DOS 3.10)
                 BX = 0
                 CX = 0

Note: If AL returns 0, you are working with a version of DOS earlier than 2.0.

INT 21H Service 31H—Terminate Process and Keep Resident

Input

AH = 31H
AL = Binary Exit Code
DX = Size of memory request in paragraphs

Note: Exit code can be read by a parent program with Service 4DH. It can also be tested by ERRORLEVEL commands in batch files.

INT 21H Service 32H—Internal to DOS

INT 21H Service 33H—Control-Break Check

Input	Output

AH = 33H
AL = 0 → Check state of ^Break
      Checking

   = 1 → Set the state of ^Break
      Checking

(DL = 0→ Turn it Off.
DL = 1 → Turn it On.)

DL = 0 → Off
DL = 1 → On

INT 21H Service 34H—Internal to DOS

INT 21H Service 35H—Get Interrupt Vector

Input	Output

AH = 35H
AL = Interrupt Number

ES:BX = Interrupt's Vector

INT 21H Service 36H—Get Free Disk Space

Input	Output

AH = 36H
DL = Drive Number (0 = Default
              1 = A...)

AX = 0FFFH→Drive Number Invalid
AX = Number of Sectors/Cluster
BX = Number of available Clusters
CX = Size of a Sector (512)
DX = Number of Clusters

Note: Files are stored in clusters, the smallest allocatable unit on a disk.

INT 21H Service 37H—Internal to DOS

INT 21H Service 38H—Returns Country-Dependent Information

Input   *Output*

AH = 38H   Filled in 32-byte block (see below)
DS:DX =   Address of 32-byte block
AL = 0

The 32-byte block looks like this:

2 Bytes DATE/TIME Format
1 Byte of currency symbol (ASCII)
1 Byte set to 0
1 Byte thousands separator (ASCII)
1 Byte set to 0
1 Byte decimal separator (ASCII)
1 Byte set to 0
24 Bytes used internally

The DATE/TIME format has these values:
0 = USA (H:M:S M/D/Y)
1 = EUROPE (H:M:S D/M/Y)
2 = JAPAN (H:M:S D:M:Y)

Note: In DOS 3 + , you can set, as well as read, these values.

INT 21H Service 39H—Create a Subdirectory

Input   *Output*

AH = 39H   No Carry→ Success
DS:DX point to ASCIIZ string   Carry→AH has error value
        with directory name   AH = 3 Path Not Found
                                             AH = 5 Access Denied

INT 21H Service 3AH—Delete a Subdirectory

Input   *Output*

AH = 3AH   No Carry→ Success
DS:DX point to ASCIIZ string   Carry→AH has error value
        with directory name   AH = 3 Path Not Found.
                                             AH = 5 Access Denied or
                                                     Subdirectory not
                                                     empty

INT 21H Service 3BH—Change Current Directory

Input

AH = 3BH
DS:DX point to ASCIIZ string
           with directory name

Output

No Carry→ Success
Carry→AH has error value
           AH = 3 Path Not Found

INT 21H Service 3CH—Create a File

Input

DS:DX points to ASCIIZ file
name
CX = Attribute of File
AH = 3CH

Output

No Carry → AX = File Handle

Carry → AL = 3 Path not found
           = 4 Too many files open
           = 5 Dir full, or previous
                   Read-Only file exists

INT 21H Service 3DH—Open a File

Input

DS:DX points to ASCIIZ filename.
AL = Access Code---⌐
AH = 3DH   ↓
[Access Codes: AL = 0   File Opened for Reading.
                AL = 1   File Opened for Writing.
                AL = 2   File Opened for Reading and Writing.]
[Access Code DOS 3 + : isssraaa
                i = 1 → file is not to be inherited by child processes
                i = 0 → file handle will be inherited
                sss = 000 → Compatibility Mode
                sss = 001 → Deny All
                sss = 010 → Deny Write
                sss = 011 → Deny Read
                sss = 100 → Deny None
                 r = reserved
                aaa = 000 → Read Access
                aaa = 001 → Write Access
                aaa = 010 → Read/Write Access]

Output

No Carry → AX = File Handle
Carry → AL = Error Code
               (Check Error Table.)

INT 21H Service 3EH—Close a File Handle

Input

BX holds a valid File Handle.
AH = 3EH

Output

Carry → AL = 6 → Invalid handle

INT 21H Service 3FH—Read from File or Device

Input

DS:DX = Data Buffer Address
CX = Number of bytes to read
BX = File Handle
AH = 3FH

Output

No Carry→ AX = Number of bytes read
Carry→ AL = 5   Access Denied
        AL = 6   Invalid Handle

INT 21H Service 40H—Write to File or Device

Input

DS:DX = Data Buffer Address
CX = Number of bytes to write
BX = File Handle
AH = 40H

Output

No Carry→ AX = Number of bytes written
Carry→ AL = 5   Access Denied
        AL = 6   Invalid Handle

Note: Full disk is NOT considered an error: Check the number of bytes you want to write (CX) against the number actually written (returned in AX). If they do not match, the disk is probably full.

INT 21H Service 41H—Delete a File

Input

DS:DX = ASCIIZ file name
AH = 41H

Output

No Carry→ Success
Carry→ AL = 2   File Not Found
        AL = 5   Access Denied

Note: No wildcards allowed in file name.

INT 21H Service 42H—Move Read/Write Pointer

Input

Output

BX = File Handle
CX:DX = Desired offset
AL = Method Value--⌐
AH = 42H   ↓
[Method Values (AL):

    AL = 0   Read/Write Pointer moved to CX:DX from the start of the file.
    AL = 1   Pointer incremented CX:DX bytes.
    AL = 2   Pointer moved to end-of-file plus offset (CX:DX).]

No Carry→DX:AX = New Location of Pointer
Carry→AL = 1 Illegal Function Number
    AL = 6 Invalid Handle.

INT 21H Service 43H—Change File's Attribute

Input

Output

DS:DX = ASCIIZ Filestring
AL = 1→ File attribute changed.
    CX holds new attribute.
AL = 0→ File's current attribute
    returned in CX.
AH = 43H

No Carry→Success
Carry→AL = 2 File Not Found
    AL = 3 Path Not Found
    AL = 5 Access Denied
If AL was 0, CX returns the attribute.

INT 21H Service—44H I/O Control

INT 21H Service 45H—Duplicate a File Handle

Input

Output

BX = File Handle to duplicate
AH = 45H

No Carry→AX = New, duplicated Handle
Carry→AL = 4 Too many files open
    AL = 6 Invalid Handle

INT 21H Service 46H—Force Duplication of a File Handle

Input

BX = File Handle to duplicate
CX = Second File Handle
AH = 46H

Output

No Carry→Handles refer to same "stream"
Carry→AL = 6 Invalid Handle

INT 21H Service 47H—Get Current Directory on Specified Drive

Input

AH = 47H
DS:SI point to 64 byte buffer
DL = Drive Number

Output

No Carry→ Success, ASCIIZ at DS:SI
Carry→AH = 15 Invalid Drive Specified

Note: Drive letter is NOT included in returned ASCIIZ string.

INT 21H Service 48H—Allocate Memory

Input

AH = 48H
BX = Number of paragraphs
        requested

Output

No Carry→AX:0000 memory block address
Carry→AL = 7 Memory control blocks
                destroyed
    AL = 8 Insufficient Memory, BX
                contains maximum allowable
                request.

INT 21H Service 49H—Free Allocated Memory

Input

AH = 49H
ES = Segment of block being
        freed

Output

No Carry → Success
Carry → AL = 7 Memory Control Blocks
                Destroyed
        = 9 Incorrect Memory Block
                Address

INT 21H Service 4AH—SETBLOCK

Input

AH = 4AH
ES = Segment of block to modify
BX = Requested size in paragraphs

Output

No Carry → Success
Carry → AL = 7 Memory Control Blocks
                    Destroyed
           = 8 Insufficient Memory;
                    BX holds maximum
                    possible request.
           = 9 Invalid Memory Block
                    Address

INT 21H Service 4BH—Load or Execute a program (EXEC)

Input

AH = 4BH
DS:DX = ASCIIZ string with drive,
                pathname, file name
ES:BX = Parameter Block Address (see below)
AL = 0 → Load and execute the
                program.
       3 → Load but create no
                PSP, don't
                run. (Overlay)

Parameter Block for AL = 0:

        Segment Address of environment to pass. (Word)
        Address of command to put at PSP + 80H (DWord)
        Address of default FCB to put at PSP + 5CH (DWord)
        Address of 2nd default FCB to put at PSP + 6CH (DWord)

Parameter Block for AL = 3:

        Segment Address to load file at (Word).
        Relocation Factor for image (Word).

Output:

        No Carry → Success
        Carry:
                AL = 1 Invalid Function Number
                        2 File Not Found on Disk.
                        5 Access Denied.
                        8 Insufficient Memory for requested operation.
                        10 Invalid Environment
                        11 Invalid Format

Output

See Below.

INT 21H Service 4CH—Exit

Input

AH = 4CH
AL = Binary Return Code.

[Note: This service can end a program.]

INT 21H Service 4DH—Get Return Code of Subprocess

Input   *Output*

AH = 4DH   AL = Binary Return Code from Subprocess
              AH = 0 If subprocess ended normally
                   1 If subprocess ended with a ∧Break
                   2 If it ended with a critical
                       device error
                   3 If it ended with Service 31H

INT 21H Service 4EH—Find First Matching File

Input   *Output*

DS:DX→ASCIIZ filestring   Carry→ AL = 2 No Match Found
CX = Attribute to   AL = 18 No More Files
match
AH = 4EH   No Carry→DTA filled as follows:
                         21 Bytes: reserved
                         1 Byte: Found Attribute
                         2 Bytes: File's Time
                         2 Bytes: File's Date
                         2 Bytes: Low Word of Size
                         2 Bytes: High Word of Size
                         13 Bytes: Name and Extension
                             of found file in ASCIIZ
                             form (NO pathname)

Note: The data buffer used in FCB services is the DTA, or Disk
Transfer Area. See earlier services.

INT 21H Service 4FH—Find Next Matching File

Input	*Output*

Use Service 4EH BEFORE 4FH.
AH = 4FH
	Carry→ AL = 18 No More Files
	No Carry→DTA filled as follows:
	    21 Bytes: reserved.
	    1 Byte: Found Attribute.
	    2 Bytes: File's Time.
	    2 Bytes: File's Date.
	    2 Bytes: Low Word of Size.
	    2 Bytes: High Word of Size.
	    13 Bytes: Name and Extension
	            of found file in ASCIIZ
	            form (NO pathname).

Note: The data buffer used in FCB services is the DTA, or Disk Transfer Area. See earlier services.

INT 21H Services 50H-53H—Internal to DOS

INT 21H Service 54H—Get Verify State

Input	*Output*
AH = 54H	AL = 0→ Verify is OFF 1→ Verify is ON

INT 21H Service 55H—Internal to DOS

INT 21H Service 56H—Rename File.

Input	*Output*

DS:DX = ASCIIZ filestring to be
           renamed
ES:DI = ASCIIZ filestring that
           holds the new name
AH = 56H
	No Carry→Success
	Carry→ AL = 3 Path Not Found
	       AL = 5 Access Denied
	       AL = 17 Not Same Device

Note: File CANNOT be renamed to another drive.

INT 21H Service 57H—Get or Set a File's Date and Time

Input	Output

Input

BX = File Handle

AL = 0→Get Date and Time . . . .

AL = 1→Set Time to CX . . . .
     Set Date to DX

Output

No Carry:

CX returns Time
DX returns Date

File's date and time set

Carry→AL = 1 Invalid Function Number
           6 Invalid Handle

The time and date of a file are stored like this:

Time = 2048xHours + 32xMinutes + Seconds/2

Date = 512x(Year-1980) + 32xMonth + Day

INT 21H Service 58H—Internal to DOS

INT 21H Service 59H—Get Extended Error DOS 3+

Input

AH = 59H
BX = 0

Output

AX = Extended Error
BH = Error Class
BL = Suggested Action
CH = Locus

Note: This error handling service is very lengthy, and involves the many DOS 3+ extended errors.

INT 21H Service 5AH—Create Unique File DOS 3+

Input

AH = 5AH
DS:DX = Address of an
     ASCIIZ path
     (ending with "\")
CX = File's Attribute

Output

AX = Error if Carry is set
DS:DX = ASCIIZ path and filename

INT 21H Service 5BH—Create a New File DOS 3+

Input

AH = 5BH
DS:DX = Address of an
        ASCIIZ path
        (ending with "\")
CX = File's Attribute

Output

AX = Error if Carry is set
   = Handle if Carry is not set

INT 21H Service 5CH—Lock and Unlock Access to a File DOS 3+

Input

AH = 5CH
AL = 0 → Lock byte range
     1 → Unlock byte range
BX = File handle
CX = Byte range start (high word)
DX = Byte range start (low word)
SI = No. bytes to (un)lock (high word)
DI = No. bytes to (un)lock (low word)

Output

If Carry = 1, AX = Error

INT 21H Service 5E00H—Get Machine Name DOS 3+

Input

AX = 5E00H
DS:DX = Buffer for computer name

Output

DS:DX = ASCIIZ computer name
CH = 0 → Name not defined
CL = NETBIOS number
AX = Error if Carry set

INT 21H Service 5E02—Set Printer Setup DOS 3+

Input

AX = 5E02H
BX = Redirection list index
CX = Length of Setup String
DS:DI = Pointer to printer setup buffer

Output

AX = Error if Carry is set

INT 21H Service 5E03—Get Printer Setup DOS 3+

Input

AX = 5E03H
BX = Redirection list index
ES:DI = Pointer to printer setup buffer

Output

AX = Error if Carry is set
CX = Length of data returned
ES:DI = Filled with printer
         setup string

INT 21H Service 5F03—Redirect Device DOS 3+

Input

AX = 5F03H
BL = Device Type
      = 3 → Printer Device
      = 4 → File Device
CX = Value to save for caller
DS:SI = Source ASCIIZ device name
ES:DI = Destination ASCIIZ network path with password

Output

AX = Error if Carry is set

INT 21H Service 5F04H—Cancel Redirection DOS 3+

Input

AX = 5F04H
DS:SI = ASCIIZ device name or path

Output

AX = Error if Carry is set

INT 21H Service 62H—Get Program Segment Prefix DOS 3+

Input

AX = 62H

Output

BX = Segment of currently
      executing program

INT 21H Service 67H—Set Handle Count DOS 3.30

Input

AX = 67H
BX = Number of allowed open handles
(up to 255)

Output

AX = Error if Carry is set

INT 21H Service 68H—Commit File (Write Buffers) DOS 3.30

Input   *Output*

AX = 68H   BX = File Handle

[Note: 68H is the last of the DOS 3.3 INT 21H services.]

INT 22H—Terminate Address

INT 23H—Control Break Exit Address

INT 24H—Critical Error Handler

AH filled this way:

0 Diskette is write protected.
1 Unknown Unit
2 The requested drive is not ready.
3 Unknown command
4 Cyclic Redundancy—Check error in the data
5 Bad request structure length
6 Seek Error
7 Media Type Unknown
8 Sector not found
9 The printer is out of paper.
A Write Fault
B Read Fault.
C General Failure

If you just execute an IRET, DOS takes an action based on the contents of AL. If AL = 0, the error is ignored. If AL = 1, the operation is retried. If AL = 2, the program is terminated through INT 23H.

INT 25H—Absolute Disk Read

Input

AL = Drive Number
CX = Number of Sectors to Read
DX = First Logical Sector
DS:BX = Buffer address

Output

No Carry→ Success
Carry→ AH = 80H Disk didn't respond
        AH = 40H Seek failed
        AH = 20H Controller failure
        AH = 10H Bad CRC error check
        AH = 08   DMA overrun
        AH = 04   Sector not found
        AH = 03   Write protect error
        AH = 02   Address Mark missing
        AH = 00   Error unknown

Note: Flags left on the Stack after this INT call because information is returned in current flags. After you check the flags that were returned, make sure you do a POPF. Also, this INT destroys the contents of ALL registers.

INT 26H—Absolute Disk Write

Input

AL = Drive Number
CX = Number of Sectors to Write
DX = First Logical Sector
DS:BX = Buffer address

Output

No Carry→ Success
Carry→ AH = 80H Disk didn't respond.
        AH = 40H Seek failed.
        AH = 20H Controller failure
        AH = 10H Bad CRC error check
        AH = 08   DMA overrun
        AH = 04   Sector not found
        AH = 03   Write protect error
        AH = 02   Address Mark missing
        AH = 00   Error unknown

Note: Flags left on the Stack after this INT call because information is returned in current flags. After you check the flags that were returned, make sure you do a POPF. Also, this INT destroys the contents of ALL registers.

INT 27H—Terminate and Stay Resident

Input

DS:DX = point directly after
        end of code which is
        to stay resident

INTs 28H-2EH—Internal to DOS

INT 2FH—Multiplex Interrupt

INT 30H-3FH—DOS Reserved

INT 40H-5FH—Reserved

INT 60H-67H—Reserved for User Software

INTs 68H-7FH—Not Used

INTs 80H-85H—Reserved by BASIC

INTs 86H-F0H—Used by BASIC Interpreter

INTs F1H-FFH—Not Used

Index

About the Author

Steven Holzner earned his BS degree at MIT and a Ph.D. at Cornell, where he was a lecturer in physics. He has travelled to over 30 countries, lived for a year each in Hong Kong and Hawaii, and spends summers in Austria. Steven now resides in Southern California, next to the beach. He just quit his job to take a year long vacation in Santa Cruz.